A REVIEW OF THE GREEK AND OTHER INSCRIPTIONS
AND PAPYRI PUBLISHED BETWEEN 1988 AND 1992

New Documents Illustrating Early Christianity

• Volume 10 •

A Review of the Greek and Other Inscriptions and Papyri Published between 1988 and 1992

Editors

S. R. Llewelyn and J. R. Harrison

Associate Editor

E. J. Bridge

Ancient History Documentary Research Centre
(an arm of the Ancient Cultures Research Centre)
Macquarie University, N.S.W. Australia

William B. Eerdmans Publishing Company
Grand Rapids, Michigan / Cambridge, U.K.

© 2012 Macquarie University
All rights reserved

Published 2012 by Wm. B. Eerdmans Publishing Co.
2140 Oak Industrial Drive N.E., Grand Rapids, Michigan 49505 /
P.O. Box 163, Cambridge CB3 9PU U.K.
www.eerdmans.com

Published in association with
The Ancient History Documentary Research Centre,
Macquarie University, NSW 2109, Australia

ISBN 978-0-8028-4520-7

The Ancient History Documentary Research Centre
(Directors: Professor S. N. C. Lieu and Professor A. M. Nobbs)
within the Ancient Cultures Research Centre of the Faculty of Arts at Macquarie University
fosters research and professional development in association with other organisations interested
in the documentation of the ancient world

Committee for *New Documents Illustrating Early Christianity*
P. W. Barnett (Chairman), J. Dalrymple, J. R. Harrison, E. A. Judge, A. M. Nobbs, R. B. Tress

Editorial correspondence should be addressed to
Prof. A. M. Nobbs, Ancient History Documentary Research Centre,
Faculty of Arts, Macquarie University,
NSW 2109, Australia

Typeset by Dr. E. J. Bridge, Department of Ancient History, Macquarie University

TABLE OF CONTENTS

PREFACE			vii
Introduction			viii
Abbreviations			
Textual Sigla			
Acknowledgements			

PHILOSOPHY

1	What makes a Philosophical School?	E.A. Judge	1
2	Choosing 'the strait and narrow'	E.A. Judge	6

MAGIC

3	Overcoming the 'strong man'	J.R. Harrison	10
4	All Grades of Angels	J.R. Harrison	16
5	Incantation for Spirit Possession of a Boy	M. Almond	20

CULT AND ORACLE

6	Livia as Hecate	J.R. Harrison	25
7	Family Honour of a Priestess of Artemis	J.R. Harrison	30
8	Artemis triumphs over a Sorcerer's Evil Art	J.R. Harrison	37
9	A 'worthy' *neopoios* thanks Artemis	J.R. Harrison	48

PUBLIC LIFE: CAESARIAN ACCESSION

10	The Crux of *RG* 34.1 Resolved? Augustus on 28 BC	E.A. Judge	55
11	The 'grace' of Augustus paves a Street at Ephesus	J.R. Harrison	59
12	Diplomacy over Tiberius' Accession	J.R. Harrison	64
13	How to celebrate Hadrian's Accession	B. Bitner	76

PUBLIC LIFE: BENEFACTION AND BUSINESS

14	Antiochus IV Epiphanes in Athens	G. Davis / S.R. Llewelyn	87
15	A Governor transmits an Imperial Privilege	B. Sanderson	92
16	Customs Law of the Roman Province of Asia	J. Ogereau	95
17	Honouring the Repairer of the Baths at Colossae	A.H. Cadwallader	110

HOUSEHOLD

18	Divorce Agreement	D.C. Barker	114
19	Insolent Women	E. Mathieson	119

| 20 | Sale of a Horse | D. Keenan-Jones | 123 |
| 21 | 'Every dog has its day' | J.R. Harrison | 126 |

JUDAICA

22	The Temple Warning	S.R. Llewelyn / D. van Beek	136
23	Pay Slip of a Roman Soldier at Masada	S.R. Llewelyn	140
24	The Babatha Archive and Roman Law	G. Rowling / S.R. Llewelyn	142
25	Dedicatory Inscription at Ostia Synagogue	E. Piccolo	154
26	The Names of Jewish Women	E.A. Judge	156

CHRISTIANITY

27	'Diogenes the Christian'	P. McKechnie	159
28	A Difficult (?) Request to 'beloved father' Diogenes	E.J. Bridge	164
29	Belated Greetings to Everyone	E.J. Bridge	170

INDEXES

Introduction	175
1. Selected Subjects	176
2. Words	207
Greek	207
Latin	211
Hebrew	214
Aramaic	214
3. Ancient Authors and Works	215
4. Inscriptions	228
5. Papyri	236
6. Biblical, Qumran and Rabbinic Works	252
Hebrew Bible	252
Apocrypha	254
Pseudepigrapha	255
Qumran	255
Rabbinical	255
New Testament	258

PREFACE

This collection represents a co-operative effort coordinated by Stephen Llewelyn, the principal editor of the second pentad of the series. A consolidated index for this pentad carefully compiled by Jon Dalrymple on the model of that for volumes 1-5 is included, and for financing that thanks are due to the Ingram Moore Estate Fund for an enabling grant. Stephen Llewelyn has worked generously to foster contributions from other researchers at Macquarie University. As well as their work, the volume contains entries from scholars from associated institutions.

The contribution of his co-editor, James Harrison, is integral to the final shape of the volume and the whole owes much to his drive and intellectual overview of the field.

For completion of many of the technical aspects, Edward Bridge played an important part, alongside some earlier input from Michael Theophilos.

The Ancient History Documentary Research Centre, which oversaw the first nine volumes, is now an arm of the larger Ancient Cultures Research Centre, a Macquarie University Centre under the overall direction of Naguib Kanawati. The support of the University and Faculty of Arts for documentary research in Ancient Cultures is gratefully acknowledged.

The series has been fostered since its inception by Edwin Judge.

Professor Alanna Nobbs
Deputy Director (with Professor Samuel Lieu)
Ancient Cultures Research Centre
Macquarie University
October 2011

INTRODUCTION

The tenth volume in the *New Documents Illustrating Early Christianity* series has collected documentary evidence which appeared in publications between the years 1988 and 1992, a five-year net. However, the collected documents represent only part of a much larger number of documents of potential interest. Of these the more significant texts have been chosen to be representative for the base years and with their associated discussions thematically grouped under the headings of Philosophy, Magic, Cult and Oracle, Public Life: Caesarian Accession, Public Life: Benefactors and Business, Household, Judaica and Christianity. In all there are twenty-nine separate documents discussed.

As always, the intended reader of *New Docs* is the researcher, teacher or student in biblical studies and other related fields. The series is offered as a tool to broaden the context of studies in these fields. In order to assist the reading of the Greek text, the translation has attempted to reflect, as far as practicable, the formal structure of the document. This means that the translation is line-by-line, with doubtful and restored readings marked by sigla in the English translation. Naturally, one cannot translate the Greek document into flowing English if at the same time one pays strict regard to formal structures. Thus something of a compromise has resulted.

The Greek of the documentary texts is not that which one has come to expect from the published literary texts of antiquity. This is particularly the case with orthography. Spelling was not standardised and persons invariably wrote as they heard the word pronounced. The correct spelling will generally be indicated below the document in its critical apparatus. Most quotations from other ancient texts or secondary sources are also translated to assist the English reader. Exceptions exist. For example, where the reader's access to an adequate translation can be assumed or when the quotation is paraphrased in the preceding sentence, translation may be omitted. If we have used the translation of another author, this is acknowledged in the text. Our own translations, however, are those not otherwise acknowledged.

Abbreviations

Abbreviations follow standard conventions, except where altered for clarity.
- Journals—as in *L'Année philologique*.
- Papyrological works—as in S.R. Pickering, *Papyrus Editions held in Australian Libraries* (North Ryde 1984); and ibid., *Papyrus Editions: Supplement* (North Ryde 1985).
- Epigraphical works according to generally used conventions (see LSJ), preceded where necessary by I. (e.g. I. Ephesus).
- Ancient authors, biblical and patristic works—generally as in LSJ, BAGD, and Lampe.

Textual sigla

αβ̣	letters not completely legible
....	4 letters missing
...	indeterminate number of letters missing
[αβ]	letters lost from document and restored by editor
[±8 letters]	about 8 letters lost
⟨αβ⟩	letters omitted by scribe and added by editor
⟪αβ⟫	editorial correction of wrong letters in the text
(αβ)	editor has resolved an abbreviation in the text
{αβ}	letters wrongly added by scribe and cancelled by editor
⟦αβ⟧	a (still legible) erasure made by scribe
`αβ´	letters written above line
ᾱ	letter stands for a numerical equivalent
v., vv., vac.	one, two, several letter spaces left blank (vacant) on document
m.1, m.2	first hand (manus), second hand

Acknowledgements

The efforts of a number of people need to be acknowledged and thanked in this introduction. Together with myself, Edwin Judge, Jim Harrison and Eddie Bridge formed the editorial committee for this volume. Judge and Harrison have read all the manuscripts, as well as contributing a number of articles under their own names. Bridge has assisted with editing the entries and has formatted the whole work. He has also contributed two entries. Jon Dalrymple has worked tirelessly through volumes 6 to 10 of *New Documents Illustrating Early Christianity* to create new, cumulative indices which now form the second part of this volume. Other contributors to the volume are Mathew Almond, Don Barker, Brad Bitner, Alan Cadwallader, Gil Davis, Duncan Keenan-Jones, Paul McKechnie, Erica Mathieson, Julien Ogereau, Ester Piccolo, Giles Rowling, Bianca Sanderson, Dionysia van Beek. Their contributions are much appreciated.

Finally, we wish to acknowledge the contribution of the New Documents committee and more particularly its chairman Paul Barnett, treasurer Dick Tress, secretary Jon Dalrymple, without whose enduring support the present volume would not have been possible.

S.R. Llewelyn
October 2011

PHILOSOPHY

§1 What makes a Philosophical School?

Bursa   Marble bases   II

Ed.pr. – G. Mendel, *BCH* 33 (1909) 407-410, nos 407, 409; S. Şahin, *ZPE* 24 (1977) 257-258; I. Hadrianoi (ed. E. Schwertheim, 1987) nos 51, 52; T. Corsten, (ed.), *Die Inschriften von Prusa ad Olympum* (Bonn 1991) 34-36 (= I. Prusa Olymp. 17-18)

17

(vac.) Ἀγαθῆι (vac.) τύχηι·	(vac.) For good (vac.) fortune.
κατὰ δόγμα τῆς βουλῆς	By resolution of the council
καὶ τοῦ δήμου Π. Ἀβιάνι-	and people (honouring) P. Aviani-
ον Βαλέριον Λυσιμά-	us Valerius Lysima-
5 χου υἱὸν φιλόσοφον	chus's son, philosopher,
τὸν φιλόπολιν ?? Τ. ??	the city's friend; T.
Ἀβιάνιος Ἀρριανὸς	Avianius Arrianus
⚭ τὸν φίλον. ⚭	(honours) (his) friend.

18

(vac.) Ἀγαθῆι τύχηι· (vac.)	(vac.) For good fortune. (vac.)
Τ. Ἀουιάνιον Βᾶσσον	(Honouring) T. Avianius Bassus
Πολύαινον στωϊκὸν φ[ι]-	Polyaenus, Stoic phi-
λόσοφον ?? Ἀουιάνιος Ἀ-	losopher. Avianius A-
5 πολλώνιος φιλόσοφος	pollonius, philosopher,
κατὰ τὸ δόγμα τῆς πό-	by resolution of the ci-
λεως τῆς Ἁδριανῶν	ty of (the) Hadrianoi
τῶν πρὸς τῶι Ὀλύ[μπωι]	facing (Mt) Olympus
τὸν ἑαυτοῦ φί[λον]	(for) his personal friend
10 [ἐκ τ]ῶν ἰδίων [ἀνέστη]-	from his own (means) [erect]-
(vac.) σεν. (vac.)	(vac.) ed (this.) (vac.)

Given the authorisation of 18 *by resolution of the city of Hadrianoi*, Schwertheim (following Şahin) had taken both inscriptions into I. Hadrianoi. But since they have been preserved with a group including I. Prusa Olymp. 13, which contains reference to a Bithyniarch, Corsten (p. 3) took both 17 and 18 as coming from Prusa (the fact that both had in a later age been built there into the 'Castle Gate', Hisar Kapısı, does not of course itself settle the matter). Hadrianoi lies in Mysia, some 50 km SSW across the Rhyndacus, with the boundary between Bithynia and the Roman province of Asia running along the intervening Mt Olympus. On the public life of Bithynia in particular we have not only the speeches of Dio Chrysostom but the letters of Pliny from his governorship, so that its cultural scene in general may be assessed (Bekker-Nielsen, Harris, Stephan).

Corsten might well have added that specifying the city's actual name (Hadrianoi) may itself imply that 18 was *not* designed for display there (whereas the identity of the city in 17 was taken for granted). He suggests that Apollonius may have been a citizen of Hadrianoi who nevertheless belonged to 'the school of philosophers' in Prusa, while the honorand, Polyaenus, was a citizen of Prusa who had perhaps undertaken office in Hadrianoi or had otherwise come forward there as a benefactor. Yet since Apollonius was paying for 18 anyway we should still need to ask why Hadrianoi was mentioned at all: was public initiative required to validate (or enhance) the honour?

In the *Lexicon of Greek Personal Names* (*LGPN*) Vol. V^A (2010) Corsten lists Apollonius and Polyaenus (no. 18) under Prusa (or, in brackets, Hadrianoi), but Arrianus and Lysimachus (no. 17) simply under Prusa. One must indeed allow the possibility that the two documents do not belong together geographically; or, given the coincidence of content, that they all come from Hadrianoi (a suggestion of Şahin). Schwertheim identified the stone of 18 as an altar, not a base, while the disposition of the texts on the two stones varies.

Their juxtaposition has nevertheless led Corsten to classify the four (or five?) individuals mentioned as 'a school of philosophers', fortified by their all being members of the same Roman *gens* (Avianii are not otherwise attested in either of the cities concerned, nor in the more extensively documented and indexed Ephesus, Philippi or Thessalonica, but several are recorded in the inscriptions of Rome itself). He takes the explicit definition of the relationships by the two dedicators as 'friendship' to refer to the formal constitution of the 'school' as a lawful association, and assumes that its philosophical commitment was to Stoicism, since Polyaenus is so identified.

It is not uncommon for an individual to be identified in the documents as *philosophos*, not necessarily because of the famous stereotype (Zanker, cf. Plin. *Ep.*, 1.10.5–7). For a range of epigraphic philosophers see Tod, Robert, Habicht and Barnes (the last also treats Christians seen as philosophers, as does Stroumsa; cf. Horsley, *New Docs* 4 257–258, on the singular 'philosopher-nun' of I. Nikaia 1.550). For the papyri see Pruneti. In Ephesus the philosophers so named are not specified as part of the regular training system. By contrast the sophists and their *paideutai* ('pupils') enjoy privileges determined by the proconsul himself (I. Eph. 216, *l.* 8). The *mathetai* ('students') request a public tribute for their *sophistes*, Soteros (I. Eph. 1548). A triumviral edict grants exemptions to 'the *paideutai* and the *sophistai* or the *iatroi*'; i.e. medical practitioners (I. Eph. 4101, *l.* 10). For the interaction between philosophy and the community in general see André, Bowersock, Hahn and Manning.

Inspired by the Jew who leases a 'hall' (*exedra*) and basement from two 'nuns' (*monachai apotaktikai*, P. Oxy. 3203), Horsley contests the common translation of *scholē* (Acts 19:9) as 'lecture-hall' (*New Docs* 1 129-130), as though it were an enclosed chamber. Rather, it suggests a more public meeting-point. 'Paul embarks on his daily discussions and debate ... with others who have their own philosophies and *modus vivendi* ... a group of people to whom addresses were given during their leisure hours.' Tyrannus may well have been the benefactor who had embellished the venue. The rhetoric of Acts 19:10 gives the impression of easy accessibility.

It is indeed the case that *scholē* ('leisure') retains its primary sense (cf. Latin *otium*), of the condition under which philosophy may best be practised. As with I. Prusa Olymp. 17–18, it is not usually part of the Greek text at all when we choose to speak of a philosophical 'school' (the meanings we have now assigned to the inherited word impose themselves even when the original is not present, cf. the similar problem we face with the term 'religion'). Note the difficulty in clarifying the physical arrangements even for the most famous school of all, the Academy (Billot). The Pompeian mosaic (frontispiece to Goulet's *Dictionnaire*, cf. Billot) imaginatively displays the leisurely and casual setting; contrast the formality of the Ostia grave relief (Zanker, *Mask*, 261, fig. 140) where a schoolteacher is presented as an idealised philosopher, yet emphatically formal, as the wooden codices and writing desks of the pupils make clear.

In the Latin inscriptions of Rome the term *schola* or *scola* appears already to indicate a purpose-built structure. The inscriptions of Ephesus (though not of Prusa or Hadrianoi) record by contrast the provision of *exedrae*, essentially the semi-circular open face of an existing building (I. Neilsen, *Brill's New Pauly* 5, 2004, cols 261–262), suitable for public gathering. Stertinius Orpex was responsible for one set into a wall of the stadium (I. Eph. 2113). A monument to T. Flavius Sophron, *libertus Augusti*, was set up on the right side of an *exedra* 'as you entered' (I. Eph. 2261, *l.* 4). Another, under Domitian, connected stoa and agora with its array of statues (I. Eph. 3005). Seating (συμψέλια, Lat. *subsellia*) was provided in the one connected with the stoa and its walls (I. Eph. 3065).

Using the modern senses of the term 'school' it is therefore not at all obvious that we should think of a particular building dedicated to philosophical discussion between teachers and students. Nor is it much more plausible to envisage a 'school' in the sense of a likeminded community of specialists sustained by a shared social life. In particular there is a shortage of documentary or other evidence to support the specific proposal of Corsten that the people named in 17 and 18 were members enrolled in a *Verein* (sc. a formal association in law). Nor does the reference (p. 35, on *ll.* 3-5) to I. Prusa Olymp. 24 secure the point since those creating that monument are explicitly ἑταῖροι (*l.* 2, 'companions', sc. enrolled members) in a κοινόν (*l.* 8, the generic term covering the several more explicit categories of Greek formal 'association', Judge, 'On this Rock', 621-624). Our inscriptions lack any comparable indication — contrast cases such as the cultic groups of Dionysius at Philadelphia (Judge, 'On this Rock', 624) or of Agrippinilla at Torre Nova (Judge, 'On this Rock', 627-628). Both of these also appear to have been based on a family network, but show very elaborate structural rules. Philosophy however might also be passed on in a family as with *IG* X 2.1.145, *ll.* 6-9, Sosibius *philosophos*, son of Sosibius the *philosophos*.

Across the whole millennium of the Greek philosophical 'schools', in the grander sense of an intellectual tradition sustained through many generations, it is rare to find clear evidence of any ongoing formal structure (Dorandi). Those who come closest to it, and then only in particular instances, are the Pythagoreans and Epicureans (Judge, 'On this Rock', 633-636). We may set aside of course the classic establishments of Athens and Alexandria (Watts).

It is unusual in the inscriptions to find a *philosophos* identified by his dogmatic position as our Polyaenus is (18, *ll*. 3-4). Stoicism in this period seems to have often been taken for granted, with the philosopher typically ranging across several fields, so to name one a Stoic implies a more consistent position (Dillon, Gill, Reydams-Schils, Strange). From Ephesus we have an Alexandrian 'eclectic' (I. Eph. 789), while the city's benefactor Heraclides, priest of Artemis, is honoured for his 'scholarly power' (τὴν ἐν τῷ μαθήματι δύναμιν, I. Eph. 683^A, *l*. 5), which implies a profession as philosopher. Two others are identified as Platonic: I. Eph. 3901, 4340. From Rome there are Stoics attested in *CIL* 6.9784, 9785, and an Epicurean in *CIL* 6.37813.

In the Greek cities of Asia Minor it is clear that philosophers also enjoyed public recognition, hence the many tributes to individuals identified as such. Yet without more explicit evidence (e.g. I. Eph. 616, a *philosophos* honoured for several no doubt costly appointments) it is better to see them as independent gurus, distinguished from and no doubt often critical of the practitioners of rhetorical persuasion, mastery of whose arts was a necessity for public leadership in the city, a strenuous training hardly suggestive of *scholē*. The sophists thus had a formal stake in public education (Winter), whereas the philosophical 'schools' dogmatically maintained the freedom of their leisurely intellectual discussions. But of course by the second century in particular such a master as Dio Chrysostom of Prusa shows how one might seriously embrace both of these functions at different times in one's life (Jones, Stanton, Swain).

Bibliography

J.-M. **André**, 'Les écoles philosophiques aux deux premiers siècles de l'Empire', *ANRW* 2.36.1 (1987) 5-77; J. **Barnes**, 'Ancient Philosophers', in *Philosophy and Power in the Graeco-Roman World* (eds, G. Clark et al.; Oxford 2002) 293-306; T. **Bekker-Nielsen**, *Urban Life and Local Politics in Roman Bithynia* (Aarhus 2008); M.-F. **Billot**, 'Académie (topographie et archéologie)', in *Dictionnaire des philosophes antiques*, Vol. 1 (ed., R. Goulet; Paris 1989) 693-785, esp. p. 783 for the later stages; G.W. **Bowersock**, 'Philosophy in the Second Sophistic', in *Der Philosoph und die Gesellschaft* (ed., J. Hahn; Stuttgart 1989) 157-170; H. **Cancik** and H. **Schneider** (eds), *Brill's New Pauly*, Vol. 5 (Leiden 2004); J.T. **Dillon**, *Musonius Rufus and Education in the Good Life* (Lanham 2004); T. **Dorandi**, 'The Organization and Structure of the Philosophical Schools', in *The Cambridge History of Hellenistic Philosophy* (eds, K. Algra, et al.; Cambridge 1999) 55-62; C. **Gill**, 'The School in the Roman Imperial Period', in *The Cambridge Companion to the Stoics* (ed., B. Inwood; Cambridge 2003) 33-58; M. **Haake**, *Der Philosoph in der Stadt* (Munich 2007); M. **Haake**, 'Philosopher and Priest: The Image of the Intellectual and the Social Practice of the Elites in the Eastern Roman Empire', in *Practitioners of the Divine* (eds, B. Dignas, et al.; Cambridge, Mass. 2008) 145-165; Ch. **Habicht**, 'Zu den Inschriften, in denen Philosophen genannt sind', *Die Inschriften des Asklepieions* (Altertümer von Pergamon 8.3, Berlin 1969) 162; J. **Hahn**, *Der Philosoph und die Gesellschaft* (Stuttgart 1989); B.F. **Harris**, 'Bithynia: Roman Sovereignty and the Survival of Hellenism', *ANRW* 2.7.2 (Berlin 1980) 857-901; G. **Herman**, *Ritualised Friendship and the Greek City* (Cambridge 1987); C.P. **Jones**, *The Roman World of Dio Chrysostom* (Cambridge, Mass. 1978) 8-13; C.P.

§1 What makes a Philosophical School?

Jones, *Culture and Society in Lucian* (Cambridge, Mass. 1986) 24-32; E.A. **Judge**, 'Kultgemeinde', *RAC* 22 (2007) 393-438, esp. 405-408; E.A. **Judge**, 'On this Rock I will build my *ekklesia*', *The First Christians in the Roman World* (Tübingen 2008) 619-668, esp. 633-636; C.E. **Manning**, 'School Philosophy and Popular Philosophy in the Roman Empire', *ANRW* 2.36.7 (1994) 4995-5026; P. **Pruneti**, 'Il termine φιλόσοφος nei papiri documentari', in F. Adorno et al. (eds), *Hodoi dizesios: Le vie della ricerca* (Florence 1996) 389-401; G. **Reydams-Schils** et al. (eds), *The Roman Stoics: Self, Responsibility and Affection* (Chicago 2005) 99-113; L. **Robert**, *Bulletin Épigraphique* 84 (1958) 513-516; G.R. **Stanton**, 'Sophists and Philosophers: Problems of Classification', *AJP* 94 (1973) 350-364, esp. (on Dio) 353-354, 359-361; E. **Stephan**, *Honoratioren, Griechen, Polisbürger: Kollektive Identitäten innerhalb der Oberschicht des kaiserzeitlichen Kleinasien* (Göttingen 2002) 199-222; S.K. **Strange**, et al. (eds), *Stoicism: Traditions and Transformations* (Cambridge 2004); G.G. **Stroumsa**, *Barbarian Philosophy* (Tübingen 1999); S. **Swain**, *Hellenism and Empire* (Oxford 1996); S. **Swain** (ed.), *Dio Chrysostom: Politics, Letters and Philosophy* (Oxford 2000); M.N. **Tod**, 'Sidelights on Greek Philosophers', *JHS* 77 (1957) 132-141; E.J. **Watts**, 'Academic life in the Roman Empire', *City and School in Late Antique Athens and Alexandria* (Berkeley 2006) 1-23; B.W. **Winter**, *Philo and Paul among the Sophists* (2nd edn, Grand Rapids 2002) 19-39, 256-260 (on P. Oxy. 2190); P. **Zanker**, *The Mask of Socrates: The Image of the Intellectual in Antiquity* (Berkeley 1995).

E.A. Judge (Macquarie University)

§2 Choosing 'the strait and narrow'

Philadephia (Lydia)   Marble block   early I[p]

Ed. pr. — J. Keil and A. von Premerstein, *Bericht über eine Reise in Lydien* (Denkschrift Ak. 53.2; Wien 1908) 34-35, no. 55, fig. 28; Petzl, *EA* 20 (1992) 1-5, pl. 1; Peek, *GVI* (1955) no. 1805 (= Pfuhl-Möbius II [1979] no. 2087, pl. 300 = *SEG* XLII 1081).

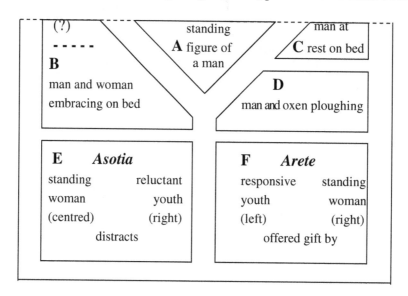

Οὐ γενόμαν Σάμιος [κ]εῖνος ὁ Πυθαγόρας,   I was not born (as) that Pythagoras of Samos,
ἀλλ' ἐφύην σοφίῃ τᾶτὸ λαχὼν ὄνο[μα],   but I have become one by wisdom, winning the same name,
[τὸν] πόνον {ον} ἐνκρείνας αἱρετὸν [ἐν βιότῳ]   (since) I judged effort to be preferable [in life]

4 [   ]ρα[   ]ουτο[   ] ...

The interpretation of this monument, often cited but now lost, has been further discussed by Petzl. However our translation reflects Staab's refinement. It is a funerary tribute to a Pythagoras, who was probably depicted in facet A of the schematic device. He has been called Pythagoras not at birth but as a complimentary by-name (cf. Horsley, *New Docs* 1, 89-96, and *ADB* 4, 1992, 101-117). The subsequent publication of *LGPN* V[A] (2010) justifies this. Though the name had been common enough in the Aegean islands, as well as in Athens and Ionia, and was typically Hellenistic, our text is the sole attestation from anywhere in Lydia of any period. The earthquake-prone rural backwater (Hemer) is an unlikely seat for a strenuous school of philosophy. To be like the legendary Pythagoras was an intellectual compliment, by no means implying any historic link. Josephus says the Essenes practised the same discipline as the Pythagoreans (Judge 2008, 639). Clement of Alexandria called Philo a Pythagorean (Runia).

§2 Choosing 'the straight and narrow'

The epigram may well have been completed by the fragmentary fourth line. But instead of two elegaic couplets it is metrically an unexpected series of pentameters. 'These dull verses' dismisses a similar case (Gow and Page, 363). This apparently arbitrary inelegance is further disfigured by incongruous dialect forms and vulgarism (Brinkmann, 616). The diagrammatic relief above it is so far unparalleled in several respects, but even without the name Pythagoras its message is clear. We know from the satirist Persius (AD 36–63) 3, *ll.* 56-57, how the letter Υ was used with its 'Samian' branches to demonstrate the right path to the young. The seventh-century Isidore (*Etymologies*, 1.3.7-8) cites this passage, explaining in detail the function of Υ as a 'mystical' letter, and attributing the device (as on our monument) to Pythagoras himself.

The surviving photograph (copied repeatedly, presumably from ed.pr.) is difficult to read in every detail, but the main point is not in doubt. It concerns the youth, who is to reject the prospect of immediate sensual ease (facet B) in favour of physical effort (D) (cf. the *ponos* of the epigram, *l.* 3) before enjoying one's rest (C). In spite of the damage at the top left-hand corner of the relief there appears to be a protuberance still visible, justifying the proposal of Brinkmann that a further facet, the counterpart of C, must be assumed.

The (undated) Latin poet Maximinus, describing the same Y-based scene as our relief, states that the easy way on the left side culminates in 'plunging its captives head-first onto the jagged rocks' (*praecipitat captos volvitque per aspera saxa*, A. Riese, *Anthologia Latina*, fasc. 2, Leipzig 1870, no. 632). Cumont (followed by others) describes this image as though it was still to be seen on our stone, and he then links it with his major interest in the afterlife. But the relief is not concerned with that at all, any more than with the ancient Egyptian 'Book of the Two Ways' (Lesko and Hermsen), which was concerned entirely with the topography of the afterlife and the alternative journeys within that. The biblical and classical 'two ways' motifs address the balance (or ethical choice) between hardship and comfort in this life, and what the proper order for these should be.

The words ἀσωτία and ἀρετή were inscribed above the heads of the women in E and F respectively, though not visible in the reproduced photographs. *Asotia* ('profligacy', its adverb being used of the 'prodigal' son in the parable of Jesus, Luke 15:13; cf. the noun in equally graphic contexts: of drunkenness, Eph 5:18; of insubordination, Titus 1:6; of wallowing, 1 Pet 4:4) does not feature in the Pythagorean literature (not in Iamblichus, Clark; or the 'Golden Verses', Thom). Nor does it commonly arise in connection with κακία ('badness') in general (not indexed in Sluiter–Rosen). No other depiction of *Asotia* is recorded by *LIMC* II.2 (1984) 669, and for that matter *Arete* is only rarely depicted. In the (Pythagorean?) *Tablet* of Cebes *asotia* appears as one of several vices, while the two ways are ἀρετή and ἀπάτη (Fitzgerald and White, 24). In the *Nicomachean Ethics* 4.1 (1119^b-1120^a) Aristotle defines *asotia* as ruination through the wasting of one's goods.

In his *Works and Days* (287-292) Hesiod confronts 'foolish' Perses, his brother, with the choice between easy 'Immorality' (Κακότης, not just 'Inferiority' surely as M.L. West translates it), a smooth and accessible path, and the 'Virtue' (Ἀρετή) in front of which the immortals have put 'sweat': this track is long and steep, rough to start with, but easy going once you reach the top, for all the trouble. Yet 'immorality' is taken up in crowds.

Closer still in theme to our relief, and of ongoing fascination in traditional mythology, is the dilemma of the young Hercules (Xenophon, *Mem.* 2.1.21-33). Faced with the invitations of two women, seductive Vice (Κακία) and slender Virtue (Ἀρετή), he must make the right choice. Virtue requires a life of labour, but only she gives undying fame (Blanshard).

At the end of his days, Moses offered the children of Israel a commandment that was already 'in your heart, ready to be kept' (Deut 30:14, tr. *NEB*). But it was also a choice, either for life and good, or death and evil (v. 15); blessing or curse (v. 19). Idolatry is the hazard (v. 17). 'Love the Lord your God ... that is life for you' (v. 20).

In the Sermon on the Mount, Jesus put it more starkly: 'Enter by the narrow gate; ... for the gate is narrow and the way is hard (*AV* 'strait' and 'narrow') that leads to life, and those that find it are few' (Matt 7:13-14, cf. Luke 13:24). In either instance of the saying it is bare of any introductory context, but there follow parables, different between themselves, pointing to the end: 'out of my sight, you and your wicked ways' (Matt 7:33); 'some who are first will be last' (Luke 13:30).

The two ways are set in the *Didache* as the framework for an ordered catalogue of the whole doctrinal, procedural and moral curriculum of the apostolic tradition. The same framework seems to lie behind the *Epistle of Barnabas* where it 'pervades the entire epistle' (Kraft, 5). But the difficulty of tracing any literary pedigree for the motif should warn us against any assumption of a fixed form (Hagner, Jefford, Keener, Malherbe, Niederwimmer, Prigent, Snell, Syreni, van de Sandt and Flusser). Moreover, the crucial principle of choosing one's own course in life has been lost. The figure of the narrow gate seems peculiar to the gospels.

Such themes are not part of any analytical school tradition. We are witnessing rather sayings of folk wisdom which pass in one form or another from culture to culture without the benefit of any pedigree, just as happens with metaphors in language itself. Albrecht Dihle has traced various tropes of 'popular ethics' (Judge, 'Popular Ethics'), the 'golden rule' (Dihle, *Die goldene Regel*), the 'canon of the two virtues', piety and philanthropy (Dihle, *Der Kanon*) – cf. the pattern seen in the Decalogue – as well as the four cardinal virtues of Hellenic culture. Though canonised once added to Paul's three lasting responses, trust, care and hope (Dihle, *Ruperto-Carola*), they still faced the test of 'the strait and narrow'.

Bibliography:

D.L. **Balch**, 'Neopythagorean Moralists and the New Testament Household Codes', *ANRW* 2.26.1 (1992) 380-411; A. **Blanshard**, *Hercules: A Heroic Life* (London 2005) 32-38; A. **Brinkmann**, 'Ein Denkmal des Neupythagoreismus', *Rheinisches Museum* 66 (1911) 616-625; G. **Clark**, *Iamblichus: On the Pythagorean Life* (Liverpool 1989); F. **Cumont**, *Recherches sur le symbolisme funéraire des Romains* (Paris 1942) 432-430, at 423; F. **Cumont**, *Lux perpetua* (Paris 1949) 278-281; A. **Dihle**, 'Demut', *RAC* 3 (1956) 735-778; A. **Dihle**, *Die goldene Regel* (Göttingen 1962); A. **Dihle**, 'Ethik', *RAC* 6 (1964) 646-797; A. **Dihle**, *Der Kanon der zwei Tugenden* (Cologne 1968); A. **Dihle**, 'Gerechtigkeit', *RAC* 10 (1977) 233-360; A. **Dihle**, 'Von der Hoffnung', *Ruperto-Carola* 44 (1992) 7-16; K. **Ferguson**, 'The Roman Pythagoreans', in K. Ferguson, *Pythagoras: His Lives and the Legacy of a Rational Universe* (London 2010) 163-180; J.T. **Fitzgerald** and L.M. **White**, *The tabula of Cebes* (Chico 1983); P. **Gottlieb**, *The Virtue of Aristotle's Ethics* (Cambridge 2009); A.S.F. **Gow** and D.L. **Page**, *The Garland of Philip*, Vol. 2 (Cambridge 1968) 363; D.A. **Hagner**, 'The Two Ways', *Matthew 1-13* (WBC; Dallas 1993) 177-180; C.J. **Hemer**, 'Philadelphia', *The Letters to the Seven Churches of Asia in their Local Setting* (Sheffield 1986) 153-177; E. **Hermsen**, *Zwei Wege des Jenseits: Das altägyptische Zweiwegebuch und seine Topographie* (Göttingen 1991) 431-438; G.H.R. **Horsley**, 'Names, Double', *ABD* 4 (1992) 1011-1017; C.N. **Jefford**, *The Sayings of Jesus in the Teaching of the Twelve Apostles* (Leiden 1989) 22-92; C.N. **Jefford**, *Apostolic Fathers and the New Testament* (Peabody 2006) 127; C.L. **Joost-Gaugier**, 'Pythagoras in the Roman World', *Measuring Heaven* (Ithaca 2006) 25-43; E.A. **Judge**, 'A Woman's Behaviour', *New Docs* 6 (1992) 18-23; E.A. **Judge**, *The First Christians in the Roman World* (Tübingen 2008) 609, 634, 639; E.A. **Judge**, 'Popular Ethics', in *Jerusalem and Athens* (Tübingen 2010) 71-74; C.S. **Keener**, *Commentary on the Gospel of Matthew* (Grand Rapids 1999) 250-251; J. **Keil** and A. **von Premerstein**, *Bericht über eine Reise in Lydien* (Denkschrift Ak. 53.2; Wien 1908) 34-35, no. 55; R.A. **Kraft**, *Barnabas and the Didache* (New York 1965) 134-162; L.H. **Lesko**, *The Ancient Egyptian Book of Two Ways* (Berkeley 1972); A.J. **Malherbe**, *Moral Exhortation: A Greco-Roman Sourcebook* (Philadelphia 1986) 135-142; K. **Niederwimmer**, *Didache: A Commentary* (Minneapolis 1998) 59-124; J.C. **Paget**, *The Epistle of Barnabas* (Tübingen 1994) 49-51; W. **Peek**, *Griechische Vers-Inschriften (GVI)* (Berlin 1955) no. 1805; G. **Petzl**, 'Zum neupythagoreischen Monument aus Philadelphia', *EA* 20 (1992) 1-5; P. **Prigent**, *Épître de Barnabé* (Paris 1971) 15-20; E. **Pfuhl** – H. **Möbius**, *Die ostgriechischen Grabreliefs* II (Mainz 1979) 2087; C. **Riedweg**, 'Hellenistic "Forgeries" and Neo-pythagoreanism', in C. Riedweg, *Pythagoras, his Life, Teaching and Influence* (ed., C. Riedweg; Ithaca 2005) 119-128; D.T. **Runia**, 'Why does Clement of Alexandria call Philo "The Pythagorean"?', in D.T. Runia, *Philo and the Church Fathers: A Collection of Papers* (Leiden 1995) 54-76; I. **Sluiter** – R.M. **Rosen** (eds), *Kakos: Badness and Anti-value in Classical Antiquity* (Leiden 2008); B. **Snell**, 'Das Symbol des Weges', *Die Entdeckung des Geistes: Studien zur Entstehung des europäischen Denkens bei den Griechen* (Göttingen [4]1975) 219-230; B. **Snell**, 'The Call to Virtue', *The Discovery of the Mind* (New York 1953) 153-190; G. **Staab**, *Pythagoras in der Spätantike* (Munich 2002) 27-30; K. **Syreni**, 'The Sermon on the Mount and the Two Ways Teaching of the Didache', in *Matthew and the Didache* (ed., H. van de Sandt; Assen 2005) 87-103; H. **Theslef**, *Pythagorean Texts of the Hellenistic Period* (Abo 1965); J.C. **Thom**, '"Don't walk on the highways": The Pythagorean *akousmata* and Early Christian literature', *JBL* 113 (1994) 93-112; J.C. **Thom**, *The Pythagorean Golden Verses* (Leiden 1995) 171; H. **van de Sandt** – D. **Flusser**, *The Didache: Its Jewish Sources and its Place in Early Judaism and Christianity* (Assen 2002) 55-270; L. **Zhmund**, *Wissenschaft, Philosophie und Religion im frühen Pythagoreismus* (Berlin 1997).

E.A. Judge (Macquarie University)

MAGIC

§3 Overcoming the 'strong man'

Provenance unknown   Inscription on a cameo   AD 25-50

Ed. pr. — A.A. Barb, 'Three Elusive Amulets: I. A "Gnostic": Cameo', *JWI* 27 (1964) 1-9, pl. I a-b; M.-L. Vollenweider, Deliciae leonis: *Antike geschnittene Steine und Ringe aus einer Privatsammlung* (Mainz 1984) 290-293, no. 508, pl. (= *SEG* XXXIV 1666); R.W. Daniel and P.J. Sijpesteijn, 'Remarks on a Magical Inscription', *JWI* 51 (1988) 169 (= *SEG* XXXVIII 1924).

The cameo, in a private collection, portrays on the front Hermes clad in a chlamys holding a caduceus and a tortoise. At his left a theta, at his right a chi. Barb suggested Θ(εὸς) Χ(ριστός) or Θ(εὸς) Χ(θόνιος); Vollenweider preferred Θ(οτ) and Χ(ελώνη) ('tortoise'), and questioned Barb's suggested identification of Vibia Paulina. Four different Vibii took consulships in AD 5, 16, 17, and 21 (or 22). Our discussion uses Barb's dating as a springboard, without reference to what may have influenced him in offering it.

	Greek	Translation
	Ἰαω	Iao
	Ἀβρασα<ξ>	Abrasa<x>
	Ἀδωναι ἅ-	Adonai, h-
4	γιον ὄνομ-	oly nam-
	<α> <δ>εξιαὶ δυ-	<e>, <f>ortunate po-
	νάμις φυλ-	wers, pro-
	άξατ<ε> Οὐε-	tec<t> Vi-
8	βίαν Παυ-	bia Pau-
	λεῖναν	lina

2 ΑΒΡΑΣΑΣ, lapis 5 ΟΝΟΜΙΛ, lapis 7 ΦΥΛΙΑΞΑΤΣ, lapis

The inscription on our cameo has inherent interest because of its early first-century AD date and the possibility that it might belong to the world of Jewish magic. First, in regard to the issue of dating, the corpus of the magical papyri mostly postdates the New Testament, with only two of the papyri in Karl Preisendanz' edition of the *Papyri Graecae Magicae* (Vol. 1, 1928; Vol. 2, 1931) belonging to the first-century AD. This raises the methodological question whether we can legitimately make use of the magical papyri, largely originating from the third century AD onwards, to throw light on our first-century New Testament texts. D.E. Aune ('Apocalypse of John', 483) and A.D. Nock (*Essays*, 187) are confident that the essential formulae of Graeco-Egyptian magic had started to take shape by New Testament times. Since our cameo inscription reveals a formulaic ritual of mid first-century AD magic, it provides us with the opportunity to test whether the later magical papyri drew upon these earlier traditions or (at least) had continuity with them.

Second, because of our inscription's Jewish echoes (i.e. 'Iao', 'Adonai'), we need to determine whether the inscription belongs to the world of Jewish magic or to the world of non-Jewish magic (H.D. Betz, 'Jewish Magic', *passim*). The diversity of types and modes of the Jewish magical tradition is now well known to us through (a) the translations of *Jannes and Jambres* and the *Prayer of Jacob* (J.H. Charlesworth, *Old Testament Pseudepigrapha*, 427-444, 715-723); (b) the exorcisms of the Qumran corpus (M.O. Wise, 'By the Power of Beelzebub', 637-650; 4Q510, 4Q560, 11Q11); (c) the Aramaic inscriptions (J. Naveh and S. Shaked, *Amulets and Magic Bowls*; *Magical Spells*); (d) Hebrew and Aramaic incantations (L.H. Schiffman, and M.D. Schwartz, *Incantation Texts*); (e) the work of Jewish alchemists (R. Patai); and (f) the *Sepher Ha-Razim* (M. Morgan). We are therefore faced with an important methodological question: are the Jewish components of our cameo inscription being employed in the context of non-Jewish magic or of Jewish magic? And how do we determine this?

It is unclear who composed the wording of the apotropaic inscription on our cameo. Did Vibia Paulina hire or approach a 'professional' magician for the rendering of the words, or did she herself compose the text for the stone-cutter to engrave? Given the brevity of the inscription, the latter possibility is, in my opinion, more likely. This cameo, therefore, points to the ubiquity of popular magic in the first century AD, where people sought to protect themselves by means of inscribed cameos and amulets against unspecified evil forces or the fickle turns of Fate. The text addresses a series of deities by their magical names. As much as several of these names reveal the syncretistic world of first-century magic (J.M. Hull, *Hellenistic Magic*, 27-37), the dynamic occurring here is different. Vibia Paulina, by virtue of her knowledge of their names, is attempting to compel or manipulate the deities to fulfil her wish for personal protection. What, then, is the significance of each name?

(a) The magical name 'Iao' is a Greek transliteration of the divine name *yhw* ('Yahia'), a shorthand way of referring to *yhwh* ('Yahweh'), the covenant name of God (Judg 5:5; cf. v. 3; Deut 6:4; 26:16-19 etc.). The name may have become associated with various deities in the underworld of magic (R. Ganschinietz, 'IAŌ' 698-721; D.E. Aune, 'Iao' cols. 1-12; M.M. Smith, *God in Translation*, 277-288) because of the reputation that Moses held in Graeco-Roman antiquity as a powerful magician (J.G. Gager, 'Moses the Magician'; cf. *PGM* V 108). 'Iao' appears regularly in the magical papyri (e.g. *PGM* I 300; III 146, 312, 945; VII 220; VIII 61; XII 63, 263-266, 285; XV 15; CI 4; CV 1-15 etc; cf. 4Q Lev[b] LXX) and in the curse tablets (J. Gager, *Curse Tablets*, 63, 64, 67, 70 n. 95, 94, 100, 101, 104, 136, 137, 144, 216, 225: cf. Smith, *God in Translation*, 278, n. 15).

(b) The name 'Abrasax' (or 'Abraxas') was assigned to a popular deity, a solar god (*PGM* I 300-305: 'Iao and you, Michael, who rule heaven's realm, I call, and you, archangel Gabriel, down from Olympos, Abrasax, delighting in dawns, come gracious who view sunset from the dawn, Adonai'). The letters of the name 'Abrasax' had the numerical value of the magic number 365 (*PGM* IV 331-332; VIII 49, 611; XIII 156, 466 etc.).

(c) 'Adonai' (or 'Adonaios') is the name of a deity in the magical papyri (e.g. *PGM* I 305, 310; III 147, 221; XII 63 ['by order of the most high God Iao Adoneai

ABLANATHANALBA'], CXXIII F.14 etc.), though its Jewish origin ('Lord') is indisputable (e.g. Isa 3:15; 6:8, 11; 10:24).

(d) 'Holy name' also occurs in the magical papyri (*PGM* III 570: 'I invoke your holy name from every side'; *PGM* CXXV f: 'I conjure you by your holy name'). The famous Paris magical papyrus (*PGM* IV 3007-3086: *ll.* 3070-3071) adjures the possessed 'with his holy name, IAEOBAPHRENEMOUN formula'. A curse tablet from Rome against a rival charioteer uses the plural form (*IGRR* I §117): 'I conjure you up, holy beings, and holy names: join in aiding this spell, and bind, enchant, thwart, strike, overturn, conspire against, destroy, kill, break Eucherius, the charioteer, and all his horses, tomorrow in the circus at Rome' (cf. *PGM* I 312-313: 'I adjure [ὁρκίζω] these holy and divine names that they send me the divine spirit …'). Last, a charm of Solomon (*PGM* IV 870-875; cf. CI 52) also uses the plural form: 'Hear me, that is, my holy voice, because I call upon your holy names, and reveal to me the thing which I want, through the NN man or little boy, for otherwise I will not defend your holy and undefiled names'.

(e) Finally, 'fortunate powers' (<δ>εξιαὶ δυ|νάμις) is P.J. Sijpesteijn's emendation of A.A. Barb's original reading (*SEG* XXIV 1666). Instead of <δ>εξιαὶ δυ|νάμις, Barb had initially reconstructed the text as the 'unattested adjective ἀέξιος or the rare ἀ(λ)έξιος, qualifying the feminine vocative plural δυνάμις (δυ|νάμεις)' (*SEG* XXXVIII 1924, p. 555). Sijpesteijn (*JWI* 51 [1998] 169) argued for his emendation of Barb's text because of the mistakes made by the engraver. What is the significance of the 'fortunate powers' that the petitioner summons here? In my opinion, this is an open-ended 'catch all' title for all the other beneficent deities not addressed by the names in (a) to (c) above. The emendment of the plural <δ>εξιαὶ δυ|νάμις clearly indicates that a plurality of deities is envisaged here, a fact confirmed by the plural form of φυλ|άξατ<ε>.

Several observations are apposite at this juncture. First, most of the magical names in this early first-century AD cameo inscription are replicated in the later papyri and curse tablets. This supports the argument of Aune and Nock that the formulae of magic were already taking definitive shape by the New Testament era. If this cameo inscription is representative, we can cautiously use the magical papyri as background for understanding the New Testament texts, without the charge of anachronism disqualifying their relevance at the outset.

Second, while there are undoubtedly Jewish terms in our cameo inscription, in this case we are definitely operating in the world of non-Jewish magic. There is no indication of Jewish monotheism, given the plural forms noted above; neither is there any reference to the angelic world, or to the Old Testament scriptures (or even to inter-textual echoes of them), apart from the magical names 'Iao' and 'Adonai', widely used in syncretistic contexts. Rather, the Jewish components in the text are merely enlisted as part of the arsenal of divinities summoned to accomplish the spell. By contrast, H.D. Betz ('Jewish Magic', 63, my emphasis), speaking of healing charms, sums the tenor of Jewish magic thus:

§3 Overcoming the 'strong man'

> What seems characteristic of both the Jewish and Christian magic is that the whole arsenal of means is put together to work against what is thought to be *one* enemy causing the malady. Implied in these forms of magic is an enormous concentration of the forces of creation and, in the Christian context, of redemption, in the battle against the evils of illness. The *one* God confronts the evil one.

What relevance, then, does this inscription have for New Testament studies? The syncretistic mixture of the magical names of Jewish and Graeco-Roman deities in our cameo inscription perhaps provides us imaginative insight into the techniques employed by the Jewish exorcists at Ephesus (Acts 19:13; cf. Matt 12:27; Luke 11:19; Josephus, *A.J.* 8.42-49 [cf. T. Sol. 12.4]; *PGM* IV 1233; IV 3007-3086: *ll.* 3020-3021: 'I adjure [ὁρκίζω] you by the god of the Hebrews, Jesus'). The exorcists had added the name of Jesus to their arsenal of Jewish magical names (Acts 19:13b [ὁρκίζω ὑμᾶς τὸν Ἰησοῦν ὃν Παῦλος κηρύσσει], 15), in order to summon Jesus' power by invoking his name (*PGM* IV 3007-3086; IV 1227-1264; cf. IV 86-87; LXXXV 1-6; XCIV 17-21). By knowing his name (cf. *PGM* III 494-501: H.-J. Klauck, *Magic*, 99), the Jewish exorcists thought that they could 'tap into his wondrous power, coercing him to do their bidding' (S.R. Garrett, *Magic and the Demonic*, 93).

Of particular interest in our cameo inscription, too, is the appeal to beneficent 'powers' (<δ>εξιαὶ δυ|νάμις), over and above the specific names of the magical deities. Luke is at pains to emphasise in Acts that the pneumatic 'power' of the risen and ascended Jesus was operative in his disciples (Acts 1:8 [λήμψεσθε δύναμιν ἐπελθόντος τοῦ ἁγίου πνεύματος]; 2:22 [ἄνδρα ἀποδεδειγμένον ἀπὸ τοῦ θεοῦ εἰς ὑμᾶς δυνάμεσι]; 3:12; 4:7, 33; 6:8; 8:13 [δυνάμεις μεγάλας]; 10:38 [ἔχρισεν αὐτὸν ὁ θεὸς πνεύματι ἁγίῳ καὶ δυνάμει]; 19:11 [δυνάμεις τε οὐ τὰς τυχούσας]). The power of Jesus triumphs over the magicians (8:4-13; 13:4-12; 19:11-20) and their occult powers (8:10b: ἡ δύναμις τοῦ θεοῦ ἡ καλουμένη Μεγάλη; cf. the magical charm cited by R.P. Casey, 'Simon Magus', 153, n. 3 [ἐπικαλοῦμαί σε τὴν μεγίστην δύναμιν ἐν τῷ οὐρανῷ]). Seemingly, the triumph of Christ over Satan, demons and practitioners of magic meant that Satan's end had come in advance (Mark 3:26b). On δύναμις in the magical papyri and its relation to the angelic 'powers' in Ephesians 1:21, see C.E. Arnold, *Ephesians*, 53-56.

Finally, the emphasis on the petitioner's knowledge of the 'holy name' in the cameo inscription (ἅ|γιον ὀνομ‖<α>) is reminiscent of Markan pericope where the man with the unclean spirit identifies Jesus the exorcist in this manner: 'Have you come to destroy us? I know who you are, the Holy One of God (ὁ ἅγιος τοῦ θεοῦ)' (Mark 1:24; cf. 3:11 ['Son of God']; 5:7 ['Son of the Most High God']). While at one level we are witnessing here the demons' clairvoyant knowledge of Jesus' identity, nonetheless the 'I know you' formula is well attested in the magical papyri (Hull, *Hellenistic Magic*, 67; cf. *PGM* VIII 13: 'I know you, Hermes, who you are and where you come from and what your city is: Hermopolis'; III 570, *supra*; IV 870-875, *supra*). As noted, magical adjurations also referred to the holy names of deities (e.g. *PGM* VII 388: 'I adjure [ὁρκίζω] you, holy names of Cypris'; cf. *PGM* VII 444: 'I conjure you, lord Osiris, by your holy names'). Thus the demon(s) in the possessed man are trying to deflect, by means of their magical incantations, the power of Jesus though their knowledge of his name (Garrett, *Magic and the Demonic*, 92). Therefore the demon uses the technical language of exorcism, known to us through the magical papyri, in response to Jesus' power as an exorcist (Mark 5:7: ὁρκίζω σε). Elsewhere in the Gospels there is reference to Jesus' name being employed in exorcisms, positively (Mark 9:38-39) and negatively (Matt 7:22). Significantly, in contrast to the magical papyri, Jesus does not use the formulae of adjuration (ὁρκίζω) to expel the demon (S. Eitrem, *Demonology*, 9, 20), but simply commands (Mark 5:8: ἔξελθε) the unclean spirit to exit the man (Garrett, *Magic and the Demonic*, 92; cf. S. Shauf, *Theology as History*, 202-210). For discussion of how Jesus used a variety of simple imperatives, over against the long magical formulae of his contemporaries, in healings and exorcisms, see Eitrem, *Demonology*, 25-27. For a Christian amulet (III-IV AD), invoking as protection an array of angelic and divine names (including Jesus), see Gager, *Curse Tablets*, §125, 232-234.

The superiority of Jesus, as Hull notes (*Hellenistic Magic*, 70), is demonstrated by the fact that he normally does not have to enquire regarding the name of the demon(s) (*pace*, Mark 5:9). Usually he silences them, leaving them no recourse on their part (Mark 1:25-26; 3:11; 5:8). In the one case where Jesus does enquire about the name of the spirits (Mark 5:9), it is significant that the unclean spirits not only have to beg Jesus to refrain from tormenting them and from sending them out of the country (Mark 5:10), but also they have to seek his permission to enter the herd of swine before plunging into the lake (5:11-13). Visual cues, such as the prostration of the spirits, in the presence of the demoniac falling before Jesus (Mark 5:6: προσεκύνησεν; cf. G. Twelftree, *Jesus the Exorcist*, 147-148), also underscore how the demonic world was being routed through him.

In conclusion, over against the magical practitioners of his day, who displayed an intricate knowledge of the multiplicity of spirit names, Jesus congregated the demonic opposition to his ministry under one figure alone: Beelzebul (Mark 3:23-27; Luke 10:17-20). The πονηρὰ πνεύματα, obedient to their leader, were being overcome by the presence of the πνεῦμα θεοῦ in Jesus (Matt 12:28; Luke 4:17 [Isa 61:1]). Jesus does not use the Name of God in expelling demons (Eitrem, *Demonology*, 6), nor does he invoke in prayer the Holy Spirit to work through him in exorcising demons. Seemingly, the Spirit's power was continuously available to Christ and operative in his conflict with the demonic world (Luke 4:1-2). Therefore, precisely because the Pharisaic experts in exorcism were unable to overcome the 'strong man' (Luke 11:19; cf. vv. 17-18, 20-23), Jesus asserted that their clients would be re-possessed by even more spirits than was originally the case (11:24-26).

Bibliography

C.E. **Arnold**, *Ephesians: Power and Magic. The Concept of Power in Ephesians in Light of Its Historical Setting* (Cambridge/New York 1989); D.E. **Aune**, 'Magic in Early Christianity', *ANRW* II.23.1 (1987) 1507-1557; D.E. **Aune**, 'The Apocalypse of John and Graeco-Roman Revelatory Magic', *NTS* 33/4 (1987) 481-501; D.E. **Aune**, 'Iao', *RAC* 17 (1994) cols. 1-12; H.D. **Betz**, *The Greek Magical Papyri in Translation, Including the Demotic Spells. Volume One: Texts* (Chicago and London 1986); *id.*, 'Jewish Magic in the Greek Magical Papyri (*PGM* VII 260-271)', in *Envisioning Magic: A Princeton Seminar and Symposium* (eds, P. Schäfer and H.G. Kippenberg; Leiden 1997) 45-63; G. **Bohak**, *Ancient Jewish Magic: A History*

(Cambridge/New York 2008); R.P. **Casey**, 'Simon Magus', in *The Acts of the Apostles. Volume V: Additional Notes to the Commentary* (eds, F.J. Jackson, K. Lake; Grand Rapids repr. 1979) 151-163; J.H. **Charlesworth**, 'Prayer of Jacob', in *The Old Testament Pseudepigrapha Volume 2* (ed., J.M. Charlesworth; Garden City 1985) 715-723; M.W. **Dickie**, *Magic and Magicians in the Greco-Roman World* (New York 2001); S. **Eitrem**, *Some Notes on the Demonology in the New Testament* (Oslo 1950); C.A. **Faraone** (ed.), *Magika Hiera: Ancient Greek Magic and Religion* (New York 1991); E. **Ferguson**, *Demonology of the Early Christian World* (New York/Toronto 1984); *Moses in Graeco-Roman Paganism* (Nashville/New York 1972); J.G. **Gager**, *Curse Tablets and Binding Spells from the Ancient World* (New York/Oxford 1992); J.G. **Gager**, 'Moses the Magician: Hero of an Ancient Counter-culture?', *Helios* 21 (1994) 179-188; R. **Ganschinietz**, 'IAŌ', *PRE* (1914) 698-721; S.R. **Garrett**, *Magic and the Demonic in Luke's Writings* (Minneapolis 1989); S.R. **Garrett**, 'Light on a Dark Subject and Vice Versa: Magic and Magicians in the New Testament', in *Religion, Science and Magic* (ed., J. Neusner, et al.; New York/Oxford 1989) 142-165; T. **Haviainen**, 'Pagan Incantations in Aramaic Magic Bowls', in *Studia Aramaica* (eds, M.J. Geller, et al.; Oxford/New York: Oxford 1995) 53-60; J.M. **Hull**, *Hellenistic Magic and the Synoptic Tradition* (London 1974); C.D. **Isbell**, *Corpus of the Aramaic Incantation Bowls* (Missoula 1975); H.C. **Kee**, *Medicine, Miracle and Magic in New Testament Times* (Cambridge 1986); H.-J. **Klauck**, *Magic and Paganism in Early Christianity: The World of the Acts of the Apostles* (Edinburgh 2000); A. **Lange**, 'The Essene Position on Magic and Divination', in *Studies on the Texts of the Desert of Judah* (eds, F.G. Martinez, A.S. van der Woode; Leiden 1997) 377-435; G. **Luck**, *Arcana Mundi: Magic and the Occult in the Greek and Roman World* (Baltimore and London 1985); M. **Morgan**, *Sepher Ha-Razim: The Book of the Mysteries* (Chico 1983); J. **Naveh** and S. **Shaked** (eds), *Amulets and Magic Bowls: Aramaic Inscriptions of Late Antiquity* (Jerusalem 1985); J. **Naveh** and S. **Shaked** (eds), *Magical Spells and Formulae: Aramaic Incantations from Antiquity* (Jerusalem 1993); A.D. **Nock**, 'Greek Magical Papyri', in *Essays on Religion and the Ancient World* (Oxford 1972) 176-194; R. **Patai**, *The Jewish Alchemists: A History and Source Book* (Princeton 1994); A. **Piertesma** and T.R. **Lutz**, 'Jannes and Jambres', in *The Old Testament Pseudepigrapha Volume 2* (ed., J.M. Charlesworth; Garden City 1985) 427-436; L.H. **Schiffman** and M.D. **Swartz**, *Hebrew and Aramaic Incantation Texts from the Cairo Geniza* (Sheffield 1992); S. **Shauf**, *Theology as History, History as Theology: Paul in Ephesus in Acts 19* (Berlin 2005); M. **Smith**, 'The Jewish Elements in the Magical Papyri', in *Studies in the Cult of Yahweh: New Testament, Early Christianity and Magic*, Vol. 2 (eds, M. Smith, S.J.D. Cohen; Leiden 1996) 242-256; M.M. **Smith**, *God in Translation: Deities in Cross-Cultural Discourse in the Biblical World* (Tübingen 2008); G.H. **Twelftree**, *Jesus the Exorcist: A Contribution to the Study of the Historical Jesus* (Peabody 1993); M.O. **Wise**, 'By the Power of Beelzebub: An Aramaic Incantation Formula from Qumran (4Q560)', *JBL* 113/4 (1994) 627-650; E. **Yamauchi**, 'Magic or Miracle? Diseases, Demons and Exorcisms', in *Gospel Perspectives: The Miracles of Jesus*, Vol. 6 (eds, D. Wenham, C. Blomberg; Sheffied 1986) 89-183.

J.R. Harrison (Macquarie University)

§4 All Grades of Angels

Provenance unknown Oval chalcedony gem AD 150-250
(Eastern Mediterranean)

Ed. pr. — A.M. Nagy, 'Ein kaiserzeitlicher Talisman', *AA* (1992) 99-108 (= *SEG* XLII 1692).

The inscription is found on both the obverse and reverse of a bone-coloured oval chalcedony gem, now in the Museum of Fine Arts, Budapest. In the centre of the gem on the obverse is engraved an eagle holding a wreath in its beak. The spell is displayed clockwise around the eagle, with the remainder of the text being continued and completed on the reverse side.

Ἄνγελος Ἰαω διδοίμης πᾶσαν πρᾶξιν	Angel Iao, may you give all success
καὶ δύναμιν καὶ χάριν καὶ συνοσεί-	and power and favour and assist-
αν {ι} Ἀσκληπιακῷ μετὰ τῶν	ance to Asklepiakos with (the help of) the
4 πρωτανγέ-	first ang-
λων καὶ μ-	els and
εσανγέλων	middle angels
καὶ τελεαν-	and final ang-
8 γέλων ἰς πά-	els through-
ντα τὸν βί-	out (his) life
ον καὶ σώμα-	and bod-
τος προφύ-	ily prote-
12 λαξιν Ἀβρ-	ction, Abr-
ασαξ ΔΑΥ	asax O Da(mnamene)us
ἀεί	for ever.

2 l. συνουσίαν   8 l. εἰς

This inscription poses several puzzles for translators. First, A.M. Nagy, the editor of the inscription, notes that διδοίμης (l. 1) is an uncertain reading (p. 99). No matter how we handle the presence of διδοίμης on the obverse, it is clear from the flow of the sentence that a second person singular predicate must stand as the conclusion. However, if διδοίμης is the correct restoration, then διδοίμης must be an unattested variant that was formed from the first person singular optative διδοίμην. Therefore διδοίμης must be a variant of the second person singular middle optative form διδοῖο. Second, Nagy (p. 104) also observes that the angelic triad is presently unknown (ll. 3-8), with the words μεσάνγελος (ll. 5-6) and τελεάνγελος (ll. 7-8) being new words. Third, several other unattested words are noted by Nagy (pp. 102, 103-104). While προφύλαξις (ll. 11-12) is an unattested word, some of its cognates (προφυλάσσειν ['to protect'];

§4 All Grades of Angels

προφυλακτικόν ['protective']) are technical terms of magic. Likewise ΔΑΥ (*l.* 13) is either an unattested magical term or the abbreviation of the vocative (Δα(μναμενε)ύ) of Δαμναμενεύς (the alternative which we have adopted in our translation). Fourth, because the word Ἰαω is indeclinable in Greek, Ἄνγελλος Ἰαω (*l.* 1) must be either possessive or appositional. Thus, as Nagy comments (p. 103), the meaning can be 'Iao's angel' or 'Iao, the angel'. Certainty on this issue is not attainable, but it is clear that one deity is primarily being summoned (*l.* 1: the singular form διδοίμης), with others being asked in a subordinate role to help in effecting the spell (*ll.* 3-8, 12-13).

At the beginning of the inscription (*ll.* 1-3), the petitioner expresses the wish — ensuring thereby that hybris is not displayed by making a demand — that the Angel Iao might give to Asklepiakos a series of blessings. On the magical deities 'Iao' (*l.* 1) and 'Abrasax' (*ll.* 12-13), mentioned above, see my discussion in §3 in this volume. In the case of Damnameneus (*l.* 13), the deity was the son of Poseidon and Thalatta (the Sea). Not only is he invoked in a love spell of attraction (*PGM* IV 2780: 'prudent Damnameneus'), but also his name is one of the Ephesia Grammata ('Ephesian letters'), that is, the famous ancient Greek magical formulae dating from the fifth to the fourth century BC.

We know nothing, however, about Asklepiakos, the potential recipient of the divine beneficence petitioned on the gem. Nonetheless, the name is well known to us from inscriptions and papyri of the first five centuries AD (Nagy, p. 100, n. 14). If the spell were effective, Asklepiakos could expect to receive πᾶσαν πρᾶξιν καὶ δύναμιν καὶ χάριν καὶ συνοσείαν (*ll.* 1-3). On χάρις in the magical papyri and its relation to Paul's understanding of grace, see J.R. Harrison, *Paul's Language of Grace*, 90-95. On δύναμις in the magical papyri and its relation to the angelology of Ephesians, see C.E. Arnold, *Ephesians*, 53-56. As far as πρᾶξις, Nagy (p. 102) argues that the word generally refers to 'measures' accomplished, but in the technical language of magic it mainly refers to 'individual charm practices'. This is the sense of πρᾶξις in Acts 19:18 where it refers to a 'magical practice' or a 'magical procedure'. However, in the context of our inscription, it is more accurately translated 'success'. The word συνοσεία — a variant of συνουσεία — 'means an association, either with mortals in the community of love, or with gods by the emotion of soul, or by the contemplative spirit' (Nagy, p. 102). Nagy concludes that the more 'earthly' understanding of 'association' is what predominated in the magical books. Thus we have translated the word as 'assistance'. Finally, we learn that Asklepiakos, because of all these blessings (*ll.* 1-3), would be protected from disease (*ll.* 10-12: σώματος προφύλαξιν) and all through his life (*ll.* 10-12: ἰς πάντα τὸν βίον).

What is especially intriguing about this gem inscription is the unprecedented description of a hierarchy of 'first angels and middle angels and final angels'. The petitioner asks Iao for the help of these other angelic creatures in blessing Asklepiakos. The *SEG* editor suggests that 'probably we have clumsy translations into Greek of concepts expressed in another language' (*SEG* XLII 1692, p. 491).

In the case of the πρωτάνγελος ('first angel'), however, there is mention of Apollo as the 'first angel of Zeus' (*PGM* I 300; cf. P. Athanassiadi and M. Frede [eds.], *Pagan Monotheism*, 17-18). In this highly syncretistic lamp divination, named after the god Apollo (*PGM* I 262-347), the Lord Apollo is summoned for revelation and healing (*PGM* I 298-305; see Nagy, p. 104, n. 39 for literary references):

> O Lord Apollo, come with Paian.
> Give answer to my questions, lord, O master,
> leave Mount Parnassos and the Delphic Pytho
> whene'er my priestly lips voice secret words,
> first angel of [the god], great Zeus. Iao,
> and you, Michael, who rules heaven's realm,
> I call, and you, archangel Gabriel,
> down from Olympos, Abrasax, delighting
> in dawns, come gracious who views sunset from
> the dawn, Adonai ...

In sum, there is no real precedent in the magical books for this graphic description of a hierarchy of angels of differing status assisting the main deity Iao in effecting the spell.

It might be argued that the hierarchical language of our inscription matches the intricate language of 'power' that Paul employs in discussing the angelic and demonic world in his epistles, particularly in Romans, Ephesians and Colossians. However, Paul displays none of the detailed interest in angelic hierarchy evinced here. Paul unifies the demonic world under one figure, Satan, whose end-time defeat has been proleptically announced through the cross (1 Cor 2:6-8; Eph 1:20-22; 4:9-10 [cf. 1 Peter 3:18-22]; 6:12-20; Phil 2:10; Col 2:15, 20 [cf. 1:13]). Paul concentrates more on Satan's threat to believers than on the activities of his demonic cohorts (Rom 16:20; 1 Cor 5:5; 7:5; 2 Cor 2:11; 4:4; 6:15; 11:3, 14; 12:7; Eph 2:2; 4:27; 6:11, 16; 1 Thess 2:18; 3:5; 2 Thess 2:9; 3:3; 1 Tim 1:20; 3:6, 7; 5:15; 2 Tim 2:26). In this regard, it is probably a mistake to attribute an 'elaborate demonology' to Paul, as does C.F.D. Moule ('St Paul and "Dualism"', 221). Only occasionally does Paul mention the activity of the demonic world (Rom 8:38; 1 Cor 10:20-21; 2 Cor 12:7; 1 Tim 4:1). As E. Ferguson states (*Demonology*, 146-147): 'Paul does see the evil spiritual forces as subordinate to Satan and functioning as one under his leadership. Otherwise, he pays no attention to the interrelationship of spiritual beings'.

To be sure, Paul regularly refers to principalities, powers, authorities, thrones, dominions, world rulers, spiritual hosts, and elemental spirits (Rom 8:38; 1 Cor 2:6, 8; 15:24; Gal 4:3, 9; Eph 1:21; 2:2; 3:10; 6:12; Col 1:16; 2:8, 10, 15, 20). But this does not necessarily imply an apocalyptic preoccupation with angelic or demonic hierarchies, or an obsession with the intricate hierarchies of Graeco-Roman or Graeco-Egyptian demonology, as seen in our magical gem. He mentions the (unnamed) archangel in 1 Thessalonians 4:16, but evinces none of the intense interest of Second Temple Judaism in the number of archangels or their names. More likely Paul's language of power is either polemically occasioned by local issues — such as the presence of Jewish and Graeco-Roman magic at Ephesus (Arnold, *Ephesians: Power and Magic*), or the existence of folk beliefs and Jewish apocalypticism at Colossae (C.E. Arnold, *Colossian Syncretism*; T.J. Sappington, *Revelation*) — or by his desire as a Hellenistic Jew, schooled in the LXX, to interact with the cosmology of popular philosophy (C. Forbes, 'Paul's Principalities'; 'Pauline Demonology').

Bibliography

C.E. **Arnold**, 'The "Exorcism" of Ephesians 6:12 in Recent Research: A Critique of Wesley Carr's View of the Role of Evil Powers in First-century AD Belief', *JSNT* 30 (1987) 71-87; C.E. **Arnold**, *Ephesians: Power and Magic. The Concept of Power in Ephesians in Light of Its Historical Setting* (Cambridge/New York 1989); C.E. **Arnold**, *Powers of Darkness: Principalities and Powers in Paul's Letters* (Downers Grove 1992); C.E. **Arnold**, 'Returning to the Domain of the Powers: *stoicheia* as Evil Spirits in Gal 4:3, 9', *NovT* 38 (1996) 55-76; C.E. **Arnold**, *The Colossian Syncretism: The Interface Between Christianity and Folk Belief at Colossae* (Grand Rapids 1996); P. **Athanassiadi** and M. **Frede** (eds), *Pagan Monotheism in Late Antiquity* (Oxford 1999); D.E. **Aune**, 'Principalities (*Archai*)', in *Dictionary of Deities and Demons in the Bible* (ed., K. van der Toorn, et al.; Grand Rapids ²1999) cols 144-150; P. **Benoit**, 'Pauline Angelology and Demonology: Reflections on the Designations of the Heavenly Powers and on the Origin of Angelic Evil according to Paul', *Religious Studies Bulletin* 3 (1983) 1-18; M. **Black**, '*Pasai exousiai autoi hypotagesontai*', in *Paul and Paulinism: Essays in Honour of C.K. Barrett* (eds, M.D. Hooker, S.G. Wilson; London 1982) 73-82; S.G.F. **Brandon**, 'Angels: the History of an Idea', in *Religion in Ancient Society: Studies in Ideas, Men and Events* (ed., S.G.F. Brandon; London 1973) 354-370; G.B. **Caird**, *Principalities and Powers: A Study in Pauline Theology* (Oxford 1956); W. **Carr**, *Angels and Principalities: The Background, Meaning and Development of the Pauline Phrase* hai archai kai hai exousiai (Cambridge 1981); F. **Cumont**, 'Les anges du paganisme', *RHR* 72 (1915) 159-182; M. **Dibelius**, *Die Geisterwelt im Glauben des Paulus* (Göttingen 1909); S. **Eitrem**, *Some Notes on the Demonology in the New Testament* (Uppsala 1966); O. **Everling**, *Die paulinische Angelologie und Dämonologie* (Göttingen 1888); E. **Ferguson**, *Demonology of the Early Christian World* (New York/Toronto 1984); C. **Forbes**, 'Paul's Principalities and Powers: Demythologising Apocalyptic?', *JSNT* 82 (2001) 61-88; C. **Forbes**, 'Pauline Demonology and/or Cosmology? Principalities, Powers and the Elements of the World in their Hellenistic Context', *JSNT* 85 (2002) 51-73; J.R. **Harrison**, *Paul's Language of Grace in its Graeco-Roman Context* (Tübingen 2003); J.R. **Harrison**, 'In Quest of the Third Heaven: Paul and his Apocalyptic Imitators', *VC* 58/1 (2004) 24-55; T.J. **Kraus**, 'Angels in the Magical Papyri: the Classical Example of Michael, the Archangel', in *The Concept of Celestial Beings: Origins, Development and Reception* (ed., F.V. Reiterer; Berlin/New York 2007) 611-628; J.Y. **Lee**, 'Interpreting the Demonic Powers in Paul's Thought', *NovT* 12 (1970) 54-69; H.C. **MacGregor**, 'Principalities and Powers: The Cosmic Ground of Paul's Thought', *NTS* 1 (1954-1955) 17-28; C.F.D. **Moule**, 'St Paul and "Dualism": The Pauline Conception of Resurrection', in C.F.D. Moule, *Essays in New Testament Interpretation* (Cambridge 1982) 200-221; D. **Ogden** (ed.), *Magic, Witchcraft and Ghosts in the Greek and Roman Worlds: A Sourcebook* (Oxford 2002); T.J. **Sappington**, *Revelation and Redemption at Colossae: The Ascetic-Mystical Piety of Jewish Apocalypticism and the Soteriology of Colossians* (Sheffield 1991); H. **Schlier**, *Principalities and Powers in the New Testament* (Edinburgh/London 1961); H. **Schlier**, 'The Angels according to the New Testament', in *The Relevance of the New Testament* (New York 1968) 172-192; E. **Schweizer**, 'Slaves of the Elements, Worshippers of Angels: Gal 4:3, 9 and Gal 2:8, 18, 20', *JBL* 107 (1998) 455-468; W. **Wink**, *Naming the Powers* (Philadelphia 1984).

J.R. Harrison (Macquarie University)

§5   Incantation for Spirit Possession of a Boy

Fayum   Lead tablet, 12.5x10.7 cm   III or IV

Ed. pr. — P.J. Sijpesteijn, 'Ein Herbeirufungszauber', *ZPE* 4 (1969) 187-191; F. Maltomini, 'πανάτιμος: non attestato *ZPE* 87 (1991) 253-254 (= *SEG* XLI 1619 = Suppl. Mag. II 66 = Trismegistos 102449).

T. Moen s.n. (formerly in private collection of A.M. Hakkert). There is a single break on one of the lower edges, otherwise the tablet is intact. Crease lines in the lead reveal that it had been folded in antiquity, by first bending the right and left thirds of the tablet inwards and then folding top to bottom. The folds would have reduced the size to approximately 4 cm by 3 cm. The tablet's provenance is Egypt. Based on reports from the French antiquities-dealers who brought the piece to Europe, it had been discovered in the Fayum, the fertile region of lower Egypt west of the Nile valley which has yielded a wealth of textual and archaeological sources for all periods of Egyptian history. The tablet is inscribed in Greek, in a hand representative of the 3rd/4th century AD.

```
      [magical characters]
      [magical characters]
      [magical characters] τουραιαρ[.]υητιρωχοχε
      μα βαντεανα αγ\α/τα αμαψουουρου
 5    αναапαντο ροδαμιτ σατραπερκμηφ
      θυρσερψε[.]αμαχθεν θουφ καρχρηθχρωινε
      κρομιορφι ζθο θονινευκτευ θωουθιθωθ
      Ἰάω τεωαντισιρονμυραε βωδρομω ω
      αλεου παον ενεπαντιενε λυμβρεκλαρυζ
10    κρογεακετοριψαραβαθαεο παχνευχανωρ
      φοβερομματεπανεργετ<α>σεσενγενβαρ-
      φαραγγησομοιβασκο/βερωουνηρ
      θωβαφ θαμβαμιοψνωοιμφυτι
      σθομψιμ φιηιοινδυσδωμηλελωθε
15    Αδυναις α´ ιοιναθαψαωσεν βιρααριν
      δαλημα´ γαθοαθαγεν γη ψουανε
      πουραθα[.]ουαμωθ ἀέἠἰὁὐώ επεη
      ωιουθευα[.] υυυ ιιι θεσμαοαθαα
      ἐλθέ λάλησον εἰσκρίθητι              Come! Speak! Enter
20    ἐμοὶ Ἀλεξάνδρῳ ὃν [ἔ]τεκε             me — Alexander, whom Didymê
      Διδύμη πάνητί μοι εἰρηνικῶς           bore! Appear to me peacefully,
      διὰ φωνῆς ἀβόφως.                     through the voice, without causing fear!
```

4 pap. αγοτα; emended by the scribe. **12** diagonal stroke in the middle of the word appears on the tablet, extending upward to the line above. **21** ed. pr. Πανάτιμος 'always unhonoured', *l.* φάνηθι. **22** ἀφόβως.

§5 Incantation for Spirit Possession of a Boy

This piece is obviously a magical artefact. Two and half lines of symbols open the text, followed by another sixteen lines of largely indecipherable words, consisting of long streams of syllables and awkward phonetic combinations. These comprise the *voces magicae*, one of the most familiar motifs for all periods of Hellenic and Egyptian magic. Though most of the potent words are unknown to us, some are attested in other texts: σατραπερκμηφ in *l*. 5 ('the great satrap Kmeph') appears in the Greek magical papyri. In *l*. 7, θωουθιθωθ is related to Hermetic literature (the 'twice great Thoth'), and even linguistically linked to Egyptian with the duplicated thetas reflecting the ideogrammatic nuances of the earlier language. In line 11 we find derived from Greek epithets φοβερομματε ('with eyes causing fear') and πανεργετα ('all causing'). Extending through lines 11-12 is σεσενγενβαρφαραγγης, one of the unexplainable yet well attested words in *PGM*. These words reveal the mixed Graeco-Egyptian traditions that are the foundation of much magical literature. It is interesting to note that the scribe has made a correction in line 4 (αγοτα to αγατα), which suggests that he was copying the formula from another source – most likely a magical handbook, several of which are extant and record the effective *voces* and *characteres* to be inscribed on amulets.

Most magic seems to have been based on authoritative traditions, and this is particularly true of spells with a textual component. One can easily imagine that the efficacy of a spell depended on its precise inscription, and even our magician shows his respect for textual tradition with his correction in line 4. However in contrast to this respect is the fact that the tradition is often demonstrably, though unintentionally, corrupted. The person who inscribed this tablet used spaces to separate what he (or his source) thought to be the individual magical words, however most of the words that are known to modern scholars have not been distinguished in this way; for example running without a break from lines 11 to 12 is φοβερομματεπανεργετασεσενγενβαρφαραγγησομοιβασκοβερωουνηρ. This suggests that despite the importance attached to tradition, in reality the origins and meaning behind much of this spidery language had been long lost, even to the practising magician of late antiquity. Perhaps the best attested example of this phenomenon is the use of the word αβλαναθαναλβα. The word's efficacy comes from its being a palindrome; however many sources, presumably not realising this, alter the spelling and deprive the word of its original value; e.g. αβραναθαναβρα London MS Or 5987, αβλαναθαληβα *Hippiatrica*, αβλαναθαλααβλα *PGM* LXXI, αβλαναθαναθαναβλα *PGM* XVII.

Although this piece is clearly a magical text, the purpose of the document is not so easy to discern. Perhaps due to considerations of space, which for amulet-texts are likely related to pecuniary considerations, the injunction is presented in quite laconic phrases. The consistent use of imperatives compels an unnamed object to attend a certain Alexander, son of Didymê. Though Alexander is the narrator of the spell, demonstrated by the use of the first-person pronoun in *ll*. 20-21, it does not necessarily mean that Alexander was the writer. Amulets require a degree of literacy we may imagine not possessed by the broader population, allowing the rise of a professional class of magicians contracted to produce a document from the client's perspective. It is interesting to note that in such a situation the efficacious power lies not within the magician, but in the inscribed words, these being tailored to empower the narrator rather than the scribe.

The anonymity of the spell's object, and the authoritative language through which it is addressed, suggest that the target is some preternatural being. This being is commanded to appear to Alexander, to enter him and to speak, presumably through him as a medium; this text appears to be a spell for an oracular possession.

The basis for this may be found in the use of the verb εἰσκρίθητι in line 19 (passive aorist imperative of εἰσκρίνειν, 'cause to enter'), which has a strong association with oracular magic. Iamblichus, in his *De mysteriis* (III.13), remarks on those who 'rejecting the sacred laws and ordinances, and other religious ceremonies, think that the standing on characters is alone sufficient, and that by doing this for one hour, they can cause a certain spirit to enter (εἰσκρίνειν νομίζουσί τι πνεῦμα).[1] What Iamblichus is glibly referring to is a deviant form of divination; he attacks the use of characters (χαρακτῆρες — i.e. magical symbols and probably words also) and seemingly the very notion of the εἴσκρισις, thereby presenting the process as something removed from civilly acceptable oracular science. It is clear that Iamblichus' target is a type of divination which for him, by its methodology, falls into the realm of magic — his target is our Alexander. The verb appears in other primary magical literature; *PGM* VII 429-458, despite not being oracular in nature, is a spell for controlling spirits. The instructions allow the user to cast them from or to send them into a person (ὁρκίζει δαίμονας καὶ εἰσκρίνει) presumably with malicious intent.

The inscribed portion of the spell does not specify from where — on the hierarchy of gods, daemons and spirits — the conscripted messenger should come, though this detail may have been expressed by the magician in a verbal component. Many of the magical papyri, particularly those with clear Egyptian influences, link oracular practice with the earthly manifestation of gods; Plutarch (*De defectu oraculorum* 414e) also confirms for us that certain 'fools' did believe in divine possession, but explains that it would be beneath the dignity of a god to enter a human and to prophesy through mortal lips. Other oracular texts are commonly directed towards the multitude of intermediaries between deities and men, or even address the earth-bound spirits of the dead.

Possessive oracular magic is not as well attested among ancient literary sources as are the professional centres of divination such as at Delphi and Siwah. Nor do they seem particularly well represented by the documentary evidence, with none as closely linked to the actual procedure as this text. However the methodology is well known from descriptions in both Egyptian and Greek magical handbooks. Although this particular text has no Christian connotations, it arises from the same religious landscape of the Mediterranean and Near East as the emerging Christian movements, and comparable motifs are to be found therein.

---

[1] Iamblichus, *de Mysteriis*, trans. T. Taylor (1821).

§5 Incantation for Spirit Possession of a Boy

Possession is a prominent theme in the synoptic gospels, in which Jesus has a series of hostile encounters with 'demoniacs' (δαιμονιζόμενοι) in the towns of Judaea. Treated with greater prominence since Wrede's hypothesis of the 'Messianic secret', is the recognition of Jesus' nature by the daemon-possessed; a recognition which comes to them on sight, without the gradual process of revelation to which others are bound. The most dramatic of these encounters is set in a synagogue at Capernaum (Mark 1:23-26), where a possessed man enters and upon seeing Jesus cries, 'What have you to do with us, Jesus of Nazareth? Have you come to destroy us? I know who you are, the Holy One of God'. Jesus' rebuke is directed not at the man, but at the preternatural being speaking through him — this idea is clearly built upon the same foundation as our text; that the possessed are able to communicate secret knowledge.

This motif of possession even retained a place among some of the early churches. Particularly notable is the second-century charismatic Marcus, a professed Christian leader whom Irenaeus accuses of duping his followers into believing that, through his theatrical invocation, heavenly *Charis* had entered them and used them as a medium for prophecy (Irenaeus, *Adversus haereses* 1.13).

Sijpesteijn suggests, in his edition of our text (p. 187), that the tablet itself would have been buried in a cemetery as part of the ritual. This position is shared by the *ZPE* editor, Koenen, and is based upon their reading πανάτιμος in line 21. They interpret this word, which is unattested elsewhere, as an adjective meaning 'wholly without honour'; and by ascribing to it the religious motif 'honour (of resurrection)', they associate it with the spirit of an ἄωρος (untimely dead) or a βιαιοθάνατος (suffering a violent death).

The subjection of such a restless spirit is a common magical motif, and there are necromantic rituals requiring a cemetery for their efficacy and even body-parts such as bones; since this text does call upon a spirit of some kind, it is entirely possible that such elements comprised part of its methodology. However there is no evidence for it in the language of the spell, since πανάτιμος is not a reliable reading. Maltomini, who was able to examine the actual tablet, responded that the letter transcribed elsewhere as α is in fact almost entirely lacunose; a single, vertical line is all that remains of the character's lower portion, suggesting η as a more appropriate reconstruction. Further, the final letter, presented by Sijpesteijn as ι, has left only the slightest, unidentifiable trace. The translation provided above has followed Maltomini's interpretation of the damaged word, offering πανητι μοι (with classical orthography φάνητί μοι), 'appear to me'.

In Maltomini's introduction to the text he asserts that Alexander, the medium for the oracle, was most likely a child. The use of children, specifically young boys, for divination is well attested in both the Greek and Demotic magical papyri; the texts detail how a boy, occasionally with an emphasis on his purity (*PGM* VII 540-578; *PDM* XIV 65), is to be made the centre of elaborate rituals for communion with gods or spirits. However there is a distinct contrast to our text, in that most of the magical papyri do not effect possession of the boy, but rather summon a spirit on the assumption that only the boy can see and hear them; that is, the boy hears and repeats the oracle, he does not produce it (cf. *PGM* V 1-54, VII 540-578, XIII 734-759; *PDM* XIV 1-295). *PGM* IV 88-93, however, corresponds more closely with our text, since part of the invocation, which is written in Coptic, implores the spirit, 'enter into the boy today!'

The oracular possession of young boys is documented in literary sources. Apuleius recalls a certain magician named Nigidius, who was believed to entrance boys by song (*ab eo carmine*) and so induce them to prophesy (*Apologia*, 42.6-8). Apuleius theorises that this may be possible because a boyish or simple nature can be lured by song to a remembrance of his divine origins and thence perceive (*praesagare*) the future (43.3). Also Hippolytus, in his heresiological catalogue, describes boys in the company of magicians who, following appropriate rituals, seem to be possessed by a divinity (εἶτα θεοφορεῖσθαι δοκῶν ὁ παῖς). From there the boy — assumed to be in on the act — flies into a fit and cries out dramatic and incomprehensible things (*Refutatio omnium haeresium* 4.28.8-9, 41).

However this is again a situation where there is no direct evidence in the text to support such a *Sitz im Leben*. Indeed the language of the tablet may even provide an argument against it; the elaborate invocations recorded in the magical papyri generally refer to the boy in the third person, emphasising his passive role in the procedure (*PGM* IV 850-929 'Reveal to me concerning the thing which I want, through... the little boy!'; VII 540-578: 'Come to me, spirit that flies in the air... enter into the boy's soul!'; *PDM* XIV 30-45: 'Appear to this youth without alarming!') — but this text is written from the first-person perspective ('Enter me!'), and does not correlate with the traditional formulaic rôle of the youth.

Bibliography

H.D. **Betz** (ed), *The Greek Magical Papyri in Translation (including the Demotic Spells)* (Chicago 1986) (= *PGM/PDM*)
[For further discussion, see bibliography under §3 above. For the use of a boy as a medium see also S.I. **Johnston** 'Charming Children: The Use of the Child in Ancient Divination', *Arethusa* 34 (2001) 97-117; and M. **Nelson**, 'Narcissus: Myth and Magic', *CJ* 95 (2000) 363-389. — eds.]

M. Almond (Macquarie University)

CULT AND ORACLE

§6   Livia as Hecate

Tralleis			Fragment of a marble base (?)			AD 14-37

Ed. pr. — A.-E. Contoléon, *BCH* 10 (1886) 516 §6 (= F.B. Poljakov, *Die Inschriften von Tralleis und Nysa*. Teil I: *Die Inschriften von Tralleis* [Bonn 1989] = I. Tralleis 11).

ἱερεὺς Τιβερίου Καίσαρος	A priest of Tiberius Caesar
καὶ Ἑκάτης Σεβαστῆς	and of Hecate Augusta
τοὺς Ἑρμᾶς ἀνέθηκεν	erected the herms.

This inscribed fragment of (probably) the marble foundation of a Hermes statue, known to scholars for well over a century, was found in the ruins of Tralleis in ancient Lydia. The old city of Tralleis now lies within the modern city of Aydin in Turkey. The Greek text of the inscription records the erection of herms by a priest — or priests — of Tiberius Caesar and of Hecate Augusta. The original editor of the inscription, A.-E. Contoléon (*BCH* 10, 516 §6), identified the cult 'of Hecate Augusta' as one devoted to the worship of Livia Augusta (59 BC–AD 24), the widow of Augustus and the mother of Tiberius. Contoléon identified 'Hecate Augusta' of the inscription as Livia — later named Julia Augusta after Augustus' death — because she has a priest in common with Tiberius Caesar. At first glance, it might seem that our inscription envisages a joint priesthood. However, A.D. Nock (*Essays on Religion*, 232) has also viably argued that one man may well have held both priesthoods, citing several inscriptional parallels for proof. Although certainty on this issue is unattainable, Nock's case remains convincing.

Contoléon's conclusion of regarding identification of 'Hecate Augusta' is correct. Although Tiberius was scrupulous in refusing the divine honours of priests, temples and statues at Rome (Tacitus, *Ann.* 1.72.1; 4.37-38; Suetonius, *Tib.* 26; *DocsAug* §102b; cf. L.R. Taylor, 'Tiberius' Refusal of Divine Honours', *passim*), the case was somewhat different outside the capital in Italy and in the provinces. For example, statues of Tiberius and Livia were dedicated at Forum Clodii in Etruria and at Cumae (R. Seager, *Tiberius*, 121), and a temple to Tiberius, Livia and the Senate was erected at Smyrna in AD 26 (Tacitus, *Ann.* 4.15, 55-56). Also the inscriptions regularly pair Tiberius with Livia in cultic matters. To cite one example, a freedwoman in Falerii makes a dedication to the Genius of Augustus and of Tiberius, as well as to the Juno of Livia (*CIL* XI 3076; Dessau, *ILS* §116).

Additionally, G. Grether ('Livia', 231-232) claims that there is numismatic evidence identifying Livia as Hecate (*BMC* Lydia 344 §§114-120). Although the editor of *BMC Lydia* identifies the coin issues as 'Livia as Demeter', Grether argues, on the basis of other similar coins (e.g. *BMC* Lydia, 341 §97 and 'Index', 389), that the 'Livia-Demeter' identification should have been Livia-Hecate, given that the goddess is identified by her attribute of the crescent moon. If Grether's arguments are sound, the numismatic evidence from Lydia seals the identification of 'Hecate Augusta' as Livia. For a brief discussion of the worship of Hecate during the Hellenistic and Roman periods, see D.E. Aune, 'Apocalypse of John', 484-489. More expansively, see H. Sarian, 'Hecate', 983-1018.

How widespread is the evidence for the worship of Livia in the provinces? Even before Augustus' death, Livia is identified as Augusta/Sebaste in the Greek East (*IG* II² 3241; *IGR* IV 249). In Ioulis on Keos (A. Chaniotis, 'Livia Sebaste', 342) a dedicatory inscription on the epistyle of a building — perhaps a sacred place dedicated to the worship of Augustus — refers to the θεοὶ Σεβαστοί, Augustus and Livia, thus:

Ὑπὲρ τῆς τοῦ θεοῦ Καίσαρος Σ-
εβαστοῦ σωτηρίας
θεοῖς Ὀλυμπίοις καὶ θεοῖς Σεβ-
αστοῖς ὁ ἀρχιερεὺς [θεῶν] Σεβ[αστῶν] Θε-
οτέ[λ]ης φιλόκαισαρ

At Lesbos and Eresus sanctuaries and temples are also set up to Augustus, Augustus' sons and Livia (*IG* XII Supp. §124).

There is also extensive evidence for Livia's identification, before and after Augustus' death, with specific deities in the western and eastern provinces of the Roman Empire. Livia is called the 'New Aphrodite' at the sanctuary of Aphrodite at Palaipaphos (E.A. Gardner, et al., 'Inscriptions', 242 §61). In Assos the city and Roman merchants honour her as the 'New Hera' (*IGR* IV 249: Θεὰ Λειουια Ἥρα νέα Σεβαστή [Gardner, et al., 'Inscriptions', 250]). At Lampsacus Livia is strangely identified as being simultaneously Hestia and the 'new Demeter' (*IGR* IV 180: Ἰουλία Σεβαστὴ Ἑστία νέα Δημήτηρ). On the coins and inscriptions of Pergamum, Livia is identified as Hera (*BMC* Mysia, 139 §348, Pl. XXVIII, 6; *IGR* IV 319). At Haluntium in Sicily there is a public dedication to Livia as 'Dea' (*CIL* X 7464; Dessau, *ILS* §119: *Liviae Augusti deae municipium*). Dedications were also made to the Juno of Livia (El-Leys in Africa [AD 3]: *CIL* VIII 16456; Dessau, *ILS* §120; cf. Ovid, *Fasti* 1.640-641; Ovid, *Pont.* 3.1.117-118, 145, 164-165), as were offerings to Livia as Ceres (*CIL* X 750). At Clazomenae the coins of Livia bore the legend Θεὰ Λιβία (*BMC* Ionia, 31 §118). Last, the fact that Chalcis held the Λειβίδηα games in her honour (*BCH* III [1879] 443) is significant because ancient games were routinely held under the patronage of various deities.

Moreover, the inscriptional evidence (R.M. Muich, *Roman divae*, 15-35) reveals that across the cities of the Empire men and women served in the cult of Livia as *flamines* (Lusitania: *CIL* X 1413; Albingavinum: *CIL* II 473), *flaminicae* (Ferrandus: *CIL* IX 1155; Cirta: *CIL* VIII 19492; VIII 6987), and *sacerdotes* (Ostia: *CIL* XIV 399; Suasa: *CIL* XI 6172; Baetica: *CIL* II 1571; Torreparedones: *CIL* II 5421). Livia's role as a divine benefactor, too, is acknowledged (Athens: Εὐεργέτις [*BCH* LI (1927) 256]; Θεὰ Εὐεργέτις [*IG* XII 7 §381 A, B]). For example, in a brief tombstone referring to *diva Augusta* (Livia), Gelos, a freedman of Julia (Augustus' daughter), singles out Livia for her role in freeing his mother Julia: *Iu]liae divai Au[gustae l(ibertae)] matr[i] ex testament[to]* (*AE* [1975] §0289).

It is also intriguing that there are informal indications of Livia's apotheosis in advance of her official apotheosis by the Senate in AD 42 (Suetonius, *Claud.* 11; cf. Ovid, *Fasti* 1.536; Valerius Maximus 6.1.*init.*). As much as Tiberius tried to restrict the spread of divine honours at Rome, Livia is presented as 'god-like' in several visual representations. First, the cameo known as Le Grand Camée de France (c. AD 23: H.M. Westropp, *A Manual of Precious Stones*, 97) shows Tiberius seated as Jupiter, with Livia at his left side, holding a poppy and corn — the attributes of Ceres — in her right hand. Second, a statue of *Ceres Augusta* from the theatre at Leptis Magna in Libya is another case in point (P. Zanker, *The Power of Images*, 236, fig. 185). The Roman official Rubellius Blandus and a wealthy woman called Suphunibal dedicated this cult image of Livia in a small temple in the city after AD 29 but six to seven years before her apotheosis (S. Wood, *Imperial Women*, 61). Third, a sardonyx (Zanker, *The Power of Images*, 234-235, fig. 184), after AD 14, shows Livia, depicted as a priestess and goddess, holding in her right palm a miniature bust of the apotheosised Augustus. In her left hand she grasps a sheaf of grain, symbol of Ceres, and wears the mural crown and *tympanon* of Cybele/Magna Mater. Fourth, in the state-sanctioned sacrifices of the Arval brethren on 30th January AD 38 a male ox is offered 'for the birthday of Julia Augusta' (J. Scheid, *Commentarii*, 33 §12). Upon Livia's deification, the divine status of Julia Augusta is made entirely clear on 17 January AD 44 (Scheid, *Commentarii*, 46 §17; cf. 12 January: 'a cow to divine Augusta'): 'The seventeenth day before the calends of February, in reason of the consecration of the divine Augusta, at the [new?] Temple a male ox to divine Augustus, a cow to [the divine Augusta])'.

In sum, it is with considerable warrant that Grether ('Livia', 245) observes of Livia's role in the imperial cult after the death of Augustus (the period to which our inscription belongs): '… since Augustus is no longer on earth but has taken his place among the divinities, his blessings must come to the Roman people through the mediation of his priestess, Julia Augusta'. What relevance, then, does our inscription have for the New Testament? Two texts from Paul's letters are instructive for the light that they throw on the critical attitude of Paul towards the imperial cult. For a discussion of Romans 1:2-5 against the imperial background of apotheosis, see J.R. Harrison, *Imperial Authorities*, 146-150.

First, a critical text for Paul's attitude to the imperial cult is Romans 1:21-23. Here Paul focuses on the dishonourable response of the Gentile world to God's natural revelation, drawing from the semantic domains of honour (ἐδόξασαν) and benefaction (ηὐχαρίστησαν) to depict the sin of human ingratitude (Rom 1:21a). Drawing upon the LXX traditions that speak of Israel exchanging the divine glory for idolatry (δόξα: Pss 4:2; 106 [LXX 105]:20; Jer 2:11; Hos 4:7; 9:11; 10:5; cf. Sir 49:5; cf. G.K. Beale, *We Become What We Worship*, 203-216), Paul states that Gentile idolaters make the same mistake in the present (Rom 1:23: ἤλλαξαν τὴν δόξαν τοῦ ἀφθάρτου θεοῦ ἐν ὁμοιώματι εἰκόνος).

Importantly, Paul nominates the types of image worshipped by the Gentiles: corruptible man, birds, quadrupeds, and reptiles. Jewish auditors familiar with the Genesis narrative would have spotted Paul's clear allusion to the subjugation of the created order (Gen 1:26b: birds, livestock, creeping things) that mankind, as the image of God (1:26a), was commanded to undertake. In an ironic reversal of the 'dominion' mandate (Gen 1:26, 28), Paul implies, human beings are subjecting themselves to created beings, including their own species, instead of to the glorious Creator of all.

But, as I.E. Rock has insightfully demonstrated (*Roman Imperial Ideology*, 303-309), there is also imperial reference in Paul's critique which Roman auditors would have discerned. Caligula had recently attempted to install his image in the Jerusalem Temple. Nero, too, was infamous for identifying himself with the Roman pantheon (Jupiter, Apollo, Hercules) and for placing his statue in the temple of Mars Ultor. Rock notes how Seneca advised the young Nero that if he demonstrated *clementia* as ruler, then 'all things will be moulded into your likeness' (*Clem.* 2.2.1). For Paul, however, the Gentile world foolishly worshipped the 'imperial likeness' instead of praising the glory and mercy of the immortal God (Rom 11:36; 16:27). In sum, the worship of Livia as Hecate and of Tiberius — along with the many other deities attached to the imperial cult — was but one example in a first-century context of the idolatry against which the Old Testament prophets had inveighed. Paul, as a first-century Jew, would not countenance his converts compromising on the issue.

Second, another important text of Paul relevant to the imperial cult, aired in a discussion of idolatry (1 Cor 8:1-11:1), is 1 Corinthians 8:5-6. As B.W. Winter has convincingly shown (*After Paul*, 269-286), Paul's christologically modified monotheism (v. 5) critiques the imperial cult with the telling phrase 'many gods and many lords' who are present 'in heaven' and 'on earth' (v. 6). J.D. Fantin (*The Lord of the Entire World*, 288) has correctly observed that the scope of Paul's polemic is 'limitless': ἐν οὐρανῷ ('in heaven') captures not only the major and minor deities but also the apotheosised Roman rulers (Caesar, Augustus, and, depending on the time of 1 Corinthians' composition, Claudius) and their family members (Livia), whereas ἐπὶ γῆς ('on earth') refers to the living ruler at Rome. Indeed, Paul dismisses the gods wholesale as λεγόμενοι θεοί ('so-called gods'), a phrase that clearly carries a derogatory tone towards the Graeco-Roman deities and their beneficent representatives, including Hecate Augusta of our inscription. Thus Paul, while endorsing the appropriateness of imperial honorific culture in certain contexts (Rom 13:1-7: v. 7 [τῷ τὴν τιμὴν τὴν τιμήν]), dismisses its innate idolatry both from a Jewish and a christological viewpoint. The heavy emphasis on the 'Lordship' of Christ in particular (v. 5) also has imperial reference, given the increasing attribution of κύριος language to Nero in inscriptions and papyri from the sixties onwards (Fantin, *The Lord*, 196-202). It is likely that this language was already informally abroad in the early fifties.

Last, it would be unwise to assume that Paul's view regarding the imperial cult commanded universal assent among the early Christians in the 50's. It is likely that some of the powerful and wealthy elite among the believers at Corinth thought that compromise with imperial idolatry was inconsequential (1 Cor 8:10; 10:14-22), being besotted by the opportunities that the imperial cult provided for social advancement (J.R. Harrison, '"Glory of Christ'", 156-188, esp. 181-187). The temptations posed for believers by the 'upwardly mobile' perspective of imperial clients made Paul all the more determined to ensure that his converts should continue to flee idolatry (1 Cor 10:14).

Bibliography

D.E. **Aune**, 'The Apocalypse of John and Graeco-Roman Revelatory Magic', *NTS* 33/4 (1987) 481-501; A **Barrett**, *Livia: First Lady of Imperial Rome* (New Haven 2002); E. **Bartman**, *Portraits of Livia: Imagining the Imperial Woman in Augustan Rome* (Cambridge 1997); G.K. **Beale**, *We Become What We Worship: A Biblical Theology of Idolatry* (Downers Grove 2008); A. **Chaniotis**, 'Livia Sebaste, Iulia Sebaste, Caius Caesar Parthikos, Domitian Anikeitos Theos: Inofficial Titles of Emperors in the Early Principate', *Acta Ant. Hung.* 43 (2003) 341-344; J.D. **Fantin**, *The Lord of the Entire World:* Lord Jesus, *a Challenge to* Lord Caesar? (Sheffield 2011); M.B. **Flory**, 'Livia and the History of Public Honorific Status for Women in Rome', *TAPA* 123 (1993) 287-308; M.B. **Flory**, 'The Deification of Roman Women', *The Ancient History Bulletin* 9 (1995) 127-134; E.A. **Gardner**, D.G. **Hogarth**, and M.R. **James**, 'Inscriptions of Kuklia and Amargetti', *JHS* 9 [1888] 242-250 §61; I. **Gradel**, *Emperor Worship and Roman Religion* (Oxford 2002); G. **Grether**, 'Livia and the Imperial Cult', *AJP* 67/3 (1946) 222-252; J.R. **Harrison**, 'The Brothers as "The Glory of Christ" (2 Cor 8:23): Paul's *Doxa* Terminology in its Ancient Benefaction Context', *NovT* 52 (2010) 156-188; J.R. **Harrison**, *Paul and the Imperial Authorities at Thessalonica and Rome: A Study in the Conflict of Ideology* (Tübingen 2011); B.A. **Levick**, *Tiberius the Politician* (London 1976); R.M. **Muich**, *The Worship of Roman* Divae: *The Julio-Claudians to the Antonines* (MA diss., University of Florida, 2004); A.D. **Nock**, *Essays on Religion and the Ancient World* Vol. 1 (Oxford 1972); S.R.F. **Price**, *Rituals and Power: The Roman Imperial Cult in Asia Minor* (Cambridge 1984); I.E. **Rock**, *The Implications of Roman Imperial Ideology for an Exegesis of Paul's Letter to the Romans: An Ideological Literary Analysis of the Exordium, Rom 1:1-17* (PhD diss., University of Wales, 2005); H. **Sarian**, 'Hecate', *LIMC* VI (1992) 983-1018; R. **Seager**, *Tiberius* (Malden ²2005); J. **Scheid**, Commentarii fratrum Arvalium qui supersunt: *Les copies épigraphiques des protocols annuels de la confrérie arvale (21 av. – 304 ap. J.-C.)* (Rome 1998); L.R. **Taylor**, 'Tiberius' Refusal of Divine Honours', *TAPA* 60 (1929) 87-110; L.R. **Taylor**, *The Divinity of the Roman Emperor* (Middleton 1931); H.M. **Westropp**, *A Manual of Precious Stones and Antique Gems* (Cambridge 2009: rpt. orig. 1874); B.W. **Winter**, *After Paul Left Corinth: The Influence of Secular Ethics and Social Change* (Grand Rapids 2002); S. **Wood**, *Imperial Women* (Leiden 1999).

J.R. Harrison (Macquarie University)

§7 Family Honour of a Priestess of Artemis

Ephesus — White marble statue base with moulding below — AD 138-161

Ed. pr. — D. Knibbe, H. Engelmann, B. Iplikçioğlu, 'Neue Inschriften aus Ephesos XI', *JÖAI* 59 (1989) 163-237, no. 8, p. 176 (= *SEG* XXXIX 1189).

. . . . O . P . . . . ΦΟ . Λ	. . . . . . O . R . . . . Pho . L . . . . . .
[Πρ]όκλου, ξυσταρχῶν κ[αὶ]	of [Pr]oklos, they being *xystarchai* a[nd]
[ν]εοποιῶν, ἱερατεύσα[σαν]	[*n*]*eopoioi*, (she) having been a priestess
[τ]ῆς Ἀρτέμιδος εὐσεβῶς	[o]f Artemis piously
5 καὶ φιλοτείμως, καὶ πάντα	and generously, and
ἐκτενῶς παρασχοῦσαν τ[ὰ]	having zealously furnished all t[hat]
διδόμενα εἰς τὴν πόλιν	(was) to be donated to the city
δηνάρια πεντακισχείλια	(to the sum of) 5,000 denarii
κατὰ το ψήφισμα τῆς βουλῆς	according to the decree of the council,
10 δοῦσαν δὲ καὶ τὰς ἐξ ἔθους	and also giving the customary
διανομάς · ἀναστήσαν-	distributions; (thus) T. Aelius Priscus
τος τὴν τειμὴν Τ. Αἰλίου	set up the honour
Σεβα(στοῦ) ἀπελ(ευθέρου) Πρείσχου	(being both) an imperial freedman (and)
ταβλαρίου τοῦ τροφέως αὐτῆ[ς]	a secretary (and) the foster-father of he[r].

A defining aspect of personal identity in antiquity was the status and wealth of one's family. Our priestess, whose name is missing from the inscription, belonged to a distinguished Ephesian family of *xystarchai* and *neopoioi*. Significantly, her ancestral pedigree, with its strong civic focus, is placed ahead of her role as a benefactor and priestess of Artemis. The fact that her foster-father was a secretary and imperial freedman is also vaunted in the conclusion of the inscription (*ll.* 13-14). There is little doubt, therefore, that the offices held by some of her family members possessed considerable social prestige and warranted their strategic placement at the beginning and end of the eulogy. As we will argue, the family is also wealthy (*ll.* 5-11) and must have belonged to the Ephesian aristocracy. Before examining the inscriptions belonging to priestesses of Artemis at Ephesus, we will discuss the role of a *xystarches* in the Mediterranean basin from the first century AD onwards and why the position of *xystarches* was an influential appointment. This entry will conclude with a discussion of the adverbs describing her activity as a priestess (εὐσεβῶς, φιλοτείμως, ἐκτενῶς) against the backdrop of the New Testament writings. The role and importance of the *neopoioi* in our inscription is not discussed in this entry; see J.R. Harrison, entry §9 below. On the role of ancestral honour in early Christianity, see Harrison, 'Excels Ancestral Honours'. On imperial freedmen, see P.R.C. Weaver, *Familia Caesaris*.

1. *Family Honour and the* xystarchai

As far as civic administration, the *xystarches* was the official in charge of the covered colonnade (*xystos*) where athletes exercised in bad weather, particularly during winter (Vitruvius, *De arch.* 5.4; Cicero, *Opt. gen.* 3.8). In the Roman period, however, the *xystarches* was more widely known as the president of the athletic association (LSJ: *IGR* 3.1171; P. Oxy. 1050; Sammelb 5275), that is, the leader of an athletic union. As civic officials, *xystarchai* are honoured in the inscriptions (e.g. P. Herrmann and H. Malay, *New Documents from Lydia* §14; W. Eck, 'P. Aelius Apollonides', 236-242). We possess letters written to them and by them, as well as letters communicating to groups across the Empire business and information involving the *xystarchai* (e.g. P. Bibl. Giss. inv. 252; *SB* X 10493; C.P. Jones, 'Three New Letters of the Emperor Hadrian', *ZPE* 161 [2007] 145-156; *CEg* 42/84 [1967] 445-452). There is mention, too, of payment being made to a *xystarches* who was the president of an athletic association at Hermopolis (*CPR* VI 41 [AD 320-324]).

The social importance of the *xystarchai* was enhanced by the role that they played in the international synod of athletes. The synod continued to develop in its social prestige across the Mediterranean basin as it underwent a process of organisational change and expansion — due to the sponsorship of the imperial rulers — from the first century (Smallwood, *Documents* §374) to the second century AD and beyond (*IG* XIV 1105; cf. Z. Newby, *Greek Athletics*, 34-35; D.S. Potter, 'Spectacle', 396-397; C.A. Forbes, 'Ancient Athletic Guilds', 238-252). Retired athletes, appointed by the imperial authorities to be permanent *xystarchai*, served as overseers of festivals around the Empire and at the central office of the synod at Rome. Hadrian had allowed the synod to establish its headquarters near the Baths of Hadrian in the capital in AD 134, a right reaffirmed in the period of our inscription by Antoninus Pius in AD 143 (*IG* XIV 1054, 1055). The status of these imperial appointments is well captured in the introduction to a (much longer) decree honouring Tiberius Claudius Rufus of Smyrna (*SIG*^{3} 1073):

> The people of the Smyrneans who hold a neocorate honor Tiberius Claudius Rufus, their own citizen, a man who won many victories and sacred victor of the synod, winning in the bouts of pancration through his courage and wisdom, appointed by decision of the emperors to the xystarchy for life of all the contests in Smyrna.

In sum, the role of the *xystarches* was not confined to the world of athletic endeavour. At the end of a successful career, an athlete could move into administration, superintending the public areas (e.g. the imperial baths) and also acting on behalf of his union. While the athletic feats of the *xystarchai* remained the main emphasis in public eulogies of them (e.g. I. Aph. XII 920; *SIG*^{3} 1073; *SB* I 5725),[1] nonetheless the honorific decrees also highlight the wider contribution of the *xystarchai* to the civic, religious, and synodal affairs of their city-states. A good example is the career is Markos Aurelios Asklepiades (c. AD 200: *IG* XIV 1102), although the inscription is presented in

---

[1] I. Aph XII 920 is available on http://insaph.kcl.ac.uk/iaph2007/). This website also includes, along with texts, translations, commentary, indices, concordance, search engines and reference materials.

abbreviated form below without his athletic achievements. For a full translation, see S.G. Miller, *Arete* §153. Significantly, the feats of Markos' father are set out in a brief vignette at the beginning, though Markos' administrative and athletic accomplishments dominate the inscription:

> I am the son of Markos Aurelios Demetrios, who was head priest and *xystarches* for life of the *Sympas Xystos* and Director of the Imperial Baths, a citizen of Alexandria and Hermopolis, a pankratiast, a *periodonikes*, and a wrestler beyond compare — I am Markos Aurelios Asklepiades, also known as Hermodoros, the oldest of the temple trustees of the great temple of Sarapis, high priest of the *Sympas Xystos*, *xystarches* for life, and the Director of the Imperial Baths; a citizen of Alexandria, Hermopolis, and Puteoli; a member of the *boule* of Naples Elis and Athens; both a citizen and member of the *boule* of many other cities; a pankratiast, an unbeaten immovable unchallenged *periodonikes* who won every contest I ever entered.

Last, in terms of their work within the gymnasium, some of the *xystarchai* are eulogised — in a manner similar to the gymnasiarchs (J.R. Harrison, 'Paul and the Gymnasiarchs') — for their pastoral role among the young men. Thus the *xystarches* at Bithynia, 'a victor at the sacred games and *xystarches* for life', is recognised 'for his goodwill and his imposition of order among the Ephebes and care of the Dogenion' (145-146 AD: *IG* II^2 3741). In sum, the family of our priestess, drawn from *neopoioi* and *xystarchai*, would have had a high social profile in Ephesus.

2. Family Honour and the Priestesses of Artemis at Ephesus

With the family honour of our priestess of Artemis having been spotlighted at the beginning and end of the inscription, the eulogy now focuses upon her payment of the *summa honoraria* (*ll.* 5-9; cf. A.D. Macro, 'The Cities of Asia Minor', 658-697; S. Cramme, *Die Bedeutung des Euergetismus*, 41-49). Civic magistrates and priests paid the substantial amount of 5,000 denarii upon entering their office, an amount determined, as our inscription informs us (*l.* 9), by the Ephesian council. Two other 'priestess of Artemis' inscriptions mention payment of 5,000 denarii. In I. Eph. III 987 *ll.* 22-24 there is reference to Vipsania Olympia's 'bestowing in addition for repairs the sum of 5,000 denarii', whereas in I. Eph. III 997, *ll.* 6-17, the contribution of the daughter of Flavia Meltine is depicted in this manner:

> [when she made] all the distributions of her priesthood and gave to the city 5,000 denarii, they — namely Flavia Meltine, her mother, daughter of Maior, and Maior her grandfather, and Maior the Younger her uncle — gave it to the city from their own funds.

S.M. Baugh ('Cultic Prostitution', 457) observes from this evidence that 'we necessarily have girls from wealthy and aristocratic families serving as priestesses of Artemis; no one else could afford the required expenses'. This impression is reinforced by the subsequent reference to additional benefactions given over and above the *summa honoraria* in our inscription (*ll.* 10-11). After an analysis of twenty Ephesian inscriptions honouring priestesses of Artemis, Baugh concludes that the priestesses were daughters of elite Ephesian families, some of whom may well have penetrated the imperial stratum ('Cultic Prostitution', 453-455). One inscription conventionally refers

§7 Family Honour of a Priestess of Artemis

to the priestess being a 'daughter of the emperor-loving M. Antonius Barus and Flavia Tertulla' (I. Eph. III 982, *ll.* 5-7; cf. 'daughter of M. Aur[elius] Hierokles Apolinarios the emperor-honouring general' [I. Eph. VII I. 3059 *ll.* 6-9]). Another inscription speaks of diplomatic contact with the Roman ruler (AD 177-180: I. Eph. III 983, *ll.* 1-15):

> Julia Pantima Potentilla, priestess and *kosmeteira* of Artemis, daughter of Julius Artemas, asiarch and prytanis, and secretary of the People, who completed all (his) offices and liturgies and an embassy to the emperors, Antoninus [and] Commodus ...

The inscription above is also important because Julia's father is an *asiarch*, a title of officials with whom Paul had contact while at Ephesus in the previous century (Acts 19:31; cf. R.A. Kearsley, 'Some Asiarchs'; cf. G.M. Rogers, 'Constructions of Women'; S. Friesen, 'Ephesian Women and Men'; S. Witetschek, 'Artemis and Asiarchs'). Could the daughter of one of these mid first-century asiarchs have been a priestess of Artemis? The question is unanswerable but not beyond the bounds of possibility.

Attention should also be drawn to I. Eph. VII 1. 3072, *ll.* 0-1, a piece of documentary evidence not discussed by Baugh ('Cultic Prostitution'). The inscription is dedicated to '[Vedia ... priestess of] most pure Artemis'. Belonging to the family of the Vedii of Ephesus, Vedia belonged to a renowned family that provided office-bearers for well over a century at Ephesus, including officials such as the asiarch, *bouleutes*, *prytanis*, *kosmeteira*, high-priest of Asia, priestess, senator and secretary. What is fascinating about I. Eph. VII 1. 3072 is the extended 'roll-call' of family members, each with their offices specified, in *ll.* 3-27. It is a spectacular catalogue of civic virtue that gives us insight into the heated competition for public status that animated the chief families at Ephesus during the first century and beyond. The family of our priestess, with members who were *neopoioi* and *xystarchai*, could not have outperformed the famous Vedii in status, but there is no sense in the inscription that her family had given up the pursuit of civic fame.

It is clear that, with the exception of the evidence of four Ephesian inscriptions (G.M. Rogers, *Sacred Identity*, 75, n. 73), the priestesses of Artemis were unmarried virgins, given that nineteen of Baugh's Ephesian inscriptions (Rogers, 456-457) designate the priestess as a 'daughter' of a father rather than a 'wife' of husband, the latter being the inscriptional convention for married women (I. Eph. III 614B; III 665; III 681; V 1655). Our inscription, also part of Baugh's overall collection of twenty, refers to the 'foster-father' of the princess, while I. Eph. VII 1. 3072, noted above, designates Vedia as 'daughter' and 'granddaughter'. Note, too, I. Eph. IV 1068 *ll.* 2-4: 'Ploutarchos the *prytanis* and gymnasiarch and his children, the priestesses of Artemis'. Thus it was unlikely that the priestess would have been much older than fourteen years old, given that upper-class girls with Roman connections married very young. It is also likely, as the aorist participle implies (*l.* 3: ἱερατεύσα[σαν]), that the tenure of a priestess was annual. This is confirmed by Charikleia, the heroine of Heliodorus' romance (*An Ethiopian Tale*, 1.22.2; cf. J.B. Connelly, *Portrait of a Priestess*, 41), who states: 'We belong to the nobility of Ephesos ... and a tradition calls on such people to undertake divine service. I became priestess of Artemis and my brother here the priest of Apollo.

The office is for a year'. Plutarch, too, points to the priestess of Artemis being a temporary office: 'At Ephesus they call each one of the servants of Artemis, first a novice, then a priestess, and thirdly an ex-priestess' (*Mor.* 795 D). Later, Plutarch compares the priestesses of Artemis to the Vestals (*Mor.* 795 E). The virginity of the priestess, therefore, would have been deemed a phase of her office rather than a life-long vocation. Undoubtedly, she would have married a male of high social status soon after she had completed her prestigious service of Artemis.

But what of the four inscriptions indicating that some priestesses of Artemis were married? There is little doubt from the evidence above that the norm was for them to be unmarried, though Baugh perhaps goes too far in proposing they were all unmarried. In some of the inscriptions, their office as a priestess is mentioned in conjunction with the decree honouring their husband. In other words, the fact that that they were priestesses of Artemis is a *past* honour, rightly recalled in the inscription, but was undoubtedly held before they were married. For example, the honour for Ti. Claudius Aelius Crispinus, an asiarch, is set up by his wife Auphidia Kuintilia, a 'priestess and high priestess of the temples in Ephesos' (I. Eph. III 637, *ll.*15-17; cf. III 894). However, two other inscriptions are erected in honour of married women: (a) Julia Atticilla, 'priestess of the most holy Artemis and high priestess of the temples in Ephesos' (I. Eph. III 617, *ll.* 7-10), wife of M. Aur. Daphnus (I. Eph. III 616); (b) Pei. Paula Aratiane, 'priestess of Artemis and well-born *theoros* of the great Olympians' (I. Eph. III 894, *ll.* 2-8), wife of G. Ioul. Ant(onios) Tertulleinos. In both cases, it could be the case that honours of the past, when they were unmarried, are being referred to in each case: but this seems unlikely in this instance. They are eulogistic decrees in honour of each priestess in her own right. Perhaps some priestesses continued in a married role at the temple of Artemis, sharing their wealth of maturity and experience with the young unmarried priestess during her annual office. Continuity in the customary cultic rituals would have been essential so that each incoming priestess could carry out the holy rites in a manner pleasing to the goddess and the Ephesians.

The cultic service of our priestess of Artemis is mentioned in highly conventional terms in our inscription (*ll.* 4-5: εὐσεβῶς καὶ φιλοτείμως). Other inscriptions of priestesses of Artemis show interest in how the priestess fulfils her responsibilities: e.g. 'worthily and piously' (I. Eph. III 980, *l.* 9); ['worthily'] (I. Eph. III 987, *l.* 13); 'purely and generously' (I. Eph. III 992A, *ll.* 6-7); 'piously and with decorum' (I. Eph. VII I. 3059, *l.* 2). However, from the scant evidence of our inscription, we do not gain much insight into what service of Artemis might have involved for the priestesses. Another first-century (?) inscription from Ephesus, however, gives us greater understanding of what duties were carried out by the priestess (I. Eph. III 987, *ll.* 1-27):

> The Council and People honored Vipsania Olympias, daughter of Lucius Vipsanius Apelles, son of Neon of the Cornelian tribe, and of Claudia Polemonis, the daughter of Pythos, having completed her term as priestess of Artemis as befits a sacred office, fulfilling both the mysteries and sacrifices worthily; she wreathed the shrine and all its precincts in the days of the goddess's manifestations, making the public sacrifices and the distributions (of money) to the State Council and to the Council of Elders, and bestowing in

addition for repairs of the basilica the sum of 5,000 denarii. She served her priestly term during the prytany of Gaius Licinnius Dionysodorus.

Additionally, J.N. Bremmer ('Priestly Personnel') notes that priestesses of Artemis reorganise the cult (I. Eph. VII I. 3059) and donate money to the hymnodoi on the birthday of Artemis (I. Eph. Ia 27, *ll*. 265-268: 'Equally he will give from the aforementioned interest each year to the priestess of Artemis 18 denarii on behalf of the hymnodoi of the goddess for distribution on the birthday of Artemis'; cf. G.M. Rogers, *Sacred Identity*). Finally, an inscription mentions that Ulpia Euodia Mudiane, priestess of Artemis, came from a family that 'often held the office of priestess and kosmeteira' (I. Eph. III 989 *ll*. 6-8; also III 980; VII I. 3034). The female office of kosmeteira was devoted to the adornment of the cultic statue of Artemis. Whether the offices of priestess and kosmeteira were held sequentially or simultaneously is uncertain.

Now that the role and family status of the priestesses of Artemis is clear, what relevance does our inscription have for the intersection of the civic and religious ideology of the Roman province of Asia with the world of the New Testament? The three adverbs that are employed concerning the service of the priestess of Artemis, although highly conventional in a Graeco-Roman context, are revealing when contrasted with the New Testament evidence. First, εὐσεβῶς is used in 2 Timothy 3:12 in a discussion of the persecutions that believers, 'wanting to live godly in Christ Jesus' (οἱ θέλοντες εὐσεβῶς ζῆν ἐν Χριστῷ Ἰησοῦ), would face in the future. In Titus 2:12 we learn that, with the appearance of the grace of God (2:11), believers should renounce impiety (τὴν ἀσέβειαν) and worldly passions, with a view to living in a sensible, righteous and godly manner (εὐσεβῶς). εὐσέβεια and εὐσεβέω are also widely used in the Pastorals (εὐσέβεια: 1 Tim 2:2; 3:16; 4:7, 8; 6:3, 5, 6; 2 Tim 3:5; Titus 1:1; cf. Acts 3:12; 2 Peter 1:3, 6, 7; 3:11; εὐσεβέω: 1 Tim 5:4; cf. Acts 17:23; εὐσεβής: Acts 10:2), with the exception of εὐσεβής (Acts 10:2, 7; 2 Pet 2:9). In the case of the Pastorals (W. Foerster, '*Eusebeia*'; F.W. Danker, *Benefactor*, 343-345; J.J. Wainwright, 'Eusebeia'; M.R. D'Angelo, 'Eusebeia'), εὐσέβεια refers to the godliness or good conduct emanating from a proper Christian lifestyle (1 Tim 2:2; 4:7; 6:11), the ethics of which are rooted in the implications of the incarnation, resurrection and ascension of Christ (3:16).

By contrast, the understanding of εὐσεβῶς in our inscription is concerned with the proper performance of cultic acts in order to maintain fitting relations between the city of Ephesus and the goddess Artemis. In antiquity a scrupulous attendance to the cultic rituals of the deity (εὐσέβεια) was of the highest moral obligation. By not properly attending to the cult one seriously risked slighting the deity, thereby rupturing the reciprocal contract between the community and the deity as far as the continuance of divine favour. Where εὐσέβεια was used of human relations in the ancient world, it was mostly in the context of duty towards parents, involving an attitude of respect and loyalty. The New Testament picks up this nuance in 1 Timothy 5:4 (J.R. Harrison, 'Benefaction Ideology').

Second, φιλοτείμως is not used in the New Testament. The cognate φιλοτιμέομαι only occurs three times in Paul's letters (Rom 15:20; 2 Cor 5:9; I Thess 4:11). In each case, the verb relates to the idea of 'aspiring to' or 'striving eagerly' (G.H.R. Horsley, φιλοτιμία, 88). Here we see another case of the New Testament's general avoidance of φιλ-compounds (*New Docs* 2, 106). Given that Paul redefined beneficence in terms of the impoverishment and dishonour displayed in the χάρις of Christ (2 Cor 8:9 [6:10b]; cf. J.R. Harrison, *Paul's Language of Grace*, 250-256), the language of 'honour' and 'friendship', underlying φιλοτιμία and its cognates, was no longer appropriate as a vehicle for expressing his new dynamic of generosity.

Third, ἐκτενῶς and its cognates are only found on three occasions (ἐκτενέστερον: Luke 22:44; ἐκτενῶς: Acts 12:5; 1 Peter 1:22) in contexts of 'fervent' prayer and love. Once again we are witnessing the transference of a significant semantic domain — the language of fervency and zeal — from the world of civic beneficence (ἐκτενῶς: IV 598; *SEG* VIII 527; XVIII 27; I. Priene 112; ἐκτενής: I. Mylasa 106; Michel 515; cf. Danker, *Benefactor*, 121), with its focus on cult in the case of our inscription, to the moral domain of the Christian lifestyle in the body of Christ.

Bibliography

M.R. **D'Angelo**, 'Eusebeia: Roman Imperial Family Values and the Sexual Politics of 4 Maccabees and the Pastorals', *BibInt* 11 (2003) 139-165; S.M. **Baugh**, 'Cultic Prostitution in New Testament Ephesus: A Reappraisal', *JETS* 42/3 (1999) 443-460; J.N. **Bremmer**, 'Priestly Personnel of the Ephesian Artemision: Anatolian, Persian, Greek and Roman Aspects', in *Practitioners of the Divine in Ancient Greece* (eds, B. Dignas and K. Trampedach; Cambridge Mass. 2008) 37-53; J.B. **Connelly**, *Portrait of a Priestess: Women and Ritual in Ancient Greece* (Princeton 2007); S. **Cramme**, *Die Bedeutung des Euergetismus für die Finanzierung städtischer Aufgaben in der Provinz Asia* (PhD diss.; University of Köln 2001); F.W. **Danker**, *Benefactor: Epigraphic Study of a Graeco-Roman and New Testament Semantic Field* (St Louis 1982); W. **Eck**, 'P. Aelius Apollonides, ab Epistulis Graecis, und ein Brief des Cornelius Fronto', *ZPE* 91 (1992) 236-242; W. **Foerster**, '*Eusebeia* in den Pastoralbriefen', *NTS* (1958-1959) 213-218; W. **Foerster**, 'εὐσεβία', *TDNT* 7 (1971) 177-182; C.A. **Forbes**, 'Ancient Athletic Guilds', *CP* 50/4 (1952) 238-252; S. **Friesen**, 'Ephesian Women and Men in Public Office during the Roman Period', in *100 Jahre österreichische Forschungen in Ephesos* (eds, H. Friesinger and F. Krinzinger; Vienna 1999), 107-113; J.R. **Harrison**, 'Benefaction Ideology and Christian Responsibility for Widows', *New Docs* 8 (1998) 106-116; J.R. **Harrison**, 'Excels Ancestral Honours', *New Docs* 9 (2002) 20-21; J.R. **Harrison**, *Paul's Language of Grace in its Graeco-Roman Context* (Tübingen 2003); J.R. **Harrison**, 'Paul and the Gymnasiarchs: Two Approaches to Pastoral Formation in Antiquity', in *Paul: Jew, Greek and Roman* (ed., S.E. Porter; Leiden 2008) 141-178; P. **Herrmann** and H. **Malay**, *New Documents from Lydia* (Vienna 2007); G.H.R. **Horsley**, 'φιλοτιμία', *New Docs* 1 (1981) 88; C.P. **Jones**, 'Three New Letters of the Emperor Hadrian', *ZPE* 161 (2007) 145-156; R.A. **Kearsley**, 'Some Asiarchs of Ephesos', *New Docs* 4 (1987) 46-55; R.A. **Kearsley**, 'Appendix: The Asiarchs', in *The Book of Acts in Its First-Century Setting* (eds, D.W.J. Gill, C. Gempf; Grand Rapids 1994) 363-376; E.A. **Judge**, 'Moral Terms in the Eulogistic Tradition', *New Docs* 2 (1982) 105-106; A.D. **Macro**, 'The Cities of Asia Minor under the Roman Imperium', *ANRW* II.7.2 (1980) 658-697; S.G. **Miller**, *Arete: Greek Sports from Ancient Sources* (rev. ed. Berkeley 1990); Z. **Newby**, *Greek Athletics in the Roman World: Victory and Virtue* (Oxford 2005); D.S. **Potter** (ed.), 'Spectacle', in *A Companion to the Roman Empire* (ed., D.S. Potter; Oxford 2006) 385-408; G.M. **Rogers**, *The Sacred Identity of Ephesos: Foundation Myths of a Roman City* (London/New York 1991); G.M. **Rogers**, 'The Constructions of Women at Ephesos', *ZPE* 90 (1992) 215-223; J.J. **Wainwright**, 'Eusebeia (Especially in the Pastoral Epistles): Syncretism or Conservative Contextualization?', *EvQ* 65/3 (1993) 211-224; P.R.C. **Weaver**, *Familia Caesaris: A Social Study of the Emperor's Freedmen and Slaves* (Cambridge 1972); S. **Witetschek**, 'Artemis and Asiarchs: Some Remarks on Ephesian Local Colour in Acts 19', *Filologia Neotestamentaria* 90 (2009) 334-355.

J.R. Harrison (Macquarie University)

§8 Artemis triumphs over a Sorcerer's Evil Art

Ephesus   Coffered slab of white marble   c. AD 165
                             1.09 x 0.89 m

Ed. pr. — D. Knibbe, 'Das "Parthermonument" von Ephesos. Parthersieg(altar) des Artemis (und Kenotaph des L. Verus) an der "Triodos"', *BerMatÖA* I (1991) 5-18; R. Merkelbach, 'Ein Orakel des Apollo für Artemis von Koloe', *ZPE* 88 (1997) 70-72; F. Graf, 'An Oracle Against Pestilence from a Western Anatolian Town', *ZPE* 92 (1992) 267-279; *JÖAI* 62 (1993) 130-132, no. 25 (= *SEG* XLI 981).

[....]Α[.]Η[ ]ΩΙΔΑΠ[---.....]ΗΣ[[ ]Α[ ]Ε[ ]ΟΙΔΑΡ[   ]ΕΣ[ ]
---]

[Ἄρ]τεμιν εὐφαρέτρειαν ἐμῆς γενεῆς γεγαυῖαν·	Artemis with a beautiful quiver, born from my race;
[π]άσης γὰρ πόλιος προκαθηγέτις ἐστὶ γενέθλης	for she is leader of the entire city from (its) origin
μαῖα καὶ αὐξήτειρα βροτῶν καρπῶν τε δότειρα·	(being the) midwife and increaser of mortals and giver of produce;
5 ἧς μορφὴν Ἐφέσοιο κομίσσατε χρυσοφάεννον,	whose form shining with gold bring (in) from Ephesus,
κάτθετε δ' ἐν νηῷ πολυγηθέες· ἣ κεν ἀλύξει	and with (much) gladness place (her) in a temple; she will provide escape from
πήματα καὶ λοίμοιο βροτοφθόρα φάρμα[κ]α λύσει	(your) sufferings and will dissolve the man-destroying poison (or 'magic') of plague
λαμπάσι πυρσοφόροις νυχίᾳ φλογὶ μάγματα κηροῦ	having melted down with (her) fire-bearing torches by nightly flame the kneaded (figurines)
τηΐξασα, μάγου κακοτήϊα σύμβολα τέχνης·	of wax, signs of (the) evil art of a sorcerer;
10 αὐτὰρ ἐπὴν τελέσητε θεῇ προστάγματ' ἐμεῖο,	however when you have completed for (the) goddess my ordinances,
ὕμνοις ἰοχέαιραν ἀπρόσμαχον ἰθυβέλειαν	worship (in awe) with hymns (the) irresistible (and) straight-hitting shooter of arrows
καὶ θυσίαις ἄζεσθε κλυτὴν ἐπιωπέα κούρην,	and worship with sacrifices (the) famous virgin (and) overseer,
ἔν τε χοροῖς ἔν τ' εἰλαπίναις κοῦραί θ' ἅμα παισὶν	and during (the) dances and (the) feasts (you) girls — together with (the) boys

παρθένον ἁλμήεσσαν ὑπὲρ χθόνα Μαίονος Ἕρμου	above (the) salty land of Maeonic Hermus
15 πάντῃ κυδαίνοντες ἀναστέφετ' εὐρέα μύρτα	praising (the) virgin in every way — crown (yourselves with) wide myrtle (wreaths)
κεκλόμενοι γαίης Ἐφεσηΐδος Ἄρτεμιν ἁγνὴν	(after) you have summoned from (the) Ephesian land (the) pure Artemis
εἰς αἰὲν ὅππως ὔμμι πέλοι ἄχραντος ἀρωγός·	in order that she might always be to you an undefiled helper;
εἰ δέ τε μὴ τελέοιτε, πυρὸς τότε τείσετε ποινάς·	but if you should not fulfil (the rites), then you will pay (the) penalty of fire.
19 (vac.) Χρηματισθεὶς ὑπὸ τοῦ Ἀπόλλωνος.	(vac.) An oracle given by Apollo.

This entry focuses on the scholarly debate over our inscription, the dispute between C.E. Arnold and R. Strelan over the nature of magical powers of Artemis, and, finally, what light our inscription throws on Luke's account of Paul's ministry in Ephesus.

1. *Scholarly Debate over the Interpretation of the Inscription*

The most extended and insightful exposition of the inscription remains the 1992 article of F. Graf ('Oracle', 267-279). After translating the inscription (pp. 267-269), Graf charts the progression of the oracle of Apollo in four stages (pp. 269-270):
- the address of the god Apollo to his petitioners (*l*. 1);
- the identification of Artemis as the beneficent leader of Ephesus (*ll*. 2-4);
- the action prescribed for the petitioners to avert the plague ravaging the town, whose identity is not identified (*ll*. 5-9);
- the rites of praise and worship to be rendered to Artemis by the town after the plague has been dispelled by the goddess (*ll*. 10-18).

After pointing to a similar oracle at Hierapolis (p. 270, n. 12), Graf discusses the iconography of Artemis in our text (pp. 274-275), concluding with a discussion of the beliefs and rituals of punitive and apotropaic magic as they relate to the inscription (pp. 274-279).

However, the inscription's context and location has generated considerable debate among its three editors during the period of 1991-1992. Graf ('Oracle', 271-273), in agreement with the original editor of the inscription (D. Knibbe, 'Das "Parthermonument"'), has argued that the context of the oracle is the plague brought back by the armies of Lucius Verus upon his return from Mesopotamia after AD 165. But, whereas Knibbe believed that citizens from Ephesus were the petitioners requesting Apollo's oracular help, Graf ('Oracle', 272) posits that the petitioners were the citizens of Sardis. Undoubtedly, Knibbe is incorrect concerning the identity of the petitioners. R. Merkelbach ('Orakel des Apollo', 70-72) has rebutted Knibbe's proposal, pointing out that the petitioners called for the image of the goddess to be brought *from* Ephesus to another site (*ll.* 5, 16; cf. Graf, 'Oracle', 16). Moreover, Merkelbach has argued that the place of ritual in *ll.* 8-10 (i.e. 'the salty lands of Maeonic Hermus') was Lake Koloe, site of a famous temple of Artemis (Strabo 13.4.5), situated to the northwest of Sardis. Additionally, Merkelbach proposed that the oracle was either Apollo of Didyma or Apollo of Klaros, as opposed to Apollo of Ephesus, Knibbe's initial suggestion ('Das "Parthermonument"'). However, on the basis of several oracles from the sanctuary of Klaros that deal with the plague, Graf ('Oracle', 271-272) argues for the oracle being Apollo of Klaros.

As noted, Graf ('Oracle', 272) has suggested that Sardis is the city of the petitioners. A sacrilege inscription (I. Eph. Ia. 2: second half IV cent. BC), cited below, demonstrates the close links between the cult of Artemis at Ephesus and at Sardis, with the mention of a sanctuary being in or near Sardis, confirming thereby the likelihood of the petitioners in our inscription being citizens of Sardis:

> The advocates on behalf of the goddess (Artemis) brought in a sentence of death, as defined in this publication of the judgement: 'When ambassadors had been sent by our city to present robes to Artemis in accordance with ancestral custom, and when the priests and the ambassadors arrived at Sardis and at the temple of Artemis, which was founded by the Ephesians, the accused violated the sanctity of the ceremonies and insulted the envoys. The verdict was death …'.

Also a *homonoia* medallion (AD 198-217: P.R. Franke and M.K. Nollé, *Die homonoia*, no. 1853) illustrates the concord existing between Ephesus and Sardis in a later period, symbolised by the cult statues of Kore and Artemis Ephesia facing each other. Finally, Graf ('Oracle', 269-271) suggests that after the image of Artemis from Ephesus was placed in the temple of Artemis at Sardis (*ll.* 5-9), the subsequent thanksgiving rituals (*ll.* 10-18) were most probably held at the sanctuary of Artemis Koloene on Lake Koloe, though on the basis of the existing evidence this suggestion remains guesswork. While our inscription was probably inscribed in Sardis, it would have been erected in Ephesus in honour of the city and her goddess because of the help given against the machinations of the sorcerer.

On crowning rituals in imperial and Graeco-Roman indigenous cults (*l.* 15) and their relevance to the New Testament, see J.R. Harrison, 'The Fading Crown'. On Graeco-Roman oracular activity (*l.* 19) and its relevance to the New Testament, see D.E. Aune, *Prophecy*; C. Forbes, *Prophecy*; L.A. Kauppi, *Foreign but Familiar Gods*, 16-34. On Graeco-Roman magic (*l.* 9), D.E. Aune, 'Magic'; C.A. Faraone, *Magika Hiera*; M.W. Dickie, *Magic and Magicians*.

2. Artemis and Magic: The Debate Between C.E. Arnold and R. Strelan

Of particular interest for New Testament scholars is the powerful role that the golden image of Artemis plays in relation to apotropaic magic in this inscription. The outbreak of the plague ('[the] man-destroying poison of plague': *l.* 7) is interpreted by the community of Sardis (?) as the work of a magician and his *defixio* (*ll.* 8-9: '[the]

kneaded figurines of wax (μάγματα κηροῦ), [the] signs of the evil art of a sorcerer'). The words μάγματα κηροῦ (*l.* 8) mean literally 'thick unguents of wax' in cases where μάγματα is used in the medical and paramedical texts (*LSJ*, 1071). However, Graf ('Oracle', 269), over against Knibbe ('Das "Parthermonument"') who translates 'wächserne Salbe' ('waxy ointment'), argues that 'a thick unguent of wax, made by a magician, makes no point in our context'. Consequently, Graf ('Oracle', 269), agreeing with the translation 'Knetfiguren aus Wachs' ('clay figures made from wax') proposed originally by Merkelbach ('Orakel des Apollo'), suggests that the kneaded wax figurines belong to the rituals associated with the *defixio* of a μάγος. If this interpretation of μάγματα κηροῦ is correct and a public disaster is being explained by reference to black magic, then, as the *SEG* editor comments (*SEG* XLI 981, 332), this 'is almost unique in the Graeco-Roman world', belonging more to Near Eastern rituals (cf. Graf, 'Oracle', 277-278).

The role of Artemis in delivering the afflicted is depicted as more 'soteriological' (*ll.* 4, 17) than magical in approach. She dissolves the poison of the plague and melts down the magician's *defixiones* with her 'flame-bearing torches' (*ll.* 6-9). Consequently, in the inscriptions we hear of Artemis referred to as Ἄρτεμις Σωτείρα (e.g. I. Eph. III 606; IV 1222). There is also a strong expectation of reciprocity demanded by Artemis' intervention on behalf of her dependants, the characteristic of a relationship between benefactor and beneficiary in antiquity (J.R. Harrison, *Paul's Language of Grace*, *passim*). Cultic ritual and praise in her honour will elicit her sustained beneficence (*ll.* 11-17), whereas ingratitude will result in the return of the dreaded poison (*l.* 18: 'you will pay the penalty of fire'). In other words, whatever role 'magic' might play in the cult of Artemis, it is within the wider context of benefaction rituals and the powerful role of Artemis as the ancestral leader of the city (*l.* 3: 'the leader of the entire city from its origin'; cf. R. Strelan, *Paul, Artemis and the Jews*, 48-52; R. Oster, 'Ephesus as a Religious Centre', 1700-1706). What is interesting in this instance is that her role as benefactor reaches beyond Ephesus to a rival Greek city-state. It attests to the truth of Demetrius' statement in Acts 19:27b about the fame of Artemis having spread well beyond the confines of Ephesus (cf. I. Eph. Ia 24 *ll.* 8-14).

Our inscription is important for New Testament social historians because it throws light on the debate between R. Strelan (*Paul*, 83-88) and C.E. Arnold (*Ephesians*, 22-24, 27, 30, 51, 67-69, 168-169, 171) over whether Artemis was an 'evil' and 'demonic' goddess in a city famed for its magic (Acts 19:19). This debate has important consequences for our understanding of Acts 19 and Ephesians as a whole. To be sure, Arnold's depiction of Artemis as 'demonic' has continuity with later Christian polemic against Artemis. For example, there is a fifth-century AD Christian inscription that celebrates the triumph of Christ over Artemis: 'Having destroyed a deceitful image of demonic Artemis, Demeas set up this sign of truth, honouring both God the driver-away of idols, and the cross, that victorious, immortal symbol of Christ' (I. Eph. IV 1351). Notwithstanding, Strelan's argument has a cumulative strength. The substance of Strelan's argument regarding the minimal role of magic in the Artemis cult is set out below:

§8 Artemis triumphs over a Sorcerer's Evil Art

(a) the evidence for the identification of Artemis with Hecate, goddess of the crossroads and magic, is slender, with Strelan rejecting Bonner's evidence from the amulets (*Paul*, 84; cf. C. Bonner, *Magical Amulets*, 262-263);

(b) there is not any sign of dread of Artemis as a deliverer among her worshippers (Strelan, *Paul*, 84-85), a conclusion confirmed by our own inscription (*ll*. 4, 10-17: *ibid.*, 88);

(c) demons in antiquity were considered either good or evil (*ibid.*, p. 85), not universally 'evil' as Arnold suggests (*Ephesians*, 85-86);

(d) only the *Ephesia grammata* connect magic explicitly with Artemis (Pausanias, as quoted by Eustathius, *Comm. ad. Hom.* 19.247; Plutarch, *Mor.* 760E), but there is no supporting iconographic evidence in this regard (Strelan, *Paul*, 87);

(e) *PGM* LXXVIII, with its ambiguous drawing of (allegedly) Artemis *multimammaea*, does not mention Artemis by name (Strelan, *Paul*, 88). For Strelan's discussion of scholarship on Artemis other than Arnold, see *Paul*, 89-94.

While Strelan's arguments are persuasive as far as Artemis' beneficent nature in antiquity, more can be said by way of modification of his case. In points (1) to (4) below, we will concentrate on the evidence of the magical papyri in Betz's collection (*Magical Papyri*), before we move on to papyrological and iconographic evidence from other sources in points (5) to (7).

First, the link of Artemis with Hecate is not as easily severed as Strelan suggests. In *PGM* IV 2711-2730 there is a clear connection between Artemis and Hecate:

> Come, giant Hekate, Dione's guard,
> O Persia, Baubo Phroune, dart-shooter,
> Unconquered, Lydian, the one untamed,
> Sired nobly, torch-bearing guide, who bends down
> Proud necks, Kore, hear, you who've parted gates
> Of steel unbreakable. O Artemis,
> Who, too, were once protectress, mighty one,
> Mistress who burst forth from the earth, dog-leader,
> All-tamer, crossroad goddess, triple-headed,
> Bringer of light, august/virgin, I call you
> Fawn-slayer, crafty, O infernal one,
> And many-formed. Come, Hekate, goddess
> Of three ways, who with your fire-breathing phantoms
> Have been allotted dreaded roads and harsh
> Enchantments.

Not only are the goddesses Hecate and Artemis paired together here, but also both goddesses are associated with the 'crossroads' in the papyrus (Artemis: 'crossroad goddess'; Hekate: 'goddess of three ways'). Hecate, too, is identified as 'torch-bearing' (*LIMC* VI [1992]: 983-1018 *s.v.* 'Hekate' §§151, 157, 257, 328; 1007 *s.v.* 'Hekate' §§251-260 Pl. 671), an aspect of the iconography of Artemis heavily underscored in our inscription (*l*. 8; cf. Graf, 'Oracle', 274-275). Therefore, contrary to Strelan, there is no doubt about the pairing of Artemis with Hecate in *PGM* IV 2711-2730. Also significant is the use of the word Δαμναμενεύς (*PGM* IV 2773, 2780), one of the famous magical *Ephesia grammata* (C. McCown, 'Ephesia Grammata'). But Strelan is surely correct in saying that this does not elevate Artemis — over against Hecate and the other underground deities — to the exalted position of 'goddess of magic' par excellence. Rather it is simply part of the syncretism that characterised the world of the magical papyri.

Second, in a prayer to Selene for any manner of spell, Hecate, Artemis and Selene are linked together in beneficence towards practitioners of magic (*PGM* IV 2811-2228), an association of deities that we will appear again in another spell (D. Wortmann, 'Neue magische Texte', *infra*):

> ... you hide your forms in shanks of lions,
> Your ankle is wolf-shaped, fierce dogs are dear,
> To you, wherefore they call you Hekate,
> Many-named, Mene, cleaving air just like
> Dart-shooter, Artemis, Persephone,
> Shooter of deer, night shining, triple-sounding,
> Triple-headed, triple-voiced Selene
> Triple-pointed, triple-faced, triple-necked,
> And goddess of the triple ways, who hold
> Untiring flaming fire in triple baskets,
> And you who oft frequent the triple way,
> And rule the triple decades, unto me
> Who'm calling you be gracious and with kindness
> Give heed ...

It is curious that Strelan spends so much effort in dismissing the questionable iconographic evidence of Bonner regarding the Hecate-Artemis link (*supra*) while ignoring the unambiguous evidence of the papyri above.

Third, the pairing of Hecate with Artemis in *PGM* IV 2711-2730 and *PGM* IV 2811-228 makes it likely that *PGM* LXXVIII is also referring to Artemis, among other deities, even though the name of Artemis is not mentioned in the love spell. As noted, Strelan (*Paul*, 88) dismisses the crude drawing of Artemis *multimammaea* on the *verso* as 'so crude as to be open to other interpretations'. However, the clue demonstrating that Hecate-Artemis is being summoned in the spell is the use of the epithet 'light-bringer' (φωσφόρος). The epithet was used of both Hecate (Euripides, *Hel.* 569) and Artemis (Pausanias 4.31.8; Cicero, *Nat. d.* 2.27: 'therefore in our country Juno is invoked in childbirth, as is Diana in her manifestation is Lucifera — 'the light-bringer' — among the Greeks'). The obverse of the silver denarius of P. Clodius M. f. Turrinus (42 BC), too, shows Diana Lucifera standing right holding two long lit torches (E.A. Sydenham, *Coinage*, §1117). This means that the crude drawing is much more likely to be Artemis *multimammaea* than Strelan is willing to concede. Moreover, it is significant that Strelan does not propose any alternative interpretation for the diagram.

However, we must resist any sweeping conclusions regarding the 'superior' magical power of Artemis from this text. *PGM* LXXVIII mentions the name of the deity 'Phnoun' — though G. Mussies ('Artemis', 96) proposes that this refers to the 'Abyss' as opposed to the Egyptian deity Nun — and concludes with a triple invocation of 'Iao'. Mussies is correct in saying that in the highly syncretistic atmosphere of the magical papyri, the individuality of each deity is hardly respected (Mussies, 'Artemis', 96). Again, Arnold's presentation of the overarching magical power of Artemis is overdrawn.

Fourth, in another magical papyrus (*PGM* III 434-435) we hear of Artemis being invoked on a particular day: '[on the 13th, say the 13th name], ARTEMI DAMNO LYKAINA'. The magical name LYKAINA ('she-wolf'), an epithet of the goddess Artemis, is also used in another spell of attraction mentioning Artemis (*PGM* IV 2550; cf. *PGM* IV 2302-2303). In that spell an offering is made in the name of Artemis and other deities (*PGM* IV 2522-2526): '[I offer you] this spice, O child of Zeus, dart-shooter, Artemis, Persephone, shooter of deer, night-shining, triple-sounding, triple-voiced, triple-headed Selene'. In conclusion, as far as the papyri in Betz's collection (*Magical Papyri*), the scarcity of reference to Artemis in the magical papyri — i.e. *PGM* III 434-435, IV 2522-2526, IV 2721-2727, IV 2811-2228, and LXXVIII — should make us wary about overestimating the role of magic in the Artemis cult. But it is certainly more pronounced than Strelan proposes.

Fifth, the same qualified conclusion emerges if we look at the evidence of the *defixiones* ('curse tablets') relating to Artemis. In a 'confession text' (AD 156/157), recording the proceedings taken against Tatia for cursing her son-in-law, there is an appeal to 'Great Artemis, Aneitis and Men of Tiamos' for deliverance from Tatia's machinations (J.G. Gager, *Curse Tablets*, §137). Divine retribution was swift against Tatia and her son Sokrateia, with the result that her remaining descendants praise the gods in a confession for their punitive power:

> Therefore great are the gods of Axionettes! They set about to have removed/cancelled the sceptre and curses that were in the temple ... The descendants of Tatia, Sokrateia and Moschas and Ioukoundos and Menekrates, constantly propitiate the gods and praise them from now on, having inscribed on (this) stele the powers/deeds of the gods.

There is little doubt that the power of Artemis over malevolent magic is celebrated in this document, but it is only in unison with the power of the two other gods addressed at the beginning of the confession text (Aneitis, Men of Tiamos). Artemis, contrary to Arnold, is not exalted as one of the most potent deities of the underworld, but neither should we play down unnecessarily her magical powers as Strelan does.

Sixth, an important love spell (D. Wortmann, 'Neue magische Texte', 60-80, Inv. T. 1, *ll*. 1-83: AD III-IV) — inexplicably omitted from Betz's collection of the papyri (*Magical Papyri*) and overlooked by Strelan — invokes the goddess of the underworld for help. She is addressed with a plurality of names: Artemis, Hecate, Persephone, and Ereschigal. The *Ephesia grammata* are used throughout the love spell, with an adjuration invoking Artemis: 'For I adjure you by the lady, Artemis DAIMON DAMNO DAMNOLUKE' (Wortmann, 'Neue magische Texte', T. 1, *ll*. 39-40). The address 'DAMNO DAMNOLUKE' is significant here because it is the magical name of Hecate-Artemis-Selene (*PGM* III 434-345). The goddess possesses the key to the gate of Hades (Tartaros), acquiring thereby authority over the deities of underworld: 'I order you (by your symbols): key, *kerykeion* (Latin: 'caduceus'), bronze sandal of Tartarouchos, gold sandal of Demeter' (Wortmann, 'Neue magische Texte', T. 1, *ll*. 57-59). Last, the love spell is brought to effect by the 'bow' of Hecate-Artemis-Selene, a feature of each goddess regularly mentioned in the magical papyri (e.g. *PGM* IV 2287, 2523, 2715, 2818, 2853). Although Artemis is not named in the papyrus extract below (Wortmann, 'Neue magische Texte', T. 1, *ll*. 48-57), seasoned practitioners of magic would have associated the 'bow' imagery with the triad of Hecate-Artemis-Selene:

> O Night-trembling One, I conjure you by your ghoulish names ATHO[M] BABATHA BARATHATH BABRITHETH BARBARARA IAOTH BRITH MARCHTHACHAMACHTHA O ARMACHAZARACHTHA and b(y the name) SANTRABIA SANTRAKATANI KANTRA, I conjure (you by) the names PHORBOR PHORBA PHORBA ARCHI . [. . NEICHAR]OPLEX, aim your bow at the heart of Matrona, daughter of Tegene, whom you have as your property. (Ensure that she is dying) with love and longing for Theodore, the son of Techosis, AMPH[. .] . THA Nature-trembling One, Night-trembling One.

However, while Arnold (*Ephesians*, 24) argues that this spell presents Artemis as one of the most powerful underworld goddesses, it is the plurality of deities addressed, along with the invocation of the *Ephesia grammata* and other magical words, which gives the spell its ultimate force.

Seventh, Strelan has overlooked the Ephesian evidence of a bronze *tessera* used as an amulet in the early Empire (J. Obermajer, 'Tesserae of Ephesos', 292-294; *SNG* von Aulock, §1875). On the obverse we see a lying deer, looking backwards, with the letters E—Φ at each side of its head, with the inscription CKωΠI. On the reverse of the bronze *tessera* is a bee with folded wings, with incomprehensible magical syllables inscribed around the iconography: KHPIΛICωΔEΠPCΠAΛVPIN. The deer accompanies Artemis in the iconography of statuary and coins. One numismatic example, picking up the 'torch' imagery of our inscription, will suffice. On the obverse of a bronze *aes* is the head of Artemis facing right with bow and quiver, whereas on the reverse are two deer facing each other on either side of the torch of Artemis (*SNG* von Aulock, §1872; cf. Homer, *Od.* 6.102-109; R. Fleischer, 'Artemis Ephesia', *LIMC* II 1 763). The bee, too, was Artemis' sacred symbol, depicted on the coins of Ephesus from VII-III BC, until the image of the goddess became the sole focus of future coin issues (Mussies, 'Artemis', 94). For a vast array of the visual evidence relating to Artemis/Diana at Ephesus and elsewhere, see *LIMC* II 2 442-628. Once again, from the evidence of the *tessera* it seems that the power of Artemis is understood in terms of apotropaic magic, protecting its beneficiaries in a manner similar to that of our inscription, but without the all-embracing implication that Arnold wants to draw in terms of the demonic status of Artemis. Thus Strelan is correct in saying that there is no magical iconography on the statues of Artemis. The closest we come to this is the zodiacal necklace on the statues — symbolic of Artemis' protection against the impersonal forces of fate (L.R. LiDonnici, 'Images',

407) — but, significantly, there is no iconographic link made between the astrological motifs and Ephesian magic.

In light of our discussion of the evidence, neither Arnold nor Strelan assesses the papyri, curse tablets, and *tesserae* with sufficient balance in discussing the magical powers of Artemis. Our inscription, as we have seen, when analysed carefully, does not support the polarised arguments of either author. An examination of Acts 19:13-41, it will be argued, endorses the same conclusion. Luke is well aware of the role of magic at Ephesus and elsewhere in the eastern Mediterranean basin, but in discussing Artemis of Ephesus he focuses his attention on other issues. The remainder of this entry focuses on the role of magic in Acts 19 and its relation to our inscription.

3. *Artemis and Magic in Acts 19*

The reference to Jewish exorcists using Jesus' name — a supplement to their arsenal of magical names in adjurations (Acts 19:13-18; cf. Josephus, *A.J.* 8.42-49; *T. Sol.* 12:4) — fits what we know of Graeco-Roman and Jewish magic (J.R. Harrison, entry §3 in this volume; S.R. Garrett, *Demise*, 92-93; H.-J. Klauck, *Magic*, 99-100; Strelan, *Paul*, 257-265). But close attention to historical detail is required if we are to understand the subtleties of Luke's account. The Jewish exorcists do not mention Jesus' name by itself in their adjuration. The actual form of their adjuration (Acts 19:13a: λέγοντες) is: 'I adjure you (Ὁρκίζω ὑμᾶς) by the Jesus *whom Paul preaches*' (19:13b). S. Shauf (*Theology as History*, 223) notes that there is no real explanation for Paul being included in the adjuration other than the fact of his own reputation as a miracle worker (e.g. Acts 13:9-11; 14:8-11; 16:16-18; 19:11; cf. Gal 3:5; 2 Cor 12:12; Acts 28:1-6). We are seeing here not only another case of the divine legitimisation of Paul's mission to the Gentiles (Acts 9:15; 26:17), but also the conviction of the exorcists that the names of early Christian 'miracle-workers' had to be invoked, as the later evidence of the Paris magical papyrus confirms (cf. *PGM* IV 3007-3086, *ll.* 3020-3021), for their exorcisms to have sufficient power.

As a brief aside at this juncture, the Jewish exorcists would have typically resorted to famous Jewish names from the Old Testament for their magical adjurations (e.g. 'Solomon': Josephus, *A.J.* 8.42-49; cf. *T. Sol.* 12:4). In this instance, however, the sons of Sceva decide to introduce the names of 'Jesus' and 'Paul' into their repertoire of adjurations. This, of course, enables Luke to establish immediately the superiority of Jesus and his Spirit-empowered workers (Acts 19:15-16; cf. 2:17, 19b ['signs on the earth below']) over the sons of Sceva. But it is also likely that the Jewish exorcists were deliberately curtailing the number of magical names invoked in this particular adjuration (Acts 19:13b). In this regard, the writer of *PGM* IV 2085-2086 criticises the spells of rival exorcists for their excessive use of magical words and names: 'For [the spell] is free of excessive verbiage, immediately carrying out as it does the preceding things with all ease'. A simple and direct formula from an especially powerful 'deity' would triumph over the complicated formulae and lists of inferior deities invoked by rivals (Eitrem, *Demonology*, 6). For Jesus, however, this futile pitting of deity against deity on the part of exorcists pointed to the imminent collapse of Satan's kingdom and household (Mark 3:24-26).

Where, then, does this leave us as far as the role of magic in Acts 19:13-18? When viewed against the practice of contemporary magic, the 'adjuration' technique of the Jewish exorcists does have magical elements: but, significantly, Luke does not identify the sons of Sceva as 'magicians', in sharp contrast to Simon (Acts 8:9-11: μαγεύων [v. 9]) and Bar Jesus/Elymas (13:6, 8: ὁ μάγος). But is there any evidence in Acts 19:19-41 for Artemis' reputation for magic attested to so eloquently in our inscription?

The incident of the magicians burning their magical books at Ephesus (Acts 19:19-20) may well have included the destruction of the *Ephesia grammata* (P. Trebilco, *The Early Christians*, 150; Garrett, *Demise*, 96-97; Klauck, *Magic*, 101-102), as well as books of magical rituals, thaumaturgic formulae, incantations, prayers and hymns. But, although there could be muted interest on Luke's part in the 'magical powers' of Artemis on this occasion, Luke devotes more attention to the operation of Jewish magic in Palestine (Samaria: Acts 8:9ff) and in the Diaspora (Cyprus: Acts 13:6ff). To be sure, we know from the Ephesian inscriptions that there were references to magicians and curses (P. Trebilco, 'Asia', 314, n. 103). But, significantly, Paul's critique of Ephesian Artemis, as presented by Luke, centres upon the fact that 'gods made with hands are not gods' (Acts 19:26; cf. 17:29). This perspective not only aligns with what we know of Paul's theology elsewhere (e.g. Rom 1:20-23; 1 Cor 8:4-6; Gal 4:8), but it also belongs to the wider polemic of Second Temple Judaism against Gentile ignorance of God and their idolatry (Deut 4:28; 27:15; Isa 37:19; 40:18-31; 41:21-24; 44:9-20; 46:5-7; 48:12-14; Ps 79:6; 115:4; Jer 10:25; Wis 13:8-9; *m. 'Abod. Zar.* 3.4).

However prominent was the role that magic played in the Artemis cult, Luke does not highlight its effects in his presentation of her worshippers in Acts 19:23-41. Luke's emphasis is more on the civic pride (Acts 19:27b, 34-35) and economic prosperity (19:24b, 25, 27a) created by the worship of Artemis in Ephesus and in the province of Asia (Shauf, *Theology as History*, 248). This was the seducing influence that the Artemis cult most obviously wielded over non-believers, notwithstanding the reputation of the goddess for magical power in syncretistic contexts. Seemingly, both Arnold and Strelan have overstated their cases in relation to Artemis and magic. As an aside to our discussion of Acts 19:23-41, Arnold is definitely correct in proposing that there is a polemic against magic in Ephesians, but whether it is directed specifically against its (alleged) concentration in Artemis is another question entirely.

Finally, there is an interesting convergence between our inscription and Acts 19:12. Just as the bringing of Artemis' image from Ephesus to Sardis meant the deliverance from the 'signs of the evil art of a sorcerer' (*l.* 9), so the bringing of Paul's sweat cloths or aprons (Acts 19:12: Klauck, *Magic*, 98-99; Strelan, *Paul*, 258-259) resulted in illnesses disappearing and evil spirits being expelled. Strelan correctly observes regarding this phenomenon (*Paul*, 259), 'To a neutral observer, there would have been no difference between the "miracles" of Paul and the "power" of the exorcists or any magician. All operated through the power of a god or demon'. Luke, however, highlights for his readers the rapid growth of the Christian community at Ephesus through the proclamation of God's word and the accompanying acts of deliverance accomplished by its divine power (Acts 19:5-7, 9-10, 15, 17-20).

Bibliography

H.C. **Ackermann** and J.-R. **Gisler**, *Lexicon Iconographicum Mythologiae Classicae: Bildlexikon der Antiken Mythologie* (Zurich: Artemis, 1981-) (=*LIMC*); C.E. **Arnold**, *Ephesians: Power and Magic. The Concept of Power in Ephesians in Light of its Historical Setting* (Cambridge/New York 1989); D.E. **Aune**, *Prophecy in Early Christianity and the Ancient Mediterranean World* (Grand Rapids 1983); D.E. **Aune**, 'Magic in Early Christianity', *ANRW* II.23.1 (1987) 1507-1557; D.E. **Aune**, 'The Apocalypse of John and Graeco-Roman Revelatory Magic', *NTS* 33/4 (1987) 481-501; H.D. **Betz**, *The Greek Magical Papyri in Translation. Volume 1: Texts* (Chicago and London 1986); C. **Bonner**, *Studies in Magical Amulets Chiefly Graeco-Egyptian* (Ann Arbor 1950); M.W. **Dickie**, *Magic and Magicians in the Greco-Roman World* (New York: Routledge, 2001); S. **Eitrem**, *Some Notes on the Demonology in the New Testament* (Oslo 1950); C.A. **Faraone** (ed.), *Magika Hiera: Ancient Greek Magic and Religion* (New York 1991); R. **Fleischer**, 'Artemis Ephesia', *LIMC* II 2 1 (1984) 755-763; C. **Forbes**, *Prophecy and Inspired Speech in Early Christianity and its Hellenistic Environment* (Tübingen 1995); P.R. **Franke** and M.K. **Nollé**, *Die homonoia-Münzen Kleinasiens und der thrakischen Randgebieten, I: Katalog* (Saarbrücken 1997); J.G. **Gager** (ed.), *Curse Tablets and Binding Spells from the Ancient World* (New York/Oxford 1992); S.R. **Garrett**, *The Demise of the Devil: Magic and the Demonic in Luke's Writings* (Minneapolis 1989); M. **Günther**, *Die Frühgeschichte des Christentums in Ephesus* (Frankfurt 1995); J.R. **Harrison**, *Paul's Language of Grace in its Graeco-Roman* Context (Tübingen 2003); J.R. **Harrison**, 'The Fading Crown: Divine Honour and the Early Christians', *JTS* 54/2 (2003) 493-529; L.A. **Kauppi**, *Foreign but Familiar Gods: Greco-Romans Read Religion in Acts* (London 2006); D. **Knibbe**, 'Das "Parthermonument" von Ephesos. Parthersieg(altar) des Artemis (und Kenotaph des L. Verus) an der "Triodos"', *BerMatÖA* I (1991) 5-18; H.-J. **Klauck**, *Magic and Paganism in Early Christianity: The World of the Acts of the Apostles* (Edinburgh 2000); L.R. **LiDonnici**, 'The Images of Artemis Ephesia and Greco-Roman Worship: A Reconsideration', *HTR* 85 (1992) 389-415; G. **Luck**, *Arcana Mundi: Magic and the Occult in the Greek and Roman World* (Baltimore and London 1985); R. **Merkelbach**, 'Ein Orakel des Apollo für Artemis von Koloe', *ZPE* 88 (1997) 70-72; C. **McCown**, 'The Ephesia Grammata in Popular Belief', *TAPA* 54 (1923) 128-140; J. **Obermajer**, 'Tesserae of Ephesos in the History of Medicine', *Med Hist* 12/3 (1968) 292-294; R. **Oster**, 'Ephesus as a Religious Centre under the Principate, I. Paganism before Constantine', *ANRW* II.18.3 (1990) 1661-1728; H. **Sarian**, 'Hecate', *LIMC* VI (1992): 983-1018; S. **Shauf**, *Theology as History, History as Theology: Paul in Ephesus in Acts 19* (Berlin 2005); R. **Strelan**, *Paul, Artemis, and the Jews in Ephesus* (Berlin/New York 1996); E.A. **Sydenham**, *The Coinage of the Roman Republic* (London 1952); W. **Thiessen**, *Christen in Ephesus: Die historische und theologische Situation in vorpaulinischer und paulinischer Zeit und zur Zeit der Apostelgeschichte und der Pastoralbriefe* (Tübingen/Basle 1995); P. **Trebilco**, 'Asia', in *The Book of Acts in its First-Century Setting* (eds, D.W.J. Gill, C. Gempf; Grand Rapids 1994) 291-362; P. **Trebilco**, *The Early Christians in Ephesus from Paul to Ignatius* (Grand Rapids 2004); D. **Wortmann**, 'Neue magische Texte', *Bonner Jahrbücher* 168 (1968) 56-111.

J.R. Harrison (Macquarie University)

§9 A 'worthy' *neopoios* thanks Artemis

Ephesus   Marble block   Undated

Ed. pr. — D. Knibbe, H. Engelmann, B. Iplikçioğlu, 'Neue Inschriften aus Ephesos XI', *JÖAI* 59 (1989) Beibl. 209/10 no. 40 (= *SEG* XXXIX 1205)

Ἀγαθῆι Τ[ύχηι]	To Good For[tune]
Εὐχαριστῶ σοι, κυρία Ἄρ[τεμι],	I give thanks to you, mistress Ar[temis],
Ἔφηβος Μηνοφιλιανός, [ἀδελφοῦ]	Ephebos Menophilianos, (from a family) of neopo[ioi], [brother],
πατρὸς πάππου νεοπο[ιῶν, νεοποι]-	father, grandfather, after serv-
5 ήσας ὡς εὐξάμην κατ[αξίως σὺν]	ing wor[thily] as I vowed as a neopoios [with]
τῷ πατρί μου Νικηφ[ορια]-	my father Nikeph[oria]-
7 νῷ καὶ συνάρχο[υσι πᾶσι]	nos and with [all] who are colleagues in off[ice].

1. *Neopoioi and the New Testament*

The editor of this inscription argues that Ἔφηβος is a name rather than the age-category of ἔφηβος. Ephebos Menophilianos, therefore, belongs to a family of *neopoioi* (consisting of his brother, father and grandfather) and had served as a *neopoios* himself. The *neopoioi* (literally, 'temple-builders') were sacred officials in the Empire who earlier, in Hellenistic times, had also exercised supervision of the citizenship. However, they had seen their role expand during the imperial age to include a wider range of civic functions. S. Dmitriev (*City Government*, 21), for example, refers to their role in arranging the inscribing of honorific decrees (e.g. Priene: *SIG*³ 273: 'let the *agonothetes* take care of the proclamation; let the *neopoios* service the inscribing'; Miletus: I. Milet. III 135), including in some instances payment for the stele as well (I. Priene 18.31-36; I. Magnesia 101.46-47). With the triumph of the Julio-Claudian house in the early Empire, however, the *neopoioi* in Asia Minor came to have increasing responsibility for the administration of the imperial cult.

An inscription, found in the ruins of a temple of Gaius at Didyma, unveils the operations of the cult of Gaius at Miletus (Dio 59.28.1). Importantly for us, the inscription speaks of the special honour of those 'who were his first *neopoioi*' (R.K. Sherk, *Roman Empire*, §43). The 'chief *neopoios*' (*archineopoios*) of the city, named Protomachos, not only supervised the other *neopoioi* but also held the offices of *sebastoneos* (an undefined temple official of the imperial cult) and *sebastologos* (the official responsible for prose eulogies of the Roman ruler). The inscription concludes with the administrative districts for which these 'Augustus-loving *neopoioi*' and the 'Gaius-loving Melesian' *neopoios* were responsible, including seven cities mentioned in the New Testament. Ephesus is not mentioned in this list, having displaced Pergamum as the capital of the province during the reign of Augustus in 29 BC (Dio 50.20.6), with the result that the proconsuls resided there (Acts 19:38) and made the city the centre of the judicial courts for the district (P. Trebilco, *Early Christians*, 14). L. Robert ('Le culte de Caligula'; cf. C. Habicht, 'New Evidence') has demonstrated that these *neopoioi*, representatives of the various districts of the province of Asia, were delegates of the *conventus* (the judicial district administering the province). Undoubtedly, each of the *neopoioi* in the inscription would have had formal or informal contact with the provincial governor when he visited each of their cities for his court hearings.

G.H.R. Horsley ('Giving Thanks to Artemis', 127) states that at Ephesus the *neopoioi* 'constituted a board of management ... responsible for the upkeep of the Temple of Artemis', including maintenance of the site and supervision of sacrifices and festivals. They were well known in Ephesus (Horsley, 'Giving Thanks', §§1, 28; cf. 8, 52, 81) and they were also present at nearby Aphrodisias (e.g. I. Aph. V 108; XII 325). A search of the Ionian inscriptions in the Packard Humanities Institute concordance revealed 27 occurrences at Ephesus for the word νεοποιός, 20 for νεοποιῶν, and 7 for νεοποιοί. Some of the Ephesian *neopoioi* exercised the role of benefactors, as the phrase *neopoioi authairetoi* ('voluntary *neopoioi*': I. Eph. III 961) indicates. The Ephesian *neopoioi* would have administered the interplay between the worship of Artemis and the imperial cult at Ephesus, if the Didyma inscription is applicable to Ephesus as well. In this regard, several of the Ephesian *neopoioi* are described as 'Augustus-loving' (φιλοσέβαστος: I. Eph. III 619; III 630; IV 1126). G.H.R. Horsley ('Inscriptions of Ephesos', 144) also refers to the wide array of administrative and religious posts (*grammateus* of the *demos*, *asiarch*, *archiereus* of the imperial cult) that the Ephesian *neopoios* T. Flavius Pythio managed to attain (I. Eph. V 1578a). Obviously, the office of *neopoios* was an important post for the upwardly mobile who wanted to advance in the cursus honorum of any significant city in provincial Asia. Undoubtedly, the officials known as *neopoioi* would have been familiar to Paul in his travels throughout the eastern Mediterranean basin, although there is no record of Paul having actually met a *neopoios*.

Notwithstanding, the silence of the New Testament regarding any encounter of the apostle with the *neopoioi* has not stopped scholars from speculating on the issue. For example, E.L. Hicks ('Demetrius the Silversmith', 401-422) famously proposed that the *neopoios* named Demetrios in I. Eph. V 1578a *ll.* 4, 6 was the same Demetrios as the silversmith mentioned in Acts 19:24-27. As textual proof, Hicks argued that the participle ποιῶν in Acts 19:24 was a mistaken memory of νεοποιῶν. W.M. Ramsay rightly challenged this imaginative construct (*Church in the Roman Empire*, 112-145; G.H.R. Horsley, 'The Silversmiths at Ephesos', 8). D.B. Saddington ('Roman Military', 2431, n. 70; P. Trebilco, 'Asia', 337-338, n. 208) sums up Hick's assumptions about I. Eph. V 1578 thus: '... the date is not certain and the name is too common to identify'. Hicks' argument, however, has again been revived by G.M. Rogers ('Demetrios of Ephesos', 877-883) in a slightly different form. Rogers claims that since the *neopoioi* took part in the enrolment of new citizens at Ephesus and elsewhere during the Hellenistic Age, Demetrius' campaign against Paul gained traction because of Ephesus' hostility to citizenship for the Jews. Once again, this theory has no foundation in the text of Acts 19:24ff. As Saddington observes ('Roman Military', 2431), it is uncertain whether *neopoioi* were still responsible for citizen enrolment by the time of Paul's visit to Ephesus, although that was the case in the Hellenistic age.

Most recently, R. Muñoz-Larrondo (*Living in Two Worlds*, 335, 342, 345) has argued that Demetrius was an imperial city official related to the Artemis cult, being 'perhaps ... a *neopoios* in charge of commerce at the temple' (p. 345). While Muñoz-Larrondo's arguments are based analogously on the role of *neopoioi* at the cult of Gaius at Miletus (Sherk, *Roman Empire*, §43) and are contextually viable in terms of Acts 19:24ff, the case still faces the fundamental objection that the identification of Demetrios as a *neopoios* is entirely speculative (Horsley, 'Inscriptions of Ephesos', 143-144). In sum, the time is long overdue for scholars to consign Hick's hypothesis to permanent rest rather than resurrecting its discredited corpse periodically.

2. *The Dynamics of Prayer in the New Testament World*

The thanksgiving (εὐχαριστῶ σοι) offered to Artemis in our inscription is entirely conventional (R. Oster, 'Holy Days in Honour of Artemis', §19 80-81), fitting what we know about how the language of 'grace' functioned in terms of the god(s) in antiquity (J.R. Harrison, *Paul's Language of Grace*, s.v. Index: 'Thanksgiving'; H.S. Versnel, 'Religious Mentality in Ancient Prayer', 1-64, esp. 42-61; cf. εὐχαριστέω: e.g. Luke 18:1; John 6:23; Acts 28:15; Rom 1:8, 21; 7:5; 14:6; 1 Cor 1:4; 14:18; Phil 1:3; Col 1:3; 3:17; 1 Thess 1:2; 2:13; 2 Thess 1:3; 2:13; Phlm 4; Rev 11:17). The reputation of Artemis ἐπήκοός as one who listened to prayer (I. Eph. II 504, *l*. 1) and who provided salvation occasioning εὐχαριστία (I. Eph. III 940, *l*. 3; 943, *ll*. 2-3; 957, *ll*. 9-10; 960, *ll*. 2-3, 9-10) was ubiquitous in the ancient world. In accordance with the practice of antiquity, prayers to Artemis and other deities would have been prayed aloud as opposed to prayed silently (P.W. van der Horst, 'Silent Prayer', 1-25). Undoubtedly, they would have been composed pieces. For an example, see the prayer written by Claudia Trophime, priestess of Artemis and *prytanis*, to Hestia (R.A. Kearsley, 'Mysteries of Artemis', 199). Note, too, the prayer to Ephesian Artemis recorded in the Acts of John by Ps.-Prochorus (C.E. Arnold, *Ephesians: Power and Magic*, 22, citing R.C. Kukala, 'Literary Witnesses of the Artemis Temple', *FiE*, 1.253; cf. S. Noegel [ed.], *Prayer*). The precise content of the thanksgiving to Artemis is not recounted in our inscription, though implicitly it is directed towards the worthy completion ([νεοποι]ήσας κατ[αξίως]) of his office of *neopoios* in a manner commensurate with his family honour and (public?) vow.

By contrast, the New Testament writers do not approach prayer in the stereotypical manner of the composer of our inscription, though the thankfulness of Ephebos Menophilianos to Artemis is undoubtedly genuine (*infra*, §3). Paul and Luke demonstrate great interest in the manner and regularity of prayer and highlight this by the addition of a rich variety of terminology to their prayer language. Believers pray with one mind (Acts 1:14: προσκαρτεροῦντες ὁμοθυμαδὸν τῇ προσευχῇ), always (Rom 1:10; Phil 1:4a; 2 Thess 1:11: πάντοτε), unceasingly (1 Thess 5:17:

ἀδιαλείπτως), with joy (Phil 1:4b: μετὰ χάρας), in the Spirit (Eph 6:18: ἐν παντὶ καιρῷ ἐν πνεύματι; Jude 1:20: ἐν πνεύματι ἁγίῳ), without anger and doubt (1 Tim 2:8b: χωρὶς ὀργῆς καὶ διαλογισμοῦ), and with the resolve of a wrestler (Col 4:12b: ἀγωνιζόμενος ὑπὲρ ὑμῶν ἐν ταῖς προσευχαῖς). The closest parallel to our inscription is Paul's command to pray 'with thanksgiving' (Phil 4:6: μετὰ εὐχαριστίας). Clearly, a distinctive dynamic animates the New Testament references to prayer.

3. *'Worthiness' and Official Duty in the New Testament World*

What differentiates this inscription from the other *neopoioi* inscriptions at Ephesus (Horsley, 'Giving thanks to Artemis') is the strong emphasis on the fact that the office of Ephebos Menophilianos was performed 'worthily' (κατ[αξίως]). In the other *neopoioi* inscriptions of Ephesus, we have reference to the official having performed the office 'uprightly and fairly' (νεοποιήσας ἁ[γνῶς καὶ κ]αλῶς: *JOAI* 59 [1989] 233/4, 68), 'piously' (νεοποιήσας εὐσεβῶς: I. Eph. III 613, 624), and 'piously and eagerly' (νεοποιήσας εὐσεβῶς καὶ φιλοτείμως: I. Eph. III 629). Caution, however, should be exercised here. In our inscription, κατ[αξίως] in line 5 has only three identifiable letters and the remaining five letters have been restored by the editor, as well as the following three letters of the preposition σύν. A search in the Packard Humanities Institute Greek epigraphy concordance database for καταξίως in the geographic regions of antiquity revealed 78 occurrences of καταξίως in inscriptions across the Mediterranean basin. The only inscription that used καταξίως of the performance of the office of *neopoios* is our inscription (i.e. *SEG* XXXIX 1205).

This is the first time that our inscription has been presented for publication, so we are dependent upon the judgement of the epigrapher editing the inscription for the restorations. καταξίως is used regularly in honorific decrees with a variety of words: τιμάω, μνάομαι, ἐπαινέω, στεφανόω, εὐδοκιμέω, ἀποδίδωμι χάριτας, etc. Its use here with νεοποιήσας, if the editor is correct, is unprecedented. The real question is whether the editor's restoration is accurate. The use of the adverb after the verb would reasonably be expected in public eulogies such as ours and καταξίως is a likely restoration, given the preponderance of its cognate ἀξίως in the honorific inscriptions. Further a preposition like σύν would also be expected to make sense of the dative clause τῷ πατρί μου Νικηφ[ορια]νῷ καὶ συνάρχο[υσι πᾶσι]. Although there is no parallel for this usage in the inscriptions searched above, and provided that the editor is correct in proposing that eight letters were required to fill in the space of the damaged portion of the inscription, the restoration has merit. Thus we have here a usage that is distinctive in terms of the inscriptional corpus of the Greek East.

The reference to Ephebos' 'vow' (ὡς εὐξάμην) in the inscription highlights his determination not to dishonour Artemis or his family and colleagues by an inadequate performance of his official duties. His pride in his personal achievement is reinforced by the mention of his brother, father (twice), and grandfather, each man having held the office of *neopoios*. Ephebos, therefore, had conspicuously upheld the family honour in the civic arena. Thus the inscription is a singular example of the civic status that the urban elites of Roman Asia sought to attain through posts in the provincial *cursus honorum*, presuming that the inscription belongs to the early period of the Empire rather than the Hellenistic age.

At the opposite end of the social spectrum stands the apostle Paul. After boasting in his weaknesses and humiliations (2 Cor 11:23c-29) in order to debunk the hybris of the interloping 'super-apostles' at Corinth (11:4-6, 12-23a), he climaxes his catalogue of 'foolishness' (11:1, 16, 17b, 21b, 23b) with a graphic vignette of social dishonour (11:30-33; cf. Harrison, *Paul's Language of Grace*, 335-340). On this occasion Paul spotlights the significance of his humiliation by an oath to God as to its veracity (11:31). Paul's radical disavowal of what was socially creditable and his identification with the humiliation of the crucified Christ (1 Cor 1:18-31; 2 Cor 13:4; Gal 2:19-20; Phil 2:5-11; 3:4-11) is a prominent feature of his thought. Paul's ready acceptance of social dishonour for the sake of Christ and his Body (1 Cor 4:9-13; 2 Cor 4:7-12; 6:8-10) must have puzzled his Graeco-Roman contemporaries who sought to maintain and surpass the achievements of their ancestors.

How, then, does the language of 'worthiness' function in the New Testament? The adverb κατ[αξίως] ('quite worthily'), used in our inscription of Ephebos' service as a *neopoios* (*l*. 5), is not found in the New Testament. Its cognate καταξιόω ('to deem worthy') is used three times in the passive form with the sense of believers being 'deemed worthy' of the Kingdom of God, though the context speaks either of suffering and dishonour (Acts 5:41; 2 Thess 1:5) or of inclusion in the resurrection age (Luke 20:35). The adverbial cognate ἀξίως is used in contexts of receiving benefactors and missionary workers worthily (Rom 16:2; 3 John 6), or believers walking worthily of their Lord's calling (Eph 4:1; Col 1:10), or conducting themselves worthily of the gospel of Christ and God (Phil 1:27; 1 Thess 2:12). In other words, the language of 'worthiness' has been wrenched by the early Christians from its context of civic honour in the inscriptions and reallocated to the social dishonour involved in discipleship, with a view to the eschatological honour of the resurrection. Thus a new reference point now defines 'worthiness' for the early Christians: namely, the gospel of the risen Lord, as opposed to the esteem of contemporaries in the honorific inscriptions. Consequently fellow believers honour the servants of Christ's gospel 'worthily' for their work.

There is little doubt that the self-humbling and dishonouring of Christ on the cross is at the centre of this new social construct of Paul. But the radical redefinition of the language of 'worthiness' on the part of the early Christians is also perhaps attributable to the impact of Jesus' teaching on importance of self-humbling (e.g. Matt 6:5-9; Mark 12:40; Luke 20:47; cf. Matt 23:12; C.A. Evans, 'Jesus' Ethic of Humility'). The parable of the *Pharisee and the Tax Collector* (Luke 18:10-14) presents a tax-collector, a client of the Roman and Herodian overlords, going up to the temple and praying: 'God, be merciful to me (ἱλάσθητί μοι), a sinner!' (18:13). The tax collector's humble prayer of repentance stands in contrast to the Pharisee's prayer of gratitude to God (18:11-12). In recounting how he excelled his contemporaries in nomistic righteousness (cf. Gal 1:14; Phil 3:5-6), the Pharisee exalts himself and denigrates others (Luke 18:11b).

The denigration of the tax collector is also conveyed by the physical position assumed by the Pharisee in the temple, provided that we take πρὸς ἑαυτόν (Luke 18:11) as modifying the aorist passive participle σταθείς ('having stood'), as opposed to modifying the imperfect verb προσηύχετο ('was praying'). If the latter alternative is correct, the Pharisee prays to himself (NASB, NIV, RSV translations). However, if the former alternative is correct, the meaning is either that the Pharisee 'stood by himself' (ESV, NRSV translations) or that 'he took up a prominent position and uttered his prayer' (J. Jeremias, *Parables*, 140; similarly, K.R. Snodgrass, *Stories with Intent*, 470). This infuses Jesus' parable with powerful symbolism in its depiction of sacred space. During the public worship at the temple, the Pharisee deliberately separates himself from the other worshippers and utters a self-righteous prayer heard by all (Luke 18:11a). By contrast, the despised tax collector stands at a distance, averting his eyes and beating his breast (18:13), presumably positioned at the centre of the temple forecourt or its entrance.

By contrast, the tax collector pleads pardon from God, as the LXX usage of ἱλάσκομαι indicates (Luke 18:13b: cf. 2 Kgs 5:18; Lam 3:42; Dan 9:19; Esth 4:17). The prayer is accompanied by the strong emotion of contrition (cf. Luke 23:48), symbolised by the tax collector beating his breast (Luke 18:13; cf. Josephus, *A.J.* 7.252). The tax collector's reverential attitude in prayer is seen in his refusal to lift his eyes to heaven because of his shame over his guilt before God (Ezra 9:6; 1 Enoch 13:5). He confesses that he is a ἁμαρτωλός ('sinner': Luke 18:13b), a term which in Luke's understanding not only expresses his moral complicity in defrauding people (cf. Luke 19:8), but also his social alienation from God's covenantal people (Luke 5:30; 7:34; 15:1; 19:2-7).

Unexpectedly, it is the tax collector, rather than the pious Pharisee, who finds God's justice (18:14a: δεδικαιωμένος). Jesus' shocking reversal of which worshipper was reckoned 'just' before God is explained by the eschatological humbling of those who exalt themselves before God (18:14b; cf. 14:11). A.J. Hultgren (*Parables*, 125) observes that here Jesus 'assumes an authority that belongs to God alone' by declaring in advance the eschatological justification of the tax collector (cf. Mark 2:3-12 par; Luke 7:47-48). In declaring the tax collector 'just', Jesus consigned the entire Pharisaic holiness system, encapsulated in miniature in vv.11-12, to the rubbish heap. Ultimately, even the temple sacrificial system is rendered obsolete through God's pardon of the tax collector's sins, even though the offering of sacrifices would continue unabated until AD 70.

In conclusion, God's vindicated elect (Luke 18:8, 14) were not the 'self-appointed guardians of Israel's national life' like the Pharisees, as N.T. Wright observes (*Jesus and the Victory of God*, 366), or, for that matter, the privileged Sadducean priesthood of the temple. Rather, with the advent of the Kingdom in Jesus, the marginalised national enemy, the tax collector, is forgiven unconditionally without any reparations required on his part (Luke 19:8; cf. 6:27-36). Notions of 'worthiness' on the part of God's worshippers, therefore, had been undermined by Jesus' parable, with its strong emphasis on humility before God and others. This possibly explains why the early believers, in contrast to our inscription, redefined the prevailing norms of social 'worth' in the Jewish and Graeco-Roman world by their use of ἀξίως and καταξιόω.

Bibliography

C.E. **Arnold**, *Ephesians: Power and Magic. The Concept of Power in Ephesians in Light of its Historical Setting* (Cambridge/New York 1989); O. **Cullmann**, *Prayer in the New Testament* (London 1995); C.A. **Evans**, 'Jesus' Ethic of Humility', *TrinJ* 13 (1992) 127-138; S. **Dmitriev**, *City Government in Hellenistic and Roman Asia Minor* (Oxford 2005); C. **Habicht**, 'New Evidence on the Province of 'Asia', *JRS* 65 (1975) 63-91; E.L. **Hicks**, 'Demetrius the Silversmith', *Exp* 4/1 (1890) 401-422; J.R. **Harrison**, *Paul's Language of Grace in its Graeco-Roman Context* (Tübingen 2003); G.H.R. **Horsley**, 'The Silversmiths at Ephesos', *New Docs* 4 (1987) 7-10; G.H.R. **Horsley**, 'Giving Thanks to Artemis', *New Docs* 4 (1987) 127-129; G.H.R. **Horsley**, 'The Inscriptions of Ephesos and the New Testament', *NovT* 34/2 (1992) 105-168; J. **Jeremias**, *The Parables of Jesus* (London ³1972); A.J. **Hultgren**, *The Parables of Jesus: A Commentary* (Grand Rapids 2000); R.A. **Kearsley**, 'The Mysteries of Artemis at Ephesus', *New Docs* 6 (1992) 196-202; R. **Muñoz-Larrondo**, *Living in Two Worlds: A Postcolonial Reading of the Acts of the Apostles* (unpub. PhD diss., Vanderbilt University, 2008), forthcoming Peter Lang; S. **Noegel** (ed.), *Prayer, Magic and the Stars in the Ancient and Late Antique World* (University Park, PA 2003); R. **Oster**, 'Holy Days in Honour of Artemis', *New Docs* 4 (1987) 74-82; W.M. **Ramsay**, *Church in the Roman Empire before AD 170* (New York/London 2000); L. **Robert**, 'Le culte de Caligula à Milet et la province d'Asie', *Hellenica* 7 (1949) 206-238; G.M. **Rogers**, 'Demetrios of Ephesos', *Belleten: Türk Tarih Kurumu* 50 (1987) 877-883; D.B. **Saddington**, 'Roman Military and Administrative Personnel in the New Testament', *ANRW* II.26.3 (1996) 2409-2435; R.K. **Sherk**, *The Roman Empire: Augustus to Hadrian* (ed. and tr.; Cambridge 1988); K.R. **Snodgrass**, *Stories with Intent: A Comprehensive Guide to the Parables of Jesus* (Grand Rapids/Cambridge 2008); P.W. **van der Horst**, 'Silent Prayer in Antiquity', *Numen* 41/1 (1994) 1-15; P. **Trebilco**, 'Asia', in *The Book of Acts in its First-Century Setting* (eds, D.W.J. Gill, C. Gempf; Grand Rapids 1994) 291-362; P. **Trebilco**, *The Early Christians in Ephesus from Paul to Ignatius* (Grand Rapids 2004); H.S. **Versnel**, 'Religious Mentality in Ancient Prayer', in *Faith, Hope, and Worship: Aspects of Religious Mentality in the Ancient World* (ed., H.S. Versnel; Leiden 1981) 1-64; N.T. **Wright**, *Jesus and the Victory of God: Christian Origins and the Question of God, Vol. 2* (Philadelphia 1996).

J.R. Harrison (Macquarie University)

PUBLIC LIFE: CAESARIAN ACCESSION

§10 The Crux of *RG* 34.1 Resolved? Augustus on 28 BC

(a) Pisidian Antioch   Limestone fragment   I^p

Ed.pr. P. Botteri, *ZPE* 144 (2003) 264 (= frag. 34 j [Drew-Bear and Scheid]).

[... P]OSTQVA[M ...]	... subsequent to ...
[... PO]TENS RE[RUM ...]	... in control of things ...
[... POPULI]QUE R[OMANI ...]	... and of the Roman people ...

(b) Asia Minor?   Aureus   28 BC

Ed.pr. *Numismatica Ars Classica* auction catalogue 5 (1992) 400 (= Simon 208–9, pl. 7.4 = British Museum accession no. CM 1995.4–1.1 = Rich and Williams, *NC* [1999] 169, plates 20-21).

Obverse:	IMP · CAESAR · – DIVI · F · COS · VI	Imp(erator) Caesar, s(on) of the god (Caesar), cons(ul) (for the) sixth time.
	Laureate head of Octavianus, right.	
Reverse:	LEGES · ET · IVRA · P · R · RESTITVIT.	Laws and rights (to the) R(oman) p(eople) did he return.
	Octavianus, togate, seated left on *sella curulis,* holding out scroll in right hand; *scrinium* (filing box) on ground to left.	

No crux of interpretation in the *Res Gestae* (= *RG*) has provoked such intense debate as that over section 34.1. Central to it all has been the origin and nature of the 'total control' ([*potitus reru*]*m om*[*n*]*ium*) over Rome asserted by Augustus with reference to the sixth consulship (28 BC). In the seventh (27 BC) he divested himself of this *potestas* by transferring the *res publica* to the *arbitrium* of the senate and people of Rome (34.2). The Praenestine calendar, preserved separately on stone, registers the date, 13 January.

In his magisterial 2nd edition of the *RG* (1883) Mommsen restored the broken text to read [*potitus*], 'having taken total control'. He used the perfect participle of the Latin verb *potiri* ('to control'), reflecting the aorist tense of the participle extant in the Greek translation, ἐγκρατὴς γενόμενος, 'becoming empowered' (the Latin present participle, *potiens*, was not in frequent use). Mommsen understood [*potitus*] to be a reference back to the oath of loyalty sworn to Octavianus in 32 BC before the battle of Actium (*RG* 25.2).

In 1951 Adcock proposed that since [*potitus*] did indeed correctly reflect the Greek aorist it should be construed as the key to the double dating (by the two successive consulships). It might then refer to an otherwise unattested occasion in 28 BC when Octavianus took total control, 'by universal consent' (*RG* 34.1).

Such an occasion might well have been a sensational and alarming bid by M. Licinius Crassus (cos. 30) for the *spolia opima*. This supreme badge of valour was available only to the commander who slew the enemy general in single combat, a feat recorded only twice hitherto across 500 years. In his proconsular command of 29 (Cassius Dio 51.24.4) Crassus had slain Deldo, king of the Bastarnae, who had crossed the Danube, threatening the Roman province of Macedonia.

Crassus was the grandson and namesake of the famous magnate who shared power with Pompeius and Caesar before the civil wars. The grandson had joined the Pompeian side, then gone over to Antonius, and finally won favour with Octavianus. But his new feat easily outshone the prestige of the new leader. He might challenge for power at Rome.

In 1957, however, Seyfarth demonstrated that [*potitus*] was itself questionable, though he retained Mommsen's text. In 1978, Krömer, citing his teacher R. Kassel, insisted it must be wrong, since *rerum potiri* (to 'be in' or 'take control of' power) is a fixed formula, not expecting an epithet such as om[n]ium ('total'). He further argued that Adcock's interpretation of the perfect tense (*potitus*) was linguistically invalid. Kassel had proposed that the adjective *potens* ('controlling') must have been the original reading. Syme 'deprecated' the case made by Krömer.

In 2003, however, Botteri printed the photograph of a new fragment from the *RG* as once displayed at Pisidian Antioch, which is our text (**a**). It had not been collected along with the 270 others found and edited between 1914 and 1928 (some of which have in the meantime disappeared). The new fragment was detected by Drew-Bear in the local museum. The photography and tabulation of all the Antiochian fragments has now been published by Drew-Bear and Scheid (2005).

Because the new fragment supplements also precisely the lines above and below the restored [*potitus*] its placement is certain, and it is now beyond question that Kassel was right. The original text did not use a participial construction, whether perfect or present tense, but indeed had the adjectival form *potens*.

This physically slight correction has been crucial for the whole concept and ideology of the *RG*. We now have a definitive new edition of the complete work by Scheid (Paris 2007). It provides a separate diplomatic transcript of each of the four extant versions, two Latin and two Greek, as well as a consolidated edition for both languages on facing pages, with French translation beneath. The introduction and commentary of Scheid completes what must rank now as the standard edition of the *RG*. It provides the foundation for all reference and historical discussion, supplanting both Mommsen's text of the nineteenth century and those of Volkmann, Gagé and Malcovati from the twentieth.

In English we now also have an historically comprehensive edition by Cooley (Cambridge 2009), which likewise outclasses all its predecessors. The Latin and Greek, as with Scheid, are on facing pages, but each with its own English translation, a valuable way of highlighting the significance of the Greek version and its bearing on the meaning of the Latin. Cooley provides an extensive historical commentary, and has listed in an appendix the quite numerous minor points at which her presentation of the texts varies from Scheid's (typically over which letters can be read for certain, and which should be marked as doubtful or conjectural).

As for what Augustus meant us to think happened in 28 BC, we must abandon the false trail long entrenched by respect for Mommsen's authority. The *RG* does not assert that Augustus 'took full control' in that year, but only that he 'was in full control'. But why then does he use a double date?

The new aureus, our text (**b**), supplies an explicit answer in his own words (for its authenticity, see Simon). Photographs of the two sides of this unique coin are reproduced on p. 259 of Cooley. Her caption reads, 'Restoration of constitutional government'. The coin itself states on its reverse, 'He returned laws and rights to the Roman people'.

Tacitus (*Ann.* 3.38.2) explains that in the sixth consulship, *potentiae securus* ('secure in his control'), the future Augustus 'abolished what he had decreed (*iusserat*) in the triumvirate' (43-33 BC, *RG* 7.1). Dio (53.1.1) notes that he formally regularised his use of the consulship both at the beginning and end of his sixth term. He states that the 'unlawful and unjust rulings' of the triumvirate terminated on the last day of that year (Dio 53.2.3).

We are still left, however, without a convincing explanation of why Octavianus moved promptly in the seventh consulship to such an elaborate celebration of the transfer of control. Why in mid-winter? Why not simply proceed to the provincial command in the time-honoured way at the end of the year just begun? Badian and Rich have argued strongly that the question of the *spolia opima* for Crassus need not even have arisen until his return and triumph in 27 BC, when it seems to have been disposed of without in the end provoking a crisis. But the news of the feat of Crassus will have become the talk of the town as soon as it arrived, long before anything could be negotiated between the stakeholders.

The new Augustus (as Octavianus was formally named on 16 January 27 BC) was not being presented as an innovator. The 'initiative' (*auctoritas*) connoted by the name reinforces the inherited ideal of the Roman nobility. A 'leader' (*princeps*) is the one whose enterprise and status saves the day, each in his own age, by whatever action Rome's future demands. There need be no plan, no constitutional reform. Only in retrospect could political science classify the gravitation of power towards the house of Caesar in such terms (see also entry §12 in this volume). Mommsen's 'principate', as a new ordering of the state, has lost its grip on our understanding of Augustus. Contrast the *Cambridge Ancient History* of 1934 with the Cambridge overviews of Crook (1996) and Gruen (2005).

Bibliography

F.E. **Adcock**, 'The Interpretation of *Res Gestae Divi Augusti*, 34.1', *CQ* 1 (1951) 130-135; E. **Badian**, '"Crisis Theories" and the Beginning of the Principate', in *Romanitas – Christianitas: Untersuchungen zur Geschichte und Literatur der römischen Kaiserzeit* (eds, G. Wirth, et al.; Berlin 1982) 18-41; P. **Botteri**, 'L'integrazione mommseniana a *Res Gestae Divi Augusti* 34,1, "potitus rerum omnium" e il testo greco', *ZPE* 144 (2003) 261-267; P.A. **Brunt** and J.M. **Moore**, *Res Gestae Divi Augusti* (Oxford 1967); A.E. **Cooley**, *Res Gestae Divi Augusti* (Cambridge 2009); J.A. **Crook**, 'Political History, 30 BC to AD 14', and 'Augustus: Power, Authority, Achievement', *CAH* 10 (Cambridge [2]1996) 70-112, 113-146; T. **Drew-Bear** and J. **Scheid**, 'La copie des *Res Gestae d'Antioche de Pisidie*', *ZPE* 154 (2005) 217-260; J. **Gagé**, *Res Gestae Divi Augusti* (Paris 1935); E.S. **Gruen**, 'Augustus and the Making of the Principate', *The Cambridge Companion to the Age of Augustus* (Cambridge 2005) 33-51; G. **Herbert-Brown**, 'Avenger of Caesar and Crassus', *Ovid and the Fasti* (Oxford 1994) 95-108; E.A. **Judge**, *The First Christians in the Roman World: Augustan and New Testament Essays* (Tübingen 2008) 33-345; E.A. **Judge**, 'Who first saw Augustus as an Emperor?', *Classicum* 33/2 (2007) 2-4; E.A. **Judge**, 'What did Augustus think he was doing?', *Classicum* 36/1 (2010) 3-6; R.A. **Kearsley**, 'Octavian and Augury: The Years 30-27 BC', *CQ* 59/1 (2009) 147-166; D. **Krömer**, 'Textkritisches zu Augustus und Tiberius (*Res gestae* c. 34 – Tac. *Ann.* 6, 30, 3)', *ZPE* 28 (1978) 127-143; D. **Krömer**, 'Grammatik contra Lexikon: *rerum potiri*', *Gymnasium* 85 (1978) 239-258; W.D. **Lebek**, '*Res Gestae divi Augusti* 34,1: Rudolf Kassels *potens rerum omnium* und ein neues Fragment des Monumentum Antiochenum', *ZPE* 146 (2004) 60; E. **Malcovati**, *Caesaris Augusti Imperatoris operis fragmenta* (Turin [1]1921, [5]1944); Th. **Mommsen**, *Res gestae divi Augusti* (Berlin [1]1865, [2]1883); J.W. **Rich**, 'Augustus and the *spolia opima*', *Chiron* 26 (1996) 85-127; J.W. **Rich** and J.H.C. **Williams**, '*Leges et iura P.R. restituit:* A New Aureus of Octavian and the Settlement of 28-27 BC', *Numismatic Chronicle* (1999) 169-213; R.T. **Ridley**, *The Emperor's Retrospect* (Leuven 2003); J. **Scheid**, *Res Gestae Divi Augusti* (Paris 2007); W. **Seyfarth**, '*Potitus rerum omnium*: Ein Beitrag zur Deutung der *RGDA*, Kapitel 34', *Philologus* 101 (1957) 305-323; B. **Simon**, *Die Selbstdarstellung des Augustus in Münzprägung und in den Res Gestae* (Hamburg 1993); R. **Syme**, *The Augustan Aristocracy* (Oxford 1986) 81, n. 122; H. **Volkmann**, *Res gestae divi Augusti* (Leipzig 1942).

E.A. **Judge (Macquarie University)**

§11 The 'grace' of Augustus paves a Street at Ephesus

Ephesus   bluish grey marble   22/21 BC
                       126 x 60 x >27 cm

Ed. pr. — C. Börker and R. Merkelbach (eds), *Die Inschriften von Ephesos*, Vol. II (Bonn 1980) §459; G. Alföldy, 'Epigraphische Notizen aus Kleinasien I. Ein beneficium des Augustus in Ephesos', *ZPE* 87 (1991)157-162 = *SEG* XLI 971; R.A. Kearsley, *Greeks and Romans in Imperial Asia* (Bonn 2001) §148 (cf. *SEG* XXXII 1135).

Latin
[Bene]ficio Ca[esaris]   By means of the [bene]fit of Ca[esar]
[A]ugusti ex rediti[bus]   [A]ugustus from (the) reven[ues]
agrorum sacroru[m]   of (the) sacre[d] lands
quos is Dianae de[dit]   which he (himself) g[ave] to Diana
via strata Sex(to) Appul[eio]   a road (was) laid under Sex[tus] Appul[eius]
pro co(n)s(ule)   (the) proco(n)s(ul)

Greek
[T]ῆι Καίσαρος τοῦ Σεβαστ[οῦ]   By means of [t]he [favou]r of Caesar August[us]
[χάριτ]ι ἐκ τῶν ἱερῶν   from the sacred reven[ues]
προσό[δων]
[ἃ]ς αὐτὸς τῇ θεᾶι ἐχαρί[σατο]   [w]hich he himself [gave] freely to the goddess
ὁδὸς ἐστρώθη ἐπὶ ἀνθυπάτ[ου]   a road was laid under (the) procons[ul]
Σέξτου Ἀππολήιου   Sextos Appoleios

This bilingual inscription was found in 1958 at Ephesus during excavations before the east wall. The oblong marble monument was situated in (what is now called) Domitian square on the eastern side of the street rising in a southerly direction. The monument is now located in the Archaeological Museum of Selçuk-Ephesus in Turkey. The Latin inscription articulates, with greater precision than its Greek translation, that the income of unspecified properties, which Augustus had given to the Artemis sanctum, provided the funds for the paving of a road. On bilingualism in Asia Minor, see R.A. Kearsley, *Greeks and Romans in Imperial Asia*. This act of Augustan beneficence had occurred when the former consul of 29 BC, Sextus Appuleius, was proconsul of Asia in 23-21 BC. A. Alföldy ('Epigraphische Notizen', 160) notes that the real *beneficium* extended by Augustus was the allocation or return of properties to the Artemis sanctum from which income was derived for the road construction work (cf. the AD 44 edict of proconsul Paullus Fabius Persicus: I. Eph. Ia 18b [Alföldy, p. 160, n. 14], *infra*). Further, Alföldy (pp. 160-162) argues that the *beneficia* of Augustus were a critical part of Augustan policy after 27 BC, with a view to creating a new social order after the dislocation of the civil wars, while demonstrating continuity with the Roman tradition of aristocratic patronage under the Republic. As examples of the wide-ranging impact of Augustus' beneficence in the provinces, Alföldy (p. 161, nn. 20-22) cites the *beneficia* made to Corsica (*CIL* X 8038 = *FIRA*² 1.72), Syria (Ulp., *Dig.* 50.15.1.1) and Africa (*AE* [1909] 158 = I. L. Afr. 301). Thus our inscription represents another instance of the Augustan 'age of grace'.

What needs to be appreciated is that Augustus had become the iconic example of beneficence in the estimation of his contemporaries and successors. A letter of the Roman proconsul to the Asian League (Priene: 9 BC) admits that 'it is difficult to return for (Augustus') many great benefactions thanks in equal measure' (*DocsAug* §98b *ll.* 46-47). The first decree of the Asian League (*DocsAug* §98b *ll.* 36-39) concerning the new provincial calendar (Priene: 9 BC) breaks into rapturous praise of Augustus' beneficence, both in terms of its extravagance in the past and as an exemplar of unsurpassable generosity for benefactors in the future:

> ... [and (since) with his appearance] Caesar exceeded the hopes of all those who had received [glad tidings] before us, not only surpassing ([ὑπερβα]λόμενος) those who had been [benefactors] before him, but not even [leaving any] hope [of surpassing him] (ἐλπίδ[α] ὑπερβολῆς) for those who are to come in the future ...

In a letter to the city of Gytheion (AD 15), Tiberius referred to 'the great size of the benefits of my father to the world' (R.K. Sherk [ed.], *The Roman Empire*, §31). In similar vein, Germanicus would later describe Augustus as 'the true saviour and the benefactor of the entire race of men' (Sherk, *Roman Empire*, §42B: AD 18-19), an accolade that would subsequently be extended to Tiberius by the people of Sardis (E.A. Judge, 'Thanksgiving to the Benefactor of the World', §10). Last, Augustus presents himself in the *Res Gestae* as a 'super-patron to the community as a whole' (E.A. Judge, 'Augustus in the *Res Gestae*', 205), devoting Chapters 15-24 to the *impensae* ('expenses') that he had incurred for the *res publica* and Rome. The imperial ideology of beneficence, therefore, would have been the immediate backdrop against which the Gentile Ephesian auditors first heard and assessed the nature and scope of the divine χάρις that Paul had announced in his preaching of the gospel. However, undoubtedly, as the new converts were taught from the LXX in the Ephesian house churches about the overflow of divine mercy in the Psalms (C. Breytenbach, 'CHARIS and ELEOS', 247-278; e.g. Rom 4:7-8 [Ps 32:1-2]), a more profound theological understanding of the extraordinary nature of God's χάρις in Christ would have emerged. Moreover, Paul's christological reinterpretation of the Psalms and his rewording of the LXX text in order to enhance the portrait of the ascended Christ's beneficence (LXX Ps 67:18 [MT Ps 68:18]: ἔλαβες δόματα τοῖς ἀνθρώποις; Eph 4:8: ἔδωκεν δόματα τοῖς ἀνθρώποις) would have startled Jewish auditors at Ephesus familiar with the Old Testament Scriptures.

There is reason to suspect that Paul, in writing to the Ephesians about divine grace (χάρις: Eph 1:2, 6, 7; 2:5, 7, 8; 3:2, 7, 8; 4:7, 29; 6:24; χαριτόω: Eph 1:6; χαρίζομαι: Eph 4:32), engages at various junctures the 'prosperity religion' that had arisen through the interaction of the imperial cult with the wealthy and powerful cult of Artemis in the city (cf. Acts 19:23-25; Dio Chrysostom, *Or.* 31.54). In this respect, corrupt members of

§11 The 'grace' of Augustus paves a Street at Ephesus

the provincial elites had exploited imperial patronage for their own economic advancement. I. Eph. Ia 18b, *ll*. 0-20, an edict of the proconsul Paullus Fabius Persicus (AD 44), reveals how the priesthoods of Artemis had became a lucrative business for the unscrupulous at Ephesus. The issue was that those selling the priesthoods paid 'no regard to blood-stock'. Rather they cheapened the priesthood by opening it up to the highest bidder as opposed to the right families who would preserve and enhance the dignity of the office:

> [for many divine buildings having either been destroyed by fire or by] collapsing in shapeless ruins, and the temple of Artemis herself, which for the province as a whole is an ornament both from the size of the work and from the antiquity of the god's cult and from the unstinting flow of the revenues that by Augustus have been restored to the goddess (διὰ τὴν τῶν προσόδων ἀφθονίαν τῶν ὑπὸ τοῦ Σεβαστοῦ ἀποκατασταθεισῶν τῇ θεᾷ), is stripped of its own resources, which both for the care and for the ornament of the offerings might have sufficed. For they are directed to the unjust desires of those who only over the common interest take the lead insofar as they expect to benefit themselves. For whenever there arrives from Rome a happy announcement, they abuse it for their own profit and, the routine of the divine building as a pretext-taking, the priesthoods as though at an auction they sell and from every class for the sale of them they invite people, and then they do not select the most suited people upon whose heads the proper crown will be set. And the revenues (προσόδους) they allocate amongst those consecrated, at whatever rate those accepting [them de]sire, with a view to embezzling as much as possible. (G.H.R. Horsley, 'Inscriptions of Ephesus', 148)

The Ephesian believers, and possibly Paul himself (Acts 19:1-20:1, 17-35), would have been aware of the corruption tarnishing the operations of the Artemis cult under its imperial sponsors in the Claudian era. The opportunity of espousing a new understanding of χάρις that contrasted with the self-serving nature of imperial grace and its clients at Ephesus was timely.

Several of Paul's 'grace' texts in Ephesians reflect an imperial benefaction background, employing the Augustan motif of 'surpassing' wealth (*DocsAug* §98b *ll*. 46-47: [ὑπερβα]λόμενος, ὑπερβολῆς; cf. Eph 2:7 [cf. 1:7]: τὸ ὑπερβάλλον πλοῦτος τῆς χάριτος αὐτοῦ). Indeed, 'wealth' terminology is a continual refrain throughout Ephesians (πλούσιος: Eph 2:4; πλοῦτος: 1:7, 18; 2:7; 3:8, 16). Moreover, Paul transfers the accompanying language of 'excess' (ὑπερβάλλω and cognates) from God's soteriological riches to Christ's soteriological power. Thus the 'surpassing' wealth of divine grace (Eph 2:7: τὸ ὑπερβάλλον πλοῦτος τῆς χάριτος αὐτοῦ) finds its counterpart in the 'surpassing' greatness of the Christ's resurrection power (1:19: τὸ ὑπερβάλλον μέγεθος τῆς δυνάμεως αὐτοῦ). Paul's language of 'wealth' in Ephesians could also be profitably looked at against the backdrop of the wealth of the Artemis cult (R. Strelan, *Paul*, 76-79), but this goes beyond the focus of this entry.

Also Paul's emphasis on the 'gift' of divine grace in Ephesians (Eph 3:7: τὴν δωρεὰν τῆς χάριτος τοῦ θεοῦ τῆς δοθείσης μοι; 4:7: ἑκάστῳ ἡμῶν ἐδόθη ἡ χάρις) resonates with the emphasis on imperial 'gift-giving' in our inscription (*SEG* XLI 971: de[dit], [χάριτ]ι, ἐχαρί[σατο]). Even Paul's reference to the 'glory' of divine grace in Ephesians (Eph 1:6a: ἔπαινον δόξης τῆς χάριτος αὐτοῦ) would have spoken into the world of imperial politics, given that the republican language of 'glory' had concentrated around the Julio-Claudian ruler and the members of his house from the time of Augustus' victory at Actium (31 BC) onwards (J.R. Harrison, '"Glory of Christ"', 156-188, esp. 174-180). It is not surprising, therefore, that the language of 'glory' is prominent in Ephesians as well (δόξα: Eph 1:6, 12, 14, 17, 18; 3:8, 16; ἔνδοξος: 5:21). In sum, the imperial context of Paul's language of 'grace' in Ephesians has to be reckoned with and the question posed whether Paul is implicitly drawing a comparison between the benefits of Christ and the munificence of the Roman ruler.

For Paul, however, the surpassing wealth of Christ's grace (Eph 1:7c; 2:7) is soteriological (2:8: τῇ γὰρ χάριτί ἐστε σεσῳσμένοι), being based on the redemption of the cross (1:7a; 2:7b) and the forgiveness of trespasses (1:7b). Here we have a radical alternative to the Julio-Claudian benefaction culture, arising from the selfless giving of one who, ironically, was crucified by an imperial prefect in a far-flung province of the Roman Empire. The unconditioned act of Christ's saving grace had pinpricked the boasting and self-advertisement of the Roman 'world-benefactor' (Eph 2:9b: ἵνα μή τις καυχήσηται) because God, unexpectedly, had given his undeserved gift to the objects of his wrath (Eph 2:3, 8b: τοῦτο οὐκ ἐξ ὑμῶν, θεοῦ τὸ δῶρον). In an honorific culture, therefore, the praise traditionally accorded to the mortal Roman ruler was now to be rendered to the eternal and beneficent God for his predestination of believers to sonship (Eph 1:6a: ἔπαινον δόξης τῆς χάριτος αὐτοῦ). The 'glory' that had formerly redounded to Augustus alone (*OGIS* 456 *ll*. 35-49; Ovid, *Tristia* 3.1.35-46, esp. *l*. 46; 5.2.49; *id.*, *Ex Ponto* 2.8.20-26; Valerius Maximus 2.8.7) was now supplanted by the glorious favour extended in Christ to his dependants (Eph 1:6b: ἧς ἐχαρίτωσεν ἡμᾶς ἐν τῷ ἠγαπημένῳ).

Further, Paul's insistence on faithfulness (Eph 2:8a: τῇ γὰρ χάριτί ἐστε σεσῳσμένοι) to God the Benefactor undermined the Roman ruler's demand for faithfulness (*pistis* or *fides* ['loyalty']) from his clients because of his 'benefits' or 'works' on their behalf (*Res Gestae* 15-24). For Paul, all human 'works' — imperial and Jewish — counted for nothing (Eph 2:9a: οὐκ ἐξ ἔργων) because of the unprecedented advent of God's grace in Christ. Additionally, God's salvation through faith had sidelined Augustus' claim that 'a large number of other nations experienced the good faith of the Roman people (Ῥωμαίων πίστεως; [(*p. R.*) *fidem*]) during my principate who had never before had any interchange of embassies or of friendship with the Roman people' (*Res Gestae* 32). God in Christ had taken the initiative in reconciling Gentiles from the nations to himself, creating thereby a new humanity that was united in peace in one body (Eph 2:11-19). This multicultural and ethnically diverse 'household', united by the Spirit, had acquired a new 'citizenship' that reversed their former alienation as 'strangers' and 'aliens' (Eph 2:20).

Finally, if the author of Ephesians is Paul — and the epistle is not the pseudonymous product of a later Pauline school — we might ask whether Paul's presentation of divine grace spoke into the age of Neronian 'grace' (*SIG*[3] 814: J.R. Harrison, *Paul's Language of Grace*, 62). One important area of intersection of Paul's gospel with the Neronian propaganda, as articulated by Seneca (3 BC—65 AD), was in the area of social relations. The diversity of gifting in the 'body of Christ' (Eph 4:7-16), founded on the beneficence of its ascended Lord (4:7b: κατὰ τὸ μέτρον τῆς δωρεᾶς τοῦ Χριστοῦ; 4:8: ἔδωκεν δόματα τοῖς ἀνθρώποις), stood in contrast to the uniformity of the Nero's 'body of state' (Seneca, *Clem.* 1.4.1—1.5.2; cf. J.R. Harrison, *Imperial Authorities*, 292-299). Seneca advises Nero that the ruler — the 'bond' of the *res publica* and the very 'breath of life' and 'soul' of the state — should exercise *clementia* ('mercy') to 'reprobate citizens'. The aim of Seneca's advice to the young Nero was to restrain any unnecessary use of sword on his part, ensuring the status quo of Julio-Claudian rule through a moderate approach to state relations.

In the view of Paul, however, diversely gifted individuals equipped the 'body of Christ' for the work of selfless service in its widest sense, with a view to building up believers in love and helping them to grow as an interdependent body into Christ as head. Here Paul envisages a work of God's grace that would ultimately transform social relations not only within the believing households of Ephesus but also within the Roman Empire more widely (Eph 5:15-6:9). The dynamism of Paul's gospel contrasted with the hierarchical set of social relations that characterised Nero's 'body of state'. A different understanding of grace, with radical social outcomes (e.g. Gal 3:28; 1 Cor 7:22; Phlm 15-16; Ephes 2:11-21), had begun to emerge in the early Empire.

Bibliography

C. **Breytenbach**, 'CHARIS and ELEOS in Paul's Letter to the Romans', in *The Letter to the Romans* (ed., U. Schnelle; Leuven 2009) 323-363; J.R. **Harrison**, *Paul's Language of Grace in its Graeco-Roman Context* (Tübingen 2003); J.R. **Harrison**, 'The Brothers as "The Glory of Christ" (2 Cor 8:23): Paul's *Doxa* Terminology in its Ancient Benefaction Context', *NovT* 52 (2010) 156-188; J.R. **Harrison**, *Paul and the Imperial Authorities at Thessalonica and Rome: A Study in the Conflict of Ideology* (Tübingen 2011); Z. **Crook**, *Reconceptualising Conversion: Patronage, Loyalty, and Conversion in the Religion of the Ancient Mediterranean* (Berlin/New York 2004); G.H.R. **Horsley**, 'The Inscriptions of Ephesos and the New Testament', *NovT* 34/2 (1992) 105-168; E.A. **Judge**, 'Thanksgiving to the Benefactor of the World, Tiberius Caesar', *New Docs* 9 (2002) 22; E.A. **Judge**, 'Augustus in the *Res Gestae*', in *The First Christians in the Roman World: Augustan and New Testament Essays* (ed., J.R. Harrison; Tübingen 2008) 182-223; R.A. **Kearsley**, *Greeks and Romans in Imperial Asia: Mixed Language Inscriptions and Linguistic Evidence for Cultural Interaction until the End of AD III* (Bonn 2001); R.K. **Sherk** (ed.), *The Roman Empire: Augustus to Hadrian* (Cambridge 1988); R. **Strelan**, *Paul, Artemis, and the Jews in Ephesus* (Berlin/New York 1996).

J.R. Harrison (Macquarie University)

§12 Diplomacy over Tiberius' Accession

Messene   Pedimental stele   AD 14

Ed. pr. — *PAAH* (1969) 104. P. Themelis, *PAAH* (1988) [1991] 57-58; *PAAH* (1990) [1993] 87-91. L. Moretti, *RPAA* 60 (1987-1988) 250-251 = *SEG* XXXVIII 340 = *SEG* XLI 328; *SEG* XLII 344; *AE* (1993) 1414.

Θεῶι Σεβαστῶı [Καίσαρι κ]αὶ Τιβερίωι Καίσ[αρι]
Σεβαστῶι, τ[οῦ γραμμ]ατέος συνέ[δρων]
καὶ ἱερέος [θεοῦ Σεβαστοῦ] Καίσαρος [- - - ca. 5 - - -]
[- - ca. 4 - -]'Αρισ[- - - - - - - - - - - - - - - - - - ---]
vac. ca. 5 cm

5   [- -]
    ἐνφάνισον δ[ὲ -]
    Διομέα ἱερέ[α -]
    οτεία τὰν θ[- ἁμεῖν καὶ πα]
    [σ]ιν ἀνθρώ[ποις -]
10 [- - -]εις θε[- -]
    [- -]
              lacuna
    δυν[- -]
    φυλάσσοντ[- πᾶσι τοῖς τὰν πόλιν κα]-
    τοικούντοις καὶ [- -]
15 ετι τελειότατα ἐκχο[- - - - - - - - - - - - - - - - - ἔμ]-
    πεδα πάντα τὰ προτει[νόμενα - - - -

To God Augustus [Caesar a]nd Tiberius Caes[ar]
Augustus, (with) t[he secr]etary of the *syne[droi]*
and priest of [God Augustus] Caesar [- - - - - - -]
[- - - - - - -] Aris[- - - - - - - - - - - - - - - - - - -]

[- -]
an[d] they manifested [- - - - - - - - - - - - - - - -]
Diomeus pries[t- -]
the [- to us and]
to [al]l me[n- -]
[- - -] [- -]
[- -]

[- -]
guarding [- - - - - - - - - - - - - - - - - - - to all in]habiting [the city]
and [- -]
most completely [- - - - - - - - - - - - - - - - -]
certainly all the off[erings - - - - - - - - - -

§12 Diplomacy over Tiberius' Accession

- -]	- - - - - - - - - - - - - - - - - - -]
ὅταν ὁ μάντις κατεύχη[ται - - - - - -	whenever the seer pray[s - - - - - - - - - -
-]	- - - - - - - - - - - - - - - - - - - -]
καὶ Καίσαρα Σεβαστὸν ἐξισ[- - - - -	and Caesar Augustus [- - - - - - - - - - - - -
-]	- - - - - - - - - - - - - - - - - - -]
εἰσφέρῃ τοὺς ἄρχοντας, ὀμν[ύειν δὲ	he might bring in the magistrates, and to
-]	sw[ear - - - - - - - - - - - - - - -]
20 ἐν ταῖς εἰσόδοις ἕκαστος ν[- - - - - -	each in the entrances (or 'revenues')[1] [-
- - - - - - - - - - - - - - - - -θεοῦ Σε]-	- - - - - - - - - - - - - - of God Au]
βαστοῦ Καίσαρος καὶ Τιβερίου	gustus Caesar and of Tiberius Caesa[r
Καίσαρο[ς Σεβαστοῦ καὶ τοῖς	Augustus and to] their [desce]nd-
ἐκγόν]-	
οις αὐτῶν· ἀμ[νοῖ]ς εὐωχείσθω ἐν	ants. Let him celebrate with l[amb]s in
τ[ῷ Σεβαστείῳ - - - - - - - - ἱερεὺς]	t[he Augusteum - - - - - - - - - let]
ὁ κατ᾽ ἔτος τοῦ Σεβαστοῦ	(the) yearly priest of Augustus be torch
δαδουχείτω [- - - - - - - - - - - - - - - - -	bearer [- - - - - - - - - - - - - - - - -]
- - - - -]	
εἰς τὸ ἱερὸν παρέρπων καὶ πρῶτος	appearing in public at the temple and
ἐκ δεξιῶν σ[- - - - - - - - - - - - - - -]	first from the right [- - - - - - - - - -]
25 μονον ἀμεῖν καὶ πᾶσιν ἀνθρώποις	only and to give light to us and to all
φωτίσαι [- - - - - - - - - - - - - - - - - -]	men [- - - - - - - - - - - - - - - - - - - -]
ναν τὸν Σεβαστόν, Τιβερίου δὲ	Augustus, and of Tiberius Caesar [- - - -
Καίσαρος ἀπ[- - - καὶ τοὺς	- and (those) who have begot]-
γεννήσαν]-	
τας αὐτὸν καὶ ἀνιέντας αὐτῷ, τὸν	ten him and who are devoted to him, the
αὐτὸν ν[- - - - - - - - - - - - - - - -]	same [- - - - - - - - - - - - - - - -]
δὲ καὶ θεὰν Λειβίαν τὰν ματέρα	and also (the) goddess Livia his mother
αὐτοῦ καὶ γ[υναίκα θεοῦ	and w[ife of god Augustus Caesar]
Σεβαστοῦ Καίσαρος]	
καὶ ᾽Αντωνίαν καὶ Λιβίλλαν, ἱερέα	and Antonia and Livilla, a priest [- - - - -
τρει[- - - - - - - - - - - - - - - - - - -]	- - - - - - - - - - - - - - - - - - - -]
30 εἰς τὸν ἑξῆς ἐνιαυτόν, ὥσπερ καὶ [-	for the next year, just [a]s also priest [-
- - - - - - - - - - - - - - - - τοῦ Σεβα]-	- - - - - - - - - - - - - - - - of Augu]-
στοῦ ἱερεὺ<ς> καὶ δαδουχείτωσα[ν -	stus and let them be torch bearer[s - - - -
-]	- - - - - - - - - - - - - - - - - - - -]
το ἐν ἁπάντοις, ὥσ[π]ερ καὶ [- - - - -	entirely, just as also [- - - - -
- -]ΔΑΙΡΟΣΑ[- - - - - -]ν δὲ κ[- -]	]DAIROSA[- - - - -] and [- - - - - - - -
	- - - - -]

---

[1] The correct translation of ἐν ταῖς εἰσόδοις (l. 20) is problematical, given the fragmentary preservation of the decree. It could refer to the 'entrances' of the 'Augusteum' (l. 22) or to a nearby building attached to the imperial cult. Equally, it could also refer to the 'revenues' associated with the imperial cult or the civic magistrates. Contextually, the first option seems more likely to me.

[- - -τ]ε θεὸν [- - -]ικαν αὐτοῦ. καὶ
ἄ[γεσθαι] πάντας τοὺς τὰν
πόλ[ιν] κατοικοῦντας

[- -]σογ[- -]αν [ἐκε]χειρίαν ἐπὶ τρεῖς
ἁμέ[ρας ἐφ]εξῆς, ἐπιτελεῖσθαι
δὲ καὶ ἀγώνας, γυμνι-

35 κὸν τῶν παίδων καὶ ἐφήβων καὶ
ἱ[ππικ]ὸν τῶν νέων ἐν τᾶι
γενεθλίῳ ἁμέρᾳ καὶ

ἀνατίθεσθαι τῶν νικησάντων ὅπ[λα
ὑ]πὸ τοῦ καθ' ἔτος ἱερέος,
ἀποστεῖλαι δὲ καὶ

πρεσβείαν εἰς Ῥώμαν ποτὶ τὸν
αὐτοκ[ρά]τορα Τιβέριον Καίσαρα,
τὰν λυπηθησο-

μέναν μὲν ἐπὶ τῷ μηκέτι ἁμεῖν
ἦμεν ἐ[μ]φανῆ τὸν θεόν,
ἀσπασομέναν δὲ Τιβέρι-

ον τὸν αὐτοκράτορα καὶ
συνχαρησομέναν ἐπὶ τῷ τὸν
ἄξιον καὶ κατ' εὐχὰν ἁμεῖν ἀγε-

40 μόνα γεγενῆσθαι τοῦ παντὸς
κόσμου, ἀποδυρουμέναν δὲ καὶ
περὶ τῶν κατεσχη-

κότων τὰν πόλιν ἀτόπων καὶ
ἱκετεύσουσαν ὅπως τύχωμες
ἐλέου τινός.

[- - -] god [- - -] of him. (It is decreed) that all inhabiting the city observe

[--] [- -] a holiday for three days successively, and also that games be completed, (namely), a gymnastic (contest) of boys and youths, and a horse (race) of young men on the occasion of the birthday and

that the shields of the victors be set up (as a votive gift) by the priest[2] of the year, and also that (the Messenians) send

an embassy to Rome to the imperator Tiberius Caesar, which, on the one hand, will grieve

that the god is no longer manifest to us and, on the other hand, will greet Tiberius

the imperator and will join in rejoicing that as a worthy (answer) to our vows

he has become leader of all the world, and which will also express bitter regret at the unwelcome (events)

that have afflicted (our) city and will beseech (him) in order that we might gain some mercy.

vacat

This highly fragmentary inscription is important for Roman historians because it expresses a provincial perspective on Tiberius' accession to rule. Apart from the literary evidence of the later writers (Tacitus, Suetonius, Dio) and our sole contemporary literary source (Velleius Paterculus), there is no documentary evidence either from Rome or the provinces reporting contemporary reactions to the death of Augustus and the transition of Julian rule from Augustus to Tiberius, the adopted son and heir of Augustus. To be sure, there are many important documents which reveal highly positive provincial perspectives on imperial rule, including the oath of the Paphlagonian businessmen to Augustus (6 BC: B.W. Jones and R.D. Milns, *Documentary Evidence*, §23), Tiberius' response to Gytheum's request about divine honours (AD 15/16: Jones and Milns, §24), and a papyrus recording the intense excitement generated by Germanicus' visit to Alexandria (AD 19: Jones and Milns, §91; cf. §78). But these provincial documents do

---

[2] Note the most recent restoration of *l.* 36, discussed *infra*.

not have quite the significance of our decree, which records the most important transition of power in the Julian house since the death of Julius Caesar. The decree also reveals aspects of the imperial cult that are relevant to the intersection of the New Testament documents with the ideology of imperial rule.

The reconstructed decree, as it stands, comprises three new fragments published by P. Themelis, combined with another previously published text:
a) the first fragment to be published (*PAAH* (1988) [1991] 57-58) was the from bottom of the decree (inv. no. 1138);
b) the second fragment, from the excavations of the Greek Archaeological Society (inv. no. 1984), was published by Themelis (*PAAH* (1990) [1993] 87-91) arguing that it is to be attached to inv. no. 1138 at the top;
c) the third fragment (inv. no. 1623) is attached to the bottom of inv. no. 986, published earlier in *PAAH* (1969) 104.

With all the new fragments re-attached, Themelis associated the reconstructed text with part of the pedimental stele *IG* V.1.1448 (inv. no. 141) (the second half of *ll*. 1-3 only, as in our text) and presented for the first time a completely new text. Stroud, the *SEG* editor (*SEG* XLI 328), notes that Themelis was apparently unaware that L. Moretti (*RPPA* 60 [1987-1988] 250-252 = *SEG* XXXVIII 340) had also connected *IG* V.1. (Kolbe, 1913) 1448 (inv. no. 141) with inv. no. 986.

Subsequent to Stroud's edition of the inscription, he reported in *SEG* XLII 344 a new restoration for *l*. 36. As authority for the restoration, he cites *AE* (1991) 1442, which was based on the fragment published in *PAAH* (1988) 57-58. The editor argues that 'we should restore [ὑ]πὸ rather than [ἀ]πὸ' (*SEG* XLII 344, p. 97). This is also included in the latest reproduction of the decree in *AE* (1993) 1414 and has been incorporated in our text of the decree above. In sum, precisely because several restorations have been suggested for *ll*. 35-36 within the short period of two years (1991-1992), Stroud is entirely justified in observing generally that 'we are in need of a new text of this important inscription based on a careful transcription from the stone' (XLI 328 p. 125).

1. *The Inscription and the Imperial Cult at Messene*

What does the text reveal about relations between Messene and the new Roman ruler Tiberius? There are speculative elements in our analysis below because of the fragmentary nature of the decree, although the actual purpose of the decree itself (*ll*. 33-41) is clear at most points. Beginning with what is reasonably certain, the stele records the decree of Messene, passed some time after Augustus had died (AD 14), to send an embassy to Rome to register the city's grief over the death of Augustus and to hail Tiberius as the new Julian ruler, the imperator, and the hegemon of the whole world. Games in honour of the new ruler's birthday are announced, with a special focus on events involving the young athletes of different ages (*paides, epheboi, neoi*) at the local gymnasium (*ll*. 34-36). Livia, too, is designated 'goddess', (*l*. 28: θεὰν Λειβίαν), but the epithet had already been applied to her well before the death and apotheosis of Augustus (J.R. Harrison, 'Livia as Hekate', §6 above).

Further, there is reference to a 'vow' (Latin: *votum*) by which Tiberius 'has become leader of all the world' (*ll.* 39-30). Priestly vows for the safety of the Roman ruler and his family were common in the Augustan principate (e.g. Augustus and his house: Dio 51.19; the illness of Germanicus: Tacitus, *Ann.*, 2.69; the safe return of Tiberius: Suetonius, *Tib.*, 38; Tacitus, *Ann.*, 3.47). Vows were also made at the *lustrum* (Suetonius, *Aug.*, 97; *Res Gestae* 9), that is, a sacrifice of propitiation made every five years. During the imperial age vows were extended for periods of five, fifteen and twenty years (*CIL* III 5706). The vow referred to in our inscription probably reflects the routine public supplications made on behalf of Augustus and family, cf. *fasti anni Juliani* (*DocsAug* 16 Jan 27 BC [p. 45]; 30 Jan 9 BC [p. 46]; 15 Dec 19 BC [p. 55]; cf. *Res Gestae* 34.1: [κ]ατὰ τὰς εὐχᾶς), or in some other prescribed priestly ritual. The decree is asserting that Tiberius' accession to rule has the blessing of the gods because of the piety that the Messsenians have demonstrated through the supplications of their priests for the safety of Rome and its ruler.

As a subsidiary motif to the embassy congratulating Tiberius, the decree alludes to certain difficulties disturbing Messene, with the result that the Messenians would petition the princeps for unspecified help (*ll.* 40-41). The *SEG* editor proposes that the 'difficulties' being alluded to was the dispute between Messene and Sparta over the territory of Dentheleatis (*SEG* XLI 328, p. 124). The Spartans supported their claim to Dentheleatis, in which the temple of Artemis Limnatis was situated (Strabo 4.4.2), on the basis of ancient annals and various documents (Pausanias 4.14.2). In response, Messene brought forward its own set of documents asserting that the entire territory of Dentheleatis, along with the temple, was their possession (Tacitus, *Ann.* 4.43). Thus both city-states hotly disputed the possession of the temple, even though its festival was common to the two. If this reconstruction is accurate, the Messenian embassy intended to throw itself upon imperial *clementia* while at Rome (*l.* 41: ἐλέου τινός) for resolution of the issue. Since Caesar, Augustus and (later) Tiberius were known for their *clementia* in various contexts, the bold approach of the Messenians to the new Julian ruler is hardly surprising. For discussion of imperial *clementia*, see T. Adam, *Clementia Principis*; B.M. Levick, 'Mercy and Moderation'; M.B. Dowling, *Clemency and Cruelty*; S. Braund, *De Clementia*. On the *clementia* of Caesar, see Julius Caesar, *BGall.* 3, 21; Cicero, *Deiot.* 8, 33, 37; *id.*, *Lig.* 5, 10, 13, 14, 16; *id.*, *Marc.* 9, 12; *id.*, *Phil.* 116; *id.*, *Vat.*, 21; *id.*, *Fam.* 6.6.8. For Augustus, see *RG* 34; Suetonius, *Aug.* 51; Tacitus, *Ann.* 1.57, 58; 2.10; *ILS* 8393 (tr. M.R. Lefkowitz and M.E. Fant (eds.), *Women's Life in Greece and Rome*, §168); Cassius Dio 43.10.3. For Tiberius, see Tacitus, *Ann.* 2.42; 4.74.

In what follows we move into more speculative territory historically because of the highly fragmentary nature of our text. In *ll.* 22-24 the rituals of imperial cult are being performed in the 'Augusteum' (*l.* 22) — though the editor has restored the word — with a feast in honour of the new ruler (*l.* 22: 'lambs'; cf. *l.* 17: 'offerings'). There is (what seems to be) a torch-lit procession headed by the priests (*ll.* 23-24, 31), with symbolic meaning attached to the rite (*l.* 25: 'to give light to us and all men'; cf. the 'sunlight'/ 'night' metaphor in reference to Caligula's rule in *SIG*³ 798). The city magistrates are also present and an oath is sworn (*l.* 19: ὀμν[ύειν]). It is possible that this ritual is a

§12 Diplomacy over Tiberius' Accession 69

local variation on an oath-swearing ceremony such as the kind carried out by the provincial businessmen at Paphlagonia (*supra*).

In terms of personnel in the imperial cult, there is reference to priests (*ll.* 3, 7, 23, 29, 30, 36) and an intriguing reference to the 'seer' (ὁ μάντις) who 'prays' (*l.* 17). It is, of course, quite possible in this instance that the seer merely 'entreats' someone to do something (*LSJ* κατεύχομαι 2, p. 926), given the fragmentary state of *l.* 17. But if 'prays' is the correct translation, what is being envisaged in regard to the imperial cult? Presumably, the seer would have read out formal prayers for Augustus and the continuing prosperity of the Julian house and Rome and for the safety of the new ruler and his family (e.g. *CIL* VI 32 323 [tr., F.C. Grant, *Ancient Roman Religion*, 178-182]; *CIL* X 8375 [tr., Grant, *Ancient Roman Religion*, 184-185]; *ILS* 137 [J.R. Harrison, *Imperial Authorities*, 67]). In other contexts, the seer may have also provided prophetic oracles in support of the Julian house (cf. *SEG* 37 1102; S.R. Llewelyn, 'Faithful Words', 8). In sum, we have here an extraordinarily rich inscription, in spite of its fragmentary preservation, allowing us keen insight into how provincial cities continued to manage the imperial cult amidst the crisis of succession created by Augustus' death and how they astutely exploited their imperial connections for their own interests upon the change of ruler.

What contribution, then, does our inscription make to our understanding of the accession of Tiberius to power, albeit from a provincial viewpoint? To what extent does our inscription reveal an astute understanding of the political realities at Rome? And what relevance does our decree have to our understanding of Paul's letters in imperial context?

2. The Problem of Succession: Handling Augustus' Death at Rome and in the Provinces

Roman historians concede that Augustus' death in AD 14 created a profound crisis in the Roman state for which there was no precedent. How the 'succession' issue would be resolved was not obvious to contemporaries (A.A. Barrett, *Caligula*, 8). It is often claimed that a series of strategic manoeuvres ensured that Tiberius' 'constitutional' accession to public position was a *fait accompli* (e.g. Barrett, *Caligula*, 8; B. Levick, *Tiberius*, 79-80; B. Severy, *Augustus*, 207; R. Syme, *Tacitus*, 410-411; Syme, *Roman Revolution*, 438-439). Several steps, it is claimed, forestalled a protracted 'succession crisis' after the death of Augustus:
  a) Tiberius had already acquired *imperium maius*, granted to him by Augustus in AD 13, as well as the renewal of his tribunician power;
  b) Augustus had nominated Tiberius in his will to be the heir to two-thirds of his estate and had bequeathed to him the title of 'Augustus';
  c) the murder of Tiberius' only potential rival, Agrippa Postumus, adopted by Augustus in AD 4, had ensured that there would be no contest for power;
  d) the state funeral and other posthumous honours to Augustus, along with Livia's adoption as Julia Augusta, had created the concept of an 'imperial family';

e) the consuls' personal oath of allegiance to Tiberius — along with the Senate, soldiers and populace — strengthened his position as princeps, reaffirming the allegiance sworn long ago to Octavian before Actium.

This construct not only ignores Augustus' conception of his place in Roman history, but also it fails to consider how Augustus envisaged that his heirs would establish their place in public life. The path of succession was not 'constitutional' in the modern sense, but rather, in the view of Augustus, was established in the same way as the houses of the Roman *nobiles* ('nobles') had traditionally established their dominance during the republic: that is, by outperforming the leading men from other noble families in a public competition for ancestral glory (Harrison, *Imperial Authorities*, 201-232). Roman nobles competed against each other through the acquisition of civic magistracies, the demonstration of *virtus* ('manliness') on the battlefield, and the creation of a strong client base locally and overseas through beneficence and diplomacy. Augustus achieved this more comprehensively than any of the houses of the Roman *nobiles* because of his unprecedented beneficence, his victory at Actium (31 BC), his personal *auctoritas* ('influence'), and, last, his *fides* ('faithfulness') to his family clients across the Empire.

However, this should not blind us to the fact that Augustus still wanted to keep the traditional paths of competition open. Augustus refused to impose in advance the 'constitutional' settlement of the 'succession' espoused by modern historians, as though such a construct was meaningful to Romans who saw politics in terms of a personal quest for fame (*fama*) and glory (*gloria*). Rather Augustus' solution was deeply traditional — his heirs had to establish their *own* military credentials and magistracies in the *cursus honorum* over their contemporaries, as Augustus had done from the second triumvirate onwards (E.A. Judge, 'Caesar's Son and Heir'; 'The Augustan Republic'; 'Eulogistic Inscriptions'; 'Merits of Augustus').

The evidence for this is clear. Augustus had expected that his grandson Gaius would only succeed to his 'position' (*statio*) of influence by demonstrating his own military 'manliness' on the battlefield (23 Sept 23 AD 1: Aulus Gellius 15.7.3; Judge, 'Caesar's Son and Heir', 100; Harrison, *Imperial Authorities*, 140-141). Suetonius (*Aug.* 56.2) tells us that Augustus 'never recommended the election of his sons to the people without adding the words: "if they deserve it"'. In his final remarks (Tacitus, *Ann.*, 1.13.2), Augustus had apparently discussed the leading men capable of taking the 'leading place' in the state (i.e. Marcus Lepidus, Gallus Asinius, Lucius Arruntius), commenting on their personal limitations and ambitions. T.E.J. Wiedemann ('Tiberius', 204) observes in this regard: '... at the beginning of Tiberius' reign, there still existed political figures whose power was independent of the backing of the princeps'. This is confirmed by the calendar of Amiternum which, on September 13 AD 16 (*DocsAug*, 52), still spoke of plurality of leaders in the Roman state: 'Holiday by arrangement of the senate because on that day the conspiracy entered into by M. Libo against the safety of Tiberius Caesar and his children, and of other leaders of the state (*aliorum principum civitatis*), and against the state itself, was condemned in the Senate'.

§12 Diplomacy over Tiberius' Accession

Tiberius evinced the same understanding of the leadership of Rome in an edict cited by Tacitus (*Ann.* 3.6; cf. Judge, 'Augustan Republic', 134-136): 'many illustrious Romans had died for their country (*res publica*) ... For the same conduct was not becoming to ordinary families or communities and to leaders of the state and to an imperial people ... statesmen (*principes*) were mortal, the state (*rem publicam*) eternal'. Moreover, although Augustus presented himself and the Julian family as the culmination of republican history in the *forum Augustum* and in the *Res Gestae* (Judge, 'Eulogistic Inscriptions'; 'Augustus in the *Res Gestae*'), it was not his intention to establish a monopoly of Julian leadership at the expense of competitors from the older noble houses. The combination of republican and Julian luminaries in the statue program of the *forum Augustum* underscores this precise point. In an edict (2 BC) Augustus states that his intention in building the *forum Augustum* was to leave a paradigm of leadership for future leaders of the state that maintained the iconic leadership of the republican leaders (Suetonius, *Aug.* 31.5; cf. *Res Gestae* 8.5):

> I have contrived this to lead the citizens to require me, while I live, and *the rulers of later times* as well, to attain the standard (*ad ... exemplar*) set by *those worthies of old*.

There is no sense in this edict that the Julian house was somehow privileged in maintaining its dominance in public life other than by the traditional mode of competition. The contemporary evidence of Velleius Paterculus (*History of Rome* 2.126.4) presents Tiberius as living in accord with the Augustan ideal of leadership: 'for the best princeps teaches his citizens to do right by doing it, and though he is the greatest among us in authority, he is still greater in the example which he sets'. In sum, Tiberius' vacillation about accepting rule of the Empire independently of the other leading men at Rome (Velleius Paterculus, *ibid.*, 2.124) should not be dismissed as a hypocritical ruse on Tiberius' part, as is the depiction in the later accounts of Tacitus and Suetonius (Tacitus, *Ann.* 1.7, 11-13; Suetonius, *Tib.* 24; cf. Dio 57.3.1-6). On Tacitus' presentation of Augustus' accession and Tiberius' rule generally, see the works of R. Ash, M.P. Charlesworth, E. Cowen, D.R. Dudley, E. Gorman, F. Klingner, R.H. Martin, R. Mellor, M.S. Sage and R. Syme, cited in the bibliography. On Dio's presentation of the accession, see P.M. Swan, *The Augustan Succession*. Rather Tiberius' indecisiveness reflects his genuine struggle to resist being typecast as the only leader of Rome.

The second problem with the 'constitutional' approach to the 'succession crisis' of AD 14 is that it overlooks the role that provincial clients played in spontaneously affirming the continued rule of the Julian family at Rome. Inevitably, this created a momentum in public perception that would have contributed to the acceptance of Tiberius as the heir of the Augustan principate. F.G.B. Millar ('Review', 327-328) has posed the important question as to how the Roman world came so quickly and easily to accept the existence of a single ruling house. In the view of Millar, a missing dimension in modern discussion is 'the positive force of popular reactions'. He states that

> ... discussion would have to start with the ways in which the political power of the Republican houses was expressed and passed from generation to generation. Then, with the Principate, weight would have to be placed not only on the measures taken by a Princeps to ensure the succession, but also on the reactions of the governed.

In terms of popular reactions to the ruler and his family in the provinces, Millar refers to the Cenotaphia Pisana of AD 3, inscribed on a marble tablet, which records the decrees of the Senate of Pisa detailing the honours given to the deceased grandsons of Augustus, Lucius and Gaius Caesar (*DocsAug*, §69; tr. R.K. Sherk, *Roman Empire*, §19). Millar also mentions a remarkable inscription (*IGRR* IV 1693) that recounts the embassy sent in a spontaneous act all the way from Aezae in the province of Asia to offer congratulations to Tiberius at Boulogne for his adoption by Augustus. This intangible declaration of the expectation of Tiberius' 'succession' on the part of provincial subjects points to an overlooked dynamic in modern scholarly discussion. We should add to Millar's evidence Velleius Paterculus' story (*History of Rome*, 2:107) of the German barbarian viewing the future emperor Tiberius for the first time: 'I, Caesar, by your kind permission, have seen the gods of whom I used once only to hear'. Last, Millar ('Review', 328) also makes the astute comment that 'A study of the *domus Augusta*, and the position of its members, in imperial documents should have a place in any discussion of continuity in the Principate'.

The evidence above sets our inscription in its proper context. The Messene decree represents the spontaneous decision of the city to honour the deceased Augustus. But, in expectation that the normal conventions of aristocratic family succession — well known to the elites of the provinces — would unfold, Messene offers congratulations to Tiberius, who was the nominated heir to the family estate and, consequently, to the family Empire (*ll.* 39-40: ἀγεμόνα γεγενῆσθαι τοῦ παντὸς κόσμου). Continuity of succession is also reinforced in the inscription by the family references to θεά Livia, Antonia and Livilla (*ll.* 28-29). The appeal for ἔλεος also establishes continuity between Tiberius and the Augustan principate because *clementia* had been a hallmark of the dictatorship of Caesar and the reign of Augustus.

The appeal to *clementia*, therefore, emphasises that for provincial subjects relations with the Roman ruler continued to operate traditionally at the level of patronage. One suspects that this may have been much more the case at Rome than has been recognised by those Roman historians who want to suggest a structural hiatus in the transition between 'Republic' and 'Empire'. The Julian house had eclipsed the houses of the Roman nobles by poaching their traditional client-base, offering beneficence on an unprecedented scale, as well as posts in the civil service and army. The Caesars, through their patronage, had redefined the traditional progression in the *cursus honorum* ('course of honours') in ways that (inadvertently) would ensure the dominance of their house. Ultimately, this would progressively stifle competition from the noble houses (e.g. Juvenal, *Sat.* 8), but this is still not the case at the period we are discussing. A close reading of Tacitus' *Annals* also reveals the existence of powerful individuals at Rome who would periodically challenge the power of the princeps and his house in various ways, with the princeps having to respond publicly to their challenges.

Having established the importance of our inscription as far as a provincial reaction to the accession of Tiberius to the Augustan principate, we have to consider what light it might thrown on the intersection of Paul's gospel with the imperial cult.

3. Paul's Gospel and the Ideology of the Imperial Cult

Our inscription intersects with Paul's letters in three areas of interest to the New Testament. First, B. Bitner (entry §13 in this volume) discusses Hadrian's accession in P. Oxy. 3781, highlighting differences in understanding in the papyrus to the terminology and concepts used of Jesus' enthronement in the New Testament. Bitner's careful study is revealing because it was precisely the early Christian preaching of the 'Kingship' of Jesus (Acts 17:7) that provoked a collision with the Roman authorities at Thessalonica (J.R. Harrison, 'Imperial Gospel'). We have seen that the city of Messene hailed Tiberius enthusiastically as the ruler of the world in his accession and petitioned him for help in a local dispute (*ll.* 39-40: ἀγεμόνα γεγενῆσθαι τοῦ παντὸς κόσμου). Such spontaneous responses of eastern Mediterranean cities towards the new imperial benefactor helps us to see why the early Christian preaching of the Kingdom of Christ could have unsettled the local civic authorities. See, too, the excellent study of J.D. Fantin (*The Lord of the Entire World*) regarding the interplay of κύριος language in the imperial cult and in the epistles of Paul.

Second, the reference to *clementia* (*l.* 41: ἐλέου τινός) — dispensed by the ruler — has interesting implications for the epistle to the Romans, a document contemporary with Seneca's *De Clementia* (AD 55-56). The believer's extension of mercy within the body of Christ stood opposed to Seneca's portrait of the ruler dispensing *clementia* to the weaker members in his own body, that is, the Roman state (*Clem.* 1.4.1—1.5.1-2). Because of the mercy of God (Rom 12:1: διὰ τῶν οἰκτιρμῶν τοῦ θεοῦ), believers were to exercise mercy in cheerfulness (12:8: ὁ ἐλεῶν ἐν ἱλαρότητι). There is no discussion in Paul, as there is in Seneca, as to whether the demands of justice had been properly met in the exercise of *clementia* ('mercy') over against the extension of *misericordia* ('pity'). The issue of 'justice' (δικαιοσύνη) for believers had been decisively settled in the cross of Christ through faith in Christ as the ἱλαστήριον (Rom 1:17; 3:24-26; 5:18-19; 8:33), notwithstanding the fact that all humanity — believer and unbeliever — would still give account of their works at the Judgement Day (Rom 2:2, 5-16; 14:10). Therefore believers could exercise mercy to anyone in the present, no matter the person's worth. Paul's 'counter-imperial' body of Christ had trumped the body of Caesar in democratising mercy and grace to the weak, without thereby compromising the demands of divine justice. For further discussion of *clementia*, see Harrison, *Imperial Authorities*, 292-299; N. Elliott, *The Arrogance of Nations*, 87-119.

Third, the reference to Augustus as 'god manifest' in our inscription (*l.* 38: ἐ[μ]φανῆ τὸν θεόν) belongs to the widespread semantic domain of 'epiphany', used of rulers and gods in antiquity. It was very common for the adjectival cognate of ἐπιφάνεια (ἐπιφανής: 'manifest', 'distinguished') to be used of the rulers of the Julio-Claudian and Flavian dynasties. For example, Julius Caesar is honoured as 'the god manifest (descended) from Ares and Aphrodite (τὸν ἀπὸ Ἄρεως καὶ Ἀφροδε[ί]της θεὸν ἐπιφανῆ) and the general saviour (σωτῆρα) of human life' (I. Eph. II 251 [48 BC]). The language of epiphany, restored by the editor in the famous Priene inscription, is also used of Augustus (*DocsAug.*, §98b, *l.* 36: [ἐπιφανείς]). Claudius is honoured on a statue base as 'Tiberius Claudius Caesar Sebastos Germanicus god manifest (θεὸν ἐπιφανῆ), saviour (σωτῆρα) of our people too' (*TAM* ii 760c). In P. Oxy. 1021 (AD 54), Claudius is designated ἐνφανὴς θεός after his death. Similarly, the language of epiphany is used of later rulers such as Trajan (P. Oxy. 2754.4 [AD 111]) and Hadrian (*New Docs* 2 §4: 'our lord and god most manifest (ὁ κύριος ἡμῶν καὶ θεὸ[ς] ἐνφανέστατος) Caesar Trajan Hadrian Augustus'). The title ἐπιφανὴς θεός is also extended to imperial family members (e.g. *DocsGaius* §134: [θεοῦ ἐπιφαν]οῦς, referring to Britannicus).

Of particular interest for Pauline scholars is the application of the language of epiphany to Caligula. In AD 40 the Roman ruler had wanted to erect his gold statue in the Jerusalem Temple as 'Gaius the new Zeus made manifest' (Philo, *Leg.* 346: Διὸς Ἐπιφανοῦς Νέου χρηματίζῃ Γαΐου)'. However, Caligula's plan came to nothing because of his assassination by the Praetorian Guard in the following year. ἐπιφάνεια, too, was used for the accession of Caligula in an inscription from Cos (*LSJ*, ἐπιφάνεια II.4: *Inscr. Cos* 391: Γερμανικοῦ Σεβαστοῦ ἐπιφάνεια). Thus it is significant that in 2 Thessalonians 2:8 Paul speaks about the revelation of the 'lawless one' in this manner:

> And then the lawless one (ὁ ἄνομος) will be revealed, whom the Lord Jesus will destroy with the breath of his mouth, annihilating him by the manifestation of his coming (τῇ ἐπιφανείᾳ τῆς παρουσίας αὐτοῦ).

Does Paul's language of Christ's 'epiphany' and the destruction of the 'lawless one' in 2 Thessalonians 2:8 (cf. v. 3) carry imperial overtones for his first-century auditors? The language of 'lawlessness' would certainly have reminded auditors of Caligula. The 'lawlessness' of the Roman ruler, seen recently in his attempted profanation of the Temple (Philo, *Leg.* 203-346; Josephus, *A.J.* 18.261-301; 2 Thess 2:3-4; cf. Mk 13:14, 21-22), pointed to the 'mystery of lawlessness' currently engulfing the empire of Rome (2 Thess 2:7). Since Philo had made a similar point about the 'lawlessness' of Caligula (*Leg.* 119; cf. Pss Sol 17:11-15) barely a decade before, it should hardly surprise us to find Paul adapting contemporary Jewish political polemic against the Roman ruler for his own eschatological ends in 2 Thess 2:7. Jewish auditors would have been sensitive to the anti-imperial resonances of such language.

Care has to be taken nevertheless in discussing the imperial reference of the language of 'epiphany' in 2 Thessalonians 2:7. Paul's epiphanic terminology is undoubtedly indebted to the Maccabean traditions regarding the saving 'epiphanies' of God on behalf of his people in times of crisis. Given that the language of epiphany was also used extensively in the inscriptions and papyri for the Roman ruler, it is a reasonable hypothesis that Graeco-Roman auditors would have heard in its use an ironical allusion to Caligula, especially in light of verses 3-4. The epiphany of the returning Christ, Paul states, would completely destroy the self-exalting opponent of God at the eschaton, including arrogant figures like the Roman ruler, the so-called 'manifest god'. If this interpretation of 2 Thessalonians 2:8 is viable, it provides a different assessment of Roman power on Paul's part to that found in Romans 13:1-7. In each case, the imperial context of Paul's discussion has to be respected and accounted for. For full discussion, see Harrison, *Imperial Authorities*, 71-95.

Bibliography

T. **Adam**, *Clementia Principis: Der Einfluß hellenistischer Fürstenspiegel auf den Versuch einer rechtlichen Fundierung des Principats durch Seneca* (Stuttgart 1970); A.A. **Barrett**, *Caligula: The Corruption of Power* (London 1989); R. **Ash**, *Tacitus* (London 2006); M.P. **Charlesworth**, 'Tiberius and the death of Augustus', *AJP* 44/2 (1923) 145-157; S. **Braund**, *De Clementia* (Oxford 2009); E. **Cowen**, 'Tacitus, Tiberius and Augustus', *Classical Antiquity* 28/2 (2009) 179-210; M.B. **Dowling**, *Clemency and Cruelty in the Roman World* (Ann Arbor 2006); D.R. **Dudley**, *The World of Tacitus* (London 1968); N. **Elliott**, *The Arrogance of Nations: Reading Romans in the Shadow of Empire* (Philadelphia 2008); J.D. **Fantin**, *The Lord of the Entire World: Lord Jesus, A Challenge to Lord Caesar?* (Sheffield 2011); E. **Gorman**, *Irony and Misreading in the Annals of Tacitus* (Cambridge 2000); F.C. **Grant** (ed.), *Ancient Roman Religion* (New York 1957); J.R. **Harrison**, 'Paul and the Imperial Gospel at Thessaloniki', *JSNT* 25/1 (2002) 71-96; J.R. **Harrison**, *Paul and the Imperial Authorities at Thessalonica and Rome: A Study in the Conflict of Ideology* (Tübingen 2011); B.W. **Jones** and R.D. **Milns**, *The Use of Documentary Evidence in the Study of Roman Imperial History* (Sydney 1984); E.A. **Judge**, 'Caesar's Son and Heir', in E.A. Judge, *The First Christians in the Roman World: Augustan and New Testament Essays* (ed., J.R. Harrison; Tübingen 2008) 90-110; E.A. **Judge**, 'The Augustan Republic: Tiberius and Claudius on Roman History', in E.A. Judge, *The First Christians in the Roman World: Augustan and New Testament Essays* (ed., J.R. Harrison; Tübingen 2008) 127-139; E.A. **Judge**, 'The Eulogistic Inscriptions of the Augustan Forum', in E.A. Judge, *The First Christians in the Roman World: Augustan and New Testament Essays* (ed., J.R. Harrison; Tübingen 2008) 165-200; E.A. **Judge**, 'Augustus in the *Res Gestae*', in E.A. Judge, *The First Christians in the Roman World: Augustan and New Testament Essays* (ed., J.R. Harrison; Tübingen 2008) 182-223; E.A. **Judge**, 'On Judging the Merits of Augustus', in E.A. Judge, *The First Christians in the Roman World: Augustan and New Testament Essays* (ed., J.R. Harrison; Tübingen 2008) 224-313; F. **Klingner**, *Tacitus über Augustus und Tiberius: Interpretationen zum Eingang der Annalen* (München 1954); M.R. **Lefkowitz** and M.E. **Fant** (eds.), *Women's Life in Greece and Rome: A Source Book in Translation* (Baltimore ³2005); B.M. **Levick**, 'Mercy and Moderation on the Coinage of Tiberius', in *The Ancient Historian and his Materials: Essays in Honour of C.E. Stevens on his Seventieth Birthday* (ed., B.M. Levick; Farnborough 1975) 123-137; B.M. **Levick**, *Tiberius the Politician* (Rev. ed.; London 1999); S.R. **Llewelyn**, 'Faithful Words', *New Docs* 9 (2002) 8-14; F.B. **Marsh**, *The Reign of Tiberius* (London 1931); R. **Mellor**, *Tacitus* (New York 1993); R.H. **Martin**, 'Tacitus and the Death of Augustus', *CQ* 5 1/2 (1955): 123-128; R.H. **Martin**, *Tacitus* (London 1981); F.G.B. **Millar**, 'Review of D. Timpe, *Untersuchungen zur Kontinuität des frühen Prinzipats* (Wiesbaden 1962)', *CR* 13/3 (1963) 327-329; M.S. **Sage**, 'Tiberius and the Accession of Tiberius', *Ancient Society* 13 (1982) 293-321; R. **Seagar**, *Tiberius* (Malden ²2005); B. **Severy**, *Augustus and the Family at the Birth of the Roman Empire* (New York 2003); R.K. **Sherk** (ed. and trans.), *The Roman Empire: Augustus to Hadrian* (Cambridge 1988); D.C.A. **Shotter**, *Tiberius Caesar* (London 2002); P.M. **Swan**, *The Augustan Succession: An Historical Commentary on Cassius Dio's Roman History, Books 55-56 (9 BC—AD 14)* (New York 2004); R. **Syme**, *The Roman Revolution* (London 1939); R. **Syme**, *Tacitus: Volume 1 and Volume 2* (Oxford repr. 1989 [1958]); D. **Timpe**, *Untersuchungen zur Kontinuität des frühen Prinzipats* (Wiesbaden 1962); B. **Walker**, *The Annals of Tacitus: A Study in the Writing of History* (Manchester 1952); T.E.J. **Wiedeman**, 'From Nero to Vespasian', in *The Cambridge Ancient History: Vol. 10. The Augustan Empire, 43 BC—AD 69* (eds, A.K. Bowman, et al.; Cambridge 1996) 256-282.

J.R. Harrison (Macquarie University)

§13 How to celebrate Hadrian's Accession

Oxyrhynchite nome 6.5 x 16 cm 25 August, AD 117

Ed. pr. – J. R. Rea, *The Oxyrhynchus Papyri* LV (London 1988) 3781 (= P. Oxy. 3781)

The text is reasonably complete and written in a quick hand.

⟦α . . . . . . ⁻ ⁻ ⟧
(vac.)
\ . . . [.] . . [. . .] . ( )/

2 Ῥάμμ(ιος) Μαρτ(ιᾶλις)
στρ(ατηγοῖς) [ ] νομ(ῶν)
χαίρε(ιν).
ἐπὶ σωτηρίᾳ τοῦ σύνπαντ(ος)
ἀνθρώπων γένους ἴστε
5 τὴν ἡγεμονίαν παρὰ τοῦ
Θεοῦ πατρὸς διαδεδέχθ(αι)
αὐτοκράτορα Καίσαρα
Τραϊανὸν Ἀδριανὸν Ἄριστ(ον)
Σεβαστὸν Γερμανικὸν Δακι-
10 κὸν Παρθικόν. εὐχόμ[ενοι]
οὖν πᾶσι θεοῖς αἰώνιον
αὐτοῦ τὴν δϵιαμονήν
ἡμεῖν φυλαχθῆναι
στεφανηφορήσομ(εν)
15 ἐφ' ἡμ(έρας) ι', ὅπερ καὶ τοῖς
ὑφ' ἑαυτοὺς νομ[οῖ]ς
φανερὸν ποιήσητε.
(ἔτους) α' Μεσορὴ
ἐπαγο(μένων) β'.
(vac.)
20 Λητο(πολίτου), Μεμφεί[τ(ου),
Ἀρσι(νοΐτου),]
Ἀφροδ(ιτοπολίτου),
Ἡρακλ(εοπολίτου),
Ὀξυρυγ(χίτου),
Ὀάσεω(ς) ζ' νομ(ῶν),
Κυνο(πολίτου),
[Ἑρμ]ο(πολίτου) [- ca. ? -]

Rammius Martialis to [the *strategoi*] of districts, greetings.
With an eye to the well-being of all mankind – Know that
he has taken up the leadership from the god his father:
Imperator Caesar
Traianus Hadrianus Optimus
Augustus Germanicus Dacicus
Parthicus. Vow[ing] (sacrifices)
therefore to all the gods that
his age-long permanence
may be preserved for us,
we shall wear garlands
for ten days. This very thing
you shall make known
to the dis[trict]s under your charge.
Year 1, Mesore
2nd intercalary day.

(Of the) Letopolite, Memphi[te, Arsinoite,]
Aphroditopolite, Heracleopolite,
Oxyrhynchite,
the Oasis of the Heptanomia, Cynopolite,
[Herm]opolite . . .

§13 How to celebrate Hadrian's Accession 77

1 The editor notes the α may suggest some form of ἀντίγραφον, 'copy'. Given the nature of the document, ἀναγραφή, 'transcription' may be another possibility. Rea also points to marks ('double curve', 'a high horizontal') which may be abbreviations of some kind. Perhaps the curve at the far right margin is a 'sinusoid curve' which in this context may denote the first regnal year of Hadrian. **2** The editor puts forward the possibility, 'of the underwritten districts' for the uncertain mark preceding νομ(ῶν). **12** διαμονήν ed. **13** ἡμῖν ed.

This letter was intended to circulate to the *strategoi* of the Egyptian districts ('nomes'), communicating instructions for the announcement of the imperial accession of Hadrian. Both the fact of its date and the language of taking up the imperial rule are of interest for the study of early Christianity.

The Circumstances of Hadrian's Accession

News of Trajan's death in Cilicia reached the 41-year-old Hadrian at Syrian Antioch, his headquarters as provincial governor, on 9 August, 117 (Dio-Xiph. 69.2; *HA Hadr.* 4.7). Inscriptional evidence points to 11 August as the date of the Hadrianic *dies imperii* (*ILS* I 318; *CIL* VI 33885.17). His eleventh-hour adoption by Trajan had not been without intrigue, yet political factors, including military support, allowed him to assume the *imperium* before senatorial confirmation (*HA Hadr.* 4.6; Dio-Xiph. 69.1-2). Hadrian's acclamation as emperor at Antioch and promulgation of the news of his accession meant that by the time the news of succession reached Rome it was a virtual *fait accompli*;[1] for a full narrative, see the recent account of Speller (23-26).

The Communication of Imperial Accession

The date of the letter demonstrates that Hadrian had rapidly transmitted – and Rammius had promptly complied with – orders for the public announcement of his accession, almost certainly before news of Trajan's death and Hadrian's acclamation at Antioch had reached the Senate at Rome. Rea conjectures that Rammius (*PIR* VII.1 [1999] no. 20; to be identified with the familiarly addressed ʽΡαμμιέ μου of an imperial letter of AD 119, *BGU* 1, 140.10 = *Chr.Mitt.* 373; cf. Trajan to Pliny, *Ep.* 10.44, 50, etc.) may have taken up his own appointment from M. Rutilius Lupus (*praefectus Aegypti* AD 113-117; *PIR* VII.1 [1999] no. 252) just after the arrival of the letter bearing news of Hadrian's accession (for other documents related to Martialis, see Bastianini, 'Lista', 283). A.R. Birley, who notes P. Oxy. 3781 (*Hadrian*, 325, n. 8), suggested that Martialis 'must surely have been in the east with Hadrian' and that one Valerius Eudaemon (appointed *ad dioecesin Alexandriae*, *HA* 15.1) 'probably came [to Alexandria] with a letter of dismissal for the Prefect Rutilius Lupus'. One might speculate that Hadrian's news arrived in a *codicillum*, or letter of appointment, also naming Martialis to the *praefectura* (cf. C. Pap. Lat. 238; Millar, 288-290; but see Rea, 16-17). Could Martialis

---

[1] Cf. Tacitus, *Hist.* 1.76: the proclamation of Otho in AD 69 by Nero's freedman Crescens who, in the tumultuous year of the four emperors, bypassed the authority of the *proconsul* Vipstanius Apronianus and prematurely let the cat out of the bag in Africa at a celebratory accession feast he gave to the common people of Carthage.

and Eudaemon have traveled together from Antioch to Alexandria, straight from Hadrian himself? Attractive as this is, it cannot be supported with firm evidence. What is certain is that the prefect of Egypt had historically been a critical imperial appointment due to the great influence he wielded as a supporter of the emperor (see Tacitus, *Hist.* 1.11; A. Bowman, *CAH* X, 679-682), and whatever the connection between Rammius Martialis and the new *imperator*, Hadrian appears to have counted on him for support.

Word from Hadrian was sent with all urgency to Alexandria, perhaps by sea given the favourable sailing season (for the usual accession announcements travelling from Rome to Alexandria, see Ramsay, 69). It is difficult to say how long sea travel from the port of Antioch in Syria to the bustling late summer harbour at Alexandria would have taken. Depending on winds, weather, and the type of vessel it may have been from a few days to over a week (see Casson, 149-162). If we are to assume that Martialis would not have delayed to draw up and send off our announcement, then the ship bearing its news must have left Antioch no later than between 15 and 20 August, perhaps earlier. Alternatively, the news may have travelled by means of the *cursus publicus*, or imperial post. This communication infrastructure, greatly developed and expanded from the time of Augustus (Suet. *Aug.* 49.3-50), could be remarkably efficient, especially in good weather and times of great need (see Casson, 182-196). Official couriers (*iuvenes*) could average 50 Roman miles a day in light conveyance (*vehiculum, cisium*). See *New Docs* 1 §9 for requisitioned transport and *New Docs* 7 §1 for the *cursus publicus*.

Once the message from Hadrian reached Alexandria, Martialis and his staff would have immediately drafted copies of the announcement, including our document. It is just possible that there was ready to hand a template for just such an occasion — one that would couch the accession announcement in the language of a new imperial age (see below for striking similarities between our document and the earlier edict of Tiberius Iulius Alexander, I. Khargeh 4, AD 69). From Alexandria the prefect sent the news and instructions to the *strategoi* (*l.* 2) of the districts (νόμοι) mentioned in *ll.* 20-23. D.W. Rathbone ('Dates', 103) argued in relation to the dissemination of third century accession announcements from Alexandria to the nomes that such news made its way up the Nile valley, reaching the districts mentioned in our document within a timeframe from one day to several weeks.[2] In a more recent unpublished paper interacting with Rathbone's study, P. Legutko presented a statistical analysis of all dated papyri between AD 76 – 255 which showed that the time interval in extant papyri with imperial date-formulas when a change in emperor occurred was 'about 49 days – between four and five times longer than the average time interval between papyri dated by the same emperor' (p. 3). From this he concluded that 'an interregnum has a large, significant effect on the time interval between the first papyrus of a new emperor and the last papyrus of his predecessor, controlling for monthly and yearly variation', a fact he suggests we might attribute to the political uncertainties and sensitivities surrounding many imperial successions (p. 5). Against this background the date of our document and

---

[2] Cf. S. Strassi's discussion of the administrative infrastructure for communication up the Nile from Alexandria ('Problemi', 89-107); and discussion of our document ('Problemi', 94).

the swiftness of Hadrian's recognition by the prefect and entire province of Egypt is even more noteworthy.

The Language and Ideology of Imperial Accession

a. Succession

The force of the opening clause of the announcement (ἴστε, *l*. 4) is carried by the infinitival διαδεδέχθαι (*l*. 6).[3] A standard term for 'succeeding to' or 'taking up' a position of authority in such contexts, διαδέχομαι (Lat. *suscipere*, not given by Mason, 36; see the evidence of Pliny below) appears more frequently in literary (Jos. *AJ* 18.33.1 of Tiberius; Cassius Dio 59.1.1 and Philo, *Leg. ad Gaium* 61.1 of Gaius; Dio Chrys. [Favorinus] *Or*. 37.5 of Periander of Athens) than documentary texts. See *DGE s.v.* διαδέχομαι for other references. Other verbs with significant semantic overlap used in succession circumstances include ἀντικαθίστημι (Cassius Dio 59.6.1) and καθίστημι (*SB* 22.15203, I BC – AD I). New Testament writers did not choose this verb with respect to taking up office or rule (but, see intertestamental succession examples in *2 Macc.* 3:9; *4 Macc.* 4:15), preferring other terms, probably under the influence of the LXX (see below). Acts 24:27 has the noun διάδοχος, 'successor', of Felix's replacement Porcius Festus (cf. *Sir.* 46:1 of Joshua as replacement for Moses). In the case of this papyrus it was a variation on a theme to style the rising emperor in terms that rendered him heir (if not son) of the god his father (παρὰ τοῦ θεοῦ πατρός).

b. Leadership

Ἡγεμονία (*l*. 5), a word which simply means 'leadership' or 'government', is the normal term in such contexts for *imperium* (Mason, *Greek Terms*, 51; cf. comments on the complexities of imperial terminology in J. Béranger, *Recherches*, 44-47, 55-61, 132-133), and is regularly coupled with ἀρχή (e.g. Dio Cassius 53.6.2, 60.2.1), forms of both terms sometimes appearing alongside ἐξουσία (Lk 20:20 of Pilate and his *imperium*). From the time of Augustus, the ἡγεμονία of the *princeps* was an imperial rule (thus the interpretive translation offered above) touted as ἐπὶ σωτηρίᾳ τοῦ σύνπαντ(ος) ἀνθρώπων γένους (*ll*. 3-4), this sentiment and language being most widely preserved in the inscriptions. In these contexts, ἐπί with the dative is best understood as telic, 'for the sake of' or 'with an eye to' (see below), while σωτηρία is best taken as universal 'safety', 'security', or 'well-being' rather than in the sense of 'health' found in private letters (see *New Docs* 1, 14, 57). The construction does not appear in the NT, with σωτηρία after ἐπί found in the genitive and accusative but not the dative (the doubted ending of Mk 16:8 has the apostles announcing the ἄφθαρτον κήρυγμα τῆς αἰωνίου σωτηρίας 'the imperishable proclamation of the well-being of the age'). Philo,

---

[3] The papyrus appears to preserve διαδεδέχ^θ, read by Rea as διαδεδέχθ(αι), apparently a perfect middle infinitival form which has no parallel among either literary or documentary texts. One would expect something like the infinitive διαδέχεσθαι or the indicative διαδέχεται. *SB* 22.15203 (I BC – AD I) has in *l*. 4 the perfect passive participle διαδεδεγμένους in a context of succession to local magistracy; P. Tebt. 3.1.725 (II BC) shows the same form in *l*. 22: διαδεδεγμέν[---.

however, writes of the well-being of the *princeps* in language akin to the accession announcement in *Leg. ad Gaium* 19.2: μέμνηται γὰρ οὐδεὶς τοσαύτην μιᾶς χώρας ἢ ἑνὸς ἔθνους γενέσθαι χαρὰν ἐπὶ σωτηρίᾳ καὶ καταστάσει ἡγεμόνος, ὅσην ἐπὶ Γαΐῳ συμπάσης τῆς οἰκουμένης ('for no one remembers such joy coming to any one country or any one nation, at the well-being and prosperity of the leader, as the whole world [experienced] at the recovery of Gaius'). An almost identical phrase is found in the well-known edict of the *praefectus Aegypti* Ti. Iulius Alexander (I. Khargeh 4 = *Docs Flav* 328, tr. Braund §600, modified, AD 68) which refers to the celebration of Galba's accession and its benefits to be mediated through the judgements and benefactions of the prefect: ἵνα <δ>ὲ εὐθυμότεροι πάντα ἐλπίζητε παρὰ τοῦ ἐπιλάμψαντος ἡμεῖν ἐπὶ σωτηρίᾳ τοῦ παντὸς ἀνθρώπων γένους εὐεργέτου Σεβαστοῦ Αὐτοκράτορος Γάλβα τά τε πρὸ<ς> σωτηρίαν | [κ]αὶ τὰ πρὸς ἀπόλαυσιν (*ll.* 7-8, 'In order that you may more confidently have expectation of the benefactor Augustus Imperator Galba, who has shone upon us for the well-being of the whole race of men, expectations both for well-being and for enjoyment'). Chalon, in his edition and commentary (*L'edit*, 43), remarks on this section of the preamble, 'Mais, maintenant que *Galba est arrivé au pouvoir pour le salut du genre humain, signe d'une ère nouvelle qui apportera au monde sécurité et prospérité*, on peut tout attendre en pleine confiance...' [emphasis added]. A true king, says Socrates in Dio Chrysostom's oration *On Kingship,* 'becomes the saviour and protector of men everywhere' (*Or.* 3.6: πάντων οὗτος ἀνθρώπων γίγνεται σωτὴρ καὶ φύλαξ). Such a ruler (think: Trajan) governs 'with an eye to their well-being and benefit' (*Or.* 3. 39: ἐπὶ σωτηρίᾳ καὶ τῷ συμφέροντι τῶν ἀρχομένων ἐπιμελεῖται).

This notion of public benefit was also present on a local scale as wealthy men and women gave extravagant gifts or took up liturgies that promoted the interests of the city. Claudia Metrodora is honoured on Chios (I. Khios McCabe 18, AD I, *ll.* 13-14) for her contribution to the baths, a gift that was ἐπὶ σωτηρίᾳ τῆς .. [-] | τουμένης πόλεως 'for the well-being of the ... ? city ...' Beginning with the Julio-Claudians, the Caesars had powerfully laid claim to the euergetic language in order to promote themselves as the benefactors of mankind. Dionysius of Halicarnassus, in speaking of early Rome (but in first-century language) captures the force of this phrase by means of contrasting phrases (*Ant. Rom.* 3.11.8): οὐκ ἐπὶ διαφθορᾷ καὶ ἐλαττώσει τῶν κοινῶν, ἀλλ' ἐπὶ σωτηρίᾳ καὶ αὐξήσει γίνεται ('not for the destruction and diminution of the commonwealth, but *for its well-being* and increase'). As Hadrian sped to secure his own claim to succession by means of his public proclamation, he (and/or his administrators) constructed an argument with a firm precedent – his taking up the leadership was for the well-being of the entire Roman world.

c. Prepositions and Purpose: ἐπί + *dat.;* ὑπέρ + *gen.;* πρός + *acc.*

The use of ἐπί + dative (ἐπὶ σωτηρίᾳ) in our document is an example of the flexibility and transitional nature of some prepositions in *koine* Greek. Moulton (p. 63) noted a century ago that ''Επί and παρά are the only prepositions in which the use with three cases is really alive; and even ἐπί illustrates [the tendency away from use with the dative].' He further noted (p. 605) that one does find ἐπί + dative expressing a sense of

§13 How to celebrate Hadrian's Accession 81

purpose in NT Greek, although as Wallace has more recently remarked (p. 376), the three basic NT uses are spatial, temporal, and causal (see BDF §235; cf. *Sir.* 46:1). It is as a subset of this causal (alternatively: locative) category that ἐπί + dative is treated by Mayser (474-475), Kühner and Gerth (501-503), and Schwyzer (467), all of whom point to instances of purpose similar to that in our text (Mayser gives as illustrative papyrological examples *SB* 6155, 7 and *BGU* 1141, 24; the others point to Xenophon, *Anab.* II.4.8 and VI.4.9). Given the high probability that our announcement was modelled on a Latin exemplar, it is also important to keep in mind this use of ἐπί + dative as a formal/administrative Greek translation equivalent to the Latin *pro salute*. Nevertheless, *koine* usage attests to a significant level of semantic overlap among ἐπί + dat., ὑπέρ + gen., and πρός + acc. used to express purpose or goal (e.g. I. Khargeh 4, *ll.* 7-8 above).

This language and construction was taken up and theologically adapted by early Christian literature with respect to the proclamation about Christ. According to Irenaeus (*Haer.* 1.18.1), God desired to send Christ ἐπὶ σωτηρίᾳ τῶν πειθομένων αὐτῷ ('for the well-being of those who trust in him'). It is a common refrain in the writing of John Chrysostom that God's work in Christ is 'for the well-being of men' (e.g. *Pasch.* 52.31, ἐπὶ τῇ σωτηρίᾳ τοῦ κοινοῦ γένους τῶν ἀνθρώπων). Augustine (*Ver. Rel.* 3.42; 7.20; cf. Paulinus Nolanus, *Ep.* 31.3.8) employs the Latin equivalent, *pro salute generis humani*. Eusebius insists that the Christian gospel is for the well-being of all men and nations (e.g. *Dem. Ev.* 6.13.20.4, ὡς ἂν ἐπὶ σωτηρίᾳ οὐ μόνον τοῦ Ἰουδαίων ἔθνους ἀλλὰ γὰρ καὶ τῶν ἐθνῶν ἁπάντων τῆς τοῦ κυρίου εἰς ἀνθρώπους καθόδου γενησομένης).

d. For the Well-Being of All Mankind: Secular Eschatology and Popular Response

In Hadrian's accession announcement, this imperial ideology takes on eschatological overtones in the second clause where the populace is enjoined to vow (εὐχόμ[ενοι], *l.* 10; prayer implying accompanying sacrifice; cf. accession announcements of Nero and Pertinax, mentioned below) which is accompanied by provision for celebration (*ll.* 14-15). The complementary infinitive φυλαχθῆναι (*l.* 13) marks the focus of the prayer as the preservation of permanence (διαμονή, *l.* 12) for the new age (αἰώνιον, *l.* 11; see evidence from Pliny below) of Hadrian's rule. From documentary evidence, it is clear that this language had wide geographical currency and the prayer-vow and celebration had real traction across varied social levels.

A statue dedication from Ephesus (I. Eph. 510A; text identical to I. Eph. 722) records a prayer for the health (ὑπὲρ τῆς ... ὑγιείας, *ll.* 1-2) of Tiberius and the permanence of the Roman *imperium* (καὶ διαμονῆς τῆς Ῥωμαίων ἡγεμονίας, *ll.* 2-3). The same language, this time for Titus (AD 79/81), appears inscribed on the restored Ephesian Augusteum (I. Eph. 412, *ll.* 1-4) and yet again in Thera for Trajan (*IG* XII 3, 324, *ll.* 1-7). Cyzicus, a city of Mysia, honored Gaius in regional dialect in his accession year (*Docs Gaius*, 401, tr. Braund, *Augustus to Nero*, §673, AD 37):

Upon the magistracy ('accession') of Gaius Caesar (ἐπὶ Γαίου Καίσαρος ἱππάρχεω{ι}, l.1) ... Since the new Helios ('Sun') Gaius Caesar Augustus Germanicus has desired kings, the bodyguards of leadership, to join in illumination with their own rays (ἐπεὶ ὁ νέος Ἥλιος Γάιος Καῖσαρ Σεβαστὸς Γερμανικὸς συναναλάμψαι ταῖς ἰδίαις αὐγαῖς καὶ τὰς δορυφόρους τῆς ἡγεμονίας ἠθέλεσεν βασιλήας, ll. 2-3) ... it is decreed by the people ... that (temples should be adorned and cult given) to vow on behalf of the permanence of the age of Gaius Caesar and of their well-being (εὔξασθαι μὲν ὑπὲρ τῆς Γαίου Καίσαρος αἰωνίου διαμονῆς καὶ τῆς τούτων σωτηρίας, ll. 20-21).

Claudius is honored in Cys (Caria) with sacrifices to the gods and to the *Augusti* 'for the permanence and health of their house for the entire age' (ὑπὲρ τῆς τοῦ οἴκου αὐτῶν εἰς ἅπαντα τὸν αἰῶνα δι|[αμο]νῆς καὶ ὑγείας, ll. 12-13 [*Docs Gaius*, 135, tr. Braund, 230, modified]). P. Oxy. 1021 (= *Docs Gaius*, 47, tr. Braund, 235) preserves Nero's accession announcement in which he is styled 'the one expected and hoped for by all the world' (ll. 5-7) and the people are called upon to celebrate by wearing garlands (στεφανηφοροῦντες, l. 15), sacrificing (l. 16), and giving thanks to the gods (ll. 17-18). Hadrian's reign was described on an inscription in Smyrna (I. Smyrna 594 = *IGRR* 4.1398) as 'in the most fortunate times of the most manifest of gods, Imperator ...' ([- ἐν τοῖς] | [εὐτυ]χεστάτοις καιροῖς τοῦ θεῶ[ν ἐμφανεστάτου Αὐτοκρά] | [τορο]ς, ll. 10-11). The stone goes on to record prayers for the permanence of his age and for the invincibility of the Roman leadership (ll. 12-13). *BGU* 646 records the prefect's edict at the accession of Pertinax (AD 193), enjoining the Alexandrians to hold a festival at which they were to offer sacrifices and prayers for the permanence of the new emperor. Such vows for the emperor, his family, and his *imperium* are well-attested at least through the fourth century (e.g. the early imperial *IG* II² 1346 from Athens and McCabe, *PHI Aphrodisias* 29, ll. 7-8; cf. *BGU* 176, AD II Arsinoite).

Although generally present throughout the principate, it becomes clear that these sentiments often blossomed in the wake of accession announcements. Three provincial reactions to Hadrian's taking office are evidenced by inscriptions (a helpful collection of older readings and brief comments is found in P.J. Alexander, *Letters*, 142-144) recording the emperor's response to their congratulatory embassies (see also Millar, *The Emperor*, 415). The Astypalaeans (*IG* XII 3, 175, AD 117-118) 'were glad at [Hadrian's] taking over the paternal rule' (ἥσθητε διαδεξαμέν[ου ἐμοῦ] | [τὴν πατ]ρῴαν ἀρχήν, ll. 8-9) and received imperial praise and confirmation of their freedom (ll. 9-10). The σύνοδος of Pergamon (*IGRR* 4.349) acted quickly, sending their congratulations in time to receive an imperial response dated November AD 117. They were commended for 'confessing feelings of joy on [Hadrian's] account' (τὴν χα|ρὰν, ὅσης ἐφ' ἡμεῖν ὡμολογεῖ|τε μετειληφέναι, ll. 12-13). Delphi, perhaps lagging a bit, joined the acclamations and but did not receive their reply until AD 118 (*FD* III 4.301). Since they 'openly showed [their] zeal for [him] by rejoicing at [Hadrian's] accession to his ancestral power and by invoking the god (Apollo) to grant [him] every good thing' (ὅτι φανερὰν [ἀπεδείξασθε τὴν πρὸς ἐμὲ προθυ] | [μίαν ὑμῶν συνηδόμ]ενοι μὲν ἐπὶ τῷ διαδέξ[ασθαί με τὴν πατρῴαν ἀρχήν, τὸν] | δὲ θεὸν δ[οῦναί μοι πάντα] ἀγαθ[ὰ] παρακαλοῦντε[ς, ll. 6-8), the Delphians received confirmation of their civic privileges (ll. 8-10; cf. I. Kor. Kent. 102, l. 7, dated c. AD 124 by Kent, where Hadrian is honoured by the Achaeans as σω]τῆρα καὶ εὐεργέτην τῆ[ς Ἑλλάδος]).

§13 How to celebrate Hadrian's Accession

Certainly those in the upper echelons of Roman society had an interest in acclaiming the new emperor. S. E. Hoffer ('Divine Comedy?') has recently shown that Pliny artfully contributed to the generating of accession propaganda for Trajan in *Ep.* 10.1-2 and the *Panegyricus*. These texts provide a window into how the Latin version of Hadrian's accession announcement would have been worded. Succession language (*suscipere*) abounds as Pliny prays (*precari*) that Trajan's age (*saeculum tuum*) would benefit all mankind (*genus humanum*). Hoffer notes, 'Trajan saved the *imperium* (imperial power/Roman Empire) by taking it up' (p. 75). 'The term "human race" conveys not only the propaganda of a world-wide empire but also *suggestio divini*, a hint that the emperor is the vice-regent of the gods in tending to humanity . . . Trajan's "reign/(golden) age" (*saeculum*) has begun, and the citizen needs only to pray for the "best" emperor's good fortune to be in keeping with the new era (*digna saeculo tuo*); the well-being of humanity will automatically follow' (p. 77). This 'Plinian trope' involves 'both "constitutional" and "theocratic" aspects' (p. 87).[4] Against this Latin background of his imperial predecessor, Hadrian's Greek proclamation achieves resonance.

The imperial claim to an inaugurated age of well-being for humanity present in our document is also attested numismatically. An early aureus and denarius issue of AD 117 (*RIC* II, Hadrian 2; cf. *RIC* II, Hadrian 534), before Hadrian returned to Rome and therefore conservative and employing stock iconography (see *RIC* II, 319-20), depicts Trajan and Hadrian on the reverse with a globe (*orbis terrarum*) held between them, portraying the 'adoptio' and making the case for Hadrian's legitimate succession to any who might doubt. On other issues, Hadrian stands upon the globe firmly grasping the rudder (*gubernaculum*, e.g. *RIC* II, Hadrian 110, AD 119-22) or celebrating his age as golden (SAEC[ulum] AUR[eum], e.g. *RIC* II, Hadrian 136). Globe and rudder together on Hadrian's coinage recalled a familiar imperial theme often expressed by the legend SALUS GENERIS HUMANI or SALUS PUBLICA (see ἐπὶ σωτηρίᾳ τοῦ σύνπαντ(ος) ἀνθρώπων γένους, our papyrus, *ll.* 3-4). Variations on this motif can be traced back into the first century (e.g. *RIC* II, Trajan 148B; *RIC* II Nerva 126; *RIC* II, Vespasian 88; *RIC* I, Galba 96; A. Birley, *Hadrian*, 83, sees the phoenix and globe on Hadrianic coinage hearkening back to Claudius's 'new *saeculum*' and suggests this imagery might be credited to 'Martialis or his advisers') while the combination and ideology may originate with Tiberius who appears as *Pontifex Maximus* with the globe and rudder (*RIC* I, Tiberius 52). Grant (*Roman*, 43-46) notes that the globe and rudder, emblems of *Fortuna*, were stressed very early in the Principate (17 BC) at the start of the 'new Augustan age' and that they resurface with a Tiberian issue of AD 34-35 celebrating the half-centenary of the *saeculum* of Augustus. He argues that this issue recalls 'the launch of the Principate in public religion' as well as 'other blessings conferred by [Augustus]' (*Roman*, 46), and that both themes resurface at accessions and Augustan anniversaries with Hadrian attempting to 'set himself beside the Founder of

---

[4] Hoffer ('Divine Comedy?' 76) also notes Pliny's use of the so-called 'pilot' metaphor in connection with divine providence, imperial accession, and universal well-being or security; see brief comments below on Heb 2:10; 12:2; Acts 5:31 and the cluster of ἀρχηγός, σωτηρία, and θρόνος.

the Empire' by means of a medallic issue of AD 119 intended to celebrate the 150th anniversary of Actium (*Roman*, 100-101; cf. related comments of R. Pudill, 31-50).

But responses were not limited merely to centralised issues of coinage, to civic entities appealing for the confirmation of rights and privileges, nor to Roman elites attempting to reinforce their relationship to the new emperor at the helm. It is not difficult to recapture the popular excitement generated around imperial accession announcements and annual celebrations, attended as they were by civic festivities. In addition to the aforementioned feast in Carthage at Otho's accession, there are other texts that yield glimpses into the popular reception of such imperial news. Pliny (*Ep.* 10.52) tells Trajan,

> We have celebrated with appropriate rejoicing, Sir, the day of your accession whereby you preserved the Empire (*diem . . . quo servasti imperium, dum suscipis*), and have offered prayers to the gods (*precasti deos*) to keep you in health and prosperity on behalf of the human race, whose security and happiness depend on your safety (*cuius tutela et securitas saluti tuae innisa est*). We have also administered the oath of allegiance to your fellow-soldiers in the usual form, *and found the provincials eager to take it, too, as a proof of their loyalty* [emphasis added].

The much discussed P. Giss. 3 conveys the sense of being in the jostle of an Egyptian crowd listening to a celebratory oration at Heptakomia in October AD 117, just months after the announcement formally issued by our papyrus. In the official draft for the public celebration, we see on stage Phoebus Apollo who, having just escorted the deified Trajan heavenward in a chariot drawn by white horses, proclaims Hadrian as the new ruler (ἄνακτα καινὸν Ἀδριανὸν ἀγγελῶ[ν], *ll*. 3-4), the one 'whom all things serve on account of his virtue and the genius of his divine father' (ὧι πάντα δοῦλα [δι᾿] ἀρετὴν κ[αὶ] πατρὸς τύχην θεοῦ, *ll*. 5-6). The People (in the script) respond by rejoicing (χαίροντες, *l.* 6), sacrificing (θύοντες, *l.* 7), and surrendering themselves to laughter (*l.* 8), drinking wine (*l.* 9), and enjoying the unguents of the gymnasium (*ll.* 10-11). All of this is a public benefaction of the *strategos* given out of reverence for the lord Hadrian (τὸ πρὸς τὸν κύριον εὐσεβὲς τοῦ στρατηγοῦ, *ll.* 12-13). *SB* 1.421 (AD 236?), an arrangement of a festal procession for the accession of Maximinus Thrax, and shows the consistency of succession language, ideology, and practice into the third century. The unknown magistrate begins, 'Since I came to know of the good news concerning the public proclamation of Caesar . . .' (ἐπεὶ γν[ώ]στ[ης ἐγενόμην τοῦ] εὐαγγελ[ίο]υ περὶ τοῦ ἀνηγορεῦσθαι Καίσαρα, *ll.* 1-2). He ends with the purpose clause (note the singular verbs) of the announcement, 'in order that, therefore, you may know and be present' (ἵν᾿ [ο]ὖν εἰδῆς καὶ παρατύχης, *ll.* 11-12; cf. παρατυγχάνω, Acts 17:17, for public gathering in Athens). Imperial accession announcements were secular (of the age) gospels, proclaimed and celebrated publicly.

Accession and Rule in the NT

Despite ongoing debate over the role of the imperial cult(s) generally and the significance of the imperial ideology to early Christians, there are some clear linguistic and conceptual resonances between our papyrus and early Christian texts. Though Christ is nowhere said to have succeeded to (διαδέχομαι) imperial rule (ἡγεμονία), he has been appointed a kingdom (Lk 22:29, διέθετό μοι ὁ πατήρ μου βασιλείαν) and been seated upon a heavenly throne (καθίζω; e.g. 'longer ending' of Mk 18:19; Heb 1:3; 8:1; 10:12; note the influence in the NT of καθίστημι from LXX Pss 2:6; 109:1), a throne that endures for the ages (Heb 1:8; LXX Ps 44:7). Jesus is presented as the one seated far above all earthly rule, authority, power, dominion, and name of this age and the coming one (e.g. Eph 1:21; Rev 11:15). Though heaven and earth be destroyed he will remain (διαμένω, Heb 1:11; LXX Ps 101:27) and his followers receive an unshakeable kingdom (βασιλεία ἀσάλευτος, Heb 12:28; *not* ἀνίκητος which is found, however, in imperial accolades and the Maccabean literature) and return worship (εὐλαβεία) as a result. Peter's speech to the Sanhedrin includes the claim at Acts 5:31 that God has exalted (ὕψωσεν) the crucified Jesus to his right hand as Leader (or Founder) and Saviour (ἀρχηγὸν καὶ σωτῆρα; see n. 3 above). Similarly, Heb 2:10 and 12:2 style the resurrected and ascended Christ as the 'Founder of salvation' (ἀρχηγὸς τῆς σωτηρίας) and 'Perfecter of our faith' (τελειωτὴς τῆς πίστεως), yet one who has been seated royally only after his suffering (διὰ παθημάτων) and enduring the cross (ὑπέμεινεν σταυρόν) on behalf of his people. Though described in terms with imperial resonance, Jesus is presented as an unlikely suffering Lord, seated on a throne, but not over the Roman world, and offering a distinct salvation to people of every nation. His is a reign which, according to the Apostle Paul in 1 Cor 15:24-28, will destroy all other authorities and powers, even the great enemy death, at which point the Lord Christ will submissively deliver his kingdom (παραδιδῷ τὴν βασιλείαν) to the Father rather than retain it for himself. The NT eschatological *loci* of ascension-enthronement-rule employ, for the most part, the distinctively Scriptural (i.e. LXX) language and concepts of διαθήκη, βασιλεία, καθίζω, and an αἰών which, in its newness and permanence overlaps with yet supersedes the age/reigns of this world.

Bibliography

F. **Adrados**, et. al., *Diccionario Griego-Español* (Madrid ²2008); P.J. **Alexander**, 'Letters and Speeches of the Emperor Hadrian', *Harvard Studies in Classical Philology* 49 (1938) 141-177; G. **Bastianini**, 'Lista dei prefetti d'Egitto dal 30 al 299', *ZPE* 17 (1975) 263-328; J. **Béranger**, *Recherches sur l'aspect idéologique du principat* (Schweizerische Beiträge zur Altertumswissenschaft, 6; Basel 1953); A. **Birley**, *Hadrian: The Restless Emperor* (London 1997); F. **Blass**, A. **Debrunner**, and R. **Funk**, *A Greek Grammar of the New Testament and Other Early Christian Literature* (Chicago 1961); A. **Bowman**, *The Cambridge Ancient History*, Vol. X (Cambridge 2008); L. **Casson**, *Travel in the Ancient World* (London 1974); D.C. **Braund**, *Augsutus to Nero: A Sourcebook on Roman History 31 BC – AD 68* (London 1985); G. **Chalon**, *L'édit de Tiberius Julius Alexander: Étude historique et exégétique* (Bibliotheca Helvetica Romana, 5; Olten 1964); M. **Grant**, *Roman Anniversary Issues: An Exploratory Study of the Numismatic and Medallic Commemoration of Anniversary Years 49 B.C. – A.D. 375* (Cambridge 1950); M. **Hammond**, 'The Transmission of the Powers of the Roman Emperor from the Death of Nero in A.D. 68 to That of Alexander Severus in A.D. 235', *HSCP* 24 (1956) 61-133; S.E. **Hoffer**, 'Divine Comedy? Accession Propaganda in Pliny, *Epistles* 10.1-2 and the *Panegyric*', *JRS* 96 (2006) 73-87; G.H.R. **Horsley**, 'A personalised Aretalogy of Isis', *New Docs* 1 (1981) 10-21; G.H.R. Horsley, 'Deferential greetings to a patron', *New Docs* 1 (1981) 56-57; Raphael **Kühner**, *Ausführliche Grammatik der griechischen Sprache* (Hannover 1966); P. **Legutko**, '"The King is Dead - Long Live the King!" Dates of Recognition Readdressed', Unpublished paper presented to the *American Philological Association*, 2004; H. **Mason**, *Greek Terms for Roman Institutions: A Lexicon and Analysis* (Toronto 1974); E. **Mayser**, *Grammatik der griechischen Papyri aus der Ptolemäerzeit. mit Einschluss der gleichzeitigen Ostraka und der in Ägypten verfassten Inschriften* (Berlin

1970); F. **Millar**, *The Emperor in the Roman World (31 B.C.-A.D. 337)* (London 1977); J.H. **Moulton**, *A Grammar of New Testament Greek* (Edinburgh ³1908); R. **Pudill**, *Hadrian: Münzen als Zeugnisse einer glanzvollen Epoche Roms* (Speyer 2008); A.M. **Ramsay**, 'The Speed of the Roman Imperial Post', *JRS* 15 (1925) 60-74; D.W. **Rathbone**, 'The Dates of the Recognition in Egypt of the Emperors from Caracalla to Diocletianus', *ZPE* 62 (1986) 101-131; O.W **Reinmuth**, *The Prefect of Egypt from Augustus to Diocletian* (Aalen 1979); E. **Schwyzer**, *Griechische Grammatik* (Handbuch der Altertumswissenschaft, 2; Munich 1939); E. **Speller**, *Following Hadrian: A Second Century Journey Through the Roman Empire* (Oxford 2003); S. **Strassi**, 'Problemi relativi alla diffusione delle disposizioni amministrative nell'Egitto romano', *ZPE* 96 (1993) 89-107; C.H.V. **Sutherland**, et. al., *The Roman Imperial Coinage*, Vols 1 & 2 (London 1923); C.H.V. **Sutherland**, 'The Historical Evidence of Greek and Roman Coins', *Greece & Rome* 9/26 (1940) 65-80; D.B. **Wallace**, *Greek Grammar Beyond the Basics: An Exegetical Syntax of the New Testament* (Grand Rapids 1996).

B. Bitner (Macquarie University)

PUBLIC LIFE: BENEFACTION AND BUSINESS

§14 Antiochus IV Epiphanes in Athens

Athens   Marble stele   178/177 BC
                      32 x 24.5 x 14.5-18.5cm

Ed pr.: S.V. Tracy, 'Greek Inscriptions from the Athenian Agora: Third to First Centuries B.C.', *Hesperia* 51.1 (1982), pp.60-62 (= SEG XXXII 131).

White marble stele with only upper left extant with moulded fillet, cavetto and ovolo. Cutter often omits crossbar of A and the central horizontal of E.

	ἐπὶ Φίλωνος ἄρχοντ[ος τοῦ μετὰ Μενέδημον, Πυανο]-	In the archonship of Philon, [the (one) after Menedemos], on the
	ψιῶνος ἐνάτει ἱστ[αμένου, ἑβδόμει καὶ δεκάτει]	ninth day (of the month) of [Pyano]psion begin[ning, on the seventeenth day]
	τῆς πρυτανείας· [ἐκκλησία κυρία ἐν τῶι θεάτρωι·]	of the presidency, [sovereign assembly in the theatre.]
4	(vac. 6) ἔδοξεν τεῖ [βουλεῖ καὶ τῶι δήμωι vac. 5]	[The boule and people] decided ...
	Ἀριστογείτων Πολυ[ca 11 εἶπεν· ἐπειδὴ]	Aristogeiton son of Poly[.... spoke: Since]
	Ἀντίοχος ὁ τοῦ βα[σιλέως Ἀντιόχου υἱός, ἀδελφὸς]	Antiochus the son of of ki[ng Antiochus,
	[δ]ὲ Σελεύκου τοῦ [βασιλέως παρὰ προγόνων]	and brother of king] Seleucus from his forbears]
8	παρειληφὼς τὴν [πρὸς τὸν δῆμον εὔνοιαν καὶ]	having inherited [good-will towards the people and]
	[ἀ]γαθὸς ὢν ἐμ [πᾶσιν ca 12 οὐ μόνον]	being good in [all ... not only]
	[ἀπ'] ἀρχῆς ὑπ[ca 26]	[from] the beginning ...
	[ca 2] ἀλλὰ κ[αὶ ca 26]	but also ...
12	[ca 4]ΡΛΙ[ca 28]	...

7 Ed pr. reads Φιλοπάτορος; J and L. Robert, παρ' αὐτῶν; C.Habicht, παρὰ προγόνων. **9-10** Robert supplies ἐμ [πᾶσιν ... οὐ μόνον ἀπ']. Cf. SEG XXXIX 138 for emendations.

The prescript of the decree records that the meeting was held on the 9th day of Pyanopsion. Tracy noted this was unusual since it was a festival day. On line 3, he restored [ἐκκλησία κυρία ἐν τῶι θεάτρωι]. However, this restoration is unlikely to be correct.

Mikalson demonstrated that the Athenians only convened the ἐκκλησία on annual or monthly festival days in an emergency.[1] This is specifically corroborated for the festival (the Stenia, first day of the Thesmophoria) by Aristophanes.[2] We have no way of knowing why the date was chosen. Tracy suggested it represented 'a suitably special occasion to honor Antiochus',[3] but this seems unsatisfactory, especially as the day of the Stenia was specifically for married women and mothers. Honorary decrees could be passed at any session of the ἐκκλησία, and were only one item on the order of business. It seems more likely that there was other, more pressing business motivating the extraordinary meeting.

The decree follows the pattern attested after ca. 340 BC in being dated according to both the conciliar and festival calendars.[4] However, a meeting held on a festival day was almost certainly not a *kuria ekklesia*.[5] Hansen has shown that such meetings were ἐκκλησίαι σύγκλητοι.[6] They could be convened at short notice, perhaps because of favourable omens, in accordance with a *psephismos*, or by the board of *strategoi* via the *boule*.[7]

Two decrees from the same period offer an analogy:
- *IG* 2² 838 (226/225 BC) – ἐκκλησί[α ἐν] τῶι θεάτρ[ωι σύγκλητος] κατὰ ψήφισμα ὅ...σιας Θορ[ίκος εἶπεν
- *IG* 2² 945 (168/167 BC) – ἐκκλησία σύγκλητος ἐν τῶι θεάτρωι

The place of the meeting was sometimes mentioned, as in the above examples, but not always. Accordingly, it is proposed we should restore either ἐκκλησία σύγκλητος κατὰ ψήφισμα or even ἐκκλησία κατὰ ψήφισμα βουλῆς. Tracy's restoration has 25 letters. The proposed restorations have 28 and 25 respectively. In any case, the inscription is non-stoichedon, fragmentary, and followed by a *vac.* in line 4, so the exact number of letters is not critical.

Until the discovery of this fragment, it had only been known that Antiochus IV was in Athens at the time when news of his brother's death (2/3 Sept.175 BC) reached him. We now know that Antiochus had been there for some time and that therefore he had been exchanged as a Roman hostage earlier than previously thought.

Antiochus had been despatched to Rome as hostage, a condition of the Treaty of Apamea. His age at this time is uncertain, though if he is to be identified with the Mithridates mentioned in Livy 33.19 and *SEG* XXXVII 859 (Antiochus IV being his later throne name), Antiochus IV was old enough in 197 BC to participate in his father's

---

[1] J. Mikalson, *The Sacred and Civil Calendar of the Athenian Year* (Princeton 1975) 7, 186-193.
[2] Aristophanes *Thesmophoriazousai* 78-80 – 'Neither the tribunals nor the Senate are sitting, for it is the third day of the Thesmophoria'. He also recorded that it was a festival day (Arist. *Thes.* 834).
[3] Tracy, 'Greek Inscriptions', 61.
[4] M. Hansen, 'When did the Athenian Ecclesia meet?' 333.
[5] For the importance of the *kyria ekklesia* see *Ath. Pol.* 43.4-5.
[6] M. Hansen, 'ἐκκλησία σύγκλητος', 149-156.
[7] *Ath. Pol.* 44.4. For such a meeting convened at short notice see Aeschines 3.67.

campaign against Sardis.[8] The length of internment as a Roman hostage was often linked to the payment schedule of the indemnity incurred, with the presence in Rome being a form of coercion in case of default.[9] Interestingly, the Treaty of Apamea specified as one condition the handing over of 20 hostages aged between 18 and 40 with a three-year rotation period. However, the terms of the treaty may not have applied to the principal hostage, namely, the king's son, for it appears that Antiochus IV, as the son of the defeated Antiochus III, was to be held for 12 years. Moreover, if one does not accept his identification with Mithridates, he may also have been under the minimum age of 18, when handed over.

The Treaty of Apamea[10] was concluded in 188 BC and Antiochus IV handed over to be released presumably in 176 BC when the war indemnity was paid. He was not the eldest son and it would appear that kings in general were reluctant to hand over their heir as this afforded Rome too great a role in the education and character formation of the future king, not to mention the suspicion it raised at home as to the loyalty of the hostage. We know very little of Antiochus IV's experience whilst a hostage. Though his presence in Rome was an instrument of coercion, the hostage was not necessarily deprived of customary comforts, be it a house provided at public expense in the case of Antiochus IV (Asconius, *Pis*. 13.16-17) or the freedom of movement and financial resources afforded Demetrius I (Polybius 31.14.3 and Diodorus Sic. 31.18). Even so, Mittag argues that the hostage's experience was negative, though it did afford him the opportunity to appreciate the cultural and social differences between Rome and the Hellenistic kingdoms.[11]

Antiochus III died in July 187 BC in a raid on the temple of Bel in Elymais (i.e. trying to raise funds to meet the heavy Roman indemnity) and was succeeded by Antiochus IV's elder full-brother, Seleucus IV.[12] This compromised somewhat the collateral value of the principal hostage. However, Antiochus remained a hostage until 178 BC (for 10 years in total) when he was replaced by Seleucus IV's son, the future Demetrius I Soter, when the latter was about 12 years old. The change of hostages at this point in time was probably sought by Rome (contra Appian, *Syr*. 45) as a result of the growing fear of an

---

[8] See discussion in P.F. Mittag, *Antiochus IV*, 34-35.
[9] J. Allen, *Hostages and Hostage-Taking*, 14, 38-66. Beside the collateral value of hostages, they played an important symbolic function as trophies of the general's victory (pp. 95-125).
[10] Polybius 21.17.3-8, Livy 37.45.11-18, Diodorus Sic. 29.10, and Appian, *Syr*., 38. For a more positive appraisal of the treaty for the Seleucid Empire, see E.S. Gruen, *The Hellenistic World and the Coming of Rome*, 643.
[11] Mittag, *Antiochus IV*, 37, 39, and M.G. Morgan, 'The Perils of Schematism', 54. Cf. also Allen, *Hostages*, 33, 144-145 and 149-167. The system was thought to civilize and Romanize the hostage and as such played a role in imperial politics. Polybius and more particularly Livy are well-known for their portrayals of Antiochus IV's adoption of Roman habits. But Allen contests this, advocating instead that he 'pursued an independent, even aggressive, foreign policy' (p. 166) and was not a 'lackey of the empire' (p. 168). Cf. also Gruen, *The Hellenistic World*, 648-650. That Polybius for his own schematic reasons misrepresented Antiochus IV's intentions in the Sixth Syrian War and misunderstood the day of Eleusis, when Popillius Laenas drew a circle in the sand and gave his famous ultimatum to the king, see Morgan, 'The Perils of Schematism', 37-76.
[12] J.D. Grainer, *Seleukid Prosopography*, 22.

alignment between Perseus of Macedon and Seleucus IV. Various evidence for this is sought: (a) the naming of Seleucus IV's first-born son, Demetrius, as Mørkholm notes 'an ominous deviation from a long established Seleucid practice of using only the names Antiochus and Seleucus for heirs to the throne' and a name with 'an obvious Macedonian connotation';[13] (b) Seleucus IV's initial, though fickle, intention to aid Pharnaces of Pontus in his war with Pergamum, a Roman ally; and (c) the marriage of Seleucus IV's daughter, Laodice, to Perseus, the king of Macedon and chief antagonist of Rome. As Mittag observes: 'Der Sohn des Königs war im Zweifelsfall ein besseres Druckmittel als der Bruder'.[14]

The release of Antiochus IV from hostage may have presented a problem, as he had been away from Antioch for a decade and his presence back home may have been unwanted. Indeed, Mittag suggests that Seleucus IV would have had little interest in taking in his brother. Athens, therefore, suggested itself as the better option; it was the cultural centre of the Hellenistic world; it was politically neutral; good relations existed between Athens and the Seleucid kings; and it afforded a good departure point for Antioch, should the need arise.[15] How Antiochus was able to support himself in Athens is unknown, though it is assumed his finances could not have been extensive in view of the support extended by Eumenes II (king of Pergamum) that enabled his return to take up the throne. The alliance between Antiochus IV and Eumenes II was of course in the interests of both parties. Indeed, the very political moves that, as suggested above, led Rome to ask for Antiochus IV's replacement with Demetrius I, also prompted Eumenes II to seek a more friendly monarch on the Seleucid throne, one who would not court involvement with Macedonia. On the other hand, the support of Eumenes was essential to Antiochus IV's attempt to attain the crown.[16]

Seleucus IV was killed by his chief minister Heliodorus on 2/3 Sept. 175 BC and news of the accession of Antiochus IV had reached Babylon by 22/23 Oct. 175 BC, a period of approximately one month and twenty days.[17] As all agree, this is perhaps too short a period for (a) news of the death to reach Athens and Pergamum respectively, (b) an offer of help to be sent from Eumenes II to Antiochus IV in Athens, and (c) Antiochus to make his way through Pergamum to Antioch. Various solutions to alleviate step (b) suggest themselves, e.g. a previous understanding between the parties for such a course of action or the presence in Athens of a Pergamene delegation authorized to initiate the travel arrangements. Be that as it may, Antiochus' long absence meant that he would have little connection with the political power structures within the Seleucid Empire. He therefore appears to have sought a quick accommodation with his brother's supporters

---

[13] O. Mørkholm, *Antiochus IV*, 34.
[14] Mittag, *Antiochus IV*, 40. Demetrius was to remain a hostage beyond the time when the indemnity was paid off (by 173 BC) and indeed even after the death of Antiochus IV himself (164 BC), as it served the geopolitical interests of Rome to keep a youth (the young son of Antiochus IV) on the Seleucid throne rather than to permit Demetrius to return. In the end Demetrius, after failing in his requests to the senate to be released (Polybius 31.2.5-6), escaped Rome in 162 BC and returned home to claim the throne.
[15] Mittag, *Antiochus IV*, 41.
[16] Mittag, *Antiochus IV*, 42-44.
[17] Mittag, *Antiochus IV*, 44-45.

which was then given expression in his marriage to the widow, Laodice, and adoption of his nephew and heir to the throne.

Bibliography

J. **Allen**, *Hostages and Hostage-Taking in the Roman Empire* (Cambridge 2006); J.D. **Grainer**, *A Seleukid Prosopography and Gazetteer* (Leiden 1997); E.S. **Gruen**, *The Hellenistic World and the Coming of Rome* (Berkeley 1984); M. **Hansen**, 'ἐκκλησία σύγκλητος in Hellenistic Athens', *GBRS* 20/2 (1979) 149-156; M. **Hansen**, 'When did the Athenian Ecclesia meet?' *GBRS* 23/4 (1982) 333; J. Mikalson, *The Sacred and Civil Calendar of the Athenian Year* (Princeton 1975); P.F. **Mittag**, *Antiochus IV. Epiphanes. Eine politische Biographie* (Berlin 2006); M.G. **Morgan**, 'The Perils of Schematism: Polybius, Antiochus Epiphanes and the "Day of Eleusis"', *Historia* 39 (1990) 37-76; O. **Mørkholm**, *Antiochus IV of Syria* (Copenhagen 1966).

G. Davis and S.R. Llewelyn (Macquarie University)

§15 A Governor transmits an Imperial Privilege

Aezani (Phrygia)　　　　　　Marble slab　　　　　　c. 17 BC
　　　　　　　　49 x 148 (till broken) x 29cm

Ed. pr. — B. Levick, S. Mitchell, J. Potter and M. Waelkens (eds), *Monumenta Asiae Minoris Antiqua, Vol. IX. Monuments from the Aezanitis recorded by C.W.M. Cox, A. Cameron, and J. Cullen* (Journal of Roman Studies Monographs, 4; London 1988) (= *MAMA* IX 13).

The inscription is on a grey-white marble slab with the letters worn and very faint, often traceable only from discolouration of stone. It was found in a court in Yagdigin, Turkey, and was said to have been brought 20 years previously from the necropolis of Aezani.

ἐκ Περγάμου	From Pergamum
Γαῖος Νώρβανος Φλάκκος ἀνθύπατος Αἰζανειτῶν	C. Norbanus Flaccus, proconsul, to the
ἄρχουσι βουλῆι δήμωι χαίρειν.	archons, boule and demos of the Aezanites, greeting.
Μενεκλῆς καὶ Ἱέραξ καὶ Ζήνων οἱ πρεσβευταὶ ὑμῶν	Menekles, Hierax and Zenon, your ambassadors
5 ἀνέδωκάν μοι Σεβαστοῦ Καίσαρος ἐπιστολὴν ἐν ἧι	have delivered to me a letter of Augustus Caesar in which
ἐγέγραπτο· συνεχώρηκεν ἀσυ[λ]ί̣α̣[ν καὶ ἀ]λησίαν	it had been written: he had conceded right of asy[lum and inviol]ability...
...	...
... συνχωρησ ...	... concede ...
πόλιν. ἐγὼ οὖν συναύξειν βουλό[μενο]ς [τὰ φ]ιλ[άνθρω-]	city. I therefore wish[ing] to augment [the im]mu[ni]ties ...
10 πα [τῆς π]όλεως ὑμῶν ἐπιτρέπω κατὰ τὸ [ἐπίκρ]ιμ̣α̣	of your city entrust according to the [decr]ee
τοῦ Καίσαρος ...	of [Caesar ...]

There is disagreement in the scholarship about which Norbanus Flaccus is the proconsul mentioned in the inscription. There are four Norbani Flacci mentioned in the consular *fasti* – the consul of 83 BC, the consul of 38 BC, the consul of 24 BC and the consul of AD 15. The eldest Norbanus Flaccus is believed to have been a *novus homo*, who was proscribed after Sulla's victory over his patron Marius,[1] and thus too old to have been the proconsul mentioned in our inscription.[2] Conversely, the consul of AD 15 is considered too young for the role. The consul of 38 BC is believed to be the son of the elder Norbanus Flaccus, and to have been praetor in 43 BC, and proconsul in Spain

---

[1] R.J. Evans, 'Norbani Flacci', 121.
[2] Evans, 'Norbani Flacci', 123-124.

between 36 and 34 BC, for which he received a triumph.[3] It is debated whether the consul of 24 BC is this consul receiving a second consulship or is the son of this consul.[4] The main argument for a second consulship is that there is only a fourteen-year gap between the two consulships, which is abnormally fast — usually there was a gap of twice that length between the consulships of fathers and sons.[5] However, this argument is complicated by the fact that there are two entries in the *fasti* for the consul of 24 BC, one with C. NO(- - - -) FLACCVS COS . . . (break in the stone), the other with (- - - -) BANO FLAC COS,[6] for no second consulship is indicated in the record despite the fact that there is sufficient space. No other details are known about the consul of 24 BC, except that he was honoured by sharing the consulship for that whole year with Augustus.[7]

Our inscription cannot be securely dated. Older authorities such as A.H.M Jones[8] have traditionally favoured an earlier date, in the early 20s BC, while more recent authorities believe that the letter was sent to Norbanus in 20-10 BC. Atkinson sets forth a convincing argument, claiming that Norbanus had to have been in Asia after the settlement of 23 BC,[9] based on a letter in Josephus by the proconsul to the people of Sardis, in which Augustus 'commands'[10] Norbanus Flaccus to ensure that the rights of the Jewish population are not infringed upon. Augustus would not have possessed the right to issue orders in a senatorial province until after 23 BC. Atkinson also believes that Augustus would not have issued such an order while Agrippa was 'exercising his proconsulare imperium'[11] in the East in 23-22 BC and 16-13 BC, or during his own tour of the eastern provinces in 21-19 BC.[12] Thus our inscription's likely *terminus post quem* is in the period after 23/22 BC.

Since the letter in Josephus makes no mention of Augustus' edict to the province of Asia, dated to 13/12 BC (the *terminus ante quem*), regarding the rights of Jews in that province, Norbanus' proconsulship must have preceded that decree. Therefore his proconsulship must have fallen between 19 and 16 BC. The Norbanus Flaccus who was consul in 24 thus appears to be the far more likely candidate. If we follow Dio's statement that there was a minimum five-year interval between the proconsulship and provincial governorship,[13] then the consulship of Norbanus Flaccus in Asia, and thus the letter recorded in our inscription, can be dated to 18/17 or 17/16 BC.[14]

---

[3] Evans, 'Norbani Flacci', 123.
[4] Evans, 'Norbani Flacci', 127.
[5] Evans, 'Norbani Flacci', 124.
[6] Fasti Cap. Cons. (*Inscrip. Ital.* 13.1, 59) C. NO(- - - -) FLACCVS (break in the stone); Fasti Fer. Latin. (ibid., p. 150f) (- - - -)BANO FLAC COS., line 10, cf. line 1, AGRIPPA COS. III, line 4, TAVRO COS. II; cf. *CIL* 6(1).2014, cited in Evans, 'Norbani Flacci', 127.
[7] Evans, 'Norbani Flacci', 126.
[8] A.H.M. Jones, 'The Imperium of Augustus', 113, n. 8.
[9] K.M.T. Atkinson, 'The Governors of the Province Asia', 322.
[10] Josephus, *A.J.* 16.171.
[11] Atkinson, 'Governors', 322.
[12] Atkinson, 'Governors', 323.
[13] Dio 53.14.
[14] Atkinson, 'Governors', 322.

Despite the damage to the inscription, it is clear that the inscription was put up by the proconsul Norbanus Flaccus in response to a letter sent to him by Augustus granting or confirming a right held by the citizens of the city. A clearer picture is afforded to us by our literary sources. Norbanus Flaccus as proconsul of Asia is mentioned by two Jewish sources — Josephus and Philo. There are two references to Norbanus in Josephus; one records his message to the people of Sardis (mentioned above) reminding them of the rights of Jews to assemble together and to send money to the Temple in Jerusalem.[15] The other is a reference to Norbanus Flaccus' letter to the people of Ephesus, in which he states that Augustus has reconfirmed these same rights.[16] Philo also records this letter to Ephesus in his work, *On the Embassy to Gaius*.[17] It has therefore been assumed that our inscription also deals with non-interference in the performance of Jewish practices.

It can be assumed from the continued appeals from the province of Asia that the rights of Jewish inhabitants to congregate and to send money to the Temple at Jerusalem continued to be refused at a local level. These Jews, however, did seem to have the support of the Roman administration to maintain their religious practices, that in part helped distinguish them from their 'pagan' neighbours. Of interest is the possibility that the letter cited by Josephus derives from an inscription similar to the one above, set up by its Jewish beneficiaries in Sardis.

Bibliography

K.M.T. **Atkinson**, 'The Governors of the Province Asia in the Reign of Augustus', *Historia* 7 (1958) 300-330; R.J. **Evans**, 'Norbani Flacci: The Consuls of 38 and 24 B.C.', *Historia* 36 (1987) 121-128; A.H.M. **Jones**, 'The Imperium of Augustus', *JRS* 41 (1951) 112-119; T. **Rajak**, 'Was there a Roman Charter for the Jews?' *JRS* 74 (1984) 107-123.

B. Sanderson (Macquarie University)

---

[15] Josephus, *A.J.* 16.171.
[16] Josephus, *A.J.* 16.166.
[17] Philo, *On the Embassy to Gaius*, 315.

§16 Customs Law of the Roman Province of Asia (*lex portorii Asiae*)

Ephesus Marble stele 75 BC – AD 62
2.82 x 1.44 x 0.305m

Edd. pr. — H. Engelmann and D. Knibbe, 'Das Monumentum Ephesenum: Ein Vorbericht', *EA* 8 (1986) 19-32; 'Das Zollgesetz der Provinz Asia: Eine neue Inschrift aus Ephesos', *EA* 14 (1989) 1-206 (text, commentary and translation). Cf. also *SEG* XXXVI 1027, p. 304; H.W. Pleket, *SEG* XXXIX 1180, pp. 367-387 (both text and commentary); C. Nicolet, *AÉ* 1989 [1992] 681, pp. 214-222; J.L. Ferrary, *AÉ* 1991 [1994] 1501, pp. 411-414 (summary); D. Knibbe, '*Lex portorii Asiae*', *JÖAI* 69 (2000) 147-173 (reconstructed original Latin version) (= *SEG* XXXIX 1180).

In 1976, the year from which the *New Docs* project began to report (cf. preface of *New Docs* 1, iv), a remarkable inscription was recovered from the ruins of Ephesus, which, to this day, has never been included or commented upon in this series. Since its discovery, the inscription itself has drawn a great deal of attention from both epigraphists and Roman historians, though it has generally not received much consideration from students of the NT. The aim of this entry is to remedy the lacuna by highlighting the importance of the inscription for a better understanding of the social world of the Roman Empire, and its administrative organisation in particular. The timing seems all the more opportune now that a magnificent critical edition has been released in the *Oxford Studies in Ancient Documents* (*OSAD*) series (Cottier et al.), a work which will no doubt remain an authoritative reference for many years to come and upon which we shall herein rely heavily.

This new publication (5th title in the series), and the series in general (which began in the year 2003; cf. bibliography), is a welcome development that invites appraisal in several respects. First of all, it represents the combined effort of experts in the field: A. Bowman and A. Cooley, the general editors, as well as M. Cottier, M.H. Crawford, B.M. Levick, O. Salomies, F.G.B. Millar and N. Purcell, to mention a few of the more familiar names, have all participated in colloquium consultations since 1999 and/or contributed to the final edition. Secondly, it comes in a much more accessible format than earlier publications. Thus, the first section of the book displays on the left page the reconstituted Greek text along with a detailed *apparatus criticus*, while on the right-hand side can be found an English translation and Knibbe's version of what *might have been* the original Latin text drafted in Rome (a speculative, but nonetheless suggestive task, which may help elucidate the rather literal, and therefore often awkward, Greek translation of the Latin original; cf. Knibbe, *lex*; *SEG* XXXIX 1180). The second section of the book provides a detailed and comprehensive (line-by-line) commentary to assist the non-expert. This is then followed by the stimulating articles of S. Mitchell, M. Corbier, G.D. Rowe, D. Rathbone and O. van Nijf., who illustrate how this document sharpens our understanding of the geographical, administrative, and social features of the province of Asia under the Julio-Claudians.

In what follows we shall simply offer a synopsis of the inscribed text, emphasising important details when necessary. We shall then focus on two small excerpts which illustrate how this inscription may help us gain some insight into the social world of the first Christian communities of Asia Minor.

Physical description and synopsis of the *lex portorii Asiae* (= *l.p.A.*)

Monumentum Ephesenum

The *monumentum Ephesenum* (the generally-agreed designation for the physical object) consists of a large, somewhat rectangular, slab (2.82 x 1.44 x 0.305 m) of 'white crystalline marble with light beige to blue-grey shading and some inconspicuous veins of quartz' (Cottier et al., 16). It was found lying face-down in the central aisle near the southern entrance of the church of St. John in Selçuk, where it had initially served as an ambo plate.[1] The damage to the stone is unfortunately rather extensive (most of the bottom section is missing), and S. Mitchell has estimated that a good quarter of the remainder of the text may have been lost (approximately 40 letters from each of the first 24 lines). This naturally renders the text intractable and irretrievable at times. According to the original editors, the stele could have been as high as 3.15 m, with an estimated width of 1.47 m, and was most likely part of a pilaster or a base of some sort (the reverse side being too rough for the stone to have been free-standing). The lettering is simple, clear and consistent, though partially or completely eroded on the surface in many places. Ligatures are frequently employed (*NH, HN, MH, ME, NE, HM, NT* being the most common), in particular in the first section of the stone or in the second half of the line, where space is often left to allow for a neat syllabic or word division. The number of letters per line is irregular, varying between 107 and 126 (probably because the stone was trimmed on the left-hand side). Syntactical breaks are either indicated by a small uninscribed space, or a more customary triangular punctuation mark, while the beginning of a new paragraph is usually signalled by a larger initial letter. Overall, it appears that the *lapidarius* was a rather scrupulous and fairly accurate copyist.

Praescriptum (AD 62) and original text of the l.p.A. (120s BC?)

The inscribed text itself comprises 64 paragraphs and 154 lines. It begins with a *praescriptum* (*ll*. 1-7) dating from the 9th of July AD 62, when the 'records of the *curatores* of the public revenues' were 'copied and checked' in the Julian Basilica in Rome, in order to be translated, inscribed on stone, and placed in Ephesus, the principal port of Asia (Cottier et al., 3). The first 30 paragraphs (or 72 lines) consist of the core clauses of the *lex* on dues for imports and exports in and out of the province of Asia by land or sea (cf. *l.* 7: νόμος τέλους Ἀσίας εἰσαγωγῆς καὶ ἐξαγωγῆς κατά τε γῆν καὶ κατὰ θάλασσαν), which seem to have been decreed in the 120s BC (Cottier et al., 8-10).

---

[1] This explains why its left-hand side has been slightly cut back to form a curved edge; see photographs online at: http://www.csad.ox.ac.uk/lex-portorii/.

§16 Customs Law of the Roman Province of Asia (*lex portorii Asiae*)

The *lex* stipulates precisely the customs rates (a 'fortieth part' or 2.5% for most goods; 5% for murex; no more than 5 denarii per slave, which was later lowered to 2.5 denarii from 17 BC onwards; cf. *ll.* 10-12, 20, 98), and establishes that customs dues on the same goods should be paid only once (cf. *l.* 16: ὑπὲρ οὗ ἄν τις πράγματος ἅπαξ < ... τῆς εἰσαγωγῆς τέλος διδότω>). It enforces customs declaration and registration of any merchandise with the collector or procurator (cf. *ll.* 13-15: τῶι τελώνηι ἢ ἐπιτρόπωι), or if neither is available, with the highest local authority (*ll.* 40-42: μεγίστη ἀρχή). It fixes the amount of the penalties incurred for tax-evasion through fraudulent declaration or failure to register: the entire merchandise is to be seized, although, if the appropriate *telos* is paid by the merchant within two days, the collector can grant the merchandise to be redeemed (*in integrum restitutio*, *ll.* 21, 45-47, 50-58.[2] Later in 72 BC, it would be decided that the fraudster ought to pay *telos* on double the amount of what has been deceitfully declared (*l.* 87).

The *lex* also gives the geographic location of the various customs offices throughout the province of Asia (e.g., Calchedon, Apollonia, Ephesus, Priene, Miletus, etc.; cf. *ll.* 22-26).[3] It determines the site and size of the customs registration posts (ἐποίκιον; a temple or sacred precinct, τέμενος, was unsuitable; the building needed to be 30 feet in length and width, etc.; cf. *ll.* 31-35, 50-58); it limits the number of customs guard-posts (παραφυλακή) as one per harbour, as well as restricts their distance from each other (no less than 80 stades; *ll.* 32-38 & 71). Finally, it gives details on the registration procedure and modalities of payment (*ll.* 42-57), and defines what are valid grounds for tax exemption (e.g., soldiers, sailors, *publicani*, *politeiai*, or peoples with special imperial privileges, were all exempt; materials for public or religious purposes, as well as goods for private use or travel purposes, could not be taxed; cf. *ll.* 58-65, 74-78, 83, 88-98, 128-133).

Addenda to the l.p.A. (75 BC – AD 62)

This first series of clauses is then followed by a long second section (*ll.* 72 ff.) recording the various amendments to the initial *lex*, which were legislated by the various consuls and (three) Neronian curators from 75 BC to AD 62.[4] Significantly, there is a noticeable gap in legislation between 72 and 17 BC, a period which was characterized (for a good part) by a certain political instability. The new modification implemented in 17 BC is thus a good indicator of renewed political stability under Augustus, who had now time to turn his attention to provincial matters such as the *l. p. A.* (cf. *ll.* 88-103).

---

[2] The formula '*in integrum restitutio*' means to restore it to the former legal '*status quo*', thereby rendering the 'offending transaction null and void' — Crook, 117; cf. Berger, 682.

[3] Not all of these places remained in the province of Asia by AD I. This is explained by the fact that the list of cities was first drafted in the 120s BC, but was never revised subsequently. Cf. Mitchell in Cottier et al., 165-201.

[4] It is significant that, with the possible exception of *ll.* 84-88, no censor is mentioned in the *l. p. A.*, which is somewhat surprising as censors were generally in charge of selling or leasing tax-farming concessions. Cf. Cottier et al., 5-7 & 135; Brunt, *Publicans*, 360, n. 18; Nicolet, *portorium*, 951, n. 49 (= Nicolet, *Censeurs*, 380).

The text then continues in typical tralatician manner, reiterating the main clauses of the *lex* concerning the period of the lease and the requirements for sureties from the *publicani*, without necessarily introducing new amendments (this tralatician style is reinforced by the repetitive use of the formula, τὰ λοιπὰ κατὰ τὸν [αὐτὸν] νόμον [ἑκάστου ἔτους], at the conclusion of each clause; cf. *ll.* 105, 108, 112, etc.). Interestingly, the *addenda* legislated in 12, 7 and 2 BC, took effect at a five-year interval, which matches the usual period for the lease of tax collection which is mentioned in the text (cf. *ll.* 108, 112, etc.), and which suggests that the *lex* was reassessed before being reconducted or modified at the end of each lease term. It is beyond the scope of this entry to review in further detail the nature and ramifications of these modifications, as well as the internal chronology of the *lex* or its actual origin — two hotly debated issues amongst Roman historians (cf. Cottier et al., 8-10). Suffice it to refer the reader to the instructive introduction and essays in the *OSAD* edition for further information.

Additional sources to consider in conjunction with the l.p.A.

As the *OSAD* editors advise, it may be helpful to examine the *l. p. A.* in conjunction with the following four documents (for full bibliography, see Cottier, et al., 11-12):
- Trajan's republication of three *senatus consulta* on the exemption of customs dues at Ephesus (*SEG* XXXI 952; cf. I. Eph. 4101; Knibbe, *Ephesos*; Bringmann).
- Hadrian's legislation on customs dues at Caunus (*SEG* XIV 639).
- An inscription on customs regulation at Myra, *c.* AD 120s (I. Kaunos, pp. 200-215).
- The *lex Antonia de Termessibus*, *ll.* 31-36, 68 (?) BC (Crawford, *RS* 1, 331-340, §19).

To this list we may add the following inscriptions, which detail precisely customs or toll fees for various items:
- The customs tariff of Zarai in the province of Africa, AD 202 (*CIL* VIII 4508; cf. Lewis & Reinhold, 146).
- The Koptos tariff, AD 90 (*OGIS* II 674; *IGRR* I 1183; cf. Lewis & Reinhold, 147).
- The tax law of Palmyra, AD 137 (*CIS* II.3.1 3913; *IGRR* III 1056; *OGIS* II 629; well covered by Teixidor; Matthews; Levick, 95-101).

Function and significance of the *lex portorii Asiae*

Significance

As we have already noted, this inscription is remarkable and significant in several respects. First of all, as the *OSAD* editors rightly emphasise, it is unique in that,

> [a]s an aggregate of regulations developed over time, the Customs Law is the most substantial and significant corpus of surviving documents [see above] that offer information both about imperial and local customs dues and their development in the Late Republic and Empire, and about the relations between the *publicani* who exacted the taxes and Roman officials and the *Aerarium Saturni* [the public treasury in the temple of Saturn in Rome]. (Cottier, et al., *Customs Law*, 2)

§16 Customs Law of the Roman Province of Asia (*lex portorii Asiae*) 99

Furthermore, it gives us a diachronic perspective on the development of the legal policies and administrative institutions of the Roman government at a critical time of transition between the Hellenistic and Roman eras. Composed under the Principate of Nero, the final form of the text itself provides important data on his reforms of the taxation system amidst intense popular resentment towards the *publicani* — itself a fairly common sentiment throughout the Republican and imperial periods.[5]

> The *societates publicanorum* originally consisted predominantly of *equites* who, at the end of the Republic, lost the supervision of the collection of **direct taxes** to the benefit of imperial slaves or freedmen (generally working under the direction of *equestrian* procurators), or other city officials, due to recurrent conflicts with censors and the senate.[6] The reforms of Caesar and Augustus however did not really affect the collection of **indirect taxes** such as customs dues, which remained the responsibility of the *publicani*.[7]

Purpose

The main purpose of the *lex* itself is rather obvious. As it plainly states in its *praescriptum*, it concerns the exaction of customs dues by *publicani*, or δημοσιῶναι in Greek (*ll*. 1-7).[8] Its function was thus to display publicly the legal arrangements regarding *portorium* dues, with a view to curb tax-evasion or smuggling by dishonest merchants, a rather common phenomenon (*ll*. 15-16, 21, 47, 50-58; cf. de Laet, 437-446; van Nijf, in Cottier et al., *Customs Law*, 291-293), as well as keep the *publicani* under control. Benefitting from somewhat opaque legislation and loose regulations, the *publicani* in general had little scruple in making abusive, if not illegal, claims on the populace.[9] As Cicero explains, on top of the usual customs dues some *publicani* would enforce additional fees for the search of the cargo (*pro spectatione*), for the exchange of currency (*pro collybo*), or for some other obscure administrative purpose (i.e., *pro cerario*, a 'wax-fee'; Cic. *Verr.* II.3.105ff., III.78.181; cf. Tac. *Ann.* XIII.51; de Laet, *Portorium*, 121). This type of financial extortion and maladministration was not restricted to the *publicani*, however, and there is plenty of evidence that corruption and rapacious attitudes affected the Roman administration on a much broader scale, including the equestrian or senatorial orders, even during the Principate — hence the need for a *repetundae* law on behalf of the *peregrini* (cf. Brunt, *Maladministration*, 53-95; *OCD*, 1308). A certain proportion of the emperors' assets had actually been acquired through *bona damnatorum* (as well as *bona caduca* and *vacantia*), that is, through

---

[5] Cf. Tac. *Ann.* XIII.50ff.; Cic. *Q fr.* I.1.33; Vell. Pat. II.92.2; *Cod. Ius.* IV 62.4 [Constantine]. Cf. also Rathbone in Cottier et al., 251-278; Brunt, *Publicans*, 357-360.
[6] Tac. *Ann.* VI.3; Livy, XLIII.16.1ff; cf. Badian, 26-47; Brunt, *Publicans*, 355-354, 388-393; Nicolet, *Censeurs*, 297-319; Youtie, 564-567; Levick, §§16, 17, 66, 67, 70.
[7] *Equites* seem to have become less involved over time, while [private] *conductores* became progressively more prominent among these *societates*. Cf. Badian, 41-43; de Laet, 398ff.; Brunt, *Publicans*, 354-432; Brunt in Jones, 180-185; Levick, §67.
[8] On the basis of *ll*. 72-74, it was initially suggested by the *edd. pr.* that the *lex* might also be regulating the *decuma* (grain tithe) and *scriptura* (tax on pasture lands), but this hypothesis has been persuasively refuted by Nicolet, *dimes*.
[9] Cf. P. Princ. 2.20; P. Amh. 2.77; *Dig.* 39.4.12; Livy, XLV 18.4: '*ubi publicanus esset, ibi aut ius publicum vanum aut libertatem sociis nullam esse*'; cf. de Laet, 58, 79-84, 437-452; van Nijf in Cottier et al., 281-297; Reinmuth.

confiscations of properties of persons rightly or wrongly condemned on criminal charges.[10]

In our text, the misconduct of the *publicani* is clearly inferred from *l.* 16, where it is stressed that no one is to pay customs dues more than once (cf. *ll.* 120-121). Similarly, in *l.* 28 the collectors are reminded that their building ought to display clearly its function 'without wrongful deceit' (χωρὶς δόλου πονηροῦ, the equivalent in Greek of *dolo malo*). The stipulations regarding the location and dimensions of customs offices also appear to be restrictive measures aimed at preventing the *publicani* from collecting customs dues anywhere they fancied, or perhaps from taxing the same goods several times in different locations (cf. *ll.* 31-38, 50-58).[11] Later, in *ll.* 78-81, a clause prohibits the *publicani* from holding up vessels containing ore and destined for Rome, lest they be required to pay double the amount on what has been held up.

This is then followed by a long tralatician series of amendments specifically aimed at clarifying the legal details of the tax-farming lease. Starting with two *addenda* in 17 BC (*ll.* 99-103), the *publicani* are reminded (for the first time in the *lex*) of their obligation to pay the lump sum by the due date (i.e., on the Ides of the same month on which they had originally contracted the lease, in the following year), in accordance with the *lex*, as well as to provide securities for their contract with *praedes* and *praedia*, viz., sureties, which from 7 BC amounted up to five times that of the *uectigal* (*ll.* 110-112, 124-126, 144-147; cf. Brunt, *Publicans*, 361). Most of the changes made to the original *lex* thus mainly concern the length of the lease, the amount of their sureties, the date for the down-payment, or the appointment of a new *magister* to manage the lease, which clearly gives the impression that the primary purpose of the *lex* was to allow the imperial administration to reassert some kind of legal and financial control over the *publicani*.

The *lex* intriguingly concludes with fragmented clauses regarding legal suits conducted against the *publicani* (*ll.* 150-153) and the adjudication of disputes between, presumably, *publicani* and defrauded merchants before Nero's procurator (cf. *ll.* 115-117, and 147-149, where the reading is uncertain as neither *publicani* nor *peregrini* appear: ἐάν τις ἀμφισβήτησις γένηται μεταξὺ ΤΑΥ[---] [± 42] ἐπιτρόπωι Νέρωνος Σεβαστοῦ τῶι τῆς ἐπαρχείας ἀφηγουμένωι). Although the details of these disputes and Nero's attempted resolution remain uncertain, this nonetheless confirms the certain embarrassment the imperial administration experienced *vis-à-vis* the conduct of the *publicani* (*ll.* 115-117).[12] Interestingly, the tax law of Palmyra states quite similarly that disputes between traders and customs 'officers' constituted the main reason for the public display of a 4.80 m wide inscription detailing the *lex* and its relevant fees.[13]

---

[10] Millar, 163-174.

[11] Cottier et al., 120-121.

[12] The objective of Nero's reform simply seems to have been to empower the local procurator to adjudicate such disputes immediately for the sake of expedience, rather than let travellers appeal to the *praetor peregrinus* in Rome; cf. Brunt, *Publicans*, 360; Nicolet, *portorium*, 945, n. 35; cf. Levick, 101-102.

[13] Cf. preamble of the *lex*, panel 1; for other examples of such disputes caused by *publicani*, see Rostovtzeff, 689, n. 100.

In conclusion, this *lex* allows us to appreciate two different social points of view, that of the imperial government and that of its subjects. As the *OSAD* editors indeed explain:

> The first perspective is reflected ... in Roman concern for the smooth working of the system of taxation through the employment of *publicani*, whose obligations ... are carefully regulated, and for the integrity of military arrangements — for the free passage of war materials, soldiers, and their equipment. As to the second point of view, restrictions on the conduct of *publicani*, mentioned long after the original establishment of the system, may well be responses to complaints from subjects; indeed, the existence of the entire document may be seen in that light. (Cottier et al., 2)

The χάρις of Augustus (*l.* 92)

92 [... εἴ τε] τούτων τῶν διοικήσεων πόλεις, ἔθνη, δῆμοι νόμωι ἢ δήμου κυρώσει ἢ συγκλήτου δόγματι ἢ χάρι<τι> Αὐτοκράτορος Καίσαρος Σεβαστοῦ δημαρ-

[... and whichever] cities, nations, (or) peoples, of these dioceses (or *conuentus*) [mentioned in *ll.* 88-91], by law, or by decision of the people, or by decree of the senate (*senatus consultum*), or by the χάρις of Imperator Caesar Augustus,

93 [χικῆς ἐξου]σίας, ἵνα μή[τε ἐν]τος τῶν ἰδίων ὅρων τέλος διδῶσιν μήτε ἐντος τῶν ἰδίων ὅρων πορρώτερον σταδίων ὀκτὼ παραφυλακὴν ἔχωσιν ...

endowed with tribunician power, in order that they should neither pay the tax [within] their own boundaries nor have a guard-post further than eight stades within their own boundaries ...

96 ... οἱ

... The

97 [αὐτοὶ προσέθηκ]αν· ὧν πραγμάτων Οὐηδίωι Πωλλίωνι συγκλήτου δόγματι ἀτέλεια δέδοται, ὅσῳ ἂν πλεῖον δηναρίων μυρίων, τούτων τῶν πραγμάτων τὸ

[same (consuls) added]: for whichever affairs exemption has been granted to Vedius Pollio by decree of the senate; by as much as (it is) more than 10,000 denarii, the

98 [τεσσαρακοστὸν μ]έρος τῶι δημοσιώνηι δοθήσεται

[fortieth] part for these things will be paid to the tax-collector.

One of the striking features of this inscription, which presents immediate relevance for the study of the NT, is the expression in *l.* 92: χάρι<τι> Αὐτοκράτος Καίσαρος Σεβαστοῦ.[14] The reader of the NT is naturally very familiar with the term χάρις, which is a favourite of Paul (he uses χάρις 97 times, χάρισμα 16 times, etc).[15] Much research has been done on this topic. Yet, as Harrison noted in his introduction, in NT scholarship the concept of χάρις has generally been treated as 'a timeless construct with

---

[14] χάριν was initially, and accurately, read by *ed. pr.*, but has since been corrected by the *OSAD edd.* so as to be more grammatically coherent with the other datives in the sentence, i.e., νόμωι ... κυρώσει ... δόγματι. Although a prepositional usage would be technically possible, χάριν (τινος), i.e., 'for the pleasure/sake of (someone)', it would make no sense here. Cf. also Harrison's four examples listed below.
[15] Cf. Harrison, *Paul's Language*, 2, n. 2.

minimal relevance to the social and theological framework of the Graeco-Roman society'.[16] What Harrison envisaged therefore was the need to conduct 'a thorough investigation of the eastern Mediterranean documentary evidence if the beneficence practised in Paul's house churches is to be accurately addressed in proper context'.[17] This was the embodiment of the oft-repeated plea that we should proceed 'city by city, and institution by institution', in our study of the NT world.[18]

By a rigorous investigation of documentary evidence, Harrison was thus able to clarify the varied semantic domain of χάρις in the Graeco-Roman context, and to propose a more nuanced interpretation of Paul's understanding of it. Based on his survey, he ascertained that χάρις 'functioned as the central term for the "favour" of benefactors towards their dependants'[19] and, in particular, that it enjoyed pride of place in imperial inscriptions to describe the Caesars' beneficence. Harrison adduced at least four telling examples of the use of χάρις,[20] which related to:

- Augustus' imperial benefaction towards Ephesus in the pavement of a road (χάριτι Καίσαρος Σεβαστοῦ θεοῦ; cf. J. & L. Robert, *BE* 5 [1965], §340; post AD 14)
- A grant of immunity from taxation by Claudius to some Egyptians (τοῦ θεοῦ Κλαυδίου χάριτι; *OGIS* 669; AD 68)
- The securing of fishing rights for the people of Istria 'by the grace of the Augusti' ([τῇ] χάριτι τῶν [Σεβαστῶ]ν; *SEG* XXIV 1108)
- The bestowal of free (ἐλεύθερος) and autonomous (αὐτόνομος) status to the people of Aphrodisias 'by the grace of the Augusti' (τῇ τῶν Σε[βασ]τῶν χάριτι; I. Eph. II 233; AD 89-90).

The obvious similarity with the expression found in the *l.p.A.* is particularly striking and strongly suggests a widespread usage of this formula. This fifth example thus confirms Harrison's already persuasive case regarding the language of imperial benefaction, and further demonstrates that, in antiquity, χάρις, imperial χάρις especially, was much more than a mere philosophical or theological abstraction. It was a favourable disposition which manifested itself in concrete action.

This instance indeed offers a vivid illustration of the socio-economic dimension of χάρις in an imperial context, which is herein expressed in the form of a reduced tax rate or a partial immunity from taxation, 'the greatest gift which an emperor could bestow'.[21] According to the *l. p. A.*, politeiai (πολειτεῖαι), nations ([ἔθ]νη), or peoples (δ[ῆμ]οι; cf. *ll.* 88-89), located *outside* (ἔξω; i.e., of 'free' status) or *within* the *formula* of the twelve dioceses (*conuentus* or assizes) of the province of Asia (enumerated in *ll.* 88-90), could only be exempt (partially or totally) from customs dues by *lex* (νόμωι), plebiscite (δήμου κυρώσει), decree of the senate (συγκλήτου δόγματι), or by the χάρις of

---

[16] Harrison, *Paul's Language*, 10; cf. Kittel, *TDNT*, 393-398.
[17] Harrison, *Paul's Language*, 8, n.29
[18] Judge, 'Social Identity', 216; cf. Harrison, *Paul's Language*, 16ff.
[19] Harrison, *Paul's Language*, 47.
[20] Harrison, *Paul's Language*, 48, 52.
[21] Millar, 425; cf. de Laet, 432-435.

§16 Customs Law of the Roman Province of Asia (*lex portorii Asiae*) 103

Augustus (*l.* 92).[22] However, such *beneficium* or *indulgentia* did not necessarily imply that πολειτεῖαι, ἔθνη, or δῆμοι, were everywhere immune from customs dues: it may simply be that they were from a different province, or they could have been required to pay *portoria* according to a different *lex* (cf. *l.* 94).

While this privilege would have certainly been unusual, it was not necessarily without precedent — generally, this was an integral part of the Caesars' politics of benefaction (cf. Veyne; Millar, 133-201). Ulpian, for example, records how in his beneficence (*beneficiis*) Augustus granted the colony of Berytus, from the 'much favoured' province of Syria Phoenice (*provincia gratiosa*), the Italian *ius*, that is, the exceptional right to immunity from *tributum soli* and *tributum capitis* (*Dig*. 50.15.1; cf. EJ 311; Levick, §88). Similarly, Nero could later boast of having freed the entire province of Achaia from taxation dues through his goodwill (εὔνοια) and χάρις (*Syll*.³ 814; *ILS* 8794; *IG* VII 2713; cf. Holleaux); while Trajan would extend the tax-immunity of physicians, teachers, and professors, initially granted by *senatus consultum* in 42 or 39 BC (*SEG* XXXI 952; cf. I. Eph. 4101; Knibbe, *Ephesos*; Bringmann).

For P. Vedius Pollio, the 'opulent, cruel and luxurious', equestrian friend of Augustus,[23] the χάρις of the emperor would be expressed in the form of reduced customs dues for what were shipments presumably (*ll.* 96-97).[24] This favour would not have been negligible for Vedius since he owned wine estates in Campania, Chios and Cos, and exported *grands crus* in Africa and Judea (amphorae bearing the stamp 'PVEPOL' have recently been discovered at Masada, Caesarea, and the Herodion; Finkielsztejn; cf. Kirbihler, 'Rufus', 263-265). The commerce of wine was probably the main source of his fortune, which may have been partly inherited from his father, most likely an equestrian named P. Vedius Rufus. A freedman himself, Rufus had amassed a considerable wealth and had risen through the ranks of Roman society to reach the level of *equites,* serving even once as a military tribune. His rapid social ascension came no doubt through his support of Caesar during the Civil Wars, an alliance which might later explain Vedius' friendship with Augustus (Kirbihler, 'Rufus'). Not much more is known about Vedius that could help explain his partial immunity, and whatever else is known of him has come to us through a less than objective literary tradition which castigated him for his cruel antics—e.g., throwing a slave to his *muraenae*.[25]

What is certain is that Vedius was a powerful equestrian who played a very important administrative role in Asia as a procurator of Augustus, even though he lacked

---

[22] Cf. an almost identical formula in the edict of Cyrene, which also relates to the exemption of financial obligations, but where the language of χάρις is missing: κατὰ νόμον ἢ δόγμα συνκλή<του ἢ> τῶι τοῦ πατρός μου ἐπικρίματι ἢ τῶι ἐμῶι; *SEG* 9, 8; EJ 311; Oliver, *Edict III*; Levick, §88.
[23] Syme, 'Vedius', 23.
[24] On Vedius see *PIR* III, #213, p. 390; *RE* 8A, 568-570; Stein, *RR*, 111; Demougin, §73; for the most complete and up-to-date summary on Vedius see Kirbihler, 'Pollio'; for epigraphic evidence see *IG* II² 4125; *CIL* IX 1703; SEG 40, 1001; I. Ilion 101 = *IGRR* IV 215.
[25] The negative treatment Vedius receives is typical of the aristocratic prejudice towards parvenus. Cf. Dio LIV.23.1; Seneca, *De ira* III.40.2; *De clem.* I.18.2; Pliny, *NH* IX, 78; Tac. *Ann*. I.10; and for a critical assessment of these literary witnesses see Syme, *Vedius*; cf. also Scott.

imperium.²⁶ Vedius eventually became so notorious that coins were minted in his honour in Tralles around the time of his death (*c.* 15 BC) — a very rare privilege for an equestrian.²⁷ A few generations later, the Vedii would be holding important positions all over Asia, but especially in Ephesus were several of them became Asiarchs and *archiereus*.²⁸ Later, in the early AD III, some Flavii Vedii would even be found in Rome entering the senatorial order (Kirbihler, *Vedii*). But before that, right after Actium (i.e. *c.* 31-30 BC), Vedius had been made responsible for implementing a διάταξις (i.e., a *constitutio*) to put in order the finances of Ephesus and the sanctuary of Artemis, on whose precinct stood a newly-built Sebasteion.²⁹ This role seems to have involved curbing corruption in the sale of priesthoods, as well as organising and partly financing the quinquennial games in honour of Augustus. It implies that Vedius played a significant part in establishing the imperial cult in Asia, not only in Ephesus but also in Athens, Ilion, or Didyma, where Sebasteions and inscriptions honouring Vedius have also been found.³⁰ Perhaps then, it was his position as 'a *quasi*-governor of Asia, acting for Augustus and serving as a model for others' that secured him such privilege.³¹ Whatever the case may be, this particular mention nonetheless remains utterly remarkable in that, apart from the consuls responsible for new amendments to the *lex*, Vedius, who is rather informally referred to here, is the only named individual in the entire inscription, a sure sign of his rather 'extraordinary' status as a recipient of Augustus' χάρις.³² Reciprocally, it also highlights Augustus' bountiful munificence towards his faithful friend.

In conclusion, this 'new' evidence unquestionably contributes to our understanding of the socio-economic dimension of χάρις, which expressed itself in the form of tangible, material benefaction. Harrison's remark thus remains extremely pertinent:

> The very one-sidedness of the Julio-Claudian disposal of χάριτες must have been striking to the contemporary observer [as demonstrated in this example]. Rivals were simply not able to compete on the same scale. The early Christians, therefore, could hardly have missed the parallel in their choice of χάρις for the unlimited beneficence of the Covenantal God and his Son.³³

---

[26] Cf. Tac. *Ann.* XII. 60; Grant, *FITA*, 382-383; on the *procuratores Augusti* see Sherwin-White, 'Procurator Augusti'.
[27] Burnett, *RPC* 1, 2634-2635, & n. 2, p. 439; *Cat. Ashmolean*, Tralles 1363; Grant, *FITA*, 382-383; *BMC* §§74 & 76, Lydia, p. 338 ; Atkinson, 283.
[28] The genealogical link with P. Vedius Pollio is not completely certain but very likely, see Kirbihler, 'Rufus'; Kirbihler, 'Vedii'; cf. Kearsley, 'Asiarch', 52, n. 21.
[29] See, e.g. I. Eph. Ia 18; cf. *CIL* III 7124; Smallwood, §380; trans. in Braund, §586; Magie, 545-546; Debord, 211-213; Demougin, §73; Scherrer; Dignas,152, n. 204 & 156, n. 224; Syme, *Revolution*, 410; Grant, *FITA*, 382-383; see also Atkinson who understands διάταξις to mean a 'benevolent fund' [cf. *New Docs* 4, §14, p. 47], but see *CIL* III 7124: *ex constitutione Vedi Pollionis*.
[30] Atkinson; Scherrer; cf. also the dedication of a Caesareum at Beneventum: *CIL* IX 1556 = *ILS* 109.
[31] Cottier et al., 142; cf. Syme, 'Vedius'; Atkinson.
[32] The 17 BC reference of the *beneficium* granted to Vedius was retained in the AD 62 edition so as to establish a legal precedent and limit future concessions; cf. Cottier et al., 218.
[33] Harrison, *Paul's Language*, 49.

Business partnership among the first Christians? (ll. 81 & 119)

78	... ἥτις ἂν γῆ ἐξ Ἀσίας εἰς Ῥώμην κατὰ τὸν γεωρυχικὸν νόμον ἐξάγηται, ὑπὲρ τῆς γῆς ταύτης σκευῶν τε, ἐν οἷς ἂν αὐτὴ ὑπάρχῃ	Whatever ore is exported out of Asia into Rome according to the *lex* concerning the mines, on the vessels containing this ore they are to
79	[τῶι τελώνηι διδ]ότων ἑκατὸν λείτρων ἀσσάρια τέσσαρα. πλεῖον ὑπὲρ τῶν πραγμάτων τούτων τέλος μὴ ὀφειλέσθω. Ἐάν τις ὑπεναντίον τούτοις κατα-	[give to the *publicanus*] four asses for a hundred pounds; (but) more *telos* is not to be owed on these things. If anyone, contrary to these (conditions),
80	[σχῇ ταῦτα τὰ σκεύη] δόλωι πονηρῶι ὥστε τὴν γῆν μὴ παρενεχθῆναι, τότε ὅσον ἂν ἦι κατεσχημένον, τούτου ὁ τελώνης τῶι παρακομίζοντι διπλοῦ ἔνοχος ἔστω	[withholds these vessels] with malicious deceit (*dolo malo*), so that the ore is not carried away, then, as much as has been withheld, of this the *publicanus* shall be liable to the carrier for double (the amount);
81	[καὶ τοῦ χρήματος] τούτου ἐνεχύρου λῆψις ἔστω κοινωνοῖς τοῖς τὰ γεωρύχια ἠργολαβηκόσιν.	[and concerning this matter] there shall be the seizure of a pledge to the κοινωνοί holding the contract for the mines.
117	οἱ αὐτοὶ προσέθηκαν· ὃς ἂν νοουίκιον δοῦλον ἢ δούλην εἰς ἐπαρχείαν Ἀσίαν εἰσάγῃ ἢ ἐξάγῃ, πρὸ[ς]	The same (consuls) added: whoever imports or exports a new male or female slave into the province of Asia is to register himself to
118	[τὸν δημοσιώνην ἢ τὸν ἐπίτ]ροπον αὐτοῦ ἀπογραφέσθω παρὰ τούτωι, ὃς ἂν φανερῶς ἐν τῶι τελωνίωι ἢ προγεγραμμένος, ἐν οἷς ἂν τόποις δημ-	[the *publicanus* or his procurator], with whoever's name is publicly displayed on the customs-office, in whatever location the *publicanus* has
119	[οσιὼν ἐποίκιον ῃ χάριν τ]ελωνίας ὑπάρχῃ καὶ τὸ σῶμα τοῦτο τῆι τῶν κοινωνῶν σφραγεῖδι σφραγισθὲν ἐξαγέτω καὶ εἰσαγέτω ...	[a post for the purpose of] (collecting) *telos*, and he must export or import this slave sealed with the seal of the κοινωνοί.

Another feature which presents some relevance for the NT is the double mention of the term κοινωνοί to refer to the *publicani* who have accepted the contract for the exploitation of the mines (κοινωνοῖς τοῖς τὰ γεωρύχια ἠργολαβηκόσιν, *l*. 81), and those who are involved in what appears to be slave trading (*l*. 119). Although the term δημοσιῶναι used throughout the *lex* to refer to the *publicani* is not employed here, it is almost certain that those who are in view in *l*. 81 are the *publicani* who hold the concession for the mines.[34] The idea implied in any case is certainly that of business partnership or association, which warrants the *OSAD* editors' translation of κοινωνοί as 'partners' (*l*. 81), or *socii* (*l*. 119) — on both occasions Knibbe uses *socius* (i.e., *societatis*) in his Latin version (Knibbe, *lex*, 165 & 170).

Epigraphic evidence from around the same period and the same area further confirms the editors' interpretation. The term appears on two funerary inscriptions from AD I, and each time it refers to *publicani*. In the first instance, it is the question of a certain Publius Curtius who is described as the agent (ἄκτωρ) of the κοινωνοί in charge of collecting the 5% manumission tax (I. Eph. 2245), while the second, bilingual epitaph makes mention of a Felix who is the slave of a man named Primio from the κοιν[ωνοί] of the 'fortieth tax of the harbour of Asia' in Miletus, precisely the customs tax that is described in the *l. p. A.* (*CIL* III 447 + add. *CIL* III 7419; *ILS* 1862; I. Milet. Herrmann II 563 inv. 92; Kearsley, *Imperial Asia*, §40, pp. 31-32). Similar references can be found in three other inscriptions estimated to date from AD I-II (I. Iasos II 416 & 417; *SEG* XXX 1658; Mitford, *ANRW* II, 7.2, p. 1327, n. 177).

But beyond these few inscriptions, there is plenty of other documentary evidence to suggest that the word κοινωνός could be employed to refer to a business associate. As early as IV-III BC we find instances of the term in inscriptions mentioning business partners involved in public works (*IG* XII 9 191), money-lending and land-leasing (I. Eph. 4), or the management of canals (*SEG* XIX 181 & 21, p. 640). A similar usage is found in an Egyptian papyrus from about the same period (c. 259/258 BC, Fayum), which employs κοινωνός as a synonym of μέτοχος, the more customary designation for associate tax-farmers in the papyri (P. Rev. L. 10_{10}, 14_9, 15_2, 18_2, 22_2; on the significance of μέτοχος, see *New Docs* 1, §40). It would appear that neither of these terms lost their business connotation over time, since the author of the Gospel of Luke could resort to a similar collocation to describe the business partnership between Galilean fishermen, *viz.*, Peter and the two brothers John and James, sons of Zebedee (μέτοχος in Lk 5:7; κοινωνός in v. 10). This generally accords with the wider usage of the term κοινωνός in the papyri, which regularly designates an associate in a legally-defined partnership between tax-farmers (P. Amh. II 92 = W. Chr. 311, AD II), farmers involved in the joint-cultivation of land (*BGU* II 530, AD I; cf. P. Bad. 19b, AD 110; P. Flor. III 370, AD 132; *BGU* II 530, AD I; P. Amh. II 94 = W. Chr. 347, AD 208), fishermen (P. Oxy. 3270.5, 8; cf. *New Docs* 3, §§4, 19), wine sellers (P. Oxy. 2342, AD 102), leather dealers (*PSI* 465; AD 268), or even prosecutors (P. Col. VI 14 [= *SB* VI 9526], AD 199-200). So common and well established was the commercial register of κοινωνός that it is actually quite difficult to find other associations for the term in the papyri and inscriptions (e.g., P. Par. 17, AD 153-154, where it seems to refer to a life-partner).

Against this background, what are we to make of Paul's designation of Timothy or Philemon as his κοινωνός (2 Cor 8:23 & Phlm 17)? How are we to interpret the Philippians' κοινωνία with Paul 'in the Gospel' (εἰς τὸ εὐαγγέλιον, Phil 1:5)? What

---

[34] Nicolet, 'dîmes', 470 & 479; cf. Brunt, *Publicans*, 396-402.

is implied is that they 'partnered' (with him) to 'the account of giving and receiving', of 'debit and credit' (ἐκοινώνησεν εἰς λόγον δόσεως καὶ λήμψεως, Phil 4:15; cf. BDAG λόγος 2b)? In a loose sense, there is little doubt that Paul has some kind of partnership in mind, one which seems to have some economic implications, judging by the accounting terminology he uses (εἰς λόγον δόσεως καὶ λήμψεως, Phil 4:15; ἀπέχω, 4:18). Historically, however, scholars have been quite reluctant to interpret Paul's usage of κοινωνία and its cognates κοινωνός and κοινωνέω in any other way than theologically. This attitude is perhaps best epitomized by Hauck for whom the 'κοινων- group ... in Paul ... has a directly religious content' (Kittel, *TDNT*, 804), a view adopted by a majority of scholars.[35] However, interestingly enough, a significant number of Pauline occurrences have very concrete, material ramifications (Rom 12:13, 15:26-27; 2 Cor 8:4, 9:13; Gal 2:9, 6:6; Phil 1:5, 4:15). The theologically-focused interpretation is all the more surprising since Hauck is willing to admit that in 'secular Greek' the 'κοινων- group is applied to the most varied relationship', such as 'common enterprises, ... legal relations', and that κοινωνός is 'a tt. [terminus technicus] for a business partner or associate' (Kittel, *TDNT*, 798).

One rare exception in scholarship who has given greater consideration to the legal and commercial connotation of κοινωνία is J.P. Sampley, who, building from the work of J. Fleury, suggested in 1980 that Paul's idea of κοινωνία in Gal 2:9 and Phil 4:15 might be best explained with regard to the Roman legal category of consensual *societas*. This proposition has been rejected as being too fanciful by a number of critics, not least by G.H.R. Horsley who was one of the first to point out the difficulties of Sampley's philological argument:

> The most fundamental problem with this hypothesis is that Sampley fails to demonstrate that κοινων- words are the normal equivalent of Latin *societas* and its related forms. While there are some points of overlap, undoubtedly, the true equivalent of κοινων- is *communis/communitas* and the like ... Sampley's argument, attributing to κοινωνία and related words the same force as *societas* in its technical Roman legal context, is philologically unsound. (*New Docs* 3, §§4, 19)

Horsley was certainly correct to criticise the lack of sophistication in Sampley's philological argument, which made little use of documentary sources. Nevertheless, in the light of the aforementioned evidence, it is possible that Horsley's critique might be overstated. Granted, we have yet to find a bilingual document wherein κοινωνία corresponds to *societas* (or *communitas* for that matter), which would give more weight to Sampley's argument (an inscription from Iasos could be such a document, where [—*sociorum*] is rendered by κοι[νωνῶν], but the reading is uncertain; see I. Iasos 417). However, there is no doubt that κοινων- words were often employed to denote some type of business partnership, which in Latin is best expressed by the words *societas* (note how epigraphists all agree in translating κοινωνός by *socius*). And although this kind of partnership most often took place between tax-collectors, tax-farming *societates* were by no means the only kind of business partnership. For example, *CIL* III, p. 950,

---

[35] Cf. Seesemann, 99: 'Die Tatsache, daß κοινωνία bei Paulus keinmal in einer profanen Bedeutung vorkommt ..., daß κοινωνία für Paulus ein religiöser Terminus ist'; cf. also McDermott, Panikulam, Hainz.

describes a *societas dani[st]ariae*, i.e., a partnership between bankers. Even the word κοινωνία could sometimes be explicitly used to describe a (legally-binding) business partnership or a commercial company, as the following examples, which come from two very different settings, illustrate:
- In P.Bour. 13, AD 98, two farmers agree to establish a partnership for the sale of lentils on a vetch market. In drafting the contract, they employ the following formula: ὁμολογοῦ[σ]ι τεθεῖσθαι [πρ]ὸς ἑαυτοὺς μετοχὴν καὶ κοινωνίαν (see translation in Frank, *Economic Survey*, 384).
- The reference to a commercial association appears on several pottery fragments from Kafizin in rural Cyprus, c. 225 BC: ἀπὸ τῆς Ζήν[ο]νος κοινωνί[ας τὸν λίνο]ν κα[ὶ το]ῦ σπέρματος (Mitford, *Nymphaeum*, §§119; cf. # 217, 218, 219, 265; *SEG* XXX 1608).[36]

It seems therefore more than reasonable to suggest that Paul could have conceived of his relationship with some of his co-workers (e.g., Timothy, Philemon), or sponsoring churches (e.g., the Philippians), as some sort of partnership whose pattern was similar to ordinary business partnerships between *publicani* or *negotiatores*. This interpretation is quite well supported both by the philological evidence derived from documentary sources, and by the contexts in which κοινων- words are found in Paul's letters — contexts which very often contain clusters of other economic or legal terms (cf. Phil 4:15-18, as noted above; Phlm 17-20: (προσ)ὀφείλω, ἐλλογέω, ἀποτίνω, ὀνίνημι, ἐγὼ Παῦλος ἔγραψα τῇ ἐμῇ χειρί). This is not to say that Paul envisaged his missionary activities as a mercantile enterprise, or that he uncritically embraced the commercial ethos of business associations (cf. 1 Cor 9; 2 Cor 2:17; 11:7-10; 12:13-18). However, he may have found mundane business partnerships, whereby associates pulled together resources and human capital to achieve a common objective, to provide a suitable model by which he could conceive of his strategic partnerships with some of his converts for the financial support of his missionary cause.

Bibliography

Plates of the *l. p. A.* can be viewed online at: http://www.csad.ox.ac.uk/lex-portorii/
Titles already published in the *OSAD* series: M. **Brosius** (ed.), *Ancient Archives and Archival Traditions* (Oxford 2003); M. **Carroll**, *Spirits of the Dead* (Oxford 2006); T. Melissa, *Image to Interpretation* (Oxford 2006); P. **Wilson** (ed.), *The Greek Theatre and Festivals* (Oxford 2007). For more information on the *OSAD* see: http://www.csad.ox.ac.uk/.
Ashmolean Museum, *Catalogue of Coins of the Roman Empire in the Ashmolean Museum* (Oxford 1975) [= *Cat. Ashmolean*]; K.M.T. **Atkinson**, 'The "Constitutio" of Vedius Pollio at Ephesus', *RIDA* 9 (1962) 261-289; E. **Badian**, *Publicans and Sinners* (Oxford 1972); A. **Berger**, *Encyclopedic Dictionary of Roman Law* (Philadelphia 1980); D.C. **Braund**, *Augustus to Nero* (London 1985); K. **Bringmann**, 'Edikt der Triumvirn oder Senatsbeschluss? Zu einem Neufund aus Ephesos', *EA* 2 (1983) 47-76; P.A. **Brunt**, 'Charges of Provincial Maladministration under the Early Principate', in *Roman Imperial Themes* (Oxford 1990) 53-95; P.A. **Brunt**, 'Publicans in the Principate', in *Roman Imperial Themes* (Oxford 1990) 354-432; A. **Burnett**, et al., *Roman Provincial Coinage* I (London 1992) [= *RPC* 1]; M. **Cottier**, et al., (eds), *The Customs Law of Asia* (Oxford 2008); M.H. **Crawford**, *Roman Statutes*, 2 Vols. (London 1996) [=

---

[36] One is compelled to correct the grammatical inaccuracy of the reading by suggesting: ἀπὸ τῆς Ζήν[ο]νος κοινωνί[ας τοῦ λίνοῦ] κα[ὶ το]ῦ σπέρματος. Hadjioannou, 257, however advises that the genitive singular of ὁ λίνος is τῷ λίνῳ or τῷ λίνων in the Cypriote dialect.

§16 Customs Law of the Roman Province of Asia (*lex portorii Asiae*)

Crawford, *RS*]; J.A. **Crook**, *Law and Life of Rome* (Ithaca 1967); P. **Debord**, *Aspects sociaux et économiques de la vie religieuse dans l'Anatolie Gréco-romaine* (Leiden 1982); S. **Demougin**, *Prosopographie des chevaliers romains julio-claudiens* (Rome 1992); B. **Dignas**, *The Economy of the Sacred in Hellenistic and Roman Asia Minor* (Oxford 2002); W. **Eck**, 'Cn. Calpurnius Piso, Cos. Ord. 7 v. Chr. und die Lex Portorii Provinciae Asiae', *EA* 15 (1990) 139-145; V. **Ehrenberg** and A.H.M. **Jones**, *Documents Illustrating the Reigns of Augustus and Tiberius* (Oxford 1949) [= EJ]; G. **Finkielsztejn**, 'P. Vedius Pollio, producteur de vin a Chios et Cos et fournisseur d'Hérode le Grand', in *Grecs, Juifs, Polonais* (Paris 2006) 123-139; J. **Fleury**, 'Une société de fait dans l'église apostolique (Phil. 4:10 à 22)', in *Mélanges Philippe Meylan*, Vol. 2 (Lausanne 1963) 41-59; T. **Frank** (ed.), *An Economic Survey of Ancient Rome* (Paterson 1959); M. **Grant**, *From imperium to auctoritas* (Cambridge 1969) [= Grant, *FITA*]; K. **Hadjioannou**, 'Review of T.B. Mitford, *The Nymphaeum of Kafizin*', *RDAC* (1982) 254-529; J. **Hainz**, *Koinonia: 'Kirche' als Gemeinschaft bei Paulus* (Regensburg 1982); J.R. **Harrison**, *Paul's Language of Grace in its Graeco-Roman Context* (Tübingen, 2003); M. **Heil**, 'Einige Bemerkungen zum Zollgesetz aus Ephesos', *EA* 17 (1991) 9-18; M. **Holleaux**, 'Discours de Néron prononcé à Corinthe pour rendre aux Grecs la liberté', *BCH* 12 (1888) 510-528; A.H.M. **Jones**, 'Taxation in Antiquity', in *The Roman Economy* (Oxford 1974); E.A. **Judge**, 'The Social Identity of the First Christians: A Question of Method in Religious History', *JRH* 11 (1980) 215-246; R.A. **Kearsley**, 'M. Ulpius Appuleius Eurykles of Aezani: Panhellene, Asiarch and Archiereus of Asia', *Antichthon* (1987) 49-56; *Greeks and Romans in Imperial Asia* (Bonn 2001); J. **Keil**, 'P. Vedius Pollio', *Paulys Realencyclopädie* 8A (1955) 568-570 [= *RE* 8A]; F. **Kirbihler**, *Les notables d'Ephèse*, Vol. 1 (PhD. diss.; Tours 2003); F. **Kirbihler**, 'P. Vedius Rufus, père de P. Vedius Pollio', *ZPE* 160 (2007) 261-271; 'Vivre à Rome pour les Flavii Vedii: l'installation d'une famille provinciale dans la capitale', in *Habiter en ville au temps de Vespasien* (ed., M.-J. Kardo; Nancy 2011) 117-138; F. **Kirbihler**, 'Pollio (Vedius)', in *Dictionnaires des philosophes antiques*, Vol. V, (ed., R. Goblet; 2011) (forthcoming); G. **Kittel** (ed.), *TDNT* (Grand Rapids 1965) [= Kittel, *TDNT*]; D. **Knibbe**, '... Ein neuer Text aus Ephesos', *ZPE* 44 (1981) 1-10; D. **Knibbe**, '*Legum dicendarum in locandis uectigalibus omnis potestas*', *JÖAI* 58 (1988) 129-134; S.J. **de Laet**, *Portorium* (New York 1975); B. **Levick**, *The Government of the Roman Empire* (London 2000); N. **Lewis** and M. **Reinhold**, *Roman Civilization*, Vol. 2 (New York 1966); D. **Magie**, *Roman Rule in Asia Minor* (Princeton 1950); J.F. **Matthews**, 'The Tax Law of Palmyra: Evidence for Economic History in a City of the Roman East', *JRS* 74 (1984) 157-180; J.M. **McDermott**, 'The Biblical Doctrine of ΚΟΙΝΩΝΙΑ', *BZ* 19 (1975) 64–77, 219–233; G. **Merola**, 'Il Monumentum Ephesenum e l'organizzazione territoriale delle regioni asiane', *MÉFRA* 108.1 (1996) 263-297; F. **Millar**, *The Emperor in the Roman World, 31 BC – AD 337* (London 1977); T.B. **Mitford**, *The Nymphaeum of Kafizin* (Berlin 1980); T.B. **Mitford**, *ANRW* II 7.2 (1980) 1285-1384; C. **Nicolet**, 'A propos du règlement douanier d'Asie: dèmosiônia et les prétendus Quinque publica Asiae', *CRAI* 134.3 (1990) 675-698; C. **Nicolet**, 'Le Monumentum Ephesenum et les dîmes d'Asie', *BCH* 115 (1991) 465-480; C. **Nicolet**, 'Le Monumentum Ephesenum et la délimitation du portorium d'Asie', *MÉFRA* 105.2 (1993) 929-959; C. **Nicolet**, *Censeurs et publicains* (Paris 2000); J.H. **Oliver**, 'On Edict II and the Senatus Consultum at Cyrene', *MAAR* 19 (1949) 105-114; 'On Edict III from Cyrene', *Hesperia* 29 (1960) 324-325; G. **Panikulam**, *Koinōnia in the New Testament* (Rome 1979); R.S. **Poole** (ed.), *A Catalogue of the Greek Coins in the British Museum* (Bologna 1963-1965) [= BMC]; O.W. **Reinmuth**, 'Two Prefectural Edicts concerning the *publicani*', *CP* 31 (1936) 146-162; J. and L. **Robert**, *BE* 5 (1965) §340; P. **de Rohden** and H. **Dessau**, *Prosopographia Imperii Romani* (Berlin 1898) [= *PIR*]; M. **Rostovtzeff**, *The Social and Economic History of the Roman Empire* (Oxford 1971); O. **Salomies**, 'Zu einigen Stellen im Zollgesetz der Provinz Asia', *ZPE* 86 (1991) 184-186; J.P. **Sampley**, *Pauline Partnership in Christ* (Philadelphia 1980); C. **Schäfer**, 'Zur Σφραγίς von Sklaven in der lex portorii provinciae Asiae', *ZPE* 86 (1991) 193-198; P. **Scherrer**, 'Augustus, die Mission des Vedius Pollio und die Artemis Ephesia', *JÖAI* (1990) 87-101; K. **Scott**, 'Notes on the Destruction of Two Roman Villas', *AJPh* 60.4 (1939) 459-462; H. **Seesemann**, *Der Begriff ΚΟΙΝΩΝΙΑ im Neuen Testament* (Giessen 1933); A.N. **Sherwin-White**, 'Procurator Augusti', *Papers of the British School at Rome* 15 (1939) 11–26; E.M. **Smallwood**, *Documents Illustrating the Principates of Gaius Claudius and Nero* (London 1967); H. **Solin**, 'Zum Zollgesetz der Provinz Asia', *ZPE* 86 (1991) 183; A. **Stein**, *Der römische Ritterstand* (Munich 1927) [= Stein, *RR*]; R. **Syme**, 'Who Was Vedius Pollio?' *JRS* 51 (1961) 23–30; *The Roman Revolution* (Oxford 1966); J. **Teixidor**, 'Le Tarif de Palmyre', *Aula Orientalis* 1 (1983) 235–252; P. **Veyne**, *Le Pain et le Cirque* (Paris 1976); H. **Wankel**, *ZPE* 85 (1991) 40; H.C. **Youtie**, 'Publicans and Sinners', *Scriptiunculae* I (1973) 554-578.

J. Ogereau (Macquarie University)

§17 Honouring the Repairer of the Baths at Colossae

Colossae   Cylindrical bomos   Late I – early II

Ed. pr. — A.H. Cadwallader, 'Honouring the repairer of the baths: a new inscription from Kolossai', *Antichthon* 46 (2012) 150-83.

The white marble bomos has small dowel holes on the base to assist in affixing the stone in a public place (the restored baths?) and larger dowel holes on the top, probably to hold a bust or small statue. It was found on Mount Honaz (Cadmus) having been removed from a field close to the mound of Colossae. The stone is heavily moulded at base and apex, the upper element and moulding containing the first five lines. The stone is considerably damaged, resulting in a fragmentary inscription with entire lines of names lost along with the text around the band (*l*. 3). The beginning of *ll*. 4 and 5 is uncertain but the ends are secure. The second part of *ll*. 6 and 7 which gives the amount of the subscription for the cost of the honour follows in meaning directly after the end of *l*. 5, that is "on the bomos from their own resources 1050 denarii". Four incised reliefs are included on the stone. A rosette has been carved at the beginning of the name in *l*. 23. A large vine leaf with exaggerated tapered point extends upwards from *l*. 25 to *l*. 19. A leaping hound is at the end of *ll*. 27-29 and a fruited fig (?) leaf at *l*. 28. These reliefs provide an *ad hoc* right hand margin indicating the maximum length of naming formulae listed on the stone. Two parallel vertical lines cut at the left hand of the names provide a sharper definition of margin. Height: 1.20m; diameter — of top rim: 0.65m at widest, of shaft: 0.50-51m, of base: 0.795m. The date is assigned by reference to the script and the naming formulae.

1	ἀγαθῆι τύ[χηι]	For good fortune.
	Κορύμβωι φιλοπά[τριδι]	For Korymbos the patriot …
	[ωεσ]	
	[…]θη εἰς ἐπισκευὴν βαλαν[είου ca. 15-17] [κ]αὶ εἰς ἐπιρουείαν	… for the repair of the baths … and for the water channel …
5	[αὐτάρ]κειαν τοῦ δήμ°υ Κ°λ°σσ [ca. 16-18]ν τῷ βωμῷ ἐξ ἰδίων	… of the Colossian people … on the bomos from their own
	Τρύφων •Β• Διοδώ[ρου] vac. ἀναλωμάτων vac.	Tryphon son of Tryphon grandson of Diodoros ‖
	Μηνογᾶς •Δ• τοῦ Ν vac. ✕ αν	Menogas son of Menogas grandson of Menogas great grandson of Menogas great great grandson of N … ‖
	Διόδοτος •Γ• τοῦ Δ[ ]	Diodotos son of Diodotos grandson of Diodotos great grandson of D. …
	[ca. 6-7] Τρυφωνᾶ τ[ ]	… son of Tryphon, great grandson of …
10	[ca. 6-7]νιου τοῦ Διο[ ]	… son of -nios grandson of Dio-

(Lines 11-18 lost)

§17 Honouring the Repairer of the Baths at Colossae

19	[ca. 10-11 το]ῦ Ζωσίμου[ος	... son of Zosimon
20	[ca. 10-11] •Β• τοῦ 'Ακρι[ ]	... son of ... grandson of Akri-
	Θεόδωρος Δημητρίου •Β• Θεοδ[ώρου]	Theodoros son of Demetrios grandson of Demetrios great grandson of Theodoros
	Δημᾶς 'Απολλωνίου τ[οῦ]	Demas son of Apollonios grandson of ...
	❀Μηνᾶς Κτησᾶ •Γ• το[ῦ]	Menas son of Ktesas grandson of Ktesas great grandson of Ktesas great great grandson of ...
	Θεόδωρος •Β• Λικιννι[ίου]	Theodoros son of Theodoros grandson of Likinnios
25	'Ηρακλέων •Β• 'Ανωτ[ ] vine leaf	Herakleon son of Herakleon grandson of Anot-
	'Ηρακλέων 'Ηρακλείδου 'Η[ρακλέων]ος	Herakleon son of Herakleides grandson of Herakleon
	Ἄτταλος Τρυφωνιώνο[υ]	Attalos son of Truphonionos
	Θεόδωρος •Β• τοῦ Δημητρίου[ ]νει^a hunting dog	Theodoros son of Theodoros grandson of Demetrios great grandson of -neias
	'Αλέξανδρος 'Ηρακλείδου[ ]ου fig leaf	Alexander son of Herakleides grandson of -os/es
30	'Απολλώνιος Β 'Αττάλου τοῦ Σκ[επα]ρνᾶ	Apollonios son of Apollonios grandson of Attalos great grandson of Skeparnas
	Εὐτύχης Ζωσίμου 'Αντιμήδου	Eutyches son of Zosimos grandson of Antimedes
	Τρύφων• Μενάνδρου •Γ• Μιννίωνος	Tryphon son of Menandros grandson of Menandros great grandson of Menandros great great grandson of Minnion
	Τυδείδης Ζωσίμου	Tydeides son of Zosimos
	Δημήτριος 'Απολλωνίου Μωκεᾶ	Demetrios son of Apollonios grandson of Mokeas
35	Κτησᾶς 'Ηρακλίδου• 'Ιουλίδος	Ktesas son of Heraklides grandson of Ioulis

Although damaged at crucial points, the inscription yields important data for the understanding of Colossae. Firstly the consistently good quality of the stone-cutting enables a reasonably confident dating of the inscription to the latter part of the first century, possibly early second century. The dominance of the Greek naming schema, along with the almost complete absence of Roman names (but note Likinnios in line 24, suggestive of servile origins), is corroborative. There is an almost axiomatic status among New Testament commentators upon the Epistle to the Colossians on the demise or rapid decline of Colossae following the 61/2 CE earthquake that severely impacted the Lycus Valley. The authority derives from J.B. Lightfoot and W.M. Ramsay. This inscription suggests that the axiom must be revised (see my "Refuting an Axiom of Scholarship"). Comparison is usually made with Laodikeia, the nearest city to Colossae (18 kms away). The Roman historian, Tacitus, noted that Laodikeia lifted itself from the ruinous effects of the earthquake (*Annals* 14.27). Because no mention is made of Colossae by Tacitus, it had been assumed that Colossae disappeared or virtually so.

Secondly, the display of independence through an elite wealthy citizen is critical for the standing of a city. Aristotle noted that "self-sufficiency" (αὐτάρκεια) was the key distinguishing mark of the State (*Politics* 1321b *cf* 2 Cor 9:8); it is tempting to restore this to *l*. 5 but a number of options are possible, none of which is decisive, given the inability to determine the beginning of *l*. 5. One of Colossae's leading citizens, Korumbos, had wealth of such significance that he could finance the repair of the baths (probably the main civic baths) as well as the construction of a main water channel, probably to supply the baths. The word ἐπιροία (the usual spelling c.f. *l*. 4) is rare in Asia Minor, though well-known in Egypt especially in irrigation works drawing from the Nile (*SB* XVIII 13747, P. Oxy. 2341). The council of citizens was significantly involved, if not in the co-financing of the restoration and construction, then certainly in benefiting from the munificence and in reciprocating with this honour for the leader who had enabled the city to display its political standing. The baths and water-supply are not only key to a city's civic status in Greek eyes (see Pausanias 10.4.1) but have a long-standing association with Colossae (see Polyaenus *Strategems* 7.16.1, Diodorus Siculus 14.18.7-8).

Thirdly, the names on the list open a significant window on the leading or at least reasonably financial citizens of Colossae shortly after Paul's death, along with their genealogies stretching back, on occasion, for a century. Sixty-six whole or partial names are still extant. Some names resonate with Paul's acquaintances (e.g. Eutyches in *l*. 31 c.f. Acts 20:9 [Eutychos], Demas in *l*. 22 c.f. Col 4:14).

Fourthly, the names are overwhelmingly Greek. This does not necessarily require that the bearers be of Greek ethnicity, at least in their origins. But it does indicate a desire, for political, commercial or other reasons, to accent the Greek commitment of these citizens of the polis. This may explain the unusual name Tydeides in *l*. 33, reminiscent of a supporting character to Odysseus in Homeric story (*Od.* 3:181, 4.280, *Il.* 5.1ff; for similar practices in neighbouring Lycia, see S. Colvin, 'Names', 44-84.) The heavy accent on the Greek ethos suggests that at least in this level of society and in the display to such society, 'Greek' was what mattered. This suggests that the familiar nullification of racial (and other) distinctions in Paul's letters (e.g. Gal 3:28, 1 Cor 12:13) has received more than a stylistic variation in Col 3:11 where "Greek" not "Jew" is placed first in the list. In Colossae, issues related to a dominant Greek culture and aspiration may have been more important, not only within Colossian society but in the ongoing negotiation of relations with Rome.

Finally, there are nevertheless a few names suggestive of other backgrounds. For all that Menogas (*l.* 7) has been called a 'Greek hypocoristic' (T. Drew-Bear, et al., *Phrygian Votive Steles*, 387) it may in origin be a theophoric name for the Phrygian god, Mên, given that the exact form appears confined to Asia Minor (e.g. *TAM* V 1. 279). The bearer of this name is the inheritor of a long succession of bearers of the name. Whilst this may accent the Greek value of stability in family and communal life, it also may suggest a conscious retention of deference to a regional deity. Tydeides (*l.* 33) for all its Homeric connections may be just the 'herophoric' name (Louis Robert's description) appropriate to the region — the Lycian word for 'son' is very similar (Colvin, 'Names', 56) and 'son' is the accent in Homer (the character's 'actual' name, Diomedes, occurs rarely). Skeparnas (*l.* 30) and Mokeas (*l.* 34) may indicate a Thracian connection (marital, ethnic?) at least in the past (*SEG* XXIX 628, *IGB* IV 2015a). Anot- in *l.* 25 is highly unusual. The *tau* may, just possibly (the letter borders on the damaged section), be a *nu* and this would clearly indicate a Thracian, even specifically Scythian, name (see *IOSPE* 1². 685). L. Zgusta suggests that Minnion (possibly from Munnion) may be Phrygian (*Kleinasiatische Personennamen*, 318, 552) or at least epichoric (L. Robert, *Noms indigènes*, 226, n. 6). The name Korymbos might trace a Lydian background (cf. L. Robert, *Noms indigènes*, 288) but is more likely to bear theophoric associations with the cult of Dionysos (and its bunches of flowers and fruit — the *coyrmboi*). How vibrant Phrygian, Lycian, Thracian, Scythian (see Col 3:11) may have been at this time is unknown. However, it is important to note that into the second century, Colossae was in need of an office of translators and interpreters (Cadwallader, 'New Inscription', 113-14) to service both the local community and commercial traders. Again this suggests that the race-nullification code in Col 3:11 is no literary embellishment on the usual Pauline formula but has local specifics, even tensions, in view.

Bibliography

A.H. **Cadwallader**, 'New Inscription [read: Two New Inscriptions], a Correction and a Confirmed Sighting from Colossae', *EA* 40 (2007) 109-118; A.H. **Cadwallader**, 'Refuting an Axiom of Scholarship on Colossae: Fresh Insights from New and Old Inscriptions', in *Colossae in Space and Time: Linking with an Ancient City* (eds, A.H. Cadwallader and M. Trainor; Göttingen 2011) 151-179; S. **Colvin**, 'Names in Hellenistic and Roman Lycia', in *The Greco-Roman East* (ed., S. Colvin; Cambridge 2004), 44-84; T. **Drew-Bear**, C.M. **Thomas** and M. **Yıldızturan**, *Phrygian Votive Steles* (Museum of Anatolian Civilizations 1999); L. **Robert**, *Noms indigènes dans L'Asie-Mineure gréco-romaine* (Amsterdam 1991 [1963]); L. **Zgusta**, *Kleinasiatische Personennamen* (Prague 1964).

A.H. Cadwallader

HOUSEHOLD

§18 Divorce Agreement

Ptolemais Euergetis   10 x 20 cm   Phamenoth AD 177

Ed. pr. — C. Préaux, 'Acte de divorce du Brooklyn Museum (P. Brooklyn Gr. 4)', *CE* 37 (1962) 323-333, pl. 325; H.C. Youtie, 'The Divorce Agreement P. Brooklyn Gr. 4 (*SB* VIII 9740)', *CE* 43 (1968) 172-175, re-edited in *Scriptiunculae* II 704-707); J.C. Shelton, 'Divorce Agreement', *Greek and Latin Papyri, Ostraca, and Wooden Tablets in the Collection of the Brooklyn Museum* (Papyrologica Florentina a cura di Rosario Pintaudi, XXII; Florence 1992) 14-15 (P. Brooklyn 8 = *SB* VIII 9740).

Our text is a copy of a divorce agreement, presumably prepared by a notary, from a τόμος συγκολλήσιμος, a roll composed of originally separate documents pasted together. Traces of the text to the right, in a different hand, are preserved.

[Ἔτους ἐπ]τακαιδεκάτου Αὐτοκράτορος Καίσαρος	[Year sev]enteen of Imperator Caesar
[Μάρκου] Αὐρηλίου Ἀντωνείνου Σεβαστοῦ καὶ	[Marcus] Aurelius Antoninus Augustus and
[Αὐτοκράτορος Κ]αίσαρος Λουκίου Αὐρηλίου Κομόδου Σεβαστοῦ	[Imperator C]aesar Lucius Aurelius Commodus Augustus
[Ἀρμενιακῶ]ν Μηδικῶν Παρθικῶν Γερμανικῶν	[Armeniaci] Medici Parthici Germanici
5 [Σαρματικῶν] Μεγίστων, μηνὸς Ἀρτεμισίου Φαμενώθ,	[Sarmatici] Maximi, the month of Artemisios Phamenoth,
[ἐν Πτολεμαίδι] Εὐεργέτιδι τοῦ Ἀρσινοείτου νομοῦ ὁμολογοῦ-	[In Ptolemais] Euergetis of the Arsinoite Nome. They mutually acknowledge,
[σιν ἀλλήλοις Ἀφρ]οδισία Σαβείνου τοῦ Μύσθου μητρὸς Ἀμμω-	[on the one hand, Aphr]odisia, daughter of Sabinus and Ammo... granddaughter of Mysthes
[. . . . . . ἀπὸ τῆς μ]ητροπόλεως ὡς (ἐτῶν) λα οὐλὴ ὀφρύϊ ἀριστερᾷ	from the metropolis, 31 years old, with a scar on her left eyebrow
[μετὰ κυρίου] Ἀχιλλᾶτος Ὠριγένους τοῦ Ἡρακλείδου μητρὸ[ς]	[with her guardian,] Achillas son of Horigenes and NN, grandson of Herakleides
10 [. . . . . ἀ]π' ἀμφόδου Θεσμοφορίου ὡς (ἐτῶν) νβ χωλαίνω(ν)	from the Thesmophorion quarter, 52 years old, with a limp.
[. . . . .] καὶ ὁ γενόμενος αὐτῆς ἀνὴρ Πτολεμαῖος	[...] and on the other hand, her former husband Ptolemaios

§18 Divorce Agreement

	[Πτολεμαίου] τοῦ Σωκράτους μητρὸς Σοήρεως ἀπὸ κώ-	[son of Ptolemaios] and Soeris, grandson of Socrates from the village of
	[μης Καραν]ίδος ὡς (ἐτῶν) λζ οὐλὴ γόνατι ἀριστ(ερῷ) συνῆρστθαι	[Karan]is, 37 years old, with a scar on his left knee,
	[αὐτούς τὴ]ν πρὸς ἀλλήλοις συνβίωσιν ἥτις αὐτοῖς	[that they] have mutually dissolved the marriage that existed between them
15	[συνεστήκει < > καὶ ἐξ]εῖναι ἑκατέρῳ αὐτῶν τὰ καθ' ἑ-	... and each their own affairs
	[αὐτὸν οἰκο]νομεῖν ὡς ἐὰν αἱρῆται· τῇ δὲ Ἀφροδισίᾳ	[is permitted to man]age as they choose and that Aphrodisia
	[σὺν ἑτέρῳ ἀ]νδρὶ ἐπισυναρμόζεσθαι ἀσυκοφαντή-	may marry another man with no danger
	[τω οὔσῃ κα]τὰ πάντα τρόπον, ἥτις καὶ ἀπέχειν	[of a court su]it; moreover, that she has received
	[παρὰ τοῦ Πτολε]μαίου ἣν προσηνέγκαντο αὐτῷ φερ-	[from Ptole]maios the dowry of
20	[νὴν χρυσικὴν] καὶ ἀργυρικὴν καὶ παράφερνα πάντα,	[gold] and silver she had brought him and all her bridal goods;
	[μηδὲν δ' ἀλλ]ήλοις ἐνκαλεῖν περὶ μηδενὸς τῶν	that they make [no] accusation about anything arising
	[τῆς συνβιώ]σεως ἀνηκόντων ⟦μηδὲ περὶ αν⟧	[from their marr]ied life;
	[τὸν δὲ Πτολε]μαῖον μηδὲ περὶ οὗ ἠγόρανεν ἡ Ἀφ-	[that Ptole]maios also makes no accusation concerning
	[ροδισία μόνη περὶ πε]δίον Ψεναρψενήσεως	Aph[rodisia's purchase, near] Psenharpsenesis
25	[c.16] ἐλαιῶνος ἀρούρης τέταρτον κα[ὶ]	[c.16] an olive grove of one quarter aroura an[d another]
	[ἄλλην περὶ κώμην Κ]ερκεσοῦχα σιτικὴν ἄρουραν	[near the village of K]erkesoucha an aroura of grain land
	[?]	[...]
	[?]	[...]
	[.........] ἀπὸ τῶν ἔμπροσθεν χρόνων	[...] from the previous years
30	[μέχρι τῆς ἐνεσ]τώσης ἡμέρας τρόπῳ μηδενί.	[up to the pre]sent day in no way at all.

2 restored from α..ηλιου. **3** l. κομμόδου **13** l. συνῆρθαι **14** l. ἀλλήλους Pap. **18** λ. ἥ **19** λ. προσηνέγκατο Pap. **23** ἠγόρασεν Pap.

From the marriage contracts and divorce agreements we learn the procedure for divorce. In the marriage contracts we learn the conditions for divorce.[1] Separation is the means which effects a divorce. The execution of a formal contract was not required for a legal divorce.[2] This separation is spelt out as either the husband sending his wife away or the wife leaving of her own free will. There is no separation contemplated that does not lead to the dissolving of the marriage contract. The act of separation is completed by the husband returning the dowry. From the divorce agreements we learn that an agreement was then drawn up between the parties wherein the divorced wife acknowledged the return of the dowry and both parties acknowledged that each one was free to marry. The agreement was a record of actions already taken to serve mainly to protect against further litigation. Divorce on demand was available to either spouse in Roman Egypt as it was elsewhere in the Roman Empire. How common it was amongst the lower classes is debated, however it would seem that it was fairly common amongst the general population.[3]

The census returns from Roman Egypt enable us to have some insight into divorce and its consequences.[4] Both divorce and remarriage are attested in the census returns. Divorce is attested in the following returns: *BGU* I 95, P. Mil. Vogl. III 193(b), P. Mil.Vogl. III 194(a), P. Mil. Vogl. III 194(b), P. Berl. Leihg. I 17, *SB* X 10219, P. Flor. III 301, *BGU* I 118 col.ii, *SB* XIV 11355, P. Fam. Tebt. 48 (using the concordance in Appendix 2 of Bagnall and Frier one has a systematic comparison of these). In two cases, P. Flor. III 301 and P. Berl. Leihg. I 17, divorced wives still live in the households of their former husbands as they are either a full or half-sister to their former husband and have little alternative but to continue to live in the family home. When the divorced wife owns a whole or part share in the house it is possible that the husband may have had to leave the home and either return to his parents' home or perhaps to another house either owned by him or to some sort of rental accommodation.[5] In the census return P. Mil. Vogl. III 194(a) we are notified that the divorced wife, Heraeis, is the declarant and owner of the houses that are the subject of the return. She has three children by her divorced husband, Heracleos, who are living with her, one of whom is married. The mother of Heraeis also lives in the house. In view of the fact that the married son and the mother of Heraeis are living in the house it seems likely that Heracleos left the house because it was owned by his former wife, leaving Heraeis to care for their children.

---

[1] For a list of the Greco-Roman marriage contracts and divorce agreements see D. I. Brewer, http://www.tyndalearchive.com/Brewer/MarriagePapyri/TableGD1.htm (accessed 2011): For the terms for divorce and their importance in understanding 1 Corinthians 7, see D.I. Brewer, '1 Corinthians 7', *TynBul* 52 (2001) 225-243.
[2] See R. Taubenschlag, *Law of Greco-Roman Egypt*, 122.
[3] For availability of divorce see Taubenschlag, *Law*, 121-125, see also R. Bagnall and B. Frier, *The Demography of Roman Egypt*, 123.
[4] Over three hundred census returns have been discovered in Egypt in varying conditions covering a period from AD 5/6 (?) to AD 257/8. The census was held every fourteen years as males became liable for the poll-tax at the age of fourteen.
[5] From the census returns we learn that where the wife owns the house in which the family lives, the husband does not own any property, therefore it is much more likely that Ptolemaios would have either moved back to his family home or into rented accommodation, see D. Barker, *Household Patterns*, 134, and D. Barker, 'The Place of Residence', 59-66.

Perhaps the actions of Heracleos were the same as those of the husband recorded in *BGU* VIII 1848 (48-46 BC), who left his wife and baby for another woman?

In our text, we learn that Aphrodisia had accumulated some property that she owned apparently independently of Ptolemaios. It also seems that there is some question of Ptolemaios's involvement in it (*l.* 23). From land registers and other evidence throughout the Roman period it appears that about one-third of landowners were women.[6] Private letters from the Roman period reveal women's involvement in agriculture management and decision making. P. Oxy. 2680 is a letter from Arsinoe to Sarapias about rent collecting and some other matters. In P. Oxy. 932, Thais writes to her estate manager (?) giving instructions on various agricultural matters, and in P. Charite 8, Aurelia Charite acknowledges that she has received half of the crop which was farmed on her ten arouras of land in a sharecropping arrangement. Our evidence for property ownership and involvement in agricultural production has been reliant on papyri from Egypt, but what of the rest of the Roman world? Tina Saavedra has compared women property owners in Roman Spain with women property owners in Egypt, using the evidence from inscriptions from Baetica (southern Spain) and papyri from Socnopaiou Nesos. She found that roughly the same proportion of one-fourth to one-third of property owners were female and that women were found to own property of every sort and engage in most of the same activities as men.[7] The major difference according to Saavedra is the relative independence which women in Baetica enjoyed in contrast to women in Socnopaiou Nesos because of the differing law in regard to guardianship.[8] By the first century, Roman women began to experience a freedom in comparison to Greek women.[9] This was mostly due to the Augustan reforms.[10] It is not surprising therefore to learn from the wax tablets recovered from Pompeii that a woman named Umbricia Januaria in AD 56 represented herself in business transactions which included a large sum of money from a banker.[11] Could Phoebe (Rom 16:1-2) be in a similar financial position? That women such as Lydia (Acts 16:15), Nympha (Col 4:15) and perhaps Chloe (1 Cor 1:11) could own property in which the household resided is attested not only in the papyri but also in archaeological remains including that of Julia

---

[6] D. Hobson, 'Women as Property Owners in Roman Egypt', 321, conducted two studies on women as property owners in Tebtunis and Socnopaiou Nesos. Her findings even though they only related to these two towns are most probably representative of villages in the Egyptian chora. She found that, 'women were involved in a substantial proportion of financial transactions and owned a fair bit of property ... ranging from 20 to 30%'.

[7] T. Saavedra, 'Women as Property-Owners', 297-312.

[8] T. Saavedra, 'Women', 311. See also J. Rowlandson (ed.), *Women & Society*, 219-220.

[9] T. Saavedra bases her argument on the regularity that Egyptian women used either their husband, son or another close male as guardian, which according to Saavedra meant that the guardian had a vested interest and authority in the property whilst in the West the guardian was usually not the husband ('Women', 310-311). See also S.B. Pomeroy, *Goddesses, Whores, Wives and Slaves*, 169-170.

[10] For the effect that these reforms had on Roman women and non-Roman women, see R.S. Ascough, *Paul's Social Network*, 65-69. See also B.W. Winter, *Roman Wives, Roman Widows*.

[11] See *CIL* IV, supplement 1, 308-310.

Felix, who owned one of the largest Pompeian residences, involving a whole city block, and was able to lease it to whomever she wished.[12]

We may also observe from the divorce agreement that the age difference between Aphrodisia and Ptolemaios is 21 years. From the Egyptian census returns we learn that in eighty-three percent of cases the husband is older than the wife and the age difference between husband and wife varies from one to thirty one years. Of that eighty-three percent forty percent are more than eleven to thirty years older. A small percentage of wives (17%) are either the same age or older than their husbands.[13]

Bibliography

R.S. **Ascough**, *Paul's Social Network: Brothers & Sisters in Faith* (Collegeville 2008) 65-69; R. **Bagnall** and B. **Frier**, *The Demography of Roman Egypt* (Cambridge 1994); D.C. **Barker**, 'Census Returns and Household Structures', in *New Docs* 4 (1987) 87-93; D.C. **Barker**, *Household Patterns in the Roman Empire with Special Reference to Egypt*, Vol.1 (PhD diss.; Macquarie University, 1994); D. **Barker**, 'The Place of Residence of the Divorced Wife in Roman Egypt', *Akten des 21. Internationalen Papyrologenkongresses,* Berlin 13-19 Aug 1995, 59-66; D.I. **Brewer**, '1 Corinthians 7 in the Light of the Jewish, Greek and Aramaic Marriage and Divorce Papyri', *TynBul* 52 (2001) 225-243; J.E. **Grubbs**, 'Divorce Documents from Roman Egypt', in *Women and the Law in the Roman Empire* (London 2002) 210-217; D. **Hobson**, 'Women as Property Owners in Roman Egypt', *TAPA* 113 (1983) 321; G.H.R. **Horsley**, 'The Purple Trade, and the Status of Lydia of Thyatura,' *New Docs* 2 (1982) 25-32; S.B. **Pomeroy**, *Goddesses, Whores, Wives and Slaves: Women in Classical Antiquity* (New York 1975); J. **Rowlandson** (ed.), *Women & Society in Greek and Roman Egypt: A Sourcebook* (Cambridge, UK 1998); T. **Saavedra**, 'Women as Property-Owners in Spain and Egypt', in *Le rôle et le statut de la femme en Égypte hellénistique, romaine et byzantine* (eds, H. Melaerts and L. Mooren; Actes du Colloque International, Bruxelles-Leuven, 27-29 Novembre 1997; Paris-Leuven 2002) 297-312.; R. **Taubenschlag**, *The Law of Graeco-Roman Egypt in the Light of the Papyri, 332BC – AD 640* (Warsaw ²1955); B.W. **Winter**, *Roman Wives, Roman Widows: The Appearance of New Women and Pauline Communities* (Grand Rapids 1998).

D.C. Barker (Macquarie University)

---

[12] *CIL* 4.1136. For women as heads of households, see G.H.R. Horsley, *New Docs* 2, 31-32, and D.C. Barker, 'Census Returns', 93.
[13] See Barker, *Household Patterns*, 88-93.

§19 Insolent Women

Oxyrhynchus	12.5 x 11.5 cm	III/IV

Ed. pr. — J.R. Rea, *The Oxyrhynchus Papyri*, Vol. LV (London 1988) 210-212 (= P. Oxy. 3815)

Only the first thirteen lines of this papyrus remain. The text of the letter is written on the recto of the papyrus, along the fibres. The address on the verso is also written along the fibres, downwards. Only the opening part of the address remains and, given the different styles of address such as the inclusion or omission of a location, it is difficult to determine the proportion missing, and hence the proportion of the letter that is lost. Ed.pr. suggests about half is missing. The papyrus has five vertical folds.

Recto

	Κυρίῳ μου υἱῷ Ἀπολλωνίῳ Εὐσέβιος	To my lord son Apollonius, Eusebius
	χαίρειν.	(sends) greeting.
	ὅτι μέλει σοι τοῦ κυρίου μου υἱοῦ Σαβείνου	That you are concerned for my lord son Sabinus,
	τεθάρρηκα. τὸ δὲ παῖδα αὐτὸν ὄντα δέεσθαι	I have confidence. With him being a child, it is essential
5	τοῦ μὴ εἰς [ἀ]ταξείαν τρέπεσθαι, καὶ περὶ τού-	that he not be directed towards ill-discipline,
	του πιστεύω ὅτι ἐντολὰς λήμψετε παρὰ	and I believe, in relation to
	σοῦ ὁ Ἐπάγαθος ὥστε αὐτῷ προσκαρτε-	this, that Epagathus will receive orders from you to stay with him.
	ρῖν. εἰ δὲ καὶ αἱ ⟦ ca. 10 ⟧ ʽπερὶ τὴν Ἀδωρᾶνʼ ἐκεῖναι ἐπι-	And if those women, ⟦ c.10 ⟧ ʽthe group around Adoraʼ, carry on in
	μένοιεν τῷ αὐτῷ στρηνι, ἀνακοπτέ-	the same brazenness, let them
10	στωσαν διὰ τῆς σῆς, τοῦ ἐμοῦ κυρίου,	be checked, my lord,
	ἐπιστρεφίας καὶ ὑπὸ τῆς ⟦ σῆς ⟧ κυρίας	by your strictness, and by that of my lady
	μου θυ[γ]ατρὸς Πτολεμαΐδος. τὴν γὰρ	daughter Ptolemais. For my
13	κυρίαν μ[ου θυ]γατέρα κ[....]..[...].	lady daughter K ...

Verso

14	κυρίῳ μου υἱῷ Ἀπολλωνίῳ [vac.]	To my lord son Apollonius ...

5 ἀταξίαν **6** λήμψεται **7-8** προσκαρτερεῖν, Pap. **9** στρήνει **9-10** ἀνακοπτέσθωσαν **11** ἐπιστρεφείας **14** corr. from αιω

This letter is one of three (P. Oxy. 3813-3815) with the name 'Apollonius' as the recipient. Their inventory numbers suggest that they were found in close proximity to one another but there is no link other than the name to connect them. The name Apollonius is common and therefore it is uncertain whether the same person is being addressed in each case. If it is the one Apollonius, the letters indicate that he is the brother of Justus (P. Oxy. 3813), Sabinus, Ptolemais and K? (P. Oxy. 3815), the father of Theodorus (P. Oxy. 3814) and son of Eusebius (P. Oxy. 3815). A.E. Hanson questions this family tree (*Gnomon* 62 [1990] 275) on the basis that it is unlikely that there would be three generations of functioning adults with the middle generation retaining five siblings. It may be that any or all of the kinship epithets are used metaphorically.[1] However, at least in the case of our text (P. Oxy. 3815), the nature of the concerns expressed favours a literal reading.

The question over the identity of the people named Apollonius renders the reference in P. Oxy. 3813, *l*. 88 to Apollonius as a hypomnematographus and ex-prytanis, and therefore, without contrary evidence, almost certainly a pagan, unhelpful in determining the religious affiliation of Apollonius in our text. There is no suggestion that he is Christian. Nonetheless, our text is of interest because of vocabulary it uses in common with the New Testament and for the evidence it gives concerning expectations of behaviour suitable for women also in common with the New Testament.

Eusebius opens the letter abruptly without the usual greeting and/or prayer. The omission became increasingly the epistolary pattern in the late fourth century[2] but is unusual in this period. It reflects perhaps the urgency of Eusebius' concern about the behaviour of his son, Sabinus, with which he opens the letter, and also of a number of women.

Eusebius describes the behaviour of Adora and her companions as στρῆνος. A search of the Duke Database of Documentary Papyri indicates that, apart from this text, στρῆνος is not attested among the documentary papyri. The noun occurs in Revelation 18:3 in reference to the 'luxury' (NRSV, NIV), 'wantonness' (RSV), 'delicacy' (KJV), 'sensuality' (NASB), of 'Babylon, the great' that has enabled merchants to become wealthy: οἱ ἔμποροι τῆς γῆς ἐκ τῆς δυνάμεως τοῦ στρήνους αὐτῆς ἐπλούτησαν. στρῆνος parallels πορνεία 'fornication' in the verse and seems likely also to carry a sexual overtone. The verb form στρηνιάω 'live in luxury, live wantonly' occurs in v. 7 with δοκέω and in v. 9 with πορνεύω. The ending in -ιαω is that of verbs of sickness.[3] The noun στρῆνος occurs once in the LXX, in 2 Kings 19:28 where it is variously translated 'arrogance' (NRSV, RSV, NASB), 'insolence' (NIV) and 'tumult' (KJV), being a translation of שאנן (š'nk). The sense is different from its earlier use in secular Greek literature, eg. Lycophron 438 (third century BC), with the meaning 'wantonness'. Στρῆνος appears in later Christian literature as 'concupisence/wantonness', for

---

[1] E. Dickey, 'Literal and Extended Use of Kinship Terms in Documentary Papyri', *Mnemosyne* 57 (2004) 131-176. See also entries §§28-29 in this volume.
[2] M. Harding, *An Examination of EYXOMAI*; H. Koskenniemi, *Studien*.
[3] Schneider, C., 'καταστρηνιάω', 631.

example, Chrysostom (d. 407), *Hom. Phile.* 1.2, and with the meaning 'insolence', Epiphanius (d. 403), *Haer.* 66.2. In the secular poet Palladas, *AP* 7.686.6 (sixth century), the connotation of sexual immorality recurs. The tendency to associate women's behaviour that flouts societal convention with promiscuity suggests that sexual innuendo applies here.

Studies in cultural anthropology suggest that any behaviour by women that flouted societal norms carried overtones of sexual immorality. The presumption of promiscuity is repeated in literary texts of the period. For example, in *Acts of Paul and Thecla* 3.8-19, Thecla's refusal to marry Thamyris and her association with Paul is understood by crowds and family as sexual impropriety. J. du Boulay comments that even a woman's suspicious absence from her home, disregard for housework and excessive gossiping carried overtones of immorality.[4]

The behaviour classed as στρῆνος in our text is such that Eusebius orders it to be 'checked' (ἀνακοπτέω), and asks Apollonius to do so with severity ἐπιστρέφεια. ἀνακοπτέω occurs once in the New Testament. St Paul uses it of the Galatians being 'prevented' (NRSV) 'hindered' (NASB) from living consistently with the gospel, Gal 5:7. ἀνακοπτέω, like στρῆνος, is infrequent in the documentary papyri. It occurs in four extant texts in addition to Eusebius' use, three of which are petitions: P. Abinn. 50 (AD 346); P. Cair. Isid. 66 (AD 299); and P. Sakaon 38 (AD 312), in a formula similar to that in our text but with behaviour checked 'by your manliness' (ὑπὸ τῆς σῆς ἀνδρείας) rather than ἐπιστρέφεια. The fourth text, P. Oxy. 2674 (AD 308), is damaged. The behaviour for which ἀνακοπτέω is appropriate in these petitions includes robbery and/or rape (P. Abinn. 50), unlawful activity (P. Cair. Isid. 66) and lawless, reckless and foolhardy behaviour (P. Sakaon 38). The verb appears to connote a strong exercise of restraint of behaviour that is serious misconduct.

The strength of the restraint for which Eusebius calls in our text is intensified by 'strictness, severity' (ἐπιστρέφεια). The word appears elsewhere among the documentary papyri generally in petitions. See, for example, P. Oxy. 1121 (third century), 2704 (AD 292), 3304 (AD 301), P. Panop. Beatty 2 (AD 300), and P. Sakaon 48 (AD 343), where it appears to be a standard word for the potential severity of lawful authority. Eusebius is asking for a strong exercise of restraint against Adora and her companions.

The relationship between Eusebius and Adora is not indicated but Adora and those with her apparently stand in a subordinate relationship to Eusebius, and also Apollonius and Ptolemais, so that their exercise of discipline is possible and appropriate. It seems unlikely that the women are relatives since no kinship epithet appears while it does for Sabinus, Apollonius, Ptolemais and K?. It may be that the women are slaves or possibly foster-daughters living in the household. If they are members of Eusebius' household, their 'brazen' behaviour would bring shame and require checking to preserve the

---

[4] J. du Boulay, *Portrait of a Greek Mountain Village*, 131-133.

family's honour.[5] Roman law of the period indicates that women's sexual purity determined the household's reputation in the community.[6]

According to literary and epigraphic sources, the ideal woman in Greek and Roman society was modest, silent, virtuous, domestic and private, devoted, nurturing and virtuous.[7] P. Haun 2.13 (third century; see *New Docs* 6, 18-23) advocates for a good woman, 'quietness' (ἡσυχίᾳ), being 'white and clean (λευκοείμονα καὶ καθάρειον) in dress', showing 'modesty (αἰδοῦς) ... decency and moderation (κοσμιότητα καὶ σωφροσύνην)', and 'management and maintenance of her household' (οἰκονομίαν τε καὶ σωτηρίαν). *AE* 828 (first-second century; see *New Docs* 3, 40-43) praises Valeria as εὔνουν φιλόστοργον σεμνὴν ἄμωμον φίλανδρον φιλότεκνον εὐνοῦχον ('kind, affectionate, dignified, blameless; she loved her husband and her children, and was faithful to her marriage').

Adora and her companions fail to exhibit the ideals of women's behaviour, showing instead στρῆνος which, with its connotations of sexual immorality, sensuality and insolence, is the opposite of the ideal. The women are to be restrained in ways that are not specified in the surviving part of P. Oxy. 3815. In Revelation 18, Babylon, the Great, is disciplined with fire, pestilence and famine.

Bibliography

J. **du Boulay**, *Portrait of a Greek Mountain Village* (Oxford 1974); E. **Dickey**, 'Literal and Extended Use of Kinship Terms in Documentary Papyri', *Mnemosyne* 57 (2004) 131-176; J. **Gardner**, *Women in Roman Law and Society* (London/Sydney 1986); J. **Hallett**, *Fathers and Daughters in Roman Society: Women and the Elite Family* (Princeton 1984); M. **Harding**, *An Examination of ΕΥΧΟΜΑΙ in the P. Oxy. Letters Illustrating 'From Cult to Life Commitment'* (MPhil diss., Macquarie University 1985); H. **Koskenniemi**, *Studien zur Idee und Phraseologie des griechischen Briefes bis 400 n. Chr* (Helsinki 1956); M.Y. **MacDonald**, *Early Christian Women and Pagan Opinion: The Power of the Hysterical Woman* (Cambridge/New York 1996); B. **Malina**, *The New Testament World: Insights from Cultural Anthropology* (Atlanta 1981); S.B. **Pomeroy**, *Goddesses, Whores, Wives and Slaves: Women in Classical Antiquity* (New York 1975); M. Z. **Rosaldo**, 'The Use and Abuse of Anthropology: Reflections on Feminism and Cross-Cultural Understandings', *Signs* 5 (1980) 389-417; C. **Schneider**, 'καταστρηνιάω', in *TDNT* 3, 631; R. **van Bremen**, 'Women and Wealth', in *Images of Women in Antiquity* (eds, A. Cameron, A. Kurht; London 1983) 223-242.

E. Mathieson (Macquarie University)

---

[5] On honour-shame as a gendered polarity in modern and ancient Mediterranean societies see B. Malina, *New Testament World*; M. Z. Rosaldo, 'Use and Abuse of Anthropology', *Signs* 5 (1980) 389-417.
[6] M.Y. MacDonald, *Early Christian Women*; J. Gardner, *Women in Roman Law and Society*, 127-131.
[7] 1 Tim 2:9-12, 5:10-14, Tit 2:3-5, 1 Pet 3:1-6; Aristotle, *On Politics* 1.13; Herodas, *Mime* 1; Tacitus *Dialogus de Oratoribus* 28f; Juvenal *Satire* 6; Plutarch, 'Advice to Bride and Groom', *Moralia*, 138A-146F, especially 142. See also J. Hallett, *Fathers and Daughters*, 7, 29f, n. 46; 38-46, 211-262 with extensive references; R. van Bremen, 'Women and Wealth', 223-242; S.B. Pomeroy, *Goddesses*, 150.

§20 Sale of a Horse

Theadelphia 7.1 x 10.2 cm 16th September AD 141

Ed. pr. — R. Pintaudi, et al., *Papyri Graecae Wessely Pragenses* (Florence 1988) 106-107 (= P. Prag. I 40).

The text is written on the recto, parallel to the fibres. On the verso, one quarter way down on the right-hand side, are traces of 3-4 letters, the first of which may be a δ and the last may be an η. The bottom is missing.

ἔτους πέμπτου Αὐτοκράτορος	Year 5 of Imperator
Καίσαρος Τίτου Αἰλίου Ἁδριανοῦ	Caesar Titus Aelius Hadrianus
Ἀντωνείνου Σεβαστοῦ Θὼθ	Antoninus Augustus, the 19th
ἐννεακαιδεκάτῃ ἐν Θεαδ(ελφείᾳ)	of Thoth, in Thead(elphia),
5 τῆς Θεμ(ίστου) μερίδος τοῦ Ἀρσινοείτ[ου]	Them(istes) district, Arsinoite
νομοῦ. ὁμολογεῖ Ἥρων	nome. Hero, son of Tyrannus,
Τυράννου ὡς φησὶν ἀπὸ ἀμφόδ(ου)	as he is called, of the district of the
Βιθυνῶν Ἰσίωνος ὡς ἐτῶν	Bithynians of the Iseon, about 40
τεσσαράκοντα οὐλὴ μετώπ(ῳ)	years old, (having) a scar in the middle of his
10 μέσωι Σώτᾳ Πτολεμαίου	forehead, agrees with Sotas, son of Ptolemaeus,
ὡς ἐτῶν τεσσαράκοντα	about 40 years old,
οὐλὴ γόνατι δεξιῷ πεπρακ(έναι)	(having) a scar on his right knee, that he has sold
αὐτῶι ἵππον ἄρενα βόλον	him a male horse shedding its
ἔχοντα ψαρὸν τοῦτον τοι-	teeth, dappled, just as it
15 οῦτον ἀναπόριφον καὶ ἀπέ-	is and not to be returned, and that
χιν τὸν ὁμολογοῦντα	Hero, the agreeing party,
Ἥρωνα παρὰ τοῦ Σώτα τὴν	has received from Sotas the
συνπεφωνημένη(ν) πρὸς	agreed-upon (sum)
[...]	[...]

15-16 l. ἀπέχειν **19** ἀλλήλους τιμὴν ἀργυρίου δραχμάς, ed. pr.

This text is an objectively framed ὁμολογία of sale. It takes the following form:
1. Date and place (*ll.* 1-6)
2. ὁμολογεῖ X to Y with descriptions of each (*ll.* 6-12), followed by two dependent accusative and infinitive constructions (X is the accusative in both):
   a. πεπρακέναι, sale item with description (*ll.* 12-15)
   b. ἀπέχιν: receipt of agreed price (*ll.* 15-)

This is a standard formula for objective contracts (Bastianini, 'vendita di animali', 75, n. 9). In line 19 the price has been lost. Figure 1 suggests that the price should have been in the region of 72 to 220 drachmae, however the few surviving papyri may not be representative. The one surviving papyrus recording the sale of a horse in the first century, gives, significantly in Latin, the price as the huge sum of 2700 drachmae (Montevecchi, 'Ricerche', 50).

The ages (*ll.* 9 and 11) of the two parties involved in the sale may not be the same, as the ages given are probably approximate, perhaps rounded to the nearest multiple of five. ἀπέχιν (*ll.* 15-16) would appear to be the present active infinitive of ἀπέχω, which we might have expected to be spelt ἀπέχειν.

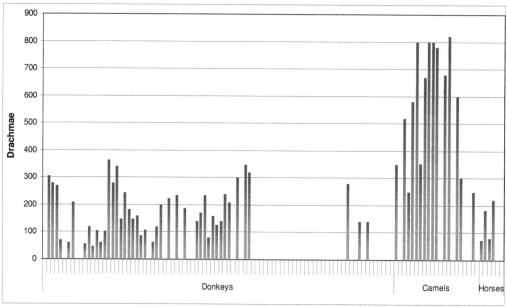

Figure 1. Transport Animal Prices in Second Century AD Egyptian Papyri (Montevecchi, 'Ricerche'; Leone, *Gli animali*; Leone, *Animali do trasporto*; Litinas 2008). Blank column spaces represent examples, like the current papyrus, where the price has not been preserved.

The sale of horses is quite rare in documentary papyri, when compared to animals such as donkeys and camels. Figure 1 shows 86 papyri recording the sale of a donkey, 21 of a camel, and only 6 of a horse. This rarity of horses is mirrored in the New Testament, as has been noted in *New Docs* 7, 128, where they only appear in military contexts. The converse is true of Roman literature, where mentions of donkeys are rare compared to those of horses (Hyland, *Equus*, 231). The choice of transport animals is another example of the socio-economic gulf separating the persons involved in the New Testament and in documentary papyri from those described in ancient literary works. While not necessarily cheaper (see Figure 1), donkeys and mules were the preferred pack animals in the Roman world (Landels, *Engineering*, 171-172), whereas horses were used primarily for military and high speed applications, such as racing and carrying of messages (Hyland, *Equus*, 231). Camels were obviously preferred in arid conditions.

Bibliography

G. **Bastianini**, 'Una vendita di animali: P. Vindob. G 31583', *ZPE* 56 (1984) 73-78; A. **Hyland**, Equus*: The Horse in the Roman World* (New Haven 1990); J.G. **Landels**, *Engineering in the Ancient World* (Berkeley 2000); A. **Leone**, *Gli animali da lavoro, da allevamento e gli ippoi nell'egitto greco-romano e bizantino* (Napoli 1992); A. **Leone**, *Animali da trasporto nell'antico Egitto: Una rassegna papirologica dalla dinastia dei Lagidi ai Bizantini* (Napoli 1998); N. **Litinas**, *References to Sales of Donkeys in the Papyri* (http://www.philology.uoc.gr/ref/sales_of_donkeys/; O. **Montevecchi**, 'Ricerche di sociologia nei documenti dell'Egitto greco-romano. III. I contratti di compra-vendita. a) Compra-vendite di schiavi e animali', *Aegyptus* 19 (1939) 11-53.

D. Keenan-Jones (Macquarie University)

Editorial note (with advice from S. Turner):

The horse is a surprisingly difficult animal to care for and so it was not generally used for agriculture and it remained scarce relative to other earlier domesticated species in antiquity. It tended to remain a "luxury" item reserved for the elite. Earlier, the development of the light, spoke-wheeled chariot was the stimulus necessary for the explosion in the number and uses of the horse, allowing the pharaohs of New Kingdom Egypt to push their hegemony into the Levant and further. The largely military use of the horse continued down into the Roman period and the situation has only changed in recent centuries with the advent of mechanized warfare.

§21 'Every dog has its day'

Termessos (Pisidia)   Limestone sarcophagus   ? Post AD 212

Ed. pr. — Termessos I, 39-42, no. 22, citing a 1991 publication in Turkish by B. Iplikçioğlu and another (= *SEG* XLI 1283)

Inscription placed on one side of the near-square undecorated sarcophagus, set out as seven hexameter lines.

1/2 .ΛΑΣ..Δ...Ο............ ΑΙ|..ΤΩ....
     Ῥοδόπ[ης ? εὐδ]αιμονια |
     ΒΑΥΛ.ΟΝ v
     Κ..Τ.ΟΝ εὐχάριτον Στέ|φανον
     παίζοντες ἐφώνουν, (vac.) ‖

4   ἐξαπίνης θανάτῳ
     μεμαραμμένον | (vac.) ἐνθάδε
     κεύθ[ει]· (vac.) |
     ἐστὶ κυνὸς τόδε σῆμα
     καταφθιμέ|νου Στεφάνοιο,
     vv

6   τὸν Ῥοδόπη δάκρυσε καὶ ὡς
     ἄνθρωπον ἔθαψεν, ‖
     εἰμὶ κύων Στέφανος, Ῥοδόπη
     δέ μ[οι] | leaf ἔκτισε τύμβον
     leaf

.LAS..D...O............AI..TO.... of Rodo[pe ? pro]sperity BAUL.ON K..T.ON (after) playing (games with) pleasing Stephanos they were crying (for him), Having suddenly wasted away to death; he li[es] here; This is (the) grave of a perished dog Stephanos. Rodope wept for this (dog) and buried him as a man. I am Stephanos (the) dog, and Rodope built m[y] grave

The owner of the dog, Stephanos, is named Aur(elia) Rodope. The *SEG* editors comment that the word K..T.ON was the pet name of Stephanos and, depending on how the three unidentifiable letters are restored, the name is either 'Koition' or 'Kittion'. Aurelia, a woman seemingly on her own, set up for herself a sarcophagus (*TAM* III I 746) in close proximity to the limestone sarcophagus of her much beloved dog. The references to 'crying' and 'weeping', although conventional, underscore the genuine emotion felt over the loss of 'pleasing Stephanos', as does the touching reference to the dog being 'buried ... as a man'. This type of heart-felt emotion for domestic dogs was widespread in the Graeco-Roman world. The final line of the epigram conveys the simple devotion of Stephanos to his owner and how that was reciprocated in the building of the grave. Other inscriptions in antiquity confirm the affection felt for pet dogs by their owners (e.g. *Anth. Lat.* 1176; 1512; *SEG* XL 1599; cf. A.L. Connolly, 'κυνάριον', 58). In what follows, we will discuss the attitude to dogs in the Graeco-Roman world and then explore its relevance to Mark 7:24-29.

The literary evidence attests to the care that Greeks and Romans exercised towards their domestic dogs and, reciprocally, the loyalty that this inspired in their pets. Here we are not focusing on the important roles that working dogs played in hunting and guarding in the world of agriculture, set out for us in the Roman agricultural treatises (Cato, Varro, Columella) and in the *Cynegetica*; that is, the specialist works on hunting written by Xenophon, Grattius, Oppian, and Nemesianus. For ancient discussions of animals, see Aristotle (*Historia Animalium*; *De Partibus Animalium*; *De Mortu Animalium*; *Parva Naturalia*; *De Generatione Animalium*), Aelian (*De Natura Animalium*) and Xenophon ('On Horsemanship': *Cynegeticus*). On dogs and hunting, see D.B. Hall, *Hounds and Hunting*; J.K. Anderson, *Hunting*; J.M. Barringer, *The Hunt*. On the visual evidence, see G.M. Richter, *Animals in Greek Sculpture*; J.M.C. Toynbee, *Animals in Roman Life and Art*. On animals in antiquity, see O. Keller, *Die antike Tierwelt*; G. Jennison, *Animals for Show and Pleasure*; S.H. Lonsdale, 'Attitudes Towards Animals'. On dogs from antiquity to the present, see D.J. Brewer, *Dogs in Antiquity*; C. Johns, *Dogs*; R.H.A. Merlen, *De Canibus*. On the use of animals, including dogs, in ancient warfare, see A. Mayor, *Greek Fire*. Our concentration, therefore, will be on household pets, given the focus of our discussion later on Jesus' encounter with the Syro-Phoenician woman (Mk 7:24-29).

In terms of the popularity and loyalty of household dogs in antiquity, the Romans and other Mediterranean peoples were besotted by the small white long-coated Melitaean, a lap-dog imported to Malta (or Meleata?) from Carthage (Pliny [The Elder], *HN* 3.26; Strabo, *Geogr.* 6.2). The man of 'Petty Pride' in Theophrastus' *Characters* understands perfectly the canine funereal culture of our inscription. He vows that 'should his Melitaean lap-dog die, he will make him a tomb and set up on it a stone to say "Branch of Melite"' (*Char.*, 93). Athenaeus tells us that the Melitaean was so popular among the Sybarians that it even accompanied their owners when they went to the gymnasium (*Deipn.*, 12.518f, 519b), whereas Aesop informs us that Meliteaen puppies were taken on sea-trips, along with apes, for the amusement of their owners during the trip (*Fab.*, 306: Chambry). Juvenal quips that women would even send their husbands to the grave in order to save their lap-dogs (*Sat.* 6.653-654). For a succinct coverage of the range of dogs known to the ancients, see J.K. Anderson ('Dogs', 490). Perhaps the most famous piece of literary evidence demonstrating the loyalty of dogs is the case involving Argos, the sporting hound of the king in Homer's *Odyssey* (14.29-36; 17.290-307). The dog greets his disguised master (Odysseus) upon his return to his household and then dies.

The importance of dogs to their owners in the Graeco-Roman world is also revealed in the iconographic evidence. The loyalty of dogs to their master is depicted on funerary *stelai* by the stereotype of the animal looking intently at its owner (e.g. Laodikeia: *MAMA* VI 27 6; E. Pfuhl and H. Möbius, *Die ostgriechischen Grabreliefs*, Tafel 46 no. 234). The attentiveness of dogs to their owners is also apparent on an Attic stele from imperial times. There we see Achilleus, rendered on the left of the stele conversing with his small dog, whose paw is extended in greeting to his master on the right (A. Conze, *Die attischen Grabreliefs IV*, 70, no. 2010, plates xviii, 443: cited J.M.C. Toynbee, *Death*, 249). This unswerving devotion of dogs to their masters, often in the face of great adversity, is matter of regular comment in the literary tradition (Plutarch, *Them.* 10.6; Pliny [the Elder], *HN* 8.61; Aelian, *Nat. an.* 1.8; 4.4; 6.25-25; 7.10, 28-29, 38, 40; 10.41, 45; 11.13; 12.35).

As far as the archaeological evidence, the physical remains of dogs are equally as revealing as the iconographic evidence. At Volos in Thessaly (VI cent. BC), there was found in the Paspalia cemetery the remains of a single individual with the bones of a dog at his feet. L.P. Day ('Dog Burials', 24) observes regarding the ambiguity of the evidence in this instance: 'The excavator suggested that the animal died from grief for its master and was buried with him, or, more likely, the dog crawled in to feed on the corpse and was unable to get out'. Further, in the afterlife the needs of much-loved pets continued to be catered for. Behind the Stoa of Attalos, located in the market place of Athens, a grave (IV cent. BC) was unearthed that contained the skeleton of a dog with a large beef bone deliberately placed near its head (J.A. Lobell and E.A. Powell, 'Man's Best Friend', 28-29). At the north wall of the Roman Yasmina cemetery in the city of Carthage, a young adult was interred in an impressive grave covered with cobbles and tiles, accompanied by the skeleton of an old dog at his feet. The find of a glass bowl, carefully placed behind the dog's shoulder, has considerable significance in a cemetery in which very few grave goods had been unearthed. Although the dog had suffered from severe physical problems, it had been exceptionally well looked after until its death in the mid-to-late teens. Michael MacKinnon, the site archaeologist from the University of Winnipeg, summed up the pathos of the find thus: 'Whether the dog represents a sacrifice — perhaps meant to 'heal' the sick person in the afterlife — or just companionship is unknown, but these two aspects need not be mutually exclusive ... this aspect of animals garnering sentimental value is a key aspect of Roman culture' (Lobell and Powell, 'Man's Best Friend', 29).

The way in which dogs accompanied their dead masters during their funeral rites is presented on sepulchral monuments in a sensitive and restrained manner. A second-century AD marble sarcophagus at the British Museum shows the deathbed scene of a child, lying on a high-backed couch surrounded by mourners, with a dog sitting beneath the couch next to the girl's slippers (V.M. Hope, *Roman Death*, plate 4). Another sarcophagus, later than the first century AD, displays the effigy of a boy holding poppies, with his little dog beside him (F. Cumont, *Recherches sur le symbolisme funéraire*, plate 41 fig. 4: cited by J.M.C. Toynbee, *Death*, 269). In the two sarcophagi above, the devotion of the dog to its owner somehow transcends the person's death, affording the deceased some continuity with the joys of life now lost, and reminding the mourning relatives of the positive relationships — symbolised by the presence of the dog — which the deceased had once possessed. Further, as S. Menache observes ('Dogs and Human Beings', 73), 'In sepulchral monuments from the late archaic to the Hellenistic period, dogs were depicted protecting their owners both against the living and against the forces of hell, thus fulfilling their function as companion animals after death as well'.

Household scenes involving children and their dogs are also commonly represented in ancient iconography. Dogs are depicted as eating from or being present at the dinner table. In a Gallic relief, we observe a boy reclining on a couch, who offers his pet dog his dinner plate to lick clean (É. Espérandieu, *Recueil général* III no. 1778; cited in F.D. Lazenby, 'Greek and Roman Household Pets', 246). In this regard, Homer (*Od.* 10.216;

cf. 17.309-310; *Il.* 22.69; 27.173; cf. *JosAs* 10:13-14; 13:8) refers to the delicate 'tit-bits' provided to dogs by their masters from the table. From the time of the sixth century BC onwards, dogs are regularly depicted on Greek vases as being positioned under the master's table waiting for food (H.M. Johnson, 'The Portrayal of the Dog', 213; Connolly, 'κυνάριον', 158). Last, a terracotta figurine from sixth-century BC Tanagra in northern Greece depicts a pet dog running away at full stretch with a piece of bread in its mouth, pilfered presumably from the family table (Lobell and Powell, 'Man's Best Friend', 35).

Other childhood scenes, involving infants and youths, show a range of interactions with dogs. In a terracotta cradle, a child is strapped comfortably inside, with a small dog curled up asleep at his feet (Espérandieu, *Recueil général* II. no. 1490; cited in Lazenby, 'Household Pets', 247). On a hydra from the Copenhagen Museum, there is a picture of a youth standing with a lyre in his right hand while his dog, standing to his left, looks up winsomely at his master after listening to (presumably) his musical performance (Lazenby, 'Household Pets', 247, fig. 1). Last, on a Greek vase from Egypt (J. Boardman, 'Greek Vase', 4) there is a picture of a boy standing on the branch of a vine, his hand held out to catch the large locust that had settled on the leaves. Tethered to the vine at the boy's feet stands a dog, with his head turned back faithfully towards its master. More examples could be given (Lazenby, 'Household Pets', 246-247), but it is clear from the ancient iconography that, notwithstanding the idealisation of its canine subjects, dogs had a positive role in the everyday routines of domestic life in the Graeco-Roman world.

In sum, although dogs did not possess the status of the human inhabitants of the household, they were nevertheless valued members of the household, as our epigram to Stephanos strikingly testifies. J. Marcus' warning (*Mark*, 463; cf. R.H. Stein, *Mark*, 351-352) to scholars about being swayed by modern sentimental attitudes towards dogs ('our canine-loving society') in discussing Mark 7:24-29 (cf. Matt 15.21-28), while methodologically sound, loses some of its force when one considers the positive attitude of the Graeco-Roman world to dogs. What light does the background evidence above throw on Jesus' encounter with the Syro-Phoenician woman?

Debate among New Testament scholars has focused on the significance of Jesus' use of the diminutive τὰ κυνάρια ('little dogs', 'puppies') in Mark 7:27 — as opposed to the normal word κύνες — in his response to the woman's request for the exorcism of her daughter (7:26). Mark's logion insists on the priority of feeding the household 'children' as opposed to the 'household' dogs who, though it is not specified in Jesus' logion, most likely sit under the table: 'Let the children (τὰ τέκνα) be fed first (πρῶτον χορτασθῆναι), for it is not fair to take the children's food (τὸν ἄρτον τῶν τέκνων) and throw it to the dogs (τοῖς κυναρίοις)'. By contrast, in Matthew's redaction of the Markan pericope (G. Jackson, *'Have Mercy on Me'*, *passim*), the first half of Mark's logion is eliminated (Mark 7:26a), the second half is converted into a question (Matt 15:26 = Mark 7:26b), and the logion itself is prefaced with a strong affirmation of the exclusivity of Jesus' mission to Israel (Matt 15:24).

Jesus' logion, it is traditionally argued, aligns with the negative attitude of Israelite society towards dogs. Jesus, like his contemporaries, transfers canine terminology pejoratively to Gentiles in verse 27 (M.E. Boring, *Mark*, 212-213; W.L. Lane, *Mark*, 262 n. 63; Marcus, *Mark*, 463-464; O. Michel, 'κύων'; V. Taylor, *Mark*, 350). M. Bird (*Jesus*, 48 n. 18) conveniently lists the texts traditionally appealed to in this regard. He also refers to a midrash on Psalm 4 which, it is argued, refers to the Gentile 'dogs' at the eschatological banquet: they will receive food to eat, but the portions are not as sumptuous as those given to the invited guests (*Midr. Ps.* 4.11; cf. Marcus, *Mark*, 464). As further proof, he cites a text from the Babylonian Talmud (*b. Hag.* 13a): 'as the sacred food was intended for men, but not for the dogs, the Torah was intended to be given to the chosen people, but not to the Gentiles'. But, like many other scholars before him, Bird does not ask whether these later rabbinic texts, post-dating the New Testament by several centuries, accurately reflect first-century viewpoints. Finally, many scholars appeal to several New Testament texts where the word κύων is used polemically in contexts of heresy and opposition (e.g. Matt 7:6; Phil 3:2; 2 Pet 2:22; Rev 22:15; cf. Gospel of Thomas 102) as extra confirmation that Gentiles were identified with 'dogs' in the Jewish world.

However, G.D. Miller ('Dogs in Ancient Israel'; cf. J. Schwartz, 'Dogs and Cats'; D.W. Thomas, '*Kelebh*, "Dog"'; A.H. Cadwallader, *Beyond the Word*, 27-34) has challenged this popular scholarly construct of Jewish attitudes towards dogs, arguing for the existence of more positive attitudes towards the animal within Israel (e.g. Job 30:1; Tob 6:2; 11:4; cf. Philo, *Praem.* 89; *b. 'Abod. Zar.* 54b). More expansively, M.D. Nanos ('Paul's Reversal', 460-469) has recently reviewed all the Jewish literature predating and postdating Paul that purportedly identifies Gentiles as 'dogs' and has concluded that none of the texts bears the weight of interpretation proposed for them. His case, I believe, is strong for the texts predating Paul. Even if some of the later 'canine' rabbinic texts (e.g. *b. Hag.* 13a *supra*; pace, on *Midr. Ps.* 4.11, see Nanos, 'Paul's Reversal') exhibit a strong anti-Gentile polemic, their use in relation to the New Testament documents is anachronistic and, therefore, problematical historically.

By contrast, other commentators have posited that Jesus' use of the diminutive τὰ κυνάρια in verse 27 qualifies to some extent the harshness of his response to the woman's request. A brief survey of the arguments advanced will suffice: e.g. H. Anderson (*Mark* 190: 'Jesus spoke half in jest'); E.P. Gould (*Mark*, 136: 'Jesus does not use the term seriously, but with a kind of ironical conformity to this common sneer'; cf. Bird, *Jesus*, 49); W.L. Lane (*Mark*, 262: 'there is no parallel to the use of the pet dogs of the household in this pejorative sense'; Jesus 'put before the woman an enigmatic statement to test her faith'); C.S. Mann (*Mark*, 321: '... the fact that the dogs in question appear to be domestic animals mitigates the saying'; cf. E. Schweizer, *Mark*, 152). Notwithstanding, all these arguments, as we will see, fall prey to philological criticism.

Several scholars are unwilling to concede any positive significance to Jesus' use of the diminutive. R.H. Gundry (*Mark*, 375), R.A. Guelich (*Mark*, 386) and R.H. Stein (*Mark*, 351 n. 2) dismiss the diminutive as insignificant, arguing that it is designed purely for stylistic effect (i.e. corresponding to the diminutive τὸ θυγάτριον in 7:25), and is commensurate with Mark's prolific use of the diminutive throughout the passage (D.C. Swanson, 'Diminutives': τό ψιχίον [7:28]; τό παιδίον [7:28, 30]). In other words, the harshness of the logion retains its full force. D. Smith ('Hard Saying') and J.D.M. Derrett ('Syrophoenician Woman') argue that there are diminutives that express contempt as much as endearment, again relativising the positive interpretation of the diminutive. Marcus (*Mark* 463) argues that in Koine Greek the diminutive is 'often indistinguishable from the regular form ... and the normal term for "little dog" is not *kynarion* but *kynidion*'. In sum, these scholars have convincingly demonstrated that it would be unwise to place any significance on Jesus' use of the diminutive in verse 27, especially given the plethora of diminutives in the Markan pericope.

A.-J. Levine ('Canaanite Woman', 413), discussing the parallel pericope of Matthew 15:21-28, speaks bluntly about attempts to 'soften' Jesus' use of 'canine' language: 'One argument holds that the use of the word for "household dogs" rather than "wild dogs" softens the insult, but this hardly makes a difference — "little bitch" is no improvement over "bitch"'. Nonetheless, the modern assumption about the inappropriateness of 'canine' language being applied to human beings does not necessarily apply in antiquity. Menache ('Dogs and Human Beings', 70) points out that Κυνίσκος and Κυνίσκα, the words for male and female puppies, 'were used by Spartans as personal names and affectionate nicknames'. A web search of the inscriptions with the Packard Humanities Institute concordance confirmed Menache's contention, with the following personal names being found in several Mediterranean regions: Κυνίσκος (*IG* II 2391; *IvO* 149; I. Kolophon 4, 6; I. Eph. II 562; *IG* XIV 643); Κυνίσκα (*IvO* 160; *IG* V.I. 1564a; *IG* V.I. 235); and Κυνάριον (*SEG* XLIV 785, p. 13). However, there are no such recorded cases in Syria or Phoenicia. Further, Cadwallader (*Beyond the Word*, 97-102) has pointed to examples of diminutives being employed as a term of abuse (*Beyond the Word*, 97 n. 44, 99, nn. 56-57), arguing that its use by Jesus aggravates the abuse of the Syro-Phoenician woman in verse 27 (*Beyond the Word*, 101). Conversely, Cadwallader (*Beyond the Word*, 220-223) provides an example of the diminutive being used to ameliorate a request (Athenaeus, *Deipn.* 359c), providing insight into the Syro-Phoenician woman's ingratiation of Jesus in verse 28. In sum, while there are positive cases of the diminutive being used as an affectionate nickname, the same diminutive can also be wielded to abuse verbally one's opponent as a 'prostitute', 'slave', or a kept 'lap-dog', or as a tactic to ingratiate oneself in relationships between social unequals.

Perhaps one way to move beyond this scholarly impasse is to recognise the Hellenistic context of Jesus' meeting with the Syro-Phoenician woman. This is a highly unusual encounter within Jesus' ministry, given that he mostly engaged with the institutions and representatives of the 'holiness system' of Second Temple Judaism, reaching out to the Jewish groups and individuals marginalised by its canons of purity (J.R. Harrison, 'Social Context'; Bird, *Jesus*). The woman, possibly a Hellenised Phoenician (Ἑλληνίς Συροφοινίκισσα τῷ γένει [Mark 7:26; cf. Matt 15:22]: G. Theissen, *Gospels*, 68-72; Cadwallader, *Beyond the Word*, 160-162; contra, Stein, *Mark*, 351), may have heard Jesus' logion somewhat differently than we moderns imagine, given the positive status of dogs in Graeco-Roman culture, for which there was some precedent, albeit very limited, in Jewish society. As Nanos argued, we have too readily assumed that the pejorative identification of 'dogs' with Gentiles had axiomatic status in Second Temple Judaism. Moreover, we must not overlook the likelihood that Jesus was speaking to this woman in Greek (S.E. Porter, 'Use of Greek'; 'Teach in Greek'). Does Jesus, therefore, accommodate himself to the woman in his response not only linguistically but also culturally, with a view to holding out for the woman the hope of participating in the eschatological banquet for Gentiles, but without thereby diminishing the priority of his mission to Israel and the nation's historic salvation privileges? Is a more subtle dynamic is occurring here than we initially imagine? Several observations are apposite here, if the Graeco-Roman background — unusually for Jesus — is seen to be determinative for his teaching on this particular occasion.

First, if the Graeco-Roman background is determinative in Jesus' response to this woman on this occasion, the 'canine' imagery in verse 27 is positive. Jesus' use of the neuter πρῶτον implies that Israel's salvation priority is not exclusive (Guelich, *Mark*, 386) and that there is a divinely appointed eschatological time-line that is unfolding in Jesus' ministry (Marcus, *Mark*, 462). The term, as Stein observes, 'brings hope to the woman'. She is part of the household living inside the house with the children, one of the Gentile 'pets' as opposed to the 'wild dogs' roaming the countryside or scavenging in the city streets (Cadwallader, *Beyond*, 24, 27; cf. Luke 16:31), or the 'guard dogs' consigned either to guard the flocks in the fields or to protect the household at the front door of the house. Note, in this regard, the mosaic from the house of Paquius Proculus at Pompeii, showing the family's guard dog on its haunches chained at a half-open door (Lobell and Powell, 'Man's Best Friend', 33), as well as the chained and snarling dog in the entrance hall mosaic, with the inscription *Cave canem* ('Beware the dog'), at Casa del Porta Tragica, Pompeii. The eschatological feast (Isa 25:6-8; Ezek 39:17-20; 1 *En* 62:12-14; *2 Bar* 29:1-4; *4 Ezra* 9:19; *T. Isaac* 6.13; IQ28a [=IQSa] *Col.* II. *ll.* 16-22; cf. D. Smith, 'Messianic Banquet'), with its 'messianic' nuptials (Mark 2:19-20), had already begun for the disciples in the ministry of Jesus. But there would be a time when the disciples fasted (Mark 2:20) and the children's food was thrown to the household dogs (7:20b), with the result that many from the east and west would take their place at the eschatological feast with Abraham (Matt 8:11; cf. Luke 6:21; 14:15-24; Matt 22:1-14). The symbolism of the two miraculous feedings of Jesus, one in Jewish territory (Mark 6:30-44) and the other in Gentile territory (8:1-10), underscores the advent of the eschatological feast and the extension of its invitation to the Gentile world (Stein, *Mark* 353).

It might be posited that the use of πρῶτον is Mark's addition to the original logion, an element of later church tradition (Rom 1:16; cf. Rom 11:17-18; Acts 13:46) that has been imported into the teaching of the historical Jesus. Is John-Mark incorporating formulations from the circles of Paul or reflecting his own contact with the apostle and his teaching (Marcus, *Mark*, 463)? However, at the time when Mark wrote his gospel, the Gentiles were already an integral part of the church's mission (Mark 13:10). Why did the salvation priority of the Jews have to be so firmly emphasised in a Syro-Phoenician context, or in a Roman context, presuming that Rome was the destination of Mark's gospel? It is a simpler hypothesis to accept that the dominical tradition has generated the later Pauline tradition in this case rather than speculate in an uninformed way about the pastoral situation of Mark's audience. Last, Taylor (*Mark*, 350) observes that πρῶτον is authentic, 'for some encouragement must have been given to the woman to prompt her witty reply in 28'.

Second, the Syro-Phoenician woman, familiar with the rituals of feeding pets in the Graeco-Roman household (Cadwallader, *Beyond*, 236), is well aware that the household dogs did not always have to wait until the children were filled (Mark 7:27: χορτασθῆναι). The feeding of the household pets sometimes occurred during the family meal, or if they were present at the meal, they could pilfer from the table, as the vase, terracotta and relief evidence above demonstrates. Thus she replies (Mark 7:27): 'Sir, even the dogs (τὰ κυνάρια) under the table eat from the crumbs of the children (ἀπὸ τῶν ψιχίων τῶν τέκνων)'. The dogs, the woman asserts, receive from the overflow of the 'messianic' extravagance in the present as much as in the future. Although the woman only asks for the 'crumbs' falling from the children's meal, nonetheless she boldly emphasises the 'already' of the advent of the eschatological feast over against the 'not yet' of its future arrival (Boring, *Mark* 214). With Jesus acceding to her request (Mark 7:29), the woman becomes a potent symbol of Jesus' openness to Gentiles on various occasions (Bird, *Jesus*, *passim*; B. Witherington, *Mark*, 233), and points symbolically to the future mission of the early church.

Finally, an alternative way of reading the pericope has been provided by the insightful and methodologically innovative work of A.H. Cadwallader, also a contributor to this volume. Cadwallader (*Beyond the Word*, 87-139) argues that, in response to the woman's request, Jesus employs a proverb of Greek rather than Jewish extraction. Jesus compounds the abuse of the woman, employing a rhythm in the proverb that was intended to offend, and casts a censorious judgment on her identity. Jesus' use of πρῶτον in verse 27, therefore, does not hold out hope of a subsequent feeding of the Gentiles but rather reinforces the pre-eminence and exclusivity of the Jews at the table (Cadwallader, *Beyond the Word*, 120-121). At this juncture, Jesus has stalled in his vocation as an exorcist and in his current ministry of outreach in the Decapolis (Cadwallader, *Beyond the Word*, 230-231). Cadwallader (*Beyond*, 141-194) skilfully delineates the social marginalisation of the Syro-Phoenician woman in Mark 7:25-26 in terms of the prevalent cultural stereotypes of the ancient world: (a) her inferiority as a woman; (b) her 'sycophantic' behaviour (7:25c, 26b); (c) the absence of any male (i.e., father or husband) in authority over her; (d) her racial inferiority as a Syro-Phoenician (7:26a), with its overtones of promiscuity, servility and occultism; (e) her failure as a mother in duty of care for her daughter (7:26b); and, last, (f) her transgression of male public space (7:25b). Notwithstanding, she is able to turn masterfully another proverb from her own culture against the crude defamatory abuse of Jesus and ingratiate herself with a social superior by means of an ameliorating use of the diminutive (Cadwallader, *Beyond the Word*, 195-242). On 'dog' as a term of abuse in the Amarna letters, see J.B. Burns, '"Devotee or Deviate"', and E.J. Bridge, 'Polite Language'.

If Cadwallader's expert analysis is correct, we are faced with the difficulty of finding a reason for the harshness of Jesus' vituperative response to the woman on this particular occasion. Perhaps it is best explained by Jesus' intense awareness of the immanent judgement facing Israel and, as the eschatological prophet announcing the restoration of Israel, Jesus demonstrates total unwillingness to be diverted in any way from that vocation. However, this solution makes Jesus' openness to Gentiles elsewhere in the gospels even more inexplicable (J. Jeremias, *Jesus' Promise*; Bird, *Jesus*). Nor does it reckon sufficiently with the fact that Jesus' prophetic vocation involved his proclamation of the eschatological pilgrimage of the nations to Zion as part of the restoration of Israel (Isa 2:2-4; 49:6; 51:5; 56:1-8 [v. 7=Mark 11:16]; 60:4-14; 66:19-21), focusing especially on the eschatological banquet for all peoples (Isa 25:6-8; Matt 8:11; 22:1-14; Luke 13:28-29; 14:16-24). For discussion, see K.H. Tan, *Zion Traditions*; S.M. Bryan, *Jesus and Israel's Traditions*; S. Freyne, *Jesus*, 92-121. Moreover, as S. Freyne has noted (Freyne, *Jesus*, 88-91), Jesus directed his prophetic oracles of judgement against Galilean towns (Corazin, Bethsaida, Capernaum: Matt 11:20-24), departing thereby from the Old Testament tradition of oracles against the wealthy Phoenician cities of Tyre and Sidon (Ezek 26-28; cf. Isa 23:1-4; Jer 25:22; Amos 1:9), and offering instead reconciliation to national enemies by moving intentionally into their territory (Luke 6:27-36; Mark 7:24, 31). If, however, Cadwallader were willing to entertain that Jesus' use of πρῶτον in verse 27 did have a sequential dimension in addition to Jewish pre-eminence, offering thereby the hope of a future feeding for the Gentiles, this difficulty in his superb exposition of the pericope would disappear.

Bibliography

H. **Anderson**, *The Gospel of Mark* (London 1976); J.K. **Anderson**, *Hunting in the Ancient World* (Berkeley 1985); J.K. **Anderson**, 'Dogs', in *The Oxford Classical Dictionary* (eds, S. Hornblower, A. Spawforth; Oxford ³2003) 490; J.M. **Barringer**, *The Hunt in Ancient Greece* (Baltimore/London 2002); M.E. **Boring**, *Mark: A Commentary* (Louisville 2006); M. **Bird**, *Jesus and the Origins of the Gentile Mission* (London/New York 2007); J. **Boardman**, 'A Greek Vase from Egypt', *JHS* 78 (1958) 4-12; D.J. **Brewer**, *Dogs in Antiquity. Anubis to Cerberus: The Origins of the Domestic God* (Warminster 2001); E.J. **Bridge**, 'Polite Language in the Lachish Letters', *VT* 60 (2010) 518-534; S.M. **Bryan**, *Jesus and Israel's Traditions of Judgement and Restoration* (Cambridge 2002); J.B. **Burns**, '"Devotee or Deviate": The "Dog" (*keleb*) in Ancient Israel as a Symbol of Male Passivity and Perversion', *Journal of Religion and Society* 2 (2000) 1-10; A. **Cadwallader**, *Beyond the Word of a Woman: Recovering the Bodies of the Syrophoenician Woman* (Adelaide 2008); A.L. **Connolly**, 'κυνάριον', *New Docs* 4 (1987) 156-159; L.P. **Day**, 'Dog Burials in the Greek World', *AJP* 88/1 (1984) 21-32; J.D.M. **Derrett**, 'Law in the New Testament: The Syro-Phoenician Woman and the Centurion of Capernaum', *NovT* 15 (1973) 161-186; É. **Espérandieu**, *Recueil général des bas-reliefs de la Gaule Romaine* (12 Volumes, Paris 1907-1947); S. **Freyne**, *Jesus, a Jewish Galilean: A New Reading of the Jesus-Story* (London/New York 2004); E.P. **Gould**, *A Critical and Exegetical Commentary on the Gospel of St Mark* (Edinburgh 1896); R.A. **Guelich**, *Mark 1-8:26* (Dallas 1989); R.H. **Gundry**, *Mark: A Commentary on his Apology for the Cross* (Grand Rapids 1993); D.B. **Hall**, *Hounds and Hunting in Ancient Greece* (Chicago/London 1964); J.R. **Harrison**, 'The Social Context', in *The Content and Setting of the Gospel Tradition* (eds, M. Harding, A. Nobbs; Grand Rapids 2010) 105-126; G. **Jackson**, *'Have Mercy on Me': The Story of the Canaanite Woman in Matthew 15.21-28* (London/New York 2002); G. **Jennison**, *Animals for Show and Pleasure* (Philadelphia repr. 2005 [1963]); J. **Jeremias**, *Jesus' Promise to the Nations* (London 1958); C. **Johns**, *Dogs: History, Myth, Art* (Cambridge, MA 2008); H.M. **Johnson**, 'The Portrayal of the Dog on Greek Vases', *CW* 12/27 (1919) 209-213; O. **Keller**, *Die antike Tierwelt*, 2 Vols. (Hildesheim repr. 1963 [German orig. 1913]); W.L. **Lane**, *Commentary on the Gospel of Mark* (NICNT; Grand Rapids 1974); F.D. **Lazenby**, 'Greek and Roman Household Pets', *CJ* 44/4 (1947) 245-252, 229-307; A.-J. **Levine**, 'Matt 15:21-28: Canaanite Woman', in *Women in Scripture: A Dictionary of Named and Unnamed Women in the Hebrew, the Apocryphal/Deuterocanonical, and the New Testament Books* (eds, C.L. Meyers, et al.; New York 2002) 411-413; J.A. **Lobell** and E.A. **Powell**, 'More Than Man's

Best Friend', *Archaeology* 63/5 (2010) 26-35; S.H. **Lonsdale**, 'Attitudes Towards Animals in Ancient Greece', *G&R* 26 (1979) 146-159; C.S. **Mann**, *Mark: A New Translation with Introduction and Commentary* (New York 1986); J. **Marcus**, *Mark 1-8: A New Translation with Introduction and Commentary* (New York 1999); A. **Mayor**, *Greek Fire, Poison Arrows, and Scorpion Bombs: Biological and Chemical Warfare in the Ancient World* (Woodstock 2003); S. **Menache**, 'Dogs and Human Beings: A Story of Friendship', *Society and Animals* 6/1 (1998) 67-86; R.H.A. **Merlen**, *De Canibus: Dog and Hound in Antiquity* (London 1971); O. **Michel**, 'κύων', *TDNT* 3 (1965) 1101-1104; G.D. **Miller**, 'Attitudes Towards Dogs in Ancient Israel', *JSOT* 32 (2008) 487-500; M.D. **Nanos**, 'Paul's Reversal of Jews Calling Gentiles "Dogs" (Philippians 3:2): 1600 Years of an Ideological Tale Wagging an Exegetical Dog', *Bib Int* 17 (2009) 448-482; S.E. **Porter**, 'Did Jesus Ever Teach in Greek?', *TynBul* 44 (1995) 195-235; S.E. **Porter**, 'Jesus and the Use of Greek: A Response to Maurice Casey', *BBR* 10/1 (2000) 71-87; G.M. **Richter**, *Animals in Greek Sculpture: A Survey* (New York 1930); J. **Schwartz**, 'Dogs and Cats in Jewish Society in the Second Temple, Mishnah and Talmud Periods', in *Proceedings of the Twelfth World Congress of Jewish Studies, Jerusalem, July 29-August 5, 1997. Division B: History of the Jewish People* (Jerusalem 2000) 25-34; E. **Schweizer**, *The Good News According to Mark* (London 1971); D. **Smith**, 'Our Lord's Hard Saying to the Syro-Phoenician Woman', *ET* 12 (1900-1901) 319-321; D. **Smith**, 'Messianic Banquet', in *Anchor Bible Dictionary*, Vol. 4 (eds, D.N. Freedman, et al.; New York 1992) 788-791; R.H. **Stein**, *Mark* (Grand Rapids 2008); D.C. **Swanson**, 'Diminutives in the Greek New Testament', *JBL* 77 (1958) 134-151; K.H. **Tan**, *The Zion Traditions and the Aims of Jesus* (Cambridge 1997); V. **Taylor**, *The Gospel According to Mark* (London 1957); G. **Theissen**, *The Gospels in Context: Social and Political History in the Synoptic Tradition* (Minneapolis 1991); D.W. **Thomas**, '*Kelebh*, "Dog": Its Origins and Some Uses of It in the Old Testament', *VT* 10 (1960) 410-427; J.M.C. **Toynbee**, *Death and Burial in the Roman World* (Baltimore/London 1971); J.M.C. **Toynbee**, *Animals in Roman Life and Art* (Ithaca 1973); B. **Witherington III**, *The Gospel of Mark: A Socio-Rhetorical Commentary* (Grand Rapids 2001).

J.R. Harrison (Macquarie University)

JUDAICA

§22 The Temple Warning

Jerusalem (a) Limestone block; 33.5 x 22.5 x 14.5 Late I BC
(b) Limestone block; 50 x 31cm

Edd. pr. — (a) C. S. Clermont-Ganneau, 'The Discovery of a Tablet from Herod's Temple', *PEQ* 3 (1871) 132-133 (= *CIJ* 2.1400 = *OGIS* II 598); and (b) J.H. Iliffe, 'The ΘΑΝΑΤΟΣ Inscription from Herod's Temple, Fragment of a Second Copy', *Quarterly of the Department of Antiquities in Palestine* 6 (1938) 1-3 + Plate I (= *SEG* VIII 169).

(a) *CIJ* 2.1400 = *OGIS* II 598 is a limestone block (33.5cm x 22.5cm x 14.5cm) with almost intact borders of 7 lines of text. It was found in secondary use in a courtyard to the north of the Temple Mount.

(b) *SEG* VIII 169 is a limestone block (50cm x 31cm) with lost right and left edges consisting of 6 lines. Its letters still show signs of red paint. The lettering and spacing are uneven and irregular, which in part is explained by the cutter's fear of running out of space. Iliffe assumes that it is the work of an inferior cutter 'intended for a less conspicuous position'. It was found in secondary use outside the Lion's Gate. Both find spots are to the north of the temple mount and thus on the opposite side from the balustrade. See below.

(a)   Μηθένα ἀλλογενῆ εἰσπο-   No foreigner is to enter
          ρεύεσθαι ἐντὸς τοῦ πε-   within the balustrade
          ρὶ τὸ ἱερὸν τρυφάκτου καὶ   around the temple and
          περιβόλου. Ὃς δ' ἂν λη-   (its) enclosed area. Whoever is
                                             caught,
5   φθῆ, ἑαυτῶι αἴτιος ἔσ-   will have himself to blame
          ται διὰ τὸ ἐξακολου-   because the incurred (penalty is)
          θεῖν θάνατον.   death.

(b)   Μη]θένα ἀλλ[ογενῆ
              εἰσπορεύεσθαι
          ἐντ]ὸς τοῦ π[ερὶ τὸ ἱερὸν τρυ-
          φάκ]του καὶ [περιβόλου. Ὃς δ'
              ἂν
          λ]ηφθῆ, αὑ[τῶι αἴτιος ἔσται
5   δ]ιὰ τὸ ἐξ[ακολουθεῖν
          θάνατ[ον.

The two inscriptions represent copies of the warning to non-Jews that stood on the balustrade of Herod's temple. Josephus describes the structure (δρύφακτος or γείσιον) as built of stone, three cubits in height, into which were set stelae at equal intervals inscribed in both Greek and Latin. He variously records a paraphrase of the inscription:

§22 The Temple Warning

μηδένα ἀλλόφυλον ἐντὸς τοῦ ἁγίου παριέναι (B.J. 5.194);

μηδένα τὸ γείσιον ὑπερβαίνειν (B.J. 6.125); and

ἑρκίον ... γραφῇ κωλῦον εἰσιέναι τὸν ἀλλοεθνῆ, θανατικῆς ἀπειλουμένης τῆς ζημίας (A.J. 15.417)

The stelae are said to forewarn of the purity law (τὸν τῆς ἁγνείας προσημαίνουσαι νόμον, B.J. 5.194), the transgression of which is ambiguously interpreted as the arrest of the culprit (τοὺς ὑπερβάντας ἀναιρεῖν, B.J. 6.126), even a Roman citizen, or as death (A.J. 15.417). For Josephus exclusion from the temple was based on the presumed ritual uncleanness of those who did not follow the laws of Moses. These persons are variously designated as ἀλλόφυλος (B.J. 5.194) or ἀλλοεθνής (A.J. 15.417).

To judge by the intact nature of *CIJ* 2.1400, the Latin translation of the warning, as commented on by Josephus, does not appear to have been cut on the same stone and therefore must have been inscribed separately. Since this practice would be unusual, it has been suggested that the Latin text was added later as necessity demanded, e.g. when Judaea passed to direct Roman rule in AD 6 (so Dittenberger, *Orientis Graeci Inscriptiones Selectae,* II.598).

The consensus view holds that the legal origin of the warning inscription was the Jerusalem priesthood. For example, in his discussion of the call to exclude Agrippa I (Josephus, *A.J.* 19.332-334), Schwartz[1] considers that the warning was based on priestly authority and reflected its position on the temple's sanctity. Krauter[2] looks at the inscription in terms of access to and exclusion from temples across Greek, Roman and Jewish religious practice and seeks to question any close connection between citizenship/ethnicity and participation in the cult. He likewise favours a priestly authorship. Lupu[3] assumes that the underlying custom or law was Jewish, and *m. Kelim* 1:8 is cited as the authority, it would appear, for the prohibition. Segal[4] also argues that a priestly authority stood behind the inscription, and believes that the text can be seen to betray its origin in the use of expressions derived from Hebrew concepts and phraseology. The suggestion, however, is problematic in that it assumes that the foreigner, as the intended reader, would understand the idiom.

In a recent study[5] we have taken a somewhat contrary position arguing from (a) the severity of the penalty compared to other Graeco-Roman temple warnings, and (b) the political purpose that the temple was to play for Herod, that the ultimate sanction of the warning rested with the king himself. The right to practise exclusion from temples was unexceptional across the Graeco-Roman world, but the punishments meted out were usually by way of fine and/or charge of impiety. This is made perfectly clear in

---

[1] D.R. Schwartz, *Agrippa I*, 124-130.
[2] S. Krauter, *Bürgerrecht und Kultteilnahme*, 144-192.
[3] E. Lupu, *Greek Sacred Law*, 19, n. 88.
[4] P. Segal, 'The Penalty of the Warning Inscription', 79-84.
[5] S.R. Llewelyn and D. van Beek, 'Reading the Temple Warning', 1-22.

Josephus' record of Antiochus III's *programma* to the Jewish authorities after his victory in the fifth Syrian War.

> μηδενὶ ἐξεῖναι ἀλλοφύλῳ εἰς τὸν περίβολον εἰσιέναι τοῦ ἱεροῦ τὸν ἀπηγορευμένον τοῖς Ἰουδαίοις, εἰ μὴ οἷς ἁγνισθεῖσίν ἐστιν ἔθιμον κατὰ τὸν πάτριον νόμον. μηδ'εἰς τὴν πόλιν εἰσφερέσθω ἵππεια κρέα μηδὲ ἡμιόνεια μηδὲ ἀγρίων ὄνων καὶ ἡμέρων παρδάλεών τε καὶ ἀλωπέκων καὶ λαγῶν καὶ καθόλου δὲ πάντων τῶν ἀπηγορευμένων ζῴων τοῖς Ἰουδαίοις· μηδὲ τὰς δορὰς εἰσφέρειν ἐξεῖναι, ἀλλὰ μηδὲ τρέφειν τι τούτων ἐν τῇ πόλει· μόνοις δὲ τοῖς προγονικοῖς θύμασιν, ἀφ' ὧν καὶ τῷ θεῷ δεῖ καλλιερεῖν, ἐπιτετρήφθαι χρῆσθαι. ὁ δέ τι τούτων παραβὰς ἀποτινύτω τοῖς ἱερεῦσιν ἀργυρίου δραχμὰς τρισχιλίας.

> No foreigner is permitted to enter within the temple's precinct which is forbidden to the Jews, except for (those) for whom after purification it is customary by tradition. Nor let one bring into the city the meat of horse, mule, wild ass, tame leopard or fox, hare or altogether of animals forbidden to the Jews. Nor is it permitted to bring their hides or even to raise any of these in the city. Only the ancestral sacrifices, from which it is necessary to offer sacrifices favourable to the god, have been permitted for use. The one who transgresses any of these (regulations) must pay to the priests three thousand silver drachmae.
>
> Josephus, *A.J.* 12.145f.

The king was the ultimate legal authority in his kingdom and the death penalty as the ultimate sanction was closely guarded by that authority. Just as Antiochus III conceded the right to a penalty to the Jerusalem priesthood, so Herod permitted the exaction of the death penalty in the case of trespass.

As to the issue of the political purpose that the temple mount's design was to play for Herod, it is essential to be aware of the two opposing structures of the *stoa basileia* and the temple with its inner courts. The gentile court stands between the two. As we observe:

> It is in the *stoa basileia* at the southern end of the pavement that Herod gave full expression to his regal status before a temple from which he, unlike his Hasmonaean predecessors, was excluded. ... the splendour of the temple and its inner courts was matched by the king's own innovative constructions in the outer court, and it was through these that most people gained access to the temple. The new structure thus advertised both the temple and Herod's rule, and by juxtaposing in such splendour the divine and the secular it highlighted the need to differentiate between the two.[6]

That the outer court became a focal point for secular activity is highlighted by Jesus' own actions in overturning the money tables of those that traded off the temple. In view of the close proximity of the holy and the profane on the new temple mount, the balustrade and its inscriptions were erected to define and protect the sanctity of the sacred space with it.

Bibliography

S. **Krauter**, *Bürgerrecht und Kultteilnahme. Politische und kultische Rechte und Pflichten in griechischen Poleis, Rom und antiken Judentum* (Berlin 2004); S.R. **Llewelyn** and D. van **Beek**, 'Reading the Temple Warning as a Greek Visitor', *JSJ* 42 (2011) 1-22; E. **Lupu**, *Greek Sacred Law* (Leiden 2005); D.R.

---

[6] Llewelyn and van Beek, 'Reading the Temple Warning', 8-9.

Schwartz, *Agrippa I. The Last King of Judaea* (Tübingen 2000), 124-130; P. **Segal**, 'The Penalty of the Warning Inscription from the Temple of Jerusalem', *IEJ* 39 (1989) 79-84.

S.R. Llewelyn and D. van Beek (Macquarie University)

§23 Pay Slip of a Roman Soldier at Masada

Masada　　　　　　　　　　16 x 12.5 cm　　　　　　　　　　AD 72 or 75

Ed. pr. — H.M. Cotton and J. Geiger, *Masada II. The Latin and Greek Documents*, (Jerusalem 1989) 35-56 (= P. Masada 722).

The papyrus, in three fragments, is assumed to be written transversa charta. The verso is blank. The text is structured with rustic capitals (3 lines) and then listings of stoppages for at least two stipendia. It is styled in the first person, though probably composed by the paymaster or his clerk. In it stoppages are listed for deduction from C. Messius' stipendium.

	IMP(ERATORE) VES]PAS[IA]N[O AU]G(USTO) IIII CO(N)[S(ULE)]		The fourth co[nsulate of Imperator Ves]pa[sianus Augustus]	
	[R]ATIO ST[IP]END[I]A		Accou]nts(?), salary	
	G(AIUS) MESSIVS G(AII) F(ILIUS) FAB(IA) BERU(TENSIS)		G. Messius, s[on of] G[aius, of the tribe] Fab[ia, from] Beiru[t.	
	[accepi st]ipendi	⋇ L	I received of my s]alary	50 denarii
5	ex eis · s[olvi]		Out of which [I have paid:	
	Hordearia	[⋇ XVI]	Barley money	[16 denarii]
6a	[?]rnius		[…]rnius	
	Sumptuarium	⋇ XX	Food expenses	20 denarii
	c[a]ligas	⋇ V	Boots	5 denarii
	lorum · fasciari(um)	⋇ II	Leather strappings(?)	2 denarii
10	tunica · linea	⋇ VII	Linen tunic	7 denarii
	accepi stipendi	⋇ LX[	I received of my salary	60 denarii
	ex eis solvi		Out of which I have paid:	
	Hordearia	⋇ XV [I	Barley money	16 denarii
14	Sumptuarium	⋇ [XX	Food expenses	[20] denarii
14a	G (aius) Antonius		G. Antonius	
15	pallium opertoriu(m)	[⋇	Overall cloak	? denarii
15a	Puplius Valerius		Puplius Valerius	
	tun[i]ca · alba	[⋇	White tunic	? denarii

3 C, Pap. 5 eos, Pap. 6 hordiaria, Pap. 7 sumtuarium, Pap. 9 linia, Pap. 10 eos, Pap. 13 hordiaria, Pap. 14 sumtuarium, Pap. 14a C, Pap.

The editors, using P. Gen. Lat. 1 recto, part 1, cols ii and iii (= Fink no.68, dated AD 81), as a point of comparison, note that P. Masada 722 is essentially a different type of account, one that covered only expenses entered against the soldier's stipendium and styled as a receipt (first person). On the other hand, P. Gen. Lat. 1 represents 'a periodical report of the amounts standing to the individual soldier's credit in the legion's *deposita*'; it is written by various hands with the legionary referred to in the third person.

Like all Latin papyri at Masada, P. Masada 722 was found at locus 1039 (casement in north-west wall), a site which, it is argued, was created as the victorious Romans sorted through their spoils shortly after the fall of the fortress. The exact date of the latter event remains a matter of dispute (i.e. either spring AD 73 or spring AD 74); see discussion by the editors on pp. 21-23. The later date is argued by W. Eck on the basis of the *cursus honorum* of L. Flavius Silva, the Roman governor of Judaea at the time of the fall of Masada.[1] The traditional date of AD 73 was established by the coordination of a chronological reference in Josephus, *B.J.* 7.409, and the assumed date in office of the Roman prefect of Egypt, T. Iulius Lupus, itself inferred from *SEG* XX 651 and P. Oxy. 1266. Although *SEG* XX 651 attests that he was in Egypt by February-March 73, uncertainty remains over the terminus of his prefecture.

The name *Messius* implies that C. Messius was a Roman citizen. He was probably a legionary in Fretensis X recruited from the Roman colony of Berytus, Syria.

Another text, P. Masada 724, is addressed to Iulius Lupus and is thus a potential peg for dating. But again there is an underdetermination in the evidence. The letter is too fragmentary to ascertain its purpose and may have:
- (a) either been received by Lupus before the fall of the fortress (assuming he was elevated to the prefecture of Egypt whilst serving in Judaea) and thus favour a date for the fall to spring AD 73; or
- (b) been written in the camp and never sent.

S.R. Llewelyn (Macquarie University)

---

[1] See also S.J.D. Cohen, 'Masada: Literary Tradition, Archaeological Remains and the Credibility of Josephus', *JJS* 33 (1982) 401, n.52.

§24 The Babatha Archive and Roman Law

Nahal Hever, Palestine   13.5 x 30.2 cm   ca AD 125
                             14.0 x 30.2 cm
                             ca 8.5 x 27 cm

Ed. pr. — N. Lewis, *The Documents from the Bar Kokhba Period in the Cave of Letters* (Jerusalem 1989) 118-120 (= P. Babatha 28-30).

No. 30 is in a different hand from that of 28 and 29. Writing is along the fibres and the back is blank. Dating is inferred from their assumed association with proceedings in AD 124-125 (see P. Babatha 13-15) against the guardians of Babatha's son.

The three copies form part of an archive of 28 documents in Nabataean, Aramaic and Greek found bundled together in a concealed crevice in the Cave of Letters. The lettering shows the use of somewhat older forms (e.g. tau) and a comparative lack of ligatures. Together with syntactic features the editor suggests that for the scribe Greek was probably a second language (Aramaic being L1). It is also noted that writing across the fibres may also have been a scribal practice in Jewish and Aramaic areas. Though found in the Judaean desert most of the documents were written in what had become after AD 106 the Roman province of Arabia.

28

Με[τα]ξὺ τοῦ [δεῖνος τοῦ δεῖν]ος	Between so-and-so son of so-and-so
ἐνκαλοῦν[τος καὶ τ]οῦ δεῖνος	the plaintiff and so-and-so (son of so-and-so)
ἐνκαλουμέ[νου μ]έχρ[ι] (δηναρίων) Βφ	the accused for up to 2,500 denarii.
ξενο[κρί]ται ἔ[στωσαν]. Ἐπεὶ	Let xenokritai be appointed. Whereas
5 ὁ δεῖνα τ[οῦ] δεῖν[ο]ς. [ὀρ]φανοῦ	so-and-so has handled the guardianship
ἐπιτροπ[ὴ]ν ἐχείρισεν,	of so-and-so, orphan,
περὶ ο[ὗ] πράγματος ἄγεται,	concerning which issue (action) is brought
ὅταν διὰ τ[ο]ῦτο τὸ πρᾶγμα	so-and-so must give to
τὸν δεῖνα τῷ δεῖνι δοῦναι	(or) do for so-and-so (something) in good
10 ποιῆσαι δέῃ ἐκ κ[α]λῆς	faith, let the xenokritai of this (action)
πίστεως, τούτου οἱ ξενοκρίται	condemn so-and-so in favour of so-and-so
τὸν δεῖνα τῷ δεῖνι μέχρι	for up to 2,500 denarii.
δην(αρίων) Βφ κατακρειν[ά]τωσαν ἐ[ὰν δὲ] μὴ φ[αί]νηται ἀπο-	But if it does not appear, let them acquit. (It has been written by ...)
15 [λυσ]άτωσαν.	

29

μεταξὺ τοῦ δεῖνος [τοῦ] δ[εῖνος]
ἐνκαλοῦντος καὶ τοῦ [δεῖνος ἐν]-
καλουμένου μέχρι (δηναρίου) [B]φ̅
  ξενο-
κρίται ἔστωσαν ἐπε[ὶ] ὁ δεῖνα
5 τοῦ δεῖνος ὀρφανοῦ
  ἐ[πι]τ[ρ]ο[π]ὴ[ν]
ἐχείρ[ι]σεν, περὶ οὗ πράγμ[ατ]ος
ἄγεται, ὅταν διὰ τοῦτο τὸ πρᾶγμα
τὸν δεῖνα τῷ δεῖνι δοῦναι ποιῆ-
σαι δέῃ ἐκ καλῆς πίστεως,
10 τούτου οἱ ξενοκρίται τὸν δ[εῖ]να
τῷ δεῖνι μέχρει δην(αρίων) B̅φ̅
κατακρεινάτωσαν, ἐὰν δ[ὲ μ]ὴ
φαίνηται ἀπολυσάτωσα[ν.]

15

20

30

με[ταξὺ τοῦ δ]ε[ῖνος]
τοῦ δ[εῖνος ἐ]ν[κ]α̣λ[ο]-
υν[τος καὶ τ]οῦ δε[ῖνο]ς
τοῦ δεῖ[νος] ἐνκαλ-
ουμέν[ου] μέχρι δ-
ηναρίω[ν B̅φ̅] (vac.)
ξεν[ο]κρίτε [ἔστω]σαν.
ἐπὶ ὁ δεῖνα [τοῦ] δεῖ-
νος [ὁ]ρφα[νοῦ ἐ]πιτ-
ροπ[ὴν] ἐ[χείρι]σεν,
περ[ὶ οὗ πράγματος]
[ἄγεται, ὅταν διὰ]
το[ῦτο τὸ πρᾶγμα]
τὸν δ[εῖνα τῷ δεῖνι]
δοῦ[ν]α̣ι [ποιῆσαι δέῃ]
ἐκ ‹κ›αλῆς [πίστε]-
ως, τ[ούτου οἱ ξενο]-
κρίτ[ε τὸν δεῖνα τῷ]
δ[εῖνι μέχρι δην(αρίων)]
B̅[φ̅ κατακρινάτω]-
[σαν, ἐὰν δὲ μὴ φαίνη-]
[ται, ἀπολυσάτωσαν.]
ἐ[γράφη διὰ   ]

28.13-14 l. κατακρινάτωσαν 29.11 l. μέχρι 30.7 l. ξενοκρίται 30.8 l. ἐπεὶ

Background

Babatha was a Jewish woman who was born in the village of Maoza just south of the Dead Sea in what is now the state of Jordan. Her date of birth (ca AD 100) and time of death (ca AD 132) are matters of conjecture based on the assumed age of her orphaned son and the fact that she never returned to retrieve her documents.

Babatha was twice married with a son, Jesus, to her first husband, also named Jesus. She was the second wife (Miriam being the first wife) in the marriage contracted to her second husband, Judah, a fact of some interest for the study of polygamy in this period.

The connection with En-gedi was through her second husband and the property she acquired through him.

Babatha appears to have been a woman of some substance in the region. This is principally indicated from the contents of the papyri which attest her property and that of her family. Further support is argued from the garments and goods found in the cave and assumed to belong to the group with which Babatha sheltered. Another line of argument might also be pursued. In the papyri she appears to pursue aggressively her perceived rights and those of her son. The absence of the 'widow's rhetoric' has been observed in her petitions; she does not appeal to her helpless state but rather to her position to preserve the interests of her son.[1] But what can be inferred from this is problematic; no doubt such a stance is to be expected given that she is asserting her ability to attend better to these than the current guardians.

She lived all her life in her home town of Maoza until her assumed flight to the cave near En-gedi. The reason for her 'flight' to Judaea in the course of the revolt is a matter of conjecture. W. Eck[2] has considered the sources for the Bar Kochba revolt from the Roman side and has drawn together useful evidence to show the seriousness of the revolt. This is reflected in the numbers of Roman legions and auxilia involved in the war, the calibre of the generals (Iulius Severus sent from Britain, Publicius Marcellus governor of Syria and Haterius Nepos governor of Arabia) who were in all probability drawn into the revolt, the exceptional measures and honours/titles (*ornamenta triumphalia* and *imperator*) awarded and the change in the name of the province after victory. Basing his argument in part on the Babatha and Salome Komaise archives, Eck suggests that not only were the Roman forces in Arabia drawn into the actions in Judaea but also that the revolt may have spilled over into the Jewish communities in the neighbouring province of Arabia.[3] If this were the case, Babatha's flight may have been as a result of the rebels' defeat there and the fear of reprisals against local Jewish communities.[4]

Equally plausible is the suggestion that sees the documents' presence in the caves as a sure sign that Babatha participated in the revolt.[5] Katzoff cheekily suggests that she may

---

[1] Hanson, 'Widow Babtha', 100. We are reminded of the Yavneh-yam ostracon (Hebrew) of the seventh century BC where the worker equally appeals in his petition to his rights rather than to pity. See Naveh, 'Hebrew Letter', 129-139.
[2] Eck, 'bar Kokhba Revolt', 76-89. Mor, 'The Geographical Scope', 107-131, questions Eck's conclusions on the geographical extent of the conflict, though not its intensity.
[3] So also Cotton, 'Some Aspects', 82. The article otherwise treats of the independence of the Roman governor of Judaea and the toparchic system (administrative units with chief village/city as centre with function of tax collection). See also Alon, *The Jews*, 595-618.
[4] From the use of witnesses and joint guardians of mixed ethnic identity, the papyri appear to attest that before the revolt relations between Jews and their Nabataean neighbours were amicable, e.g. the appointment of 'Abdo-obdas son of Ellouthas, a Nabataean, as guardian for Babatha's son. If Eck is right, then the revolt may have caused a change in ethnic relations in Arabia. See also Bowersock, *Roman Arabia*, 108.
[5] Cotton, 'Rabbis', 173.

have been driven to side with the rebels due to her frustration with Roman rule and law.[6] Indeed, it is assumed that many Jews from the southern areas sought refuge around Engedi, because it was a rebel stronghold. But the Bar Kokhba connection is argued circumstantially on the basis of (a) the date of the latest document; and (b) the find spot of the archive in the Cave of Letters where three of Bar Kokhba's letters had been found during the previous excavation season.

P. Bab. 28-30 represent the first known Greek version of the Roman legal formula of *actio tutelae*. It gives no date, location or other information over the occasion and purpose for its composition. Though written in Greek the legal system on which it rests is Roman. In other words, the language of the document does not appear to determine the legal system of the case.

Legal and other Complexities

In Roman law of the Republic an action under civil law had to be brought by the plaintiff before the praetor. The latter did not decide the dispute but determined whether the case could proceed to trial. He issued a decree which appointed the judge (or judges) and formulated in terms of the *ius civile* the issue that needed to be established. If the judge established that it was so, then the edict commanded him to condemn; if not, to acquit. The formulary system, as it is called, and associated praetorian edict was a source of legal innovation through the period of the Republic. In time the issues to be decided extended beyond those defined under the older statutory formulae of the civil law (*ius civile*). Actions could be brought on the basis of contracts entered into under good faith (*bona fides*) or between parties not contemplated by the old civil law, and exemption clauses in favour of the defendant were included in the formulae. In other words, the formulary process took into account the growing technical variability of contractual arrangements as the commercial influence and power of Rome grew. The praetors would publish annually, when they took office, the principles under which they would administer their legal jurisdiction and the formulae to be used in actions under it. Presumably other Roman magistrates (including provincial governors), who possessed legal jurisdiction, modelled their administration of justice on the praetor by emulating his edict. It is of interest that the edict, which had long ceased to be innovative, received a fixed form under Hadrian (AD 130) and thus at about the time of the Babatha archive.

The archive affords insight into the workings of courts and the legal system in a newly created Roman province (Nabataea became the Roman province of Arabia in AD 106). It is here that the speed of Romanisation is deserving of comment especially with regard to the laws governing appointment of guardians and the use of stipulation and *testatio*.[7]

---

[6] Katzoff, 'P.Yadin 21', 575.

[7] Cotton, 'Guardianship of Jesus son of Babatha', 94-108; Cotton, 'Private International Law or Conflict of Laws', 246-247; and Chiusi, 'Babatha vs the Guardians', 105-132. Roman features of guardianship are: exclusion of women from guardianship, Roman sentiment (weak as this is prepared for legal matter before governor), use of or intention to use the Roman formulary system (*actio tutelae* – nos 28-30), the use of an *epitropos tou pragmatos*, Babatha's offer to indemnify her son's guardians. But cf. Yiftach-Firanko, 'Judaean Desert Marriage Documents', 67-84, who argues that the deeds of marriage in Greek were an

See especially the above text of P. Bab. 28-30 which represent the first known Greek version of the Roman legal formulary process of *actio tutelae*. In other words, an element of the formulary process of the city of Rome administered by the praetor is appealed to in a case of legal obligation brought by a provincial residing in Arabia, an instance which Wolff describes as 'nicht unbeträchtliche Romanisierung'.[8] But the question remains how such a specifically Roman legal institution functioned in terms of provincial law. The solution lies, as Wolff notes, in the person of the Roman governor and his position as the highest legal authority in the province.[9] The legal proceedings of Babatha may be framed with reference to Roman law if the case were to be heard by *cognitio*.

Given that both in Egypt and Arabia the Jews in the documents that survive use the local legal systems with no indication of peculiar Jewish practice, Cotton asks: 'What is ... the precise meaning of the privilege successfully sought and granted to Jews by the Roman government, namely to live according to their ancestral laws and customs ...? Surely the papyri from Egypt and Arabia render the evidence for legal autonomy elsewhere very difficult to interpret.'[10] It has long been held that the Rabbinical portrayal of its legal traditions as normative is overstated for the first and second centuries,[11] though more recently there have been challenges to this.[12] But such challenges do not go all the way to explain the fact that the language of the document often appears to determine the legal system in use. Documents in Aramaic (and more so Hebrew) follow more closely Jewish legal custom (e.g. deed of marriage) whereas those in Greek do not.[13] Cotton[14] suggests that the reasons for Jewish resort to Greek documents were practical, i.e. to make the deeds valid in non-Jewish courts and able to be registered in the public archives[15] (perhaps registration was required by law as a lien existed over the husband's

---

'attempt to formulate in Greek terms and according to the Greek formulaic tradition institutions and customs of non-Greek origin'.
[8] Wolff, 'Römisches Provinzialrecht in der Provinz Arabia', 774.
[9] Wolff, 'Römisches', 785-786.
[10] Cotton, 'Guardianship', 100; and Cotton, 'Rabbis', 177.
[11] On the Hellenistic nature of marriage contracts between Jews but recorded in Greek see H. Cotton, 'Cancelled Marriage Contract', 64-86; H.M. Cotton, 'Die Papyrusdokumente', 228-247.
[12] Katzoff, 'P. Yadin 21', 545-575. The article rests its case on the legal fiction of the document which presents as a sale of dates but is in reality a contract to harvest them. Details such as (a) that the language reflects documents quoted in Rabbinic literature; (b) that the distraint is stated to be 'in lieu of dowry and debt' and no mention is made of alimentation; and (c) that the distraint is against immovable property which is the case while the dates are still on the tree, are to be explained in terms of rabbinic law governing the right of the woman to self-help to recoup her dowry. But a question still remains over the possibility that rabbinic law merely reflects local practice in this matter.
[13] The language of document determines the law, as well as the system of dating. See Cotton, 'Corpus Inscriptionum Iudaeae/Palaestinae', 329.
[14] Cotton, 'Guardianship', 101; Cotton, 'Rabbis', 169-170 84-85.
[15] A registry (ἀρχεῖον) operated in Judaea before AD 66 but was destroyed in the revolt in AD 66 (Josephus, *B.J.* 2.426-427) and/or AD 70 (Josephus, *B.J.* 6.354). According to Josephus the intention of those who burnt the archive was to curry favour with debtors. In other words, the archives were places where debts were recorded and saved and thus acted to protect the rich. In all probability the registry would, like those in Egypt, house the tax lists regularly created in the Roman census. This can perhaps be inferred from Josephus, *C.Ap.* 31, who states that genealogical records for the priesthood were situated in it and were consulted in the instance of their marriage. If priesthood afforded the individual special tax status, then it

property for maintenance and dowry payment so that a future purchaser might know of encumbrances). Cf. also oaths by the emperor's tyche. The point is argued on the basis that the signatures are in Aramaic, though the documents are in Greek.

Cotton notes the reliance of the guardian documents on Roman formulary practice and sees this as a sign of Romanisation. But one might pause for thought here. It is to be remembered that the hearing was by *cognitio* before the Roman governor, the highest legal authority in the province (Gaius 1.6).[16] All things being equal he would be prejudiced in the application of Roman legal principles. But recognition of local custom was also possible as the evidence of translations of legal collections suggests.[17] That a particular legal instrument was adopted by Babatha does not imply that she was following the law of the land.[18] On marriages (*DJD* II, 21 and P. Yadin 10) Cotton notes that the Greek documents are not translations of a Jewish *ketubah* and that this is clear in the nature of the dowry involved.[19] She also entertains the possibility of marriage by cohabitation without a written contract.

i. The Provincial Edict
At least during the Republic, Roman provincial governors issued edicts as did Cicero as governor of the province of Cilicia in 51-50 BC; he followed, he says (*Ad. Att.* 6.1.15), many clauses in the provincial edict of Q. Mucius Scaevola, including one that Greeks should conduct their disputes under their own laws ('suis legibus'). Amongst the matters he dealt with were matters that could not be dealt with without a provision in the edict ('quod sine edicto satis commode transigi non potest'), such as the possession of inheritances 'de hereditatum possessionibus', describing them as matters that were usually litigated and conducted under an edict ('quae ex edicto et postulari et fieri solent'). However many provisions were left unwritten, ἄγραφον, because he had announced that his 'edicta' would conform to those of the urban edicts, presumably that of the urban and peregrine praetors ('ad edicta urbana commodaturum').[20]

The form of the provincial edict is referred to also in Cicero's orations *In Verrem*, since Verres as proconsul of Sicily in 73-71 BC had at least in respect of granting possession of intestate estates, 'de hereditatum possessionibus', followed the urban edict except that of himself as *praetor urbanus* in 74 BC, which contained innovations Cicero attacks as corrupt: *Verr.* 2.1.44, 114-116, 118. He had also in the exercise of his jurisdiction deprived the Sicilians of their rights under the *Lex Rupilia* or the decree of the governor

---

was important for the government to regulate marriage and the religious status of offspring. Cf. Hezser, *Jewish Literacy in Roman Palestine*, 150ff.
[16] See Cotton and Eck, 'Roman Officials', 23-44. The governor's authority could be delegated to legates, tribunes and prefects under their control. Authority in some cases was also delegated to local officials. Imperial procurators, assisted by imperial freedmen, exercised legal authority in fiscal matters independent of the governor by virtue of their appointment.
[17] Modrzejewski, 'What is Hellenistic Law?', 13.
[18] For a similar argument regarding the use of the formulary system in Egypt see, Katzoff, *ANRW*, 825-833, esp. p. 831.
[19] One exception is noted, namely, the clause dealing with the son's inheritance of the dowry. See Cotton, 'Rabbis', 175-176
[20] See Buckland, 'L'Edictum provinciale', 81-96.

P. Rupilius at the time of the establishment of the province: *Verr.* 2.1.13, 32-33. Although Cicero clearly condemns Verres for this, his own provision that the Greeks should conduct their disputes under their own laws shows, as Jolowicz and Nicholas say,[21] that 'if he wished, he might have substituted some entirely different system during his term of office'. Provincial governors issued edicts at least up to AD 68 in the reign of Galba, when the prefect of Egypt issued an edict, which however contained no rules concerning the conduct of private litigation.[22]

The urban or praetorian edict, as already noted, was codified and fixed by the jurist Salvienus Julianus in about AD 130 after an edict of the Emperor Hadrian confirmed by a senatus consultum: see the constitution 'Tanta' 18; the constitution says nothing about the provincial edict and it is not clear whether codification of it was carried out at the same time. However, it is clear that the provincial edict survived in some sense since Gaius (who died after AD 178) wrote a commentary *Ad edictum provinciale XXX*, quotations from which appear in the *Digest* and which according to Honoré was written in the period AD 155-160, after the codification of the praetorian edict.[23]

ii. Guardianship

What we have in the above three documents from the Babatha archive is a Greek translation of a Roman statutory formula which is recorded by Gaius (*Institutes* 4.47). The Latin text and its translation reads:

Sed ex quibusdam causis praetor et in ius et in factum conceptas formulas proponit, ueluti depositi et commodati. illa enim formula, quae ita concepta est:	In some instances, however, the prætor permits formulas having reference to either law or fact to be employed; for example, in actions of deposit, and loan for use. The following formula:
IVDEX ESTO. QVOD AVLVS AGERIVS APVD NVMERIVM NEGIDIVM MENSAM ARGENTEAM DEPOSVIT, QVA DE RE AGITVR, QVIDQVID OB EAM REM NVMERIVM NEGIDIVM AVLO AGERIO DARE FACERE OPORTET EX FIDE BONA, EIVS, IVDEX, NVMERIVM NEGIDIVM AVLO AGERIO CONDEMNATO. SI NON PARET, ABSOLVITO,	'Let So-and-So be judge. Whereas Aulus Agerius deposited a silver table with Numerius Negidius, for which this action is brought, whatever Numerius Negidius is obliged to pay to, or do for, Aulus Agerius, in good faith, on this account, do you, judge, condemn Numerius Negidius to pay to, or do for Aulus Agerius (unless he makes restitution); and, if the case should not be proved, let him be discharged.'
in ius concepta est.	is one of law.
at illa formula, quae ita concepta est:	The following formula:
IVDEX ESTO. SI PARET AVLVM	'Let So-and-So be judge. If it appears that

---

[21] Jolowicz and Nicholas, *Historical Introduction*, 101.
[22] See Smallwood, *Docs Gaius*, §391.
[23] Honoré, *Gaius* (Oxford 1962) 69.

AGERIVM APVD NVMERIVM NEGIDIVM MENSAM ARGENTEAM DEPOSVISSE EAMQVE DOLO MALO NVMERII NEGIDII AVLO AGERIO REDDITAM NON ESSE, QVANTI EA RES ERIT, TANTAM PECVNIAM, IVDEX, NVMERIVM NEGIDIVM AVLO AGERIO CONDEMNATO. SI NON PARET, ABSOLVITO,	Aulus Agerius deposited a silver table with Numerius Negidius, and, through the fraud of the said Numerius Negidius, the said table has not been restored to the said Aulus Agerius, do you, judge, condemn Numerius Negidius to pay to Aulus Agerius a sum of money equal to the value of the property, and if the case is not proved let him be discharged';
in factum concepta est. similes etiam commodati formulae sunt.	is one of fact. Similar formulas are employed in an action of loan for use.[24]

The first formula introduced by *QUOD* concerns the issue of legal obligations arising from an agreement entered into under good faith. The fact of the deposit is not in dispute. What is to be determined are the legal obligations arising from the agreement. In the second formula introduced by *SI PARET*, it is the fact that needs to be determined by the judge. The above Greek translations are framed according to the formula *in iure*. The facts of the deposit (in our case assumed to be the funds deposited with the legal guardians of Babatha's son to be used to provide for his upkeep) are not at issue, but whether the guardians have fulfilled their obligations in good faith.

Lenel (*Das edictum perpetuum*, §124, 255) reconstructs the formula for an *actio tutelae* in the following terms:

> Quod N^s N^s A^i A^i (contraria A^s A^s N^i N^i) tutelam gessit quidquid ob eam rem N^m N^m A^o A^o dare facere oportet ex fide bona, eius iudex N^m N^m A^o A^o c(ondemnato) s(i) n(on) p(aret) a(bsolvito),

upon which the Greek versions of the formula which are in P. Bab. 28-30 appear to be based.

Guardians or tutors for Babatha's son Jesus were, as is evidenced by P. Yadin 12, appointed after the establishment of the province of Arabia: that is shown by the date and by the reference to the 'acta' (ἀπὸ ἄκτων βουλῆς) or minutes of the city council of Petra; appointment of guardians in this manner after the establishment of the province was not, so far as we are aware, in accordance with Roman law, under which, according to Gaius (*Inst.* 1, 183, 185 & 195) tutors were appointed in a province by the governor ('praeses provinciae'); see also Justin. *Inst.* 1.20. Pr., where the rule is attributed to a late Republican *Lex Julia et Titia*.

From the time of Marcus Aurelius *legati* of proconsular governors and *iuridici*, or deputy prefects of Egypt who were acting in Alexandria, might appoint (*Dig.* 1.20.2, and 26.5.1) and at any rate from the time of Ulpian (who was killed in about AD 225) all

---

[24] Translation taken from http://faculty.cua.edu/pennington/Law508/Roman%20Law/GaiusInstitutesEnglish.htm#FOURTH%20BOOK

municipal magistrates might appoint inhabitants of their area as tutors (*Dig.* 26.5.3). By the time of Justinian the jurisdiction was exercised in Rome by the consuls and in the provinces by the governors or in the case of modest estates ('non magnae facultates') by local magistrates ('magistratus') on their orders (Justin. *Inst.* 1.20.4). The provisions of the *Lex municipii Salpensani* (Riccobono, *FIRA* I 2, No. 23, c XXIX) and the *lex Irnitana* (see: J. Gonzalez, 'The Lex Irnitana', 147-243: c XXIX) both of which provide for the appointment of tutors for a ward by one of the *iiviri iure dicundo* of the municipality and under some circumstances after a decree by the *decuriones* or city councillors.

Certainly in Egypt appointments were made by local magistrates, στρατηγοί of nomes, on the direction of the δικαιόδοτης (*iuridicus*) (see P. Harris 68 a petition to the στρατηγός for such an appointment) or of the prefect (see P. Tebt. 326) or by lesser local officials such as the ἐξηγητής (P. Oxy. 888) or γραμματεὺς τῆς πόλεως (P. Oxy. 487, a petition to the ἐπιστράτηγος to give directions that the γραμματεύς make a substitutionary appointment).

The *actio tutelae* could be brought only after the termination of the tutorship (*Dig.* 27. 3. 1. 24) and accordingly would have been inapplicable since it appears that Babatha's purpose in commencing action against the tutors was to obtain for him a higher rate of maintenance while they remained tutors: see her summons and deposition of October AD 125 (P. Bab. 14 & 15).

iii. Marriage and Polygamy

Cotton argues that marriage contracts between Jews recorded in Greek are Hellenistic rather than Jewish.[25] The differentiation is made by comparison with Aramaic marriage contracts and includes: (a) that the clause 'according to the law of Moses and the Jews' is lacking in Greek contracts; (b) that the marriage settlement is essentially different, i.e. it is not a bride price paid from groom's family to bride's family but a dowry which was brought into the marriage by the bride. There are, however, peculiarities in Judaean Greek documents between Jews, for example, (a) the liability clause for maintenance of the wife and covering future property, not just the property at time of contracting, and (b) the clause that a son inherits his mother's dowry.

Satlow, *Jewish Marriage in Antiquity*, 68-89, sees marriage as a two-part procedure: betrothal (ἔκδοσις) where the father relinquishes the bride and wedding where husband assumes the rights. But betrothal so understood was a rabbinic institution and not universally practised in the second-temple period. Most marriages were without documents and the documents, those that do exist, focus on economic matters within the marriage.[26] The only Jewish legal stipulations were that male children inherit a wife's

---

[25] Cotton, 'Cancelled Marriage', 64-86.
[26] Yiftach-Firanko argues that both dowry payment and *ekdosis* was fundamental for the Greek contracts from the archive. The transfer of property through the dowry did not suffice itself to constitute marriage, but the *ekdosis* also needed to be recorded. He sees here an important difference from the Hellenistic contracts from Egypt in which the recording of the dowry sufficed to attest marriage.

marriage settlement and that her female children be supported from the husband's estate. The former may attest acceptance of polygamy. The phrase 'according to the law of Moses and the Jews', which Satlow (*Jewish Marriage*, 85-86) sees as part of a Semitic scribal tradition, parallels the phrase in an Edomite marriage deed 'according to the custom of the daughters of [Edom]' (176 BC). The question is how meaningful the phrase would be without the existence of Jewish courts to enforce the law.

On the issue of the law of marriage in the regulation of spousal property, Satlow argues that the documentary evidence, in opposition to the Talmudic literature, indicates that Jews followed local custom. In other words, the biblical *mohar* or bride price largely disappeared and was replaced by the dowry after the Hellenistic model. The dowry was subject to a guarantee clause and the Jewish stipulation that the wife's male children inherit it. Its purpose was as a payment to compensate the husband for maintaining his wife and in the case of divorce to allow the wife to sustain herself for a short period. The *ketubah* (כתובה) itself was a Babylonian fiction, envisaged as a means to compensate the woman when divorce became unilateral. In any case, the wife's access to her patrimony was largely safeguarded in practice by the use of gifts;[27] these placed the property outside the dowry and thus outside the husband's direct control. This is different from the Talmud which in seeking to restrict the wife's control over independent property envisages the dowry itself as the chief vehicle of property transmission.

The evidence from the archive suggests that polygamy was not just practised by the top echelons of society but extended somewhat down the social hierarchy, though it is possible that customs differed between regions with polygamy more widely practised in more traditional rural areas.[28] Babatha, as already observed, was the second wife in the marriage contracted to her second husband, Judah. The provision that a son inherit his mother's dowry is also construed as a further indication of polygamy, as it protected the inheritance of her children in a polygamous marriage. Of interest also is the fact that by law the bride price (*ketubah*) was reduced in the case of an already married woman. The editor assumes that this might be indicative that this 'was the best that a widow – even a young, well-to-do widow – could expect' (Lewis, *Documents*, 22). At the same time he also surmises that there may have been a shortage of men due to recent Jewish revolts. The latter, which is mere conjecture, would also place pressure on the marriage prospects of women.

iv. Language
The editor argues the influence of both Latin and Aramaic on the language of the archive. See pp.13-21. Wolff notes the following Latinisms:
1. λιβλάριος = libellarius or perhaps preferably librarius (P. Bab. 15);[29]
2. μαρτυροποίημα = testatio, perhaps to be used as a legal deposition confirming details for a related suit to be heard in Petra (P. Bab. 15);[30]

---

[27] See Llewelyn, 'Paul's Advice on Marriage', 10-18.
[28] Still, polygamy is denounced in CD 4.21 and thus one must assume that it was practised.
[29] Wolff, 'Römisches', 769, 789.
[30] Wolff, 'Römisches', 779-781, 789.

3. The use of seven witnesses to the double document;[31]
4. Use of acta in P. Bab. 12; and
5. Date by (a) consuls and Roman calendar, (b) at the beginning of a cheirograph, (c) simple declaration of receipt without appended promise not to take legal action, (d) the use of *epitropos* rather than *kurios* for a woman's guardian assumes Roman legal context which did not distinguish between the tutor of minor and of a woman, a distinction maintained in Greek as well as the Aramaic subscription to our document (κύριος, אדון / ἐπίτροπος, אפטרפא) (P. Bab. 27).[32]

On the issue of Latin influence, Lewis notes the relative isolation of the Roman province of Arabia from the inroads of Hellenism in the earlier period. Accordingly he concludes: 'the inhabitants of the new province of Arabia were so much the readier to accept and adopt many of the practices and locutions of the new government.' This was no doubt further facilitated by the direct involvement of Roman military officers rather than Greek-speaking provincial officials in the various administrative functions (e.g. P. Bab. 16, a census return).

The case of Semitisms is perhaps the more interesting given the history of the discussion of the influence of Aramaic on the formulation of the Greek in the NT. The editor lists under the category a number of features which could truly be considered Semitisms, e.g. omissions of the definite article with abstract nouns or in nouns with a dependent genitive (genitive construct type), the use of the nominative absolute participial construction (P. Bab. 18, *ll.* 36-37). But many others are what have in NT studies been or could be categorized as Septuagintalisms, e.g. the introduction of direct discourse by the participle, λέγων; the order in which the four points of the compass are given. But as the listing of Greek phrases which translate Aramaic legal formulae shows (pp. 15-16) many of the documents are framed and conceptualised through Aramaic legal idiom.

Conclusion

At the beginning it was noted that for the scribe Greek may have been a second language and that certain scribal practices might be an indication of Jewish/Aramaic custom. The question therefore arises as to how the provincial scribe came by the Roman statutory formula. Did he have access to a Roman legal text or was it part of the provincial edict? Since it was the governor who would draw up the case in terms of the formula, did he also appoint the ξενοκρίται (members of the courts), did he refer the

---

[31] The use of double documents arose to protect against the falsification of documents, the inner (upper) copy of the contract being sealed and only opened to verify the correctness of the lower text. The need for this form ceased when documents were officially registered, but the practice and use of double documents did not die out immediately. The form had so established itself that it was not altogether surrendered in all places; however, the inner text was increasingly abbreviated. This is the situation met in our archive where some of the documents are copies from the official register, but are nevertheless in the double form. Others which are originals lack seals.

[32] Wolff, 'Römisches', 790-797. Exceptions exist which may show some influence of local custom, e.g. length of guardianship and the active role of the mother in proceedings for her adult son.

case to an existing body, or did he hear the plea itself? And if the former, why should a local court be expected to apply Roman law? The texts are thus significant in so far as they bear on the relationship of the Roman governor to the legal institutions operating within his *imperium*.

Bibliography

G. **Alon**, *The Jews in their Land in the Talmudic Age 70-640 C.E.* (London 1989); G.W. **Bowersock**, *Roman Arabia* (Cambridge, MA 1983); W.W. **Buckland**, 'L'Edictum provinciale', *RB* 13 (1934) 81-96; T.J. **Chiusi**, 'Babatha vs the Guardians of her Son ...', in *Law in the Documents of the Judaean Desert* (eds, R. Katzoff, L. Schaps; Leiden 2005) 105-132; H. **Cotton**, 'The Guardianship of Jesus Son of Babatha: Roman and Local Law in the Province of Arabia', *JRS* 83 (1993) 94-108; H. **Cotton**, 'A Cancelled Marriage Contract from the Judaean Desert', *JRS* 84 (1994) 64-86; H. **Cotton**, 'The Rabbis and the Documents', in *Jews in a Graeco-Roman world* (ed., M. Goodman; Oxford 1998) 173; H.M. **Cotton**, 'Die Papyrusdokumente aus der judäischen Wüste und ihr Beitrag zur Erforschung der jüdischen Geschichte des 1. und 2. Jh.s n.Chr', *ZDPV* 115 (1999) 228-247; H.M. **Cotton**, 'Some Aspects of the Roman Administration of Judaea/Syria-Palaestina', in *Lokale Autonomie und römische Ordnungsmacht in den kaiserzeitlichen Provinzen vom 1. bis 3. Jahrhundert* (ed., W. Eck; Oldenburg 1999) 82; H.M. **Cotton**, 'Corpus Inscriptionum Iudaeae/Palaestinae: A Multilingual Corpus of Inscriptions', in *Acta XII Congressus internationalis epigraphiae graecae et latinae* (Barcelona, 2007) 329; H. **Cotton**, 'Private International Law or Conflict of Laws', in *Herrschen und Verwalten: Der Alltag der römischen Administration in der hohen Kaiserzeit* (eds, R. Haensch, J. Heinrichs; Cologne 2007) 246-247; H.M. **Cotton** and W. **Eck**, 'Roman Officials in Judaea and Arabia', in *Law in the Documents of the Judaean Desert* (eds, R. Katzoff, D. Schaps; Leiden 2005) 23-44; W. **Eck**, 'The bar Kokhba Revolt: The Roman Point of View', *JRS* 89 (1999) 76-89; J. **Gonzalez**, 'The Lex Irnitana: A New Copy of the Flavian Municipal Law', *JRS* 76 (1986) 147-243; A.E. **Hanson**, 'The Widow Babatha and the Poor Orphan Boy', in *Law in the Documents of the Judaean Desert* (eds, R. Katzoff, D. Schaps; Leiden 2005) 100; C. **Hezser**, *Jewish Literacy in Roman Palestine* (Tübingen 2001); T. **Honore**, *Gaius* (Oxford 1962); H.F. **Jolowicz** and B. **Nicholas**, *Historical Introduction to the Study of Roman Law* (Cambridge [3]1972); R. **Katzoff**, *ANRW* II 13 (1980) 825-833; R. **Katzoff**, 'P.Yadin 21 and Rabbinic Law on Widow's Rights', *JQR* 97 (2007) 575; S.R. **Llewelyn**, 'Paul's Advice on Marriage and the Changing Understanding of Marriage in Antiquity', in *New Docs* 6 (ed., S.R. Llewelyn; Macquarie University 1992) 1-18; M. **Mer**, 'The Geographical Scope of the Bar-Kokhba Revolt', in *The Bar Kochba War Reconsidered: New Perspectives on the Second Revolt against Rome* (ed., P. Schäfer; Tübingen 2003) 107-131; J.M. **Modrzejewski**, 'What is Hellenistic Law?' in *Law in the Documents of the Judaean Desert* (eds, R. Katzoff, D. Schaps; Leiden 2005) 13; J. **Naveh**, 'A Hebrew Letter from the Seventh Century B.C.', *IEJ* 10 (1960) 129-139; M.L. **Satlow**, *Jewish Marriage in Antiquity* (Princeton 2001); E.M. **Smallwood**, *Documents Illustrating the Principates of Gaius, Claudius and Nero* (London 1967); H.J. **Wolff**, 'Römisches Provinzialrecht in der Provinz Arabia (Rechtspolitik als Instrument der Beherrschung)', *ANRW* II.13, 769-789; U. **Yiftach-Firanko**, 'Judaean Desert Marriage Documents and Ekdosis', in *Law in the Documents of the Judaean Desert* (eds, R. Katzoff, L. Schaps; Leiden 2005) 67-84.

G. Rowling and S.R. Llewelyn (Macquarie University)

§25 Dedicatory Inscription at Ostia Synagogue

Ostia   Marble slab   II² – III
                         36 x 54.3 x 2.5-3.5 cm

Ed. pr. – M. Guarducci, *Epigrafia greca, Vol. 3: Epigrafi di carattere privato* (Rome 1974) 15-17 (= *SEG* XLII 916 = *JIWE* I.13).

The inscription was found in secondary usage (dated to the 4th century AD) on a marble slab in the paving of the synagogue's vestibule. The size of the letters varies from a height of 3 cm to 5 cm. The inscription consists of 6 lines: the first line in Latin and the rest in Greek. The orthographic features of the Greek inscription reflect the Jewish patterns of pronunciation and spelling in Imperial Rome.[1]

Study of the orthographic features of the text indicates that two different types of Greek characters from two different time periods are present. The first 5 lines, although the first in Latin and the rest in Greek, belong to the same hand, the Greek characters being of the 2nd century AD. The last 2 lines written on an erased surface present more recent Greek lettering corresponding to 3rd century Greek orthography. The chronological and stylistic difference can be noted in the change from a square M in the first 5 lines to a curved form in the name of Mindius Faustus.[2] Accordingly, the inscription seems to have been first inscribed in the 2nd century AD and reused in the 3rd century AD when the last 2 lines were added on the erasure of the original lines. In the 4th century AD it was then recycled in the pavement of the synagogue.

	Pro salute Aug(usti) [n(ostri)]	For the welfare of [our] Aug(ustus).
2	οἰκοδόμησεν κὲ αἰπο[ί]-	He has built and
	ησεν ἐκ τῶν αὐτοῦ δο-	made by his own gift
4	μάτων καὶ τὴν κειβωτὸν	and has dedicated
	ἀνέθηκεν νόμῳ ἁγίῳ	the ark for holy law,
6	Μίνδις Φαῦστος με-	Mindius Faustus,
	[τὰ τῶν] ἰδίω[ν].	[with his] co-religionists(?).[3]

2-3 l. καὶ ἐποίησεν.

The stone slab is a dedicatory inscription belonging to two different people and centuries. The first inscription, the dedicator of which remains unknown, probably referred to the construction of the ark of the Torah in the synagogue in the 2nd century AD. The small size of the dedication may indicate that its main object was only the small ark rather than the whole synagogue. The second usage of the inscription saw the original name of the dedicator erased and replaced by that of Mindius Faustus. The latter's dedication, based on its lettering, belongs to the 3rd century AD and refers to the redecoration of the ark of the Torah. In fact the ark of the Torah appears to have been

---

[1] L.M. White, 'Synagogue', 41.
[2] White, 'Synagogue', 39, n. 47.
[3] The last line can be only supposition. Some have taken the last line to be part of the name, resulting in Mindis Dius or Diocas. This speculation has been due to the occurrence of same name on other Ostian inscriptions. For more discussion see White, 'Synagogue', 39-40.

redecorated in the 3rd century with the addition of 2 small columns supporting an architrave with a corbel roof decorated with Hebrew symbols including a *menorah*.[4]

The use and reuse of the inscription covering the 2nd to the 4th centuries has made it an important piece of evidence for the reconstruction of the building history of the Ostia synagogue.[5] The inscription has also shed light on the social tapestry of the population of imperial Ostia.

The inscription records the dedication of the Torah ark or receptacle (קדש ארון), in Greek, but only after first indicating well wishes to the emperor in Latin. One might easily assume that *pro salute Augusti* is more a pragmatic and standard beginning to a public dedication than a sincere expression of feelings towards the Roman emperor.[6] On the other hand, the salutary formula could be seen as an indication of Mindius Faustus' membership in a group of Jews dependent in some way or other on the emperor. In fact there is evidence of two other synagogue communities from Rome called the 'Augustesians' and the 'Agrippesians', respectively (Noy, *JIWE* 2: Augustesians in nos 96, 169, 189, 194, 542, 547; Agrippesians in nos 130, 170, 549, 562). The names suggest that these communities were dependent on the imperial household.[7] Mindius Faustus could have been one member of such a particular Greek-based ethno-cultural group making up the Jewish community at Ostia. As Rome's port, the city is likely to have been a melting pot of peoples of diverse ethnic and cultural backgrounds. Of further interest is the inscription's reference to the dedicator's personal gift, τὰ αὐτοῦ δόματα (*ll.* 3-4). While the author could perhaps have meant 'from his property/house/expenses',[8] it is more likely to be a reference to a financial gift, in particular to the tenth offering or tithe. If so, the inscription contributes to our understanding of Jewish practice in Ostia and Imperial Rome. But would such an offering be called a 'gift'?

Bibliography

D. **Noy**, *Jewish Inscriptions of Western Europe* 2 (Cambridge 1995); A. **Runesson**, 'The Oldest Original Synagogue Building in the Diaspora: A Response to L. Michael White', *HTR* 92 (1999) 409-433; M. F. **Squarciapino**, *Atti del VI Congresso Internazionale di Archeologia Cristiana, Ravenna 23-30 Sept. 1962* (Vatican City 1965) 314; L.M. **White**, 'Synagogue and Society in Imperial Ostia: Archaeological and Epigraphic Evidence', *HTR* 90 (1997) 23-58; L.M. **White**, 'Reading the Ostia Synagogue: A Reply to Runesson', *HTR* 92 (1999) 435-464.

E. Piccolo (Macquarie University)

---

[4] M. Guarducci, *Epigrafia greca*, 17.
[5] See White, 'Synagogue', 23-58 and A. Runesson, 'The Oldest', 409-433.
[6] Guarducci, *Epigrafia greca*, 17.
[7] White, 'Synagogue', 42.
[8] White notes that while usually meaning 'gifts' it could also mean 'funds' or as 'rooms' referring to the house or rooms from which the synagogue was renovated ('Synagogue', 40-41, n. 49).

§26 The Names of Jewish Women

T. Ilan, 'Notes on the Distribution of Jewish Women's Names in Palestine in the Second Temple and Mishnaic Periods', *JJS* 40 (1989) 186-200; reported in *SEG* XXXIX 1618; T. Ilan, *Lexicon of Jewish Names in Late Antiquity, Part I: Palestine 300 BCE – 200 CE* (Tübingen 2002).

Ilan seeks to use 'the total of all the onomastic material available' to deduce 'the major onomastic trends' ('Notes', 186) of its chosen area and period: Palestine across half a millennium.

Table I in a 'Corpus of Women Known by Name' (Ilan, 'Notes', 193-200) itemises 247 women using 68 different names. The names are classified according to the language of their origin, as follows:

	No. of women	Percentage	No. of names	Percentage
Hebrew	145	58.7	11	16.1
Greek	45	18.2	31	45.5
Aramaic	42	17.0	14	20.5
Latin	10	4.0	8	11.7
Persian	4	1.6	3	4.4
Nabatean	1	0.4	1	1.4
Total	247	100	68	100
Salome and Mariamme	119	47.7	2	2.9

The corresponding tally for men was (in 1989) 2040, 8.2 men to 1 woman, leaving women as 10.8% of the total population as attested. 'It may be concluded that they were discriminated against in these sources' (Ilan, 'Notes', 186). In order to enquire into the causes of this, Ilan made a comparison across five source-categories, as follows:

		Men	Women	Ratio
1.	Josephus	442	40	11.5:1
2.	Gospels/Acts	92	16	5.7:1
3.	Rabbinic	605	25	24.2:1
4.	Funerary	487	152	3.2:1
5.	Papyri	375	19	19.7:1
6.	Others	42	0	
		2043	252	

Notes
1. Josephus will have taken in the Herodian 'gossip and scandal' (Ilan, 'Notes', 187) from Nicolaus of Damascus, with prominent court women.
2. 'The early Christians moved in circles less established in traditional paternalism than Judaism' (Ilan, 'Notes', 188).

§26 The Names of Jewish Women

3. Only one woman is named from the 'world of scholars', where women were 'legally barred' from the 'institutions of study' (Ilan, 'Notes', 188). The rest arise in 'semi-historical accounts, legends and judicial rulings'.
4. Bones deposited in the ossuaries 'belonged to men and women equally' (Ilan, 'Notes', 189). But while a woman's inscription often included the name of a father, husband or son, the converse was less common with a man's inscription.
5. While women are absent from military documents, they are involved fully in those relating to property, marriage and divorce.

In Ilan's *Lexicon* of 2002 these tallies were expanded by 50%, to 3193 men and 402 women. The increase results partly from a wider range of literary sources (e.g. Apocryphal, Patristic) but more likely from the flow of new data from inscriptions (esp. ossuaries) and papyri (from the Judaean desert).

Tables 7 and 8 of the *Lexicon* list the ten most frequently attested names for men and women. Alongside these tallies we set the frequencies presented in *BDAG*. One must note that all the NT names have already been counted in the *Lexicon*, while *BDAG* of course includes the very numerous classic Hebrew names from the two genealogies of Jesus (Matt 1:1-14; Luke 3:23-38).

Male Names	*Lexicon*	BDAG	Egypt	Female Names	*Lexicon*	BDAG	Egypt
Simon (Simeon)	257	9	✓✓	Mariam (Mary)	80	7	✓✓
Joseph (Joses)	231	12	✓✓	Salome	63	1	–
Judah	179	8	✓	Shelamzion	25	–	–
Eleazar (Lazarus)	177	3	✓	Martha	20	1	✓✓
Yohanan (John)	128	7	✓✓	Joanna	12	1	✓
Joshua (Jesus)	103	5	✓✓	Shiphra	12	–	–
Hananiah (Ananias)	85	4	✓✓	Berenice	10	1	✓
Jonathan	75	–	✓	Sarah	9	1	✓
Mattathias (Matthew)	63	2	✓	Imma	7	–	–
Menahem	46	–	–	Mara	7	–	–

(a) *BDAG* = Bauer's *Greek-English Lexicon of the New Testament*, 3rd edn. 2000.
(b) 'Egypt' = listed (✓) or frequent (✓✓) in the papyrological *Namenbuch* of Preisigke with Foraboschi's *Onomasticon alterum*.

In 'Notes', 191-192, Ilan discusses why the names Mariam and Salome were so 'exceptionally popular' (50% of all women had one or the other). 'One possible explanation' is that they were typically Hasmonean. In the male list, Mattathias and his five sons (John, Simon, Judas, Eleazar and Jonathan) claim 30% of the men.

The only Salome attested however from this connection is the sister of Herod the Great, while his wife is the only Mariam. The dynasty had by then long become 'loathsome to its Jewish subjects' (Ilan, *Jewish Women*, 55). The heroic generation of the Maccabees

150 years before must have included a Mariam and a Salome who inspired the flood of namesakes across the following centuries in Palestine.

Unlike Mariam, Salome did not pass into either Egyptian or Christian currency. The name was perhaps well known (e.g., from Josephus) as that of the girl who asked for the head of John the Baptist on a platter (Matt 14:6; Mark 6:22). But onomastic fashions varied greatly from region to region, as the ongoing *Lexicon of Greek Personal Names* is demonstrating. The Greek papyri of Egypt moreover extend several centuries beyond Ilan's terminal year of AD 200. The explicitly Christian allocation of personal names is not noted before Dionysius, bishop of Alexandria AD 247–264.

Bibliography

N.G. **Cohen**, 'Jewish Names as Cultural Indicators in Antiquity', *JSJ* 7 (1976) 97-128; G.H.R. **Horsley**, '... a Problem like Maria', *New Docs* 4 (1987) 229-230; T. **Ilan**, *Jewish Women in Greco-Roman Palestine: An Inquiry into Image and Status* (Tübingen 1995) 53-55; T. **Ilan**, *Mine and Yours are Hers: Retrieving Women's History from Rabbinic Literature* (Leiden 1997); M. **Peppard**, 'Personal Names and Ethnic Hybridity in Late Ancient Galilee: The Data from Beth She'arim', in *Religion, Ethnicity and Identity in Ancient Galilee: A Region in Transition* (eds, J. Zangenberg, H.W. Attridge, D.B. Martin; Tübingen 2007) 99-113. R. **Singerman**, *Jewish Given Names and Family Names: A Bibliography* (Leiden 2001).

E.A. Judge (Macquarie University)

CHRISTIANITY

§27 'Diogenes the Christian'*

Apollonia Limestone stele with a pediment c. AD 280
72 x 43 x 31 cm

Ed. pr. — J.R.S. Sterrett, *The Wolfe Expedition to Asia Minor: Papers of the American School of Classical Studies at Athens*, Vol. III 1884-1885 (Boston 1888) 555; W. Tabbernee, *Montanist Inscriptions and Testimonia: Epigraphic Sources Illustrating the History of Montanism* (North American Patristic Society, Patristic Monograph series 16; Macon 1997) no. 34 and plate 11, image 34; E. Gibson, *The 'Christians for Christians' Inscriptions of Phrygia* (Missoula 1978) 44; W.H. Buckler, W.M. Calder and W.K.C. Guthrie, *Monumenta Asiae Minoris Antiqua* (= *MAMA*), Vol. 4 (Manchester 1933) 221.

Αὐρ. ᾿Αρτέμων Αὐξά- νοντος τρὶς Δομετίου τῷ πατρὶ Αὐρ. Αὐξάνοντι τρὶς Δο- μετίου βουλευτῇ καὶ τῇ μ- 5 ητρὶ Αὐρ. Δόμνῃ Εὑρήμονο[ς] Λικινίου οἱ υἱοὶ αὐτοῦ Αὐ[ρ.] Ζωτικὸς καὶ Αὐξάνων [κ]αὶ Αὐρ. ᾿Αρτέμων ἔγονος [ἐ-] ποίησαν καὶ ἡ γυνὴ αὐτοῦ 10 ὑστέρα Αὐρ. ᾿Αμμία Νανιτ[η-] νὴ Βράδωνος Αὐρ. Αὐξάνον- τι Ζουλα(*vac.*)κίῳ βουλευτῇ δὶς Δομετίου καὶ τῇ γυνεκὶ αὐτο- ῦ τῇ π(*vac.*)ρώτῃ Αὐρ. Δόμνῃ Δο- 15 ύλου (*vac.*) Διογένου Χρηστια- (*vac.*)	Aurelius Artemon son of Auxa- non, son of Auxanon, son of Auxanon, son of Dometios, for his father Aurelius Auxanon son of Auxanon, son of Auxanon, son of Do- metios, councillor, and his mo- ther Aurelia Domne daughter of Heuremon son of Likinios. His sons Aurelii Zoticus and Auxanon, and Aurelius Artemon his grandson, made (this gravestone), and so did his later wife Aurelia Ammia Nanitene daughter of Bradon, for Aurelius Auxanon Zoulakios, councillor, son of Auxanon son of Dometios, and his first wife Aurelia Domne daughter of Do- ulos son of Diogenes, a Christ-

---

* A precursor of this entry was given as a paper to the Staff-Student Research Seminar of the Department of Classics and Ancient History in the University of Auckland as long ago as 2004. I wish to thank Prof. W.K. Lacey, and others who were present on that occasion: none of these persons, however, should be blamed for anything which is amiss in this article.

νοῦ (vac.) τ(vac.)οῖς γλυκυτάτοις   ian, for their most sweet
γονῖσιν μνήμης χάριν   parents, *in memoriam*.

In this complex gravestone from Apollonia (Mordiaeum) in the province of Galatia, the first six lines adopt the point of view of Artemon, who cites his ancestry as far back as his great great grandfather Dometios: he has buried his father Auxanon, and his mother Aurelia Domne. But from line 6 onwards the text is borrowed, presumably from an earlier gravestone which was perhaps dismantled at the time of the extant stone's dedication: there Artemon is referred to as the grandson of the (earlier) deceased, Auxanon also known as Zoulakios, who was buried together with his first wife, also called Aurelia Domne.

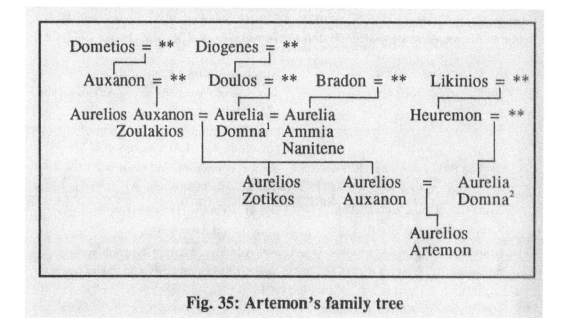

Fig. 35: Artemon's family tree

William Tabbernee in 1997 included this gravestone in his *Montanist Inscriptions and Testimonia*, although he concluded that it could not be classified as Montanist.[1] Tabbernee's summary of Artemon's family tree appears to be correct,[2] as does his dating of the stone c. 280.[3] In this article I will put forward a speculative identification of one of the members of Artemon's family, and suggest on the basis of that identification that the case for viewing this gravestone as a Montanist monument is stronger than Tabbernee thought.

---

[1] Tabbernee, *Montanist Inscriptions*, 234.
[2] Tabbernee, *Montanist Inscriptions*, 232: Tabbernee's Fig. 35 is reproduced here.
[3] Tabbernee, *Montanist Inscriptions*, 229 and 234.

§27 'Diogenes the Christian'

An interesting yet puzzling feature of the epitaph is its mention of 'Diogenes, a Christian' (*ll.* 15-16). The third letter of the word Χρηστιανοῦ is an *êta*,[4] and a flaw in the stone makes the remaining *iota* look like an *omega*. In 1884, Sitlington Sterrett read Χρηστωανου. A squeeze taken in 1930 showed W.M. Calder that there was an *iota* carved over the *omega*-shaped flaw in the stone.[5] So the grandfather of Aurelia Domne, first wife of Auxanon Zoulakios, was certainly 'Diogenes, a Christian'. Her father, Diogenes' son, was called Doulos. Doulos can be paralleled in Phrygia, although it seems an odd choice for a personal name (= 'Slave'):[6] Tabbernee cites *MAMA* VII 288 from Amorion,[7] and *MAMA* IV 263 from Pise may be added—a gravestone dedicated (coincidentally) by one Aurelius Doulos also known as Artemon.

One question which has occurred to scholars who have studied the Auxanon epitaph is whether the mention of Diogenes the Christian in the text implies that other members of the family were Christians. Tabbernee took a narrow view, noting that 'the family, which was possibly designated as Christian since Diogenes' time, is the family comprising Aurelia Domna's paternal lineage, not necessarily (or not at all!) the family into which she married'.[8] This I think unnecessarily cautious, like wondering if a petition to an emperor, recorded in an inscription, was successful or not: communities were not usually going to carve unsuccessful petitions in stone. Implicitly the family was in an overall sense a Christian one — though that is not the same thing as to say that every individual named on the stone was a Christian.

Less attention has been given to another question: *why* Diogenes is described as having been a Christian. Being a Christian was not a distinction, or an honour conferred by peers, like being a councillor (as Auxanon Zoulakios and his son Auxanon were). No doubt Christian assertiveness, or freedom (around AD 280) from fear of reprisals, is part of the answer; but even so, why Diogenes? The reminiscence concerns Grandma's grandfather, whom possibly no living family member had met, at the time when the gravestone was set up at about AD 280. Calder found that the context of the text as a whole made him hesitate to accept the phrase 'Diogenes, a Christian' at all. 'The difficulty of taking Χρηστιανός in the sense of "Christian" is obvious', he wrote.[9] 'An epitaph in which the grandfather of one of the dead is singled out as "a Christian" is not only unique: it comes close to being absurd.'

Sensitivity to the difficulty Calder perceived is in order. Accordingly, I propose that the phrase 'Diogenes, a Christian' was included in the text because Diogenes was a

---

[4] A normal spelling in papyrus documents: Judge and Pickering, 'Papyrus Documentation', 59, 67-68, with n.78.
[5] Calder, 'New Jerusalem', 422.
[6] The Pauline resonance of δοῦλος (Rom 1:1, Tit 1:1) might be thought to justify giving the name to a child in a household of suitable piety.
[7] Tabbernee, *Montanist Inscriptions*, 233.
[8] Tabbernee, *Montanist Inscriptions*, 233-234. On p. 234 Tabbernee says, 'There is no absolute evidence that anyone other than Diogenes was a Christian' — a comment which disregards in a strange way the motivation of the family members who had the gravestone made, and the implications of the context as a whole.
[9] Calder, 'Philadelphia and Montanism', 349.

memorable or important Christian — perhaps one of whom readers of this gravestone at modern Senirkent (ten kilometres from the urban centre of Apollonia at modern Uluborlu) would have heard.

Tabbernee proposed that Zoulakios and his first wife Domne were 'probably born no later than the last decade of II',[10] i.e. the 190s. He argued from the possession by the family members of the Aurelius name, positing that Zoulakios and Domne would have received it as adults, in the second decade of the third century. Domne's personal name is a pointer in the same direction. Septimius Severus married Julia Domna in 187, but at the time he was not yet emperor. In 193, the first year of Severus' reign, Julia Domna received the title of Augusta; then, in 195, she was given the additional title of Mother of the Camp. It is probable that a great many more girls empire-wide were named Domna after 193 — and accordingly it is likeliest that Aurelia Domne, daughter of Doulos son of Diogenes, was born after 193. Diogenes, then, it may be inferred, would be a memorable or important Christian born about the middle of the second century.

There is a suitable Diogenes, though his name is epigraphically attested in the shortened form 'Diogas'. He was the dedicator of the gravestone of Bishop Artemidoros at Temenothyrai (Uşak) — an inscription dated c.200-210 by Tabbernee[11] — and later (now himself called Bishop Diogas) he was the dedicator of the gravestone of Ammion, a woman presbyter, also at Temenothyrai (Uşak).[12] His own grave was marked with a Type G Uşak 1 door stone which Tabbernee dates to the second quarter of the third century,[13] a stone which in 2009 I saw on display in the garden of the Archaeological Museum at Uşak. In all these inscriptions his name is spelt as Διογᾶς or Δειογᾶς, but the use of a shortened form in those places does not imply that a fuller spelling could not be employed elsewhere. Diogas' association with the woman presbyter Ammion is sufficient to show that both were Montanists, as Tabbernee concluded,[14] even before he had discovered the 'portals of the New Jerusalem', namely Tymion and Pepouza. Pepouza is only eighteen kilometres away from Uşak, to the south.[15]

Apollonia is some 120 kilometres away from Temenothyrai/Uşak, in a south-easterly direction. The suggestion that Domne's grandfather was Diogenes/Diogas, the Montanist Bishop of Temenothyrai, involves supposing it to be probable that he, or at least his son Doulos, made that journey, possibly in order to preach the gospel of Jesus and the New Prophecy — and then that Doulos married, and (in the 190s or later) fathered Domne. But supposing this does not draw too long a bow: Montanists were energetic at spreading their message, or it would not have reached Carthage and Rome; and the road system of Phrygia and Pisidia made the journey from Temenothyrai to Apollonia feasible: Temenothyrai, Sebaste, Eumeneia, Apamea (Kelainai), Apollonia.[16]

---

[10] Tabbernee, *Montanist Inscriptions*, 234.
[11] Tabbernee, *Montanist Inscriptions*, no. 3.
[12] Tabbernee, *Montanist Inscriptions*, no. 4, dated by Tabbernee in the same decade as no. 3.
[13] Tabbernee, *Montanist Inscriptions*, no. 5.
[14] Tabbernee, *Montanist Inscriptions*, 72.
[15] Tabbernee, 'Portals', 89.
[16] Talbert, et al (eds), *Barrington Atlas*, maps 62 and 65.

Diogenes/Diogas probably grew up at Temenothyrai, near the geographical heart of Montanism, living through the decades (the 160s and 170s) when Montanism was taking its characteristic shape and being separated from majority Christianity.[17] If he came from out of town late in the second century and made a strong impression at Apollonia with his preaching,[18] the otherwise cryptic reference to Diogenes the Christian is perhaps accounted for: he would have been a local celebrity for decades afterwards, at least in Christian eyes. If it is thought plausible that Diogenes the Christian was Diogas, Bishop of Temenothyrai, then the hypothesis that the Auxanon gravestone comes from a Montanist context is reinvigorated.

Bibliography

W.H. **Buckler**, W.M. **Calder** and W.K.C. **Guthrie**, *MAMA* Vol. 4 (Manchester, 1933); W.M. **Calder**, 'Philadelphia and Montanism', *BJRL* 7 (1922-1923) 309-353; W.M. **Calder** 'The New Jerusalem of the Montanists', *Byzantion* 6 (1931) 421-425; E. **Gibson** *The 'Christians for Christians' Inscriptions of Phrygia* (Missoula 1978); E.A. **Judge** and S.R. **Pickering**, 'Papyrus Documentation of Church and Community in Egypt to the Mid-fourth Century', *JbAC* 20 (1977) 47-71; P. **McKechnie**, 'Apollonia: an Early Testimony for Christianity in Anatolia', *Epigraphica Anatolica* 41 (2008) 141-146; J.R.S. **Sterrett** 'The Wolfe Expedition to Asia Minor', *Papers of the American School of Classical Studies at Athens* 3 (1884); W. **Tabbernee** and P. **Lampe**, *Pepouza and Tymion: the Discovery and Archaeological Exploration of a Lost Ancient City and an Imperial Estate* (Berlin/New York 2008); W. **Tabbernee**, 'Portals of the Montanist New Jerusalem: the Discovery of Pepouza and Tymion', *JECS* 11.1 (2003) 87-93; W. **Tabbernee**, *Montanist Inscriptions and Testimonia: Epigraphic Sources Illustrating the History of Montanism* (Patristic Monograph series 16; Macon 1997); R.J.A. **Talbert**, et al. (eds), *Barrington Atlas of the Greek and Roman World* (Princeton 2000); C. **Trevett**, *Montanism: Gender, Authority and the New Prophecy* (Cambridge 1996).

P. McKechnie (Macquarie University)

---

[17] Trevett, *Montanism*, 26-54; Tabbernee and Lampe, *Pepouza and Tymion*, 4-7.
[18] I have argued elsewhere that at Apollonia, soon after 214, the family of Alexandros, also known as Artemon, commemorated in *MAMA* IV 222, carved a cross in the pediment of his gravestone to mark their family's Christian commitment. This is evidence for a Christian community at Apollonia early in the third century (McKechnie, 'Apollonia', 141-146).

§28 A Difficult (?) Request to 'beloved father' Diogenes

Oxyrhynchus   10.5 x 25.5 cm   IV[1]

Ed. pr. — M.G. Sirivianou, *The Oxyrhynchus Papyri*, Vol. LVI (London 1989) 117-210 (= P. Oxy. 3858).

The text is described as 'written in a careful and practiced hand based on a good literary type, a large sloping severe style'. There is no address for this letter; the back of the letter is blank. This is also the case for P. Oxy 3857 and a number of other letters, which suggests the bearer of the letter was told how to find the addressee or otherwise knew how to find him/her (*New Docs* 8, 170-171). *Nomina sacra* are contracted ($\overline{κω}$, *l.* 3; $\overline{θς}$, *l.* 25), the final *nu* at line ends is abbreviated with a high stroke (*ll.* 4, 11, 14) and dieresis (ϊνα) is found in *ll.* 9, 23.

The trapezoidal shape (9.5 cm wide at the top and 10.5 cm wide at the bottom) suggests the sheet was cut carelessly from a roll. Fold marks suggest careless folding or throwing away once read. The first fold is horizontal below the middle of the sheet, and then folded again on a vertical axis, also just off centre (Sirivianou, 117).

	τῷ ἀγαπητῷ καὶ πατρὶ	To the beloved and father,
	Διογένει Βαρὺς ὁ ἀδελ-	Diogenes: (From) Barys, the brother
	φὸς ἐν κ(υρί)ῳ χαίριν.	in the Lord. Greetings.
	εἰδώς σου τὴν ἀγάπη(ν)	Knowing your love
5	καὶ τὴν θεοσέβειαν	and your reverence of God
	ἣν ἔχεις πρὸς ἡμᾶς,	which you have for us,
	κύριέ μου πάτερ, δι' αὐ-	my lord father, for this very reason
	τὸ τοῦτο ἔγραψά σοι, ἀξι-	I wrote (= I am writing) requesting
	ῶν σε, ἵνα μὴ ἐπιβαρή-	you that I may not be a [financial] burden
10	σω τοῦ ἐλθεῖν πρὸς σέ,	to you.
	εἰδώς σου τὴν ἀσχολία(ν)	Knowing your busyness
	τοῦτο οὖν σε ἀξιῶ,	this I therefore request you,
	οὐκ ἐπιτάσσων, περὶ	not commanding (you): about
	Ὥρου, περὶ οὗ ἐλάλησέ(ν)	Horus, about whom spoke to you
15	σοι Παθερμοῦθις, πε-	Pathermpouthis—about
	ρὶ αὐτοῦ, εἰ δυνατόν	him—[that] if possible
	ἐστιν, συγχωρῆσε αὐ-	you can grant him
	τῷ ταύτην τὴν τε-	this
	τράμηνον, ἐπιδὴ πά-	four months, since
20	νοι μέτριός ἐστιν καὶ	he is (of) moderate means, and
	ἔχει χωρίον Σερηνιανῷ.	has a piece of land for Serenianus.
	τῷ γὰρ Ἀθὺρ μέλλι ἀπο-	In Hathyr he is intending to

§28 A Difficult (?) Request to 'beloved father' Diogenes

τάξε αὐτῷ ἵνα σχολάσῃ	leave (*give it up*) so that he may (thus) be unoccupied
τῇ λιτ[ο]υργίᾳ. δυνατὸς	for the (his?) service. (The) mighty
25 ὁ θ(εὸ)ς φυλάξε σε, ἔστ' ἂν	God guard you, so
ἐκτελέσῃς τὴν λιτ[ο]υρ-	you may complete the (your?)
γίαν, ἀπρόσκοπον.	service, blameless.
ἐρρῶσθε σε εὔχομε	I pray that you (will) be well
29 πολλοῖς χρόνοις.	for a long time.

2 l. Διογένῃ 3 κ̅ω̅ pap., l. χαίρειν 4 ἀγάπη͞α pap. 9 l. ἵνα 11 ἀσχολία͞ pap. 13 ουκ' pap. 14 ελαλησε͞ pap. 15 l. Παθερμοῦθεις 17 l. συγχωρῆσαι 19 l. ἐπειδὴ 19-20 l. πάνυ 22 l. μέλλει 22-23 l. ἀποτάξασθαι? 24 l. λειτουργίᾳ 25 θ̅ς̅ pap., l. φυλάξαι 26-27 l. λειτ[ο]υργίαν 28 l. ερρῶσθαί, l. εὔχομαι.

The content of the letter is that Barys asks Diogenes to grant Horus leave or an extension of leave, because he is of moderate means and occupied with some land apparently belonging to Serenianus. In the month of Hathyr Horus will give up working that land and devote himself to the λιτουργία ('service/ministry').

The use of ἐν κ̅ω̅ (= ἐν κ(υρί)ῳ; *l*.3) and ὁ θ̅ς̅ (ὁ θ(εὸ)ς; *l*. 25) shows that Barys and Diogenes are Christians. However, it is Barys' use of familial terms for both himself and Diogenes that is of particular interest. Barys calls Diogenes (τῷ) πατρί, and himself ἀδελφός (*ll*. 1-3). Later he addresses Diogenes as κύριέ μου πάτερ (*l*. 7). The use of familial terms for people who are not biological kin of the sender occurs often in the papyri. They are found, for example, in P. Mich. VIII 467.32, P. Mich. VIII 468.46-47; *UPZ* I 65.3, P. Mich. III 209, *SB* III 6263, P. Oxy. 1296, P. Oxy. 3396, P. Oxy. 3813-3815, and P. Oxy. 3859. P. Oxy. 3859 is also discussed at §29 in this volume. Note of such language is made in earlier volumes of *New Docs*, but is not discussed extensively.[1] For P. Oxy. 3857, Llewelyn (*New Docs* 8, 171) discusses the view of Treu that ἀδελφός/ἀδελφή denotes 'a full (i.e. baptised) member as distinct from a catechumen' and Sirivianou's contrasting view that θυγατέρα ('daughter'; designating Germania, who is the subject of the letter) is cultural terminology to refer to someone who is younger than both sender and recipient. For our text (P. Oxy. 3858), Sirivianou simply notes the familial terms function as 'terms of family relationship to express respect and friendship'.

The use of familial terms to describe members in one's social or religious group was widespread in the ancient world,[2] so Sirivianou's understanding that θυγατέρα in P. Oxy. 3857 simply indicates a young age is reasonable. It has been frequently argued that family/kin was the basic structure in Graeco-Roman and Jewish societies and that

---

[1] See *New Docs* 6, 158 (n. 178), 177; and *New Docs* 8, 171.
[2] This is so much so that letters using familial terms cannot be automatically assigned as 'Christian', as discussed in *New Docs* 6, 175.

various groups or social institutions were modelled on it.[3] The portrayal of Christians and the church in the New Testament has been frequently subjected to analyses based on this observation, to emphasise either Christian inclusivity and reciprocal relations[4] or patriarchal structures.[5]

The use of familial terms as terms of address outside of the biological family has a long pedigree in the Ancient Near East. For example, 'brother' is used by kings of equal status in the Amarna letters (EA 1-44, 197, 245; fourteenth century BC), and 'father' is used as an address by vassal kings in the Amarna letters to their Egyptian overseers (EA 73, 77, 82, 85, 158, 164) and occasionally to the Egyptian king (EA 199, 209, 288, 300). Familial terms also occur in Ugaritic correspondence (RS 11.872, 16.379, 34.124 and 94.2542+; c. fourteenth century BC[6]); and 'brother' was frequently used as a term of address between scribes in Egypt.[7] As commented by Wente and Hawley, the use of familial terms presupposes some level of intimacy in the relationship between speaker/sender and hearer/addressee. This is highlighted in 1 Sam 24 and 26 (24:11, 16; 26:17, 21) where David uses 'my father' (אבי) to King Saul to deny he rebels against the king, and Saul responds with 'my son' (בני) in apparent remorse. In contrast, the typical Ancient Near Eastern deferential terms in relative status contexts are 'your servant' and 'my lord', which indicate social distance between speaker/writer and hearer/recipient.[8]

Since Barys uses ἐν κ̄ω̄ and ὁ θ̄ς̄ in his letter, it can be presumed that he uses ἀδελφός and πατήρ as Christian terms of familiarity to Diogenes.[9] In the case of ἀδελφός, it takes the meaning, 'fellow believer'. This parallels the New Testament. Recipients of letters, for example, are frequently designated as ἀδελφοί (e.g. 1 Cor 10:1; 15:1; 1 Thess 2:1, 9; 2 Thess 1:3 *passim*; Heb 13:22; Jms 1:2 *passim*). Believers are designated as ἀδελφοί in 1 Pet 5:9 in reference to suffering. Paul designates Apollos with τοῦ ἀδελφοῦ (1 Cor 16:12). Similarly, Paul designates an unnamed high profile believer as ἀδελφός (2 Cor 8:18, 22) and an unnamed group of believers as ἀδελφοί (2 Cor 8:23; 9:3, 5) who will be taking a substantial gift of money to Jerusalem. Such use of ἀδελφός for believers Christians is traced back to Jesus himself in Matt 23:8, in which Jesus says that they are ἀδελφοί to each other. There is also a similar use of ἀδελφός for Jews in the speeches of Acts (3:17, 22; 22:1; 28:17). Here, Peter and Paul both appeal to Jews as a fellow Jew, using ἀδελφός as 'in-group' language to emphasise that their message about Jesus is in keeping with Jewish beliefs.

Barys' use of πατήρ for Diogenes at first sight contradicts his use of ἀδελφός for himself, since the obvious complement of πατήρ is 'son' (υἱός) rather than ἀδελφός. The same use of ἀδελφός to designate the sender and πατήρ to designate the addressee

---

[3] E.g. Judge, *Social Pattern*; Elliott, *Home for the Homeless*; Balch, *Let Wives be Submissive*.
[4] E.g. Bartchy, 'Undermining Ancient Patriarchy', 72; B.J. Malina, *New Testament World*, 122-125; Osiek and Balch, *Families*, 42-43.
[5] Osiek, 'Family in Early Christianity', 1-24; Joubert, 'Managing the Household', 213-223.
[6] See, R. Hawley, *Studies in Ugaritic Epistolography*.
[7] Wente, *Letters from Ancient Egypt*, §§116, 120, 123, 124, 139, 171.
[8] Bridge, 'Polite Language', 525.
[9] C.f. *New Docs* 6, 175.

§28 A Difficult (?) Request to 'beloved father' Diogenes

occurs also in *UPZ* I 65.3, P. Mich. III 209 and *SB* III 6263, so it should be considered as a custom amongst early Christians. πατήρ suggests some form of status difference. Here, it is probably an age difference, helped by the use of πατήρ for three different persons in P. Oxy. 3396 (*New Docs* 6, 158, n.178), its use in P. Oxy. 3859 (see §29 in this volume) and Barys' use of κύριε for Diogenes in *l.* 7 (see below). Such use of πατήρ is also found in the New Testament. Older men are designated as πατέρες in 1 Jn 2:12-14.[10] In 1 Tim 5:1, the recipient is asked to appeal to any older man (πρεσβύτερος, 'elder') as πατήρ. In keeping with what has just been said, younger men in 1 Tim 5:1 (νεωτέρικος; 'youthful/younger one') are designated as ἀδελφοί. A similar use of πατήρ to indicate an age difference is found in Acts 22:1 where Paul addresses a Jewish audience as ἀδελφοί and πατέρες.

Barys use of κύριε for Diogenes in *l.* 7, should be considered as the term that indicates formal status difference between the two. The topic of the letter, that Barys has to request a deferral of Horus' doing the λιτουργία (*ll.* 11-24), suggests that Diogenes has some supervisory authority over Barys and certainly Horus. Such a use of the vocative κύριε is in line with such language found in some of Jesus' parables (e.g. Matt 25:11; Lk 13:8). However, in the NT, κύριε is mostly used by slaves to their master in Jesus' parables, and by people to both Jesus and others whom they perceive to have some prophetic-like or other religious role (e.g. Mt 9:28 par; 17:15; Mk 7:28 par; Lk 7:6; 19:8; Jn 4:49; 14:11, 15, 19; 8:11; 9:36). It is occasionally used as a title of respect by people in no formal relationship with the hearer (e.g. Lk 19:25; Jn 20:15).[11] The same occurs in the documentary evidence. κύριε is used as a term of address to superiors in P. Giss. 61:17; 11:12, 20 (AD 119 and 118); and to rulers in P. Giss. 41 col I:4, 9, 13). κύριέ is also used in the literary texts of Epictetus (first century AD) as a term of address, for example, to high officials (*Diss.* IV 1:57), philosophers (II 7:9), and physicians (II 15:15; III 10:15). In P. Oxy. 123 there is the odd situation of a father addressing a son as κύριε, in contrast to the more expected son addressing his father as κύριε (cf. *BGU* 665:II:18).[12] This evidence, both literary and non-literary, indicates the few NT uses of κύριος as a title of respect to a superior is in keeping with societal conventions, even though it has affinities with the use of 'my lord' (אדני) and 'your servant' (עבדך) in the Old Testament as deferential terms. In the case of Barys, it is best to understand his use of κύριε to reflect societal practice rather than a Christian practice; that is, Diogenes is not necessarily a bishop or church leader.

Barys' introduction to his request about Horus, εἰδώς σου τὴν ἀσχολία(ν) τοῦτο οὖν σε ἀξιῶ, οὐκ ἐπιτάσσων, περὶ Ὥρου (*ll.*11-14), parallels Paul's introduction to his request to Philemon to release Onesimus for service: Διὸ πολλὴν ἐν Χριστῷ παρρησίαν ἔχων ἐπιτάσσειν σοι τὸ ἀνῆκον διὰ τὴν ἀγάπην μᾶλλον παρακαλῶ ('For this reason, though I am bold enough in Christ to command you on the basis of

---

[10] In 1 Jn 2:12-14, there is a repeated pattern of address to τεκνίον, πατέρες and νεανίσκοι. Is possible that τεκνίον addresses all (male) recipients, with πατέρες and νεανίσκοι differentiating them on the basis of age.

[11] C.f. Fitzmyer, 'κύριος', 329.

[12] Foerster, 'κύριος', 1045.

love …'; Philm 8-9). Sirivianou argues that Barys' desire not to command Diogenes indicates that the two men 'were about equal in rank'. However, as discussed above, Diogenes is Barys' superior. Barys writes in the way he does because he recognises that he is violating an aspect of Diogenes' 'face'; that is, Diogenes' wish for honour and respect. Specifically, Barys potentially violates Diogenes' freedom to grant or not grant the request and his language shows Diogenes that he (Barys) is aware of this potential violation.[13] Paul does the same in Philm 8-9. The difference between Paul and Barys is that Paul claims superior status over Philemon (πολλὴν ἐν Χριστῷ παρρησίαν ἔχων) whereas Barys is Diogenes' inferior. Paul *assumes* he can direct Philemon but does not want to do so; Barys indicates he cannot *presume* he can direct Diogenes. However, it is possible that Barys was able to make direct requests of Diogenes on routine matters. For both Paul and Barys, despite their differing relative statuses to their respective recipients, their respective hedging serves to indicate that their requests are non-routine.

Barys' use of λιτουργία (i.e., λειτουργία) is problematic. Does it refer to some form of public service, or to some form of *Christian* service? Sirivianou argues for the former, helped by his understanding of the phrase, ταύτην τὴν τετράμηνον, as an equivalent of the Latin *quadrimenstruum*, one of the three equal periods of four months the tax year was divided into. Looking to the New Testament does not help, since in Paul the verb equivalent λειτουργέω appears in both a 'public service' context (Rom 15:27; 2 Cor 9:12 [Christian giving]; Phil 2:17, 25, 30 [people's help]) and a cultic context (Rom 13:6; 15:16). Other documentary evidence indicates that λειτουργία meant 'public service' at or just before the time of our text (P. Brit. Mus. 1712C [unspecified service]; P. Vienna 15324 [unspecified service]; P. Gen. 81 [building a city wall]; P. Gen. 246 [mining]; P. Brit. Mus. 1564 [tax collecting]).[14] This, along with ταύτην τὴν τετράμηνον suggests that public service is being discussed by Barys. Accepting this, we have two Christians in communication, one of whom has authority over the other, on the 'secular' matter of public service, rather than a request for deferral of specifically Christian service. Barys' use of hedging indicates that the request he asks, that Horus' time of service be deferred, is a 'large' request, similar to Paul's request to Philemon to release Onesimus for service.

Bibliography

D.L. **Balch**, *Let Wives be Submissive: The Domestic Code in 1 Peter* (Atlanta 1981); S.S. **Bartchy**, 'Undermining Ancient Patriarchy', *BTB* 29 (1999) 68-78; E.J. **Bridge**, 'Polite Language in the Lachish Letters', *VT* 60 (2010) 518-534; P. **Brown** and S.C. **Levinson**, *Politeness: Some Universals in Language Usage* (Cambridge 1987); J.H. **Elliott**, *A Home for the Homeless* (Philadelphia 1981); J.A. **Fitzmyer**, 'κύριος', in *Exegetical Dictionary of the New Testament*, Vol. II (eds, H. Balz, G. Schneider; Grand Rapids: Eerdmans, 1990) 328-331; W. **Foerster**, 'κύριος', in *TDNT* 3 (1965) 1039-1058, 1081-1096; R. **Hawley**, *Studies in Ugaritic Epistolography* (PhD diss., University of Chicago, 2003); S.J. **Joubert**, 'Managing the Household', in *Modelling Early Christianity* (ed., P.F. Esler; London 1995) 213-223; E.A. **Judge**, *The Social Pattern of the Christian Groups in the First Century* (London 1960); N. **Lewis**, *Leitourgia Papyri: Documents on Compulsory Public Service in Egypt under Roman Rule* (Philadelphia 1963); S.R. **Llewelyn**, 'The Christian ΞΜΓ (Greek gamma), an Acrostic or an Isopsephism?', *New Docs* 8 (1998) 156-168; S.R.

---

[13] C.f. Brown and Levinson, *Politeness*, 171-172.
[14] N. Lewis, *Leitourgia Papyri*, 8-9, 19, 22, 24, 27-28.

Llewelyn, 'Christian Letters of Recommendation', in *New Docs* 8 (1998) 169-175; B.J. **Malina**, *The New Testament World* (Louisville 1993); C. **Osiek**, 'The Family in Early Christianity: "Family Values" Revisited', *CBQ* 58 (1996) 1-24; C. **Osiek** and D.L. **Balch**, *Families in the New Testament World* (Louisville 1997); E.F. **Wente**, *Letters from Ancient Egypt* (Atlanta 1990).

E.J. Bridge (Macquarie University)

§29 Belated Greetings to Everyone

Oxyrhynchus   26.4 x 33-22 cm   IV

Ed. Pr.—M.G. Sirivianou, *The Oxyrhynchus Papyri*, Vol. LVI (London 1989) 120-124 (= P. Oxy. 3859).

This letter is written in two columns, of which more than half of the lower left-hand side of the first column has been lost. The second column is well preserved. Each column is on a separate sheet of papyrus, with the join between them showing the papyrus has been used upside-down from normal practice. The script is 'an evidently practised and not unskilful cursive', but contrasts with 'the phonetic spelling and the bad grammar' (Sirivianou, 120). A *terminus post quem* for dating the letter is provided by the reference to a *pagus* (*l*. 13). *Pagi* replaced the former toparchies in the early fourth century. As with P. Oxy. 3857 and P. Oxy. 3858 (see §28 in this volume), there is no address on the back. Instead, the back has been used for some accounts (= P. Oxy. 3874). Sirivianou, 120, suggests the price of the solidus in these accounts indicates a date of about AD 340-350. She thinks the letter would not have been kept long before it was used for its new purpose.

The 'bad grammar' is not entirely haphazard. One feature is consistent. In the greeting list (*ll*. 25-50), when a male 'title' (*master, brother, father*) and name are placed together directly after ἀσπάζω, the dative is used (except in *l*. 46). All other 'titles' (*wife, children, daughter-in-law*), with or without names, that are further objects of ἀσπάζω are (correctly) written in the accusative. When a man's name is placed directly after ἀσπάζω without the addition of a title, it is also (correctly) written in the accusative. Women's names and 'titles' (*sister, mother*) are also (correctly) written in the accusative if they are placed directly after ἀσπάζω (except in *ll*. 49-50). The plural *you* in *l*. 50 is also put in the dative after ἀσπάζω.

Col I	Col i
τῷ δεσπότῃ μου καὶ ἀδελφῷ (vac.) Σαραπάμμων	To my master and brother, (vac.) Sarapammon:
Ὠριγένης (vac.) πλῖστα χαίρει(ν).	Horigenes (vac.) many greetings!
πρὸ μὲν πάντων εὔχομαι τῇ θείᾳ προνοίᾳ περὶ τῆς ὁλο-	Above all else (= everything) I pray for the divine providence[1] concerning
κληρίας σου ὅπως ὑγιαίνοντι καὶ εὐθυμοῦντα καὶ ἀπολα-	your full health that being in good health and taking courage, you may receive
5 βεῖν τὰ παρ' ἐμοῦ γράμματα, κύριέ μου ἄδελφε. (vac.)	the letter from me, my lord brother. ...
καθὼς ἔπεμψές μοι Παπνοῦθιν, διὰ τῶν σῶν γραμμάτων	When you sent me Papnouthis, through your letters
ἐδήλωσάς μοι ὥστε μοι ἀπαντήσω πρὸς σὲ εἰς τὴν Ὀξυρυ-	you indicated to me I may meet you in the [city] of the Oxyrhyn-
γχιτῶν καὶ ἐπὶ τὴν ἐπαύριον κατεσχέθημαι ὑπὸ Πλου-	chites, and (=but) until the next day I was detained by Plu-

---

[1] For προνοίᾳ as 'providence' and εὔχομαι τῇ θείᾳ προνοίᾳ as a formulaic prayer, see Horsley, *New Docs* 3, 143-144, and M. Choat, *Belief and Cult*, 24, 84, 152.

§29 Belated Greetings to Everyone

	τάρχῳ στρατιώτου τοῦ ἡγεμῶνος ὑπὲρ Ὡριγένους	tarchus, a soldier of the governor because of Horigenes
10	πρόφασιν τῶν ἵππων, μετὰ τὸν θεὸν οὐδέναν εὗρον	on (the) pretext of (the?) horses, after the god I found no one
	βοηθήσῃ μαι εἰ μὴ Ὡρίωνα τὸν προνοητὴν Ἀννιανοῦ.	to help me except Horion the steward of Annianus.
	μετ[ὰ] ταῦτα ἐβουλ[ήθη]ν ἀπαντῆσαι πρὸς σὲ καὶ ἤκουσα	After these things [=all this], I wanted to meet you and [=but] I heard
	[ca. 20]ου β (= δευτέρου) πάγου ποσάκις ηλ-	... (of) the second *pagus*, how often
	[ca. 20]ης ὀφιλῆς τῆς οὐσίας	... of a monetary debt
15	[ca. 20].....ηθη ἐλθῖν πρὸς σὲ	... to come to you
	[ca. 25].ιω μετὰ Ὁριγένης	... with Horigenes
	[ca. 25]. καὶ τελέσαι ὑπὲρ	... and to finish on behalf of/for the sake of
	[ca. 25]ίνομαι. μὴ νομίσῃς	I become(?)... Do not assume
	[ca. 25]... ἀνεχώρησα	... I withdrew
20	[ca. 25]υ οἶδαις καὶ σὺ τακ	... you know and (you) ??
	[ca. 25]...λαμβαν....ρ	... [[take/receive]]
	[ca. 25]υν ἔγραψά [σο]ι καὶ ου	... I wrote (or, I am writing) to you and not
	[ca. 25].καν διὰ τὴν ὁλοκλη-	... for the sake of [your? his?] (full) hea-
	[ρίαν ca. 20]ωδεευταθ.	[lth] ... ??
25	[ca. 25].Ἀμμωνίωνι. ἀσπάζω	... to Ammonion. I greet
	[ca. 20 ἀσπάζ]ω τῷ δεσπότῃ μου καὶ	... [I gre]et my lord and
	[ἀδελφῷ [ca. 6] ἀσπάζω τὴν ἀδε]λφήν μου Παλλαδία.	[brother ..., I greet] my [sis]ter Palladia.

Col II / Col ii

	ἀσπάζω τῷ δεσπότῃ μου καὶ ἀδελφῷ Εὐλογίῳ καὶ τὴν	I greet my master and brother Eulogius and
	σύνβιον αὐτοῦ καὶ τὴν θυγατέραν αὐτοῦ. ἀσπάζω τὴν ἀδελ-	his wife and his daughter. I greet
30	φήν μου Εὐκερᾶ. ἀσπάζω τῷ πατρί μου Ψῦρος καὶ τὴν σύν-	my sister, Euccesia. I greet my father Psyrus and
	βιον αὐτοῦ καὶ τὰ παιδία αὐτοῦ. ἀσπάζω τῷ ἀδελφῷ μου	his wife and his children. I greet my brother
	Ἥρωνι καὶ τὴν σύνβιον αὐτοῦ καὶ τὰ παιδία αὐτοῦ. ἀσπάζω	Heron and his wife and his children. I greet
	τῷ ἀδελφῷ μου Ἐδέσις καὶ τὴν	my brother Aedesius and his wife and

	σύνβιον αὐτοῦ καὶ τὸν υἱὸν	his son
	αὐτοῦ Θεόδουλε. ἀσπάζω τὴν μητέραν μου Ἀμροκηράκη.	Theodulus. I greet my mother Amoöcyrace(?).
35	ἀσπάζω τῷ ἀδελφῷ μου [[ατι]] Ἁρποκρατίων καὶ τὴν σύνβι-	I greet my brother [[ατι]] Harpokration and his wi-
	ον αὐτοῦ καὶ τὴν θυγατέραν αὐτοῦ. ἀσπάζω Ἐπάγαθον καὶ τὴν	fe and his daughter. I greet Epagathus and
	σύνβιον αὐτοῦ καὶ τὴν θυγατέραν αὐτοῦ καὶ τὴν γαμβρὰν αὐτοῦ.	his wife and his daughter and his daughter-in-law (or, sister-in-law).
	ἀσπάζω τῷ ἀδελφῷ μου Μαρτῖνον καὶ τὴν σύνβιον αὐτοῦ	I greet my brother Martinus and his wife
	καὶ τὰ παιδία αὐτοῦ. ἀσπάζω τῷ ἀδελφῷ μου Εὐγένις καὶ τὴν	and his children. I greet my brother Eugenis and
40	σύνβιον αὐτοῦ καὶ τὰ παιδία αὐτοῦ. ἀσπάζω τὴν ἀδελφήν μου	his wife and his children. I greet my sister
	Ἀΐα καὶ τὰ παιδία αὐτῆς. ἀσπάζω τὴν μητέραν μου Ταννοῦς	Aia and her children. I greet my mother Tannous
	καὶ τὰ παιδία αὐτῆς. ἀσπάζω τῷ ἀδελφῷ μου Πάξαμος καὶ τὴν	and her children. I greet my brother Paxamus and
	σύνβιον αὐτοῦ. ἀσπάζω Ταυῆς καὶ τὴν ἀδελφήν αὐτῆ<ς>. ἀσπάζω	his wife. I greet Taues and her sister. I greet
	τῷ ἀδελφῷ μου Ερηνες. ἀσπάζω τῷ ἀδελφῷ μου Ἀγαθαφέρον	my brother Erenes (?). I greet my brother Agathapheron
45	καὶ τὸν ἀδελφόν μου Ἐπάγαθον καὶ τὸν ἀδελφόν μου Ἀπίων.	and my brother Epagathus and my brother Apion.
	ἀσπάζω τὸν ἀδελφόν μου Σακαῦ καὶ τὸν ἀδελφόν μου Ἀμάεις	I greet my brother Sacau and my brother Amaeis.
	ἀσπάζω τῷ ἀδελφῷ μου Σιλβανὸς ὀνηλάτῃ καὶ τὴν σύνβιον	I greet my brother, Silvanus, donkey-driver, and his wife.
	αὐτοῦ. ἀσπάζω τῷ ἀδελφῷ μου Παύλου ὀνηλάτῃ καὶ τὴν	I greet my brother Paul, donkey-driver, and
	σύνβιον αὐτοῦ καὶ τὰ παιδία αὐτοῦ. ἀσπάζω τῇ ἀδελφῇ μου	his wife and his children. I greet my sister
50	Διονυσᾷ. ἀσπάζω ὑμῖν πάντες κατ᾽ ὄνομα. (vac.)	Dionysia. I greet you all by name. …
	ἐρρῶσθέ	For your health
	σε εὔχομαι πολλοῖς	I pray for many
53	χρόνοις, κύριέ μου ἄδελφε.	years, my lord brother.

1 l. Σαραπάμμωνι 2 l. πλεῖστα, χαίρει pap. 4 l. ὑγιαίνοντα 6 l. ἔπεμψάς 8 l. κατεσχέθην 8-9 l. Πλουτάρχου 9 l. ἡγεμόνος 10 l. οὐδένα 11 l. βοηθῆσαί μοι 14 l. ὀφειλῆς 15 l. ἐλθεῖν 16 l.

§29 Belated Greetings to Everyone 173

'Ὀριγένους **20** corr. from οἶδας ed. **26, 28** l. τὸν δεσπότην **27** l. Παλλαδίαν **28** l. αδελφὸν Εὐλογίον **29, 30, 32, 33, 35, 37, 38, 40, 43, 47** l. σύμβιον **29** l. θυγατέρα **30** l. Εὐκαιριαν, l. τὸν πατέρα, l. Ψῦρον **31, 33, 35, 38, 42, 44, 44, 47, 48** l. τὸν ἀδελφόν **32** l. Ἥρωνα **33** l. Αἰδέσιον **34** l. Θεόδουλον, l. μητέρα **35** l. Ἁρποκρατίωνα ed. **36, 37** l. θυγατέρα **39** l. Εὐγένιν **41** l. Ἀίαν, l. μητέρα, l. Ταννοῦν **42** l. Πάξαμον **43** l. Ταυῆν **45** l. Ἀπίωνα **46** l. Ἁμᾶιν **47** l. Σιλβανὸν ὀνηλάτην **48** l. Παῦλον ὀνηλάτην **49** l. τὴν ἀδελφήν **50** l. Διονυσίαν, l. ὑμᾶς πάντας **51** l. ἐρρῶσθαι **53** l. χρόνοις

The letter is in two halves. In the first half, and the reason for writing, Horigenes explains why he could not meet Sarapammon at Oxyrhynchus. He was detained by a soldier who was acting on orders from another(!) Horigenes who seems to have charged Horigenes with some offence relating to horses. Horigenes claims that no one assisted him, except for a certain Horion (*ll*. 8-11). Sometime later, Horigenes appeared to have been delayed or detained by news from another *pagus* (*ll*. 12-14). The reason for this is now lost, but may have had something to do with a monetary debt (*l*. 14). It may be that Horigenes endured some suffering in these difficulties (ἀνεχώρησα; *l*. 19).

The second half of the letter is a lengthy series of greetings to various people, which occupies the last three lines of the first column and the entire second column. Horigenes greets fourteen 'brothers', five 'sisters', two 'mothers' and one 'father'. In addition, two 'brothers' are also designated with δεσπότης ('lord'; *ll*. 26-28), a title which contrasts with Horigenes' use of κύριε for Sarapammon in *ll*. 5, 53 (cf. §28 in this volume), except in *l*. 1, where he also uses δεσπότης.

Overtly Christian language such as ἐν κ̄ω̄ and ὁ θ̄ς̄ is not used in this letter (contrast §28 in this volume). Rather, a circumlocution is used in Horigenes' greeting prayer for Sarapammon's health: εὔχομαι τῇ θείᾳ προνοίᾳ (*l*. 3). This, and the extensive list of greetings to people designated with familial terms, suggests Horigenes and Sarapammon are Christians, and members of the same community or group of believers. It might be that Horigenes' troubles have prompted him to remove overt Christian language, in case interception of the letter caused more trouble for him.

In a similar fashion as in §28 in this volume, Horigenes' use of ἀδελφός and πατήρ parallels the use of these terms in the New Testament. As Sirivianou notes (p. 120), the person named as 'father' in *l*. 30 'is hardly likely to be his real father'. ἀδελφός, in the designation, τῷ ἀδελφῷ μου, is the general term to cover the men of the group. The once only use of τῷ πατρί μου (*l*. 30) may indicate Psyrus is an older man, despite having a wife and family. The use of δεσπότης for two men (*ll*. 26-28) and κύριε for Sarapammon suggests that, as with §28 in this volume, πατήρ is an age marker, not a leadership marker. Likewise, ἀδελφή should be thought of as a general designation for the women in the group and μήτηρ (*ll*. 34, 41) as designating older women. This parallels the New Testament, in which ἀδελφή is the general term for believing women (Mk 3:35 // Mt 12:50; Rom 16:1; 1 Cor 7:15; 9:5; Jms 2:15). However, in 1 Tim 5:2 ἀδελφή is also used as an age-based term: older women (πρεσβυτέρας) are designated as μήτηρ and younger women (νεωτέρας) are designated as ἀδελφή, which is similar to the use of ἀδελφός and πατήρ in the preceding verse. Μήτηρ also is used in Mk 3:35 // Mt 12:50, but here it should not be thought of as designating older believing women. Instead, it should be understood as part of a rhetorical strategy to indicate everyone who does God's will is in God's 'family'.

Horigenes' use of ἀδελφός/πατήρ and ἀδελφή/μήτηρ also reveals patriarchal culture. The titles, τὴν ἀδελφήν μου and τὴν μητέραν μου, are only used for women who are not connected with a man. These women are also named. Otherwise, wives and sisters of named men are unnamed. This parallels Paul's greetings in Romans 16. There, Rufus' mother (v. 13) and Nereus' sister (v. 15) are not named, and any named women are not connected with any men. Two exceptions are Prisca in v. 3 and Junia[2] in v. 7, who are both named with their husbands and noted as husband and wife ministry teams.

The use of σύνβιος by Horigenes contrasts with the use of γυνή ('woman') in the New Testament for 'wife'. Sirivianou, 124, comments that the word (more commonly spelt as σύμβιος) 'is found from the second century onwards in the papyri. It is mainly applied to wives, and only rarely to husbands.' There is a possibility that σύμβιος reflects the Roman term *coniugium* ('joined together'), which is considered by Treggiari as being the general Latin term for marital union and 'less associated with the specifically Roman institution' of marriage.[3] For example, Cicero can use *coniugium* to refer to how a 'whole household is joined together by marriage and offspring' (*et tota domus coniugio et stirpe coniungitur*; Cicero, *De finibus*, 65). Despite the applicability of *coniugium* to either husband or wife (i.e. the term is neutral rather than patriarchal), it is used much more frequently of women than of men, no doubt as a result of the patriarchal nature of most extant texts. In this respect, Horigenes follows cultural practice, given that he writes to a man. It is therefore likely that Horigenes' designation of wives as σύμβιος is a later equivalent of the NT's use of γυνή for 'wife'.

Bibliography

M. **Choat**, *Belief and Cult in Fourth-Century Papyri* (Turnhout/Macquarie University 2006); G.H.R. **Horsley**, 'Divine Providence in a Letter of Judas', *New Docs* 3 (1983) 143-144; S. **Treggiari**, *Roman Marriage* (Oxford 1991)

E.J. Bridge (Macquarie University)

---

[2] There is a textual difficulty with Ἰουνίαν. P46, along with Coptic and Latin mss, reads Ἰουλίαν.
[3] S. Treggiari, *Roman Marriage*, 6.

CUMULATIVE INDEXES FOR VOLUMES 6 - 10

The cumulative indexes for Vols. 6-10 supersede the separate indexes in individual volumes and differ from them in that references are listed by volume and page number or, in the case of footnotes, by volume, page number and footnote, rather than volume and entry number. All index references are given in numerical order, including footnotes, e.g. 9.93 n.17.

1. Selected Subjects

– A –

Abbreviation	8.85 n.25, 158 n.9
Aberkios	6.177-181
Abrasax	10.11, 16, 17
absenteeism	6.62 n.75
abuse	8.55, 60, 68, 70, 74, 75
of power	9.60
Academy	10.3
accession	10.64-67, 82
acclamation	8.4-6, 7 n.5
accounting	8.55, 66
accounts	8.53 n.23, 59 n.56
annual return	8.75
archive	8.64
accusation	8.143
acquisition	
Athenian law	7.155 n.69
hazaqah	7.156-157
legal grounds	7.155, 156, n.72
maximum period	7.155
of property	8.141
undisturbed possession	7.137 n.24, 144-145, 155, n.70, n.71, 157
usucapio	7.154-156, 192
(see also 'forcible acquisition')	
acrostic	8.156-168, n.5; 9.121
act of association	8.53 n.23
action	
against property	8.25 n.63
for recovery	9.55
Actium	10.70, 84
actors	8.144
acts of God	6.82-86; 9.55
Adam	9.37
Adam-Christ typology	9.4
address/es	9.34, 47, 57, 65, 69, 70
collars of slaves	7.43 n.40
house-by-house census	7.41 n.37
labels on buildings	7.32 n.16
letters	8.123-125, 126 n.8, 171
notices of birth, death, flight	7.41 n.37
property records	7.41 n.37
universal address	8.127
use of temples	7.43, 43 n.40
addressees	
of Paul's letters	6.150 n.165
administrative	
district	8.49
infrastructure	9.33
staff	9.35
administration of Palestine	
census	6.123
reintegration edicts	6.118-119
sources of influence	6.91-92
the Herods	6.99
the Ptolemies	6.100-104
toparchies	6.129
Adonai	10.10, 11, 12
adoption	8.15 n.21
Aegean	10.6
aeons	8.176
Africa	10.60
afterlife	9.19
age	8.65
aggravated theft	7.147
agoranomion	6.39, 42
agoranomos	6.42, 66, 107; 7.185, 206, 208, n.41, 209
agreements	8.57
agricultural workers	9.110
agriculture	8.56
Agrippa	8.153-155, n.7
Agrippa I	10.137
Agrippa Postumus	10.69
Agrippeia	8.118
Alexandria	10.4, 78
Alexandrian	
court	8.10
Greeks	9.109
alias	9.62
aliens	10.62
alimentation capital	9.49, 90, 97
allegorising tendency	9.66
allotment	
after death	6.27-39
formal structure	6. 27 n.34
homologia	6.32-33, 38
Jewish adaptation of	6.36-38
Jewish practice	6.43-47
obligations and charges	6.31
of land	7.142, 143, n.31
ownership of property	6.33-36
parable of the wicked tenants	6.37 n.49
relation to testament	6.38-39
revocability of	6.32-36, n.39, 43
right of usufruct	6.31
Amarna	10.133, 166
ambassador	8.110
amulet	

Index 1 – Subjects

Christian	8.156	Archelaus	6.128
magical	6.192-196; 8.166	*archiphylax*	7.221
amphora	8.157, 162, 164	*archisomatophylax*	6.167
amphodarch	7.104	*archon*	9.67, 69-72
amphodogrammateus	7.41-42 n.37	aretalogies	8.174
amphodokomogrammateus	7.97-98 n.29	aristocratic models	8.108
anachoresis	8.96, 97-105, 103 n.15	ark	10.154
		army	8.68, 153-155
notification of	8.100	auxiliary units	8.155 n.14
anagnostes	9.68	military escort	8.54, 67
anakrisis	6.50 n.61	military register	8.162
ancestral *arête*	7.239	post	8.10
ancestral honours	9.20	soldier	7.23 n.1, 47, 60, 62, 65, 67, 69, 71-72, 74, 80, 84, 86-87, 164
angareia	7.13, 59-87, 59 n.8		
ἀγγαρεύειν	7.13 n.27, 60 n.11, 16		
ἀγγαρήιος	7.3	supply	7.83
ἀγγαρήιον	7.13 n.27	under Augustus	7.83
ἄγγαρος	7.4, 2-3 n.6, n.12, 4 n.13	veteran	7.47, 164
		arrest	9.42, 53, 59
(see also 'liturgy' and 'requisitioning')		Artemis	9.26-29; 10.30, 37, 48
angel	9.2, 14, 37; 10.16		
angelology	8.176	of Ephesus	6.196-201, 203-206; 10.30-36, 37-47, 59
anointing	8.178		
Antioch	10.77, 90		
Antiochus III	10.138	Antioch	
Antiochus IV	10.87-91	Pisidian	10.55
antigrapheus	9.42, 43	Antonius	10.56
antitheses	7.87	artists	9.67, 68
Antoninus Pius	6.148; 9.28, 117	asceticism	8.104
Aphrodite	10.26	Asia (Roman province of)	10.1, 49, 51, 93, 95
'apocalypse of John'	10.10	*asiarch*	10.33, 49, 103
Apollo	9.15, 17; 10.18, 39	assault	9.43, 44, 63
of Didyma	10.39	associates	8.52, 53 n.23, 55, 57, 64, 66, 78
of Klaros	10.39		
of Ephesus	10.39	association	9.2, 67, 78; 10.3, 105
Apollonia	10.159-163		
apostles	7.195	of Greeks	8.19
apostolic		asylum	7.222 n.112; 8.10, 14-15 n.19-22, 34-36, 41, 44
authorship	8.121		
emissaries	7.51-57		
1 and 2 Thessalonians	7.53-54	Athens	10.4, 6, 87
Galatians	7.53	Athenian law	7.155 n.69; 9.43
Romans	7.53	athletes	8.130, 144; 9.67
faith	8.116	privileges	8.130 n.2
parousia	7.51-54	attendance at church	7.248
support	9.2	auction	7.199, 199 n.6, 206; 8.47, 49-51, 53 n.23, 55, 57, 61; 9.32, 33, 39, 40
appeal	7.172-5		
procedure	8.65		
to Caesar	9.53		
applications for lease	8.83		
appointed time	9.65	bidding process	8.53
Arabia	10.142-153	minimal bid	8.50
Aramaic	9.84; 10.142, 151, 152	audience	8.5, 127
		Augustine	8.173, 174
arbitration	7.133, 137, 144		

Augustus	6.149; 9.4, 9, 16, 18, 22-24, 26-30, 41, 68, 90, 115, 116; 10.26, 49, 55-58, 59-63, 66, 73, 93, 97	benefactor	9.2, 4-7, 15, 16, 18, 20-22, 30, 31, 71; 10.2
		benefactors	8.149
		Berytus	10.141
		Beroea	9.50
authority	9.15, 37, 51, 60	biblical allusions	9.102
autonomy	8.110	biblical echoes	9.104
auxilia	6.153 n.173	biblical names	9.77
Avianii	10.2	biblical quotation	9.102
Avircius Marcellus	6.181	bilingual inscriptions	9.24; 10.59
awarding of a crown	8.107	bilingualism	10.59
		billeting	7.12, 60 n.11, 134 n.15, 135
– B –		birth	9.7, 41, 57, 58, 62, 64, 77, 79, 104, 116, 120, 121
Babatha	10.142-153		
Babylon	10.122		
Babylonian	10.151	bishop	10.162-163
Baienus Blastianus	6.113	Bithynia	10.1, 32
banishment	8.35	bodies of saints and martyrs	8.166 n.37
bank	8.48, 49 n.11, 50, 50 n.19, 52 n.21, 23, 53 n.28, 55 n.36, 55-56, 65, 67, 67 n.92, 84 n.22	body	9.19, 37, 42, 103
		bonded labour	6.51
		bones	9.102-105
		books	
		1 Clement	7.108 n.58
		(see also 'Clement of Rome')	
bank ledger	8.67, 99	1 John	7.246
banquet	7.237-239; 9.63, 65, 66	Acts	7.91
		adornment of	7.249-250
baptism	8.167, 176-179	'Book of the Two Ways'	10.7
delaying baptism	8.177 n.6	Ephesians	10.17
Johannine metaphor	8.177 n.8	Gospel of Egyptians	7.245, 247
Latin inscriptions	8.177 n.9	Gospel of Hebrews	7.247
magic	8.178 n.12	literary/scientific	7.251
Pauline metaphor	8.177 n.8	Mark	7.251-2
schismatic group	8.177 n.7	Paul and 1 Clement	7.107 n.56
signum fidei	8.177 n.9	touring bookseller	7.253
Bar Jesus/Elymas	10.46	version of Aquila	7.248
Bar Kokhba	10.142	(see also under 'codex')	
Basil the Great	7.159	booty	8.15 n.22
basilikogrammateus	7.41, 67, 69-71, 112-113, 121-122, 127, 199, 207	*boulai*	8.61 n.70
		boule	7.236-7, 94 n.12; 9.29, 77; 10.88
bath-attendant	9.42-44	*bouleutes*	10.33
bath-gymnasium	9.30, 31	branding	7.123 n.46
bath-house	9.42, 43	(see also under 'slave')	
bathing	8.178	break of church from Judaism	7.195
battle of Milvian bridge	8.167 n.41	breastplate	8.167
beast	8.165	brewer	9.32, 33
Beelzebul	10.14	bridal gift	9.83, 88
beer	8.65 n.77	bride's personal possessions	9.91
benediction of Amidah	8.146	bridegroom	9.64-66, 83, 86-89
benefaction	7.233-241	bride-price	9.87, 88, 92, 93
in NT	7.239-241	brigandage	8.104 n.22
ideology	8.106-113	brothel	8.39
terminology	8.113	brother	8.171; 10.166, 173

Index 1 – Subjects

burial and the *collegium funeraticium*	6.51 n.62
business loan	7.225
business ventures	9.33

– C –

Caesar	10.28
calendar	9.39-41, 84, 91, 112-115
Caligula	10.28, 74
camel	7.11, 72, 113, 113 n.2, n.3, 117 n.17, 123, 124 n.48, 165
sale of	10.124
camel-drivers	7.11, 123
cameo	10.10
Capernaum	10.23
capital	8.57
Caracalla	6.117, 118; 9.27-31, 77
catechumen	8.167, 171, 178-179
catoecic land	8.47, 47 n.1, 48 n.5, 66
celebration of the mysteries	7.184
Celtic incursion	8.107
censor	9.23
census	6.31, 119; 8.58 n.49; 9.41
census period	6.121
census returns	10.116
dates of edicts	6.121 n.137
declaration	8.37, 39 n.101, 73
declaration as proof of status	6.137
duration in Egypt	6.136
form of declaration	6.120-121
fourteen-year cycle (Egypt)	6.121
idia	6.125-126, 127
in Herod's kingdom	6.129
in Judaea by tribe	6.127-129
Luke's dating of Jesus' birth	6.123
official use of declarations	6.121-122
personal details	6.121 n.131
personal presence at lodgement	6.126-130
persons lodging a declaration	6.3, 124-125
place of lodgement	6.124-130
proof of registration	6.121 n.136
Roman administration structures	6.127-129
six-year cycle (Herod)	6.129
twelve-year cycle (Syria)	6.127
types of declarations	6.120 n.127, 121 n.129
census-motif	
Gospel of Luke	6.130 n.153
central	
administrative control	8.60
fiscal planning	8.56
imperial budget	8.68
centralisation of economic power	8.103 n.16
centralised and planned economy	8.57
ceremony	8.5
Ceres	10.27
chancellery	8.133
changing views of church	7.106
chanting	8.6
charging of interest	7.225 n.129, 231 n.164
Charis	10.23
charisma	8.6
check mark	8.67
cheirographon	6.11, 61, 62, 63, 105-111, 115, 189; 8.48 n.5, 77; 9.60
Chloe	10.117
choachytai (keepers of mummies)	7.135-138, 138, 136 n.23, 154
chora	9.50, 51, 69
chrematistai (see 'courts')	8.23; 9.46, 50-52
Christ	9.2, 4, 6, 7, 11, 12, 21, 33, 37, 44, 48, 70, 102, 103, 105, 109, 119-121; 10.13, 52, 84
Christ's redemptive work	8.177
Christian	
amulet	8.156
apologists	8.120
benefaction ethics	8.113
charity	7.49
communities	9.27, 110
funerary inscriptions	8.176, 176 n.2; 9.102, 104
households	6.54-55; 8.116
phrases	8.124
rhetoric	8.121
sign	8.166-167 n.39
symbol	8.166-167 n.39
talisman	8.166-167 n.39
ownership of slaves	6.54-55
Christianity	8.142, 177 n.6
in Egypt	7.244
relation to Judaism	7.247-248, 247 n.21
spread of	7.248, 253
christological controversy	8.158
Chrysostom, John	10.121
church	8. 113, 144, 171; 9.8, 13, 18, 50, 68, 102, 104, 112, 115, 117
Cicero	9.15, 17
circumcision	7.91, 189; 9.117

circus factions	8.4-6	origins of	7.250-256
cities		Roman innovation	7.254
Roman use of	7.72-80	style of Christian texts	7.254, 254 n.21
citizen	9.39, 109	typology	7.253
citizen body	8.2	Codex of Theodosius	7.13
citizenship	9.71, 77; 10.62	Codices	10.3
grant of	6.148 n.163	coercive power	8.66-67
civic expenditure	8.60	cohabitation	
civic life	8.120	Jewish practice	6.18 n.32
modelling	8.108	collocation	
civic celebrations	9.27	as indicator of belief	6.174-177
civic-mindedness	8.110	collusion	8.34-35
civil appeals	8.134	Colossae	9.50; 10.18, 110-113
civil disturbance	8.36		
civil unrest	7.146	commerce and the early church	7.50
class and status		communion	8.172
attitude to poor	8.75	compensation	7.172 n.33, 188, 193; 8.15-16, 35
control	8.19 n.44		
decurion class	8.104	competition	9.21
elite classes	8.120	complaints	8.68-69
elitist culture	8.121	composition of Philemon and Colossians	8.45
elitist ethic	8.112	compulsory public service (see 'liturgy')	
higher culture	8.119	confessional allegiance	8.165
lower classes	8.2	confessional texts	6.192
lower strata	8.67	confiscation of property	7.162 n.90; 8.59 n.56, 143
middle classes	7.94, 104		
poorer classes	8.103-4, 121	of Jewish property	8.146-147
poorer strata	8.96	congregations	9.50
propertied class	8.26	connivance	8.67 n.90, 100
social elite	8.134	consent	7.132, 147-148, 152, 154, 160, 193-194
classical echoes	9.104		
Claudius	6.51, 148, 153; 10.28, 82		
		consolation	8.118
Claudius Lysias	6.152-154; 9.53	Constantine	9.110, 111, 117, 118
Clement of Alexandria	7.159; 10.6		
Clement of Rome		constitutional affairs	8.111
appointment of bishops	7.107	constitutional change	8.55
choice of terminology	7.107	consular authority	9.15
death penalty	7.107	contacts and friends	8.13-14 n.17
division between priests and laity	7.107	continuity of family	8.119
'fall of early Church'	7.106	contract	8.51
hierarchy	7.106, 106 n.55	contract of service	7.220 n.101
Jewish-Christian apologetic tradition	7.110	contractors	8.81
succession of bishops	7.107	contractual agreement	7.230
τάγμα	7.107	contractual friendship	6.173
τάξις	7.107	contributions	8.149
ζῆλος, φθόνος and ἔρις	7.108	control	
cleansing	8.177	government	8.55-56, 59 n.58, 60
Cleopatra (epithets)	7.197 n.1		
cleruch	8.88, 88 n.30; 9.55	population	8.40 n.103, 45 n.109
client	9.17		
codex		status	8.19 n.44
Christian adoption	7.251	title	8.19 n.44
date of parchment texts	7.246	of tax companies	8.52 n. 23
dating of manuscripts	7.243-244	conversion	8.173
impetus to adoption	7.254	conveyance	7.229

Index 1 – Subjects

Coptic	10.23	stipulations	9.95
copying	8.141	ten-man court	7.173-174, 178
copying an *exemplum*	6.49-50; 8.137, 170	titles	6.167
		φροντιστής	7.214 n.74
Corinth	9.6-8, 11, 18, 21, 50, 79	ὡς ἐλεύθερος	7.173
		created order	8.165 n.33
corporate bodies	8.130-131, 133	creation	9.4, 38, 52, 90, 103, 112, 116
corporation	8.58, 74		
correspondence of *strategos*	8.31	creator	9.103, 104, 120
corruption	6.158 n.177; 8.60, 68, 74; 9.35, 58; 10.104	credal confessions	8.158
		creditor	9.35, 59, 60
		creeds	8.158, 167
Corsica	10.60	crime	9.43, 53
corvée	8.89, 90, 94	aggravating factors	9.43
cosmic events	8.174	criminal	9.35, 43, 61
costs of administration	8.59 n.58	criminal appeals	8.134
costs of magistracies	7.102	criticism of Rome	8.75
Council of Jerusalem	7.54	crossing	
councillor	9.77	of letters	6.172-173
court/s	8.23, 23 n.55; 9.112	of loan documents	6.107-110
		crown	7.236, 239-40; 9.1-3
archidikastes	7.201 n.9, 203-204, 203 n.21, 208 n.41, 210-212, 210 n.44, 211 n.48, 212 n.57, 215	crowning	10.39
		crucifixion	8.1-2, 1 n.1, 35
		cult	8.111; 9.4, 16, 22, 24, 27, 29-31, 43, 62, 64, 77, 79, 80, 115
avoiding litigation	7.188		
chrematistai	7.131-132, 136-137, 189, 198, 204, 204 n.22, n.23, 205 n.29, 206 n.31, 208, 208 n.41, 210, 210 n.44, n.45, 212-215, 212 n.61, 214 n.69, n.71, 217 n.91	cultic buildings	8.150
		cultic smothering	8.75
		curator	9.108
		curse	8.4
		curse tablets (see also *defixiones*)	10.43
		cursus publicus	7.13-22
circular notice	7.189	*a diplomatibus*	7.71, 84, 84 n.76
court decision	7.220	abuse	7.76, 80-85, 85 n.78
δικαστήριον	7.174, 218	administration	7.13, 19-20 n.63
documentation	7.174, 176, 180	*agentes in rebus*	7.2, 2 n.4, 56
eisagogeus	7.198	ἁλιάδες	7.2 n.1
ἐπὶ τῆς διαλογῆς procedure	7.212-215	ἁλιαδίτης	7.2
ἐπιδέκατον	7.172	*animalia publica*	7.19, 19 n.58
ἐπιπεντεκαιδέκατον	7.172	Augustus' innovation	7.15, 56, 73
iuridicus	7.212	*beneficiarii*	7.17 n.50, 19 n.60
judgement in default	7.189	cost of running	7.19, 19 n.63
judges	7.212 n.61	*cursus clavularis*	7.2, 20 n.64
judicial status	7.175	*cursus velox*	7.1-2, 2 n.1, 20 n.64, 49
κατάστασις	7.213		
κρίσις	7.211-212	development	7.13-14
λαοκριταί	7.137, 175	δημοσία ὁδός	7.79
legal competence	7.173	*diploma*	7.15 n.40, 16-18, 16 n.47, 18 n.52, 19 n.62, 20, 20 n.65, 71-72, 72 n.39, 77, 80-85, 83
legal cost	7.172-173		
μαρτυρίαι	7.176		
οἱ κιδασταί	7.174, 176		
out-of-court charge	7.177-178		

	n.66, n.67, 84 n.69, n.72, n.73, 85 n.77, 87
evectio	7.14, 85, 85 n.77
frumentarii	7.2, 2 n.4, 17, 19, 20, 56
general guidelines	7.81
γραμματηφόρος	7.2, 49, 49 n.4, 59
hospitium	7.14, 60 n.12, 72, 80, 81 n.59, 82, 83 n.66
inefficiency and waste	7.81 n.60
information service	7.15, 17, 20, 56
Italy	7.19 n.62
Jewish and NT evidence	7.85
keeping records	7.67
legatio libera	7.14, 16, 84, 84 n.71
λιτουργία	7.79; 10.168
liturgies and requisitions	7.15
magister officiorum	7.20 n.65
manicipes	7.19 n.63, 21
mansio	7.15 n.37, 17 n.50, 18, 18 n.57, 67 n.33, 72, 73 n.41, 83 n.66
μερισμὸς διπλῶν	7.71
militarisation	7.17 n.51
munera	7.79
munus and *locatio*	7.83
mutatio	7.18, 18 n.57, 73
obligations on subject populations	7.62-87, 82 n.61
parangariae	7.13
paraveredi	7.13
penalties	7.67
post and transport	7.14
praefectus praetorio	7.17, 20, 84
praefectus vehiculorum	7.2, 17 n.51, 19, 19 n.63, 20, 20 n.67, n.68, n.70,72
praetoria	7.15 n.37
provincial differences	7.13
regerendarius	7.20
regulations of Maximus	7.67, 69
remedies to address abuses	7.85 n.78
role of provincial governors	7.80-85
Roman innovation	7.18
secret service	7.56
sodalitates iuvenum	7.15, 18, 22, 73 n.44
speculatores	7.19
speed	7.15, 19 n.59
statio	7.17, 17 n.50, n.51, 73 n.41
stationarii	7.17 n.51
statores	7.14
structure and organisation	7.15, 18-22
tabellarii	7.14, 15 n.39, n.40, 16-19, 16 n.47, 17 n.49, 43 n. 42, 47, 83-84
tabernae	7.14 n.37
tesserarius	7.16 n.47
tractoria	7.85 n.77
veredi	7.13
via militaris	7.15
(see also '*angareia*' and 'requisitioning')	
custody	8.46
of books	8.55
customary gratuities	8.68 n.95
customs law	10.95-109
customs regulations	8.61
Cyprus	10.46
Cyrus	9.71

– D –

damages	7.172
injury	7.164
property	7.165
damnation	8.178-9
Darius	9.71
dative	
for duration of time	6.62
daughter	9.34, 57, 63, 64, 78, 83, 84, 86, 88-92, 95, 96
day of preparation	9.115
day of rest (*otium*)	9.112, 114, 118
day of resurrection and judgement	8.167 n.43
day of the Lord	9.58
day-books	8.67, 87, 141
Dead Sea	10.143
death	8.118-9
debtor	9.35, 59, 60, 61
debtor prison	8.67; 9.61
Decalogue	10.8
decisions of emperors	8.137
declaration	
of disappearance	8.102
of guarantor	8.51
of obligation	9.86
of animals and boats	7.63 n.19
decline in productivity	8.103 n.15
deferral	9.110
defixiones	10.43
deity's power	8.173
dekania	9.78
deliberative exercises	8.120, 120 n.9
delict of *plagium*	8.35

Index 1 – Subjects

delivery	
of *epistolae*	8.134 n.23
of *libelli*	8.133 n.20
Delphi	
sacral manumission	6.72-76, 79-81; 10.22
demand for satisfaction	7.188
Demeter	10.25
Demetrios of Phaleron	7.169
democracy	8.110
democratic constitutions	7.237
demons	10.14
demos	7.236-7
dependent females	9.63
depopulation	8.100
destitute widows	8.113 n.44
Deutero-Pauline letters	6.22
diadochos	6.167
diagramma	9.51, 60
diagraphe	6.5-6, 6 n.8, 11
διαθήκη in LXX and NT	6.43
diaspora	9.69, 80
dictation	9.86
Didyma	10.4
dikasteria	9.51
Diocletian	9.67, 68
Dionysiac artists	9.67
Dionysus	9.67
diploma	6.48
directors	8.57
disguising of identity	8.12 n.9
dislocation	
economic, social	8.104
political relationships	8.59, 104
dismission	6.37
display of corpse	8.1 n.1
distraint	8.50 n.19, 52 n.23, 54, 54 n.33, 57, 9.35, 49
divine deliverance	9.5
divine honours	9.16, 22
divine name	9.36
divorce	7.192-193; 8.143; 9.88-92, 96, 97; 10.114-118
agreement	10.115
deeds of divorce	6.6
initiating divorce	6.15-16, 15 n.25
divus	6.133 n.155
doctors	8.144
documentary evidence	
bias in data	6.143
documentation	7.137, 201-202
ἀγορανόμιον	7.208
ἀποδείξεις	7.137
γραφεῖον	7.201, 208
δημόσιος χρηματισμός	7.208-9 n.41
δημοσίωσις	7.202-203, 202 n.13, 203 n.21, 214 n.71, 216
διαγραφή	7.119, 201, 214 n.71
καταλογεῖον	7.208
συγγραφή	7.201
συγχώρησις	7.210, 215-6
χειρόγραφον	7.201, 203, 203 n.20, 214 n.71, 215-216
(see also 'courts')	
dog	10.126-135
dogmatic formulations	8.176
domestic affairs of cities	8.42
domestic codes or *Haustafel*	6.18-19; 7.194
Domitian	9.23-26
domus Augusta	10.72
donations	9.77-79
donkey	
importance of	7.113
δημόσιοι and ἰδιωτικοὶ ὄνοι	7.113
donkey-driver	7.96-7, 102, 123, 123 n.47, 163 n.2
requisitioning of	7.58, 63-4 n.23
sale of	10.124
standard burden	7.113
τριονία ὀνηλασία	7.82, 122 n.35, 123 n.46
use outside nome	7.113, 127
Doric dialect	6.23
dowry	6.1-18, 31 n.38; 9.49, 83, 86-90, 92-97; 10.115
LXX	6.12-13 n.16
as a metaphor	6.16 n.30
παραφερνα	6.4-5
προίξ to φερνή	6.2-4
προσφορά	6.4
provision of	6.2, 10
return of	6.2-3, 13
Roman practice	6.4 n.2
to regulate marriage	6.3-4
dreams	7.135 n.16

– E –

earthquake	8.174; 9.22, 29
Easter	8.178; 9.120
Eastern religions	8.173
ecclesiastical terms	9.68
eclipse	8.174
economic decline	8.103
ecumenical synod	9.67
edicts	8.42, 74

prefects	8.61	military *epikrisis*	6.148 n.162
aediles	8.26	proof of ancestry	6.136-139
education		taxation	6.136
classical curriculum	8.121	epiphany	10.73
educational system	8.120	*episcopus*	9.68
elitist culture	8.121	*epistates*	7.221, 138-9 n.26;
epideictic oratory	8.120		9.60
higher culture	8.119	*epistrategos*	6.142, 142 n.160,
instruction	8.178-9		144; 7.97, 102,
integrity of teachers	8.121 n.13		123 n.46, 124, 124
moral teachings	8.178-179		n.52, 139
pragmatikai	8.120	equestrian order	8.57
rhetor	8.119, 144	equestrian status	7.140
rhetoric	8.118	escape	9.43, 57, 58
rhetorical exercise	8.120	eschatological birth pangs	9.7
rhetorical training	8.120	eschatological judgement	7.223
teaching of church	8.177	eschatology	8.44
efficiency of government	8.40 n.103	and celibacy	6.16-17
Egypt	10.20, 146, 166	and slavery	6.54, 55
Egyptian		*eschaton*	7.154; 9.2, 4;
court	9.50		10.74
judges	9.51	esoteric legitimisation	8.171-172
magic	10.20-24	Essenes	10.6
marriage	9.49, 90	ethical model	8.108
name	9.33, 35	ethnic laws	9.51
eighteen benedictions	9.78	ethnicity	9.51, 52
ekdikos	9.29	eucharist	8.167 n.44, 177-
ekklesia	9.2		178; 9.117
ekthesis	7.242	*eucheion*	9.70, 71
elder	9.2, 15, 68-71, 74	*euergetes*	9.5, 15, 17
elders (γεραιοί)	7.79 n.50, 110 n.70	(see also 'benefactor')	
ellipsis	6.67-69, 132	evening	9.108, 109, 112,
emancipation	9.118		113, 114
embassy	8.107, 107 n.1, 133	examination	8.178
emperor	9.23-25, 27, 29-31,	of Christians	8.142
	109, 117, 118	execution	8.1; 9.53, 60, 61,
emperor's court	9.109		95, 96, 108, 109
empire and communication	7.57	*exegetes*	6.142
enchoric law	9.51	*exemplum*	7.136 n.19, 138-9
entrepreneurial class	9.33		n.26
envoy	9.109	exorcism	8.178
ἐπείκτης	7.50	of demons	7.154
ephebe	6.145	exorcists	
ephebic list	8.118	Jewish	10.45
Ephesia grammata	10.41, 44	extortion	8.68, 70, 75
(see also Artemis)		extra-judicial custom and habit	7.167
Ephesians			
epistle to	6.201-202	– F –	
Ephesus	9.24-31, 50; 10.18,		
	30; 10.35, 37-47,	faith	9.103
	49, 59-63, 95	faithful words	9.9
Epicureans	10.4	faithfulness of animals	8.115 n.55
epikrisis	6.126, 132-140,	familial terms	10.166
	145, 148 n.162	familial titles	8.171
education	6.136	family	9.17, 25, 27, 30,
form of	6.135		31, 34, 35, 43, 60,

Index 1 – Subjects

	63, 77, 85, 87, 89, 91, 92	penalty	7.132-134, 136, 136 n.20, 138
piety	8.114	removal	9.55
tree	8.86	foreign communities	9.17
famine	9.7, 8, 25	formula of introduction	9.35
farewell	9.63	formulary system	9.108
farthing	9.59	Fortuna	10.83
fasting	8.178	founder	9.16, 22, 78
fate	9.116; 10.11	foundlings	8.39 n.99
father	10.166, 173	four cardinal virtues	10.8
favour, asked of friend	8.22 n.52	fraud	9.55
Feast of Unleavened Bread	9.113	fraudulent claims	7.167
feasts in sanctuary of Dionysos	7.237	free city	8.58 n.54
federation of councils	9.71	freedman	8.42 n.105; 9.22; 10.103
Felix	8.153, 154		
festival days	9.112	Jewish	6.18 n.31
festival of Dionysos	7.239	*Lex Junia*	6.51, 151 n.168
Festival of Pan	9.67	Junian Latinity	6.151-152
festival of the Lark	7.238	freedom	8.110
festivals	9.112	four types of	6.62
Festus	9.53	frequency of quotation of John's gospel	
financial			7.246-247
burden	8.96	Friday	9.113, 115
houses	9.68	friend and ally of Romans	9.31
liability	8.57, 68	funding of festivals	7.238
loss	8.55 n.35	funeral activities	9.78
official	9.32	funerary	
period	8.57 n.45	epigraphy	9.102
procurator	8.59, 154	inscription	8.119, 152 n.1, 176
year	9.40	monument	9.77
fine	8.53, 54	*topos*	8.119 n.5
(see also 'penalty')			
fiscal		– G –	
conceptions	8.56		
domicile	8.99, 200 n.12, 123	Gabinius	6.129
governance	9.47	Gabriel	10.18
policies	8.110	Gaius	9.11; 10.48, 70, 81
risks	8.56	Galatia	9.24; 10.160
fiscus	7.210	Galba	10.80, 148
flattery	9.22	games	8.5, 129, 131
font	8.177	*gematria*	8.157, 165, 165 n.34; 9.87
forced sale	7.208 n.40		
forcible acquisition	7.130-162; 9.55	genitive absolute	6.132
action against dispossession or trespass		genre of 'lives'	8.121
	7.155 n.68	Gentile/s	9.2, 76-80; 10.130, 132
Athenian law	7.147-151		
charges	7.133	gentile	
		court	9.97
compensation	7.132-133, 140, 143, 134 n.10	benefactors	8.149
		Germanicus	10.60, 66
degree of force	7.152	*gerousia*	9.69-72
demotic law	7.132 n.5	Geta	9.28, 30, 31
disturbance of possession	7.134	gift of property	7.156
force or consent	7.132 n.3	giving evidence	8.36
Graeco-Roman law	7.132-147	*gnomon* of the *idios logos*	6.39, 107; 7.175
		glory	10.61

Gnosticism	6.54 n.65; 8.178; 9.117 n.36	grazing rights	8.48 n.5
gnosticism and the gospel of John	7.244-248	Greek bible	8.166, 166 n.37
God-fearers	9.73, 75, 77, 79, 80	cities	9.50, 115
gold medals	9.67	city-states	8.74
goldsmiths	8.67 n.89	civic title	9.71
Goliath	6.162-164	colonists	8.150
good government	9.25	court	9.50-52, 97
gospel as manual	7.253	ethical tradition	6.18
government of Greek city	8.5	ideas	9.19
governor	9.15, 24-26, 41, 52, 53, 68, 97, 109	law	9.50, 51, 94, 95
		legal usage	9.93
grace	10.61	marriage	9.49, 87
graffiti	8.6, 111 n.19, 163	names	9.64, 77, 117
grain		Greek and Latin in inscriptions	9.24; 10.56
ἀπαίτησις	7.114	greeting	8.123-124
collection of grain revenue	7.113-117, 114 n.8, n.9, 115 n.12	groom's obligations	9.95
		guarantee/s	8.51, 52 n.23, 56-58, 68; 9.32, 33, 40, 43, 46, 48-50, 83, 84, 88, 90-93, 95, 97
collection of grain revenue and NT	7.127-129		
classical diet	7.113		
ἐπιγένημα	7.115		
γενηματοφύλακες	7.114, n.8		
πράκτορες σιτικῶν	7.114, 115 n.11, 140	guarantees and guarantors	7.98, 208 n.41, 209
		guarantor	8.50-51, n.19, 53, 56, 57, 66, 67 n.90; 9.32, 33, 48, 49, 52
πρεσβύτεροι γεωργῶν	7.114, 115 n.10		
πρεσβύτεροι κώμης	7.120, 115 n.10		
προσμετρούμενα	7.114		
quantity collected	7.114	guard	9.39, 42, 43, 59
sitologoi	7.116-117, 119, 121, n.32, 126 n.56, 127 n.59	guardian/s	8.88 n.30; 9.49, 50, 94, 95, 97; 10.117, 143
σπέρματα	7.114	gubernatorial behaviour	9.15
theft of wheat	7.115	guest	9.63-66
grain transport		guilds	7.123-127, n.40-41; 8.5 n.3, 67 n.89, 69; 9.39, 106
collection of transport charges	7.117-121		
δημόσιοι ὄνοι	7.82, 123, 124 n.50		
disbursement of transport charges	7.121-123	*cisiarii* and *iumentarii*	7.16
δραγματηγία	7.118	γραμματεὺς κτηνοτρόφων	7.95 n.17, 122
ἐπισπουδασμοῦ φόρετρον	7.118	of κτηνοτρόφοι	7.117, 121
καταγωγή	7.117	of transport workers	7.123-7
λόγοι καταγωγῆς σίτου	7.117	penalties for members	7.123 n.41
ναύκληρος	7.62 n.17, 121, n.31, 32	silversmiths of Ephesus	7.123 n.43
		guilt	8.174
ναῦλον	7.121 n.31	*gymnasiarch*	10.32
ὁρμοφύλακες	7.122	gymnasium	8.108 n.2, 112
παραγωγή	7.117	class	6.136-139
payment procedure	7.122, 119 n.25	Gytheion	10.60
σακκηγία	7.118		
supply of transport	7.127	– H –	
φόρετρον	7.72, 117-121, 118 n.20, 126		
		Hades	10.43
(see also 'camel', 'donkey' and 'guilds')		Hadrian	6.148, 149; 8.136; 9.9, 29, 77; 10.31, 73, 76, 81, 82, 145
grammateus	7.237		
grapheion	6.7, 61, 110, 127		
grave	9.39, 104	Hadrianoi	10.1-2
grave robbers	9.102	Halicarnassus	9.4

Index 1 – Subjects

handmaiden	9.90, 91	hostage	10.88
harassment	8.103	house-church	9.50
Haustafeln	7.191 n.100, 194; 8.40	household	10.62
		household relations	8.114
hazaqah	6.37, 95-98, n.106, 112, 105; 8.142	householder	7.191-192
		humiliation	9.44
date of	6.97-98	hymn	9.119-121
healing	8.173	*hyperalla*	8.72
heavenly sign	8.167	*hypographe*	6.107
Hebrew	10.137, 145	*hypotheke*	8.50 n.19; 9.33, 48
Hecate	10.41		
Hecate Augusta	10.25	– I –	
heir	9.90, 91		
Hellenistic		Iamblichus	10.7
diplomatic discourse	9.17	Iao	10.10, 11, 12, 16, 42
historiography	7.23-25, 25 n.87		
law	9.55, 96	*iatroi*	10.2
royal theory	9.47	identification	8.12; 9.77
Hellenisation	8. 2 n.4; 9.33	identity, disguise of	8.12 n.9
Hellenised Jew/s	8.153; 9.96	*idiologos*	7.123 n.41
hendiadys	9.37	idolatrous pollution	8.150
herald	8.50	idolatry	10.29
Hercules	10.8	ignorance	8.175
Hermes	10.10, 25	illegal dispossession	7.147
Herod	6.42, 99, 129, 130; 9.41; 10.138, 156	illicit act	8.122
		illiteracy	6.30
Herod Antipas	6.99	image of God	9.38
Highest God	9.79	imitation	9.21
hierarchical structure of church 7.253		of meritorious actions	8.108
(see also under Clement of Rome)		immortality	9.19
Hierapolis	10.38	immovable property	7.148-149
high-priestess of Asia	6.25-27	imperial	
holiness and justice	6.206-209	agents	8.59 n.59
Holy Spirit	10.14	archive	8.136
holy war	7.154	authority	8.136
homily	8.121, 127	budget	8.68
homologia	6.32, 38	business affairs	8.59
homonoia	10.39	coins	8.113
honorific		constitutions	8.142
conventions	9.2	court	8.5
descriptions	8.108	policy	8.5
inscriptions	7.233-241; 8.114, 149; 9.3, 7, 20, 21	cult	9.4, 16, 22, 24, 27, 29-31; 10.28, 67, 104
honour	9.1, 2, 3	edicts	7.81; 8.70
in early Christianity	9.2	*epistula*	7.76, 80
of parents	8.116 n.56	estates	7.118 n.21
system	9.2	fiscus (see *fiscus*)	
horoscopes	8.156 n.1	freedmen	7.84
horse/s	10.173	generosity	8.68 n.95
in antiquity	10.124-125	halls	9.30
sale of	10.123-125	laws	8.61
horsemanship	8.88 n.30	*mandata* (ἐντολαί)	7.80
Horus	9.37, 62, 64	officials	8.60
hosios and *dikaios*	6.206-209	policy	8.5
hospitality	7.55 n.20; 8.171; 9.13, 50	post	8.59, 144
		(see also *cursus publicus*)	

privileges	8.110	888	8.161 n.21
procurator	8.59, n.56, n.59, 153	χμγ	8.4, 156 ff.
provinces	8.59, n.56, n.58, 60	ϙθ	8.157, 161, n.18, n.22, 166 n.37, 169, 172
provincial councils	9.68		
respect for law	8.136 n.41	Israel	10.8
revenue	8.60	iteration	8.65 n.75
rule	8.58	Iunia Theodora	6.24-25
scrinium	8.133, 134		
subscripts (see rescripts)		– J –	
whim	8.68 n.95		
imperial and official visits	7.63 n.23, 65	Jerusalem	9.14, 21, 41, 50, 53, 66, 69, 72, 117
impiety towards parents	8.115 n.55		
impressed labour	6.185 n.196	Jerusalem temple	8.145
imprisonment	8.54; 9.59, 60, 61	Jesus	9.11, 12, 16, 33, 37, 41, 52, 53, 55, 58, 65, 66, 70, 85, 98, 99-101, 103, 111; 10.8, 85, 129-130, 138
incantations			
Aramaic	10.11		
Hebrew	10.11		
indigenous court	9.52		
indulgence	8.41, 132, 136 n.41		
influences on legal systems		Jesus' travels	7.89
disposition of property	6.32-33, 36-38	Jew/s	10.28, 93, 145
marriage	6.4, 6-9, 12-14	Jewish	
inheritance	6.27; 7.156, 192; 8.59 n.56; 9.2, 91-95	ancestry	8.155; 9.20
		colony	8.149
		community	9.31, 69-71, 77, 79, 84
co-heirs	7.140		
debtor's heir	7.216	confiscation of property	8.146-7
disputed will	7.189	contractual forms	9.97
heir	6.38-39	court	9.52, 53, 71, 96
NT metaphor	6.39	cultural continuity	9.96
patrimony	7.149, 151	diaspora	8.127
Roman law and custom	6.39-40	disputes with elements	8.155
suus heres	7.148	gifts in contemplation of death	6.36-38, 96 n.107
testament	7.220		
information		Hellenised Jew	8.153
laying of	8.13, 17, 54	knowledge of ancestry	6.128
receipt of	8.19, 25	law	8.142; 9.4, 53, 88, 89, 92, 94-97
initiation	8.178		
instruction	8.178-179	magic	10.11
instrumental dative	9.55	marriage	9.84, 87-89, 95, 96
intellectuals of church	166 n.38	names	8.53 n.24
intermarriage	9.72	revolt	8.145-146
interpolation	8.128	Samaritans	8.150 n.7
interpretation of scripture	7.226	Schismatics	8.149
interruption of communication	7.139	system of time	9.112
introspection	8.174-175	terms	10.12
inundation of Nile	7.140	week	9.114, 118
invitations	9.62-66	Jewish-Christian community of Antioch	7.252
invocation to Poseidon	8.163		
Ionia	10.6	Jewish-Gentile question	8.174
irrigated crops	8.56	Jews	9.19, 69, 72, 73, 77, 79, 80, 84, 85, 91, 93, 96, 109, 114, 115; 10.166
Isis	9.36, 62		
isopsephism	8.171; 9.87		
666	8.165	outrage against Jews	8.146

Index 1 – Subjects

Johannine dialogue	8.149 n.4
Johannine vocabulary	9.101
John's Gospel	9.11, 100
Jordan	10.143
Josephus	9.11, 19, 71, 111, 114, 115; 10.6, 45
journeys	9.26, 58, 102, 116
Judaea	10.140, 144
Hellenisation	6.164
Judaism	9.19, 33, 77, 79, 80, 112, 114
influences on	6.36-38, 91-92
law of inheritance	6.32, 45
marriage	6.12-14
Judaism and Hellenism	7.191 n.100, 227
judgement in default	7.189
judge/s	7.212 n.61; 8.87, 136
judicial	
business	9.110
decision	8.137; 9.60, 61
dialogue	9.109
hearing	8.73
reform of Ptolemy II Philadelphos	7.202
status	7.175
Julia Augusta	10.25
Julius Caesar	9.9; 10.67
Jupiter	10.27
jurisdiction	9.47, 50-53
of local courts and judges	8.42
Justin Martyr	9.79, 115, 11

– K –

ketubbah	9.83-97
king	8.107; 9.36, 37, 40 n.4, 45, 47, 51, 63 n.3, 66
Kingdom of Heaven	7.154 n.66
kings of Israel	8.112
kinship	
relationships	8.115-116
responsibilities	8.113
Klaros	10.39
koina	8.58 n.54
koine	7.236
koine paraphrase	6.23
koinodikion	9.51
koinon	9.27
komarches	7.58, 58 n.1, 96-7, 97 n.29, 114
komogrammateus	7.58 n.1, 96, 97 n.29, 101, 113, 114, 119, 126 n.56, 211
Kore	10.39

kouretes	6.196-201
kurios	10.152

– L –

labour contracts – see *paramone*	
lamentation	8.145
language	
analogy of language	7.110
antecedents of verb	8.14 n.17
aorist in verbs of sending or going	7.51 n.9
arrangement of letters	8.160
Attic juristic vocabulary	7.169
boasting phraseology	7.239
case endings	8.158 n.9
Christian	6.85, 158 n.178, 174-177; 8.171
circumstantial participle	7.140, 147
cohesive ties	7.207
connotation	7.111
definite article	8.22 n.52
ellipsis	7.35, 207
elitist culture	8.121
epideictic oratory	8.120
epithet	8.162
expressive present	8.158
fossilisation	8.83 n.16
generalised audience	8.127
genitive absolute	7.207 n.35
Greek alphabet	8.159
higher culture	8.119
imperatival infinitive	8.13 n.16
Johannine metaphor	8.177 n.8
language of *clientela*	9.17
language of excess	9.20, 21
language of service	7.105-111
language of zeal	9.21
Latin language	10.151
Latin loan word	7.86
legal terms and concepts	7.152 n.54
lexical cohesion	7.207
metaphor	7.153-154, 161
metaphor of well-ordered city	7.108
nature of metaphor	6.40, 43, 53
Pauline metaphor	8.177 n.8
phonology	8.159, 164
play on words	8.128
predicative adjective	8.25, n.26
protasis	8.10
political register	7.109
religious and cultic register	7.109, 110
rhetor	8.119, 144
rhetoric	8.118
rhetorical exercise	8.120
rhetorical licence	7.150, 151
rhetorical usage of 'force'	7.2 n.53

semantic association	7.161		200, 202, 202 n.14, n.18, 205 n.29, 218-219, 219 n.99, 220 n.102, n.103, 224
semantic field	7.174		
stylistic values	8.120		
topos	8.118-119 n.5, 120, 176		
translation	8.136 n.39	*diagramma*	7.172, 186
use of article	8.92 n.49	*prostagma*	7.62, 77 n.49, 134, 137, 155, 178 n.64
use of διά with γράφω	7.54 n.19		
word order	8.158	revenue laws	8.49 n.11
Latin	10.148, 151, 152	Roman law	8.42, 58, 142
laokritai	9.46, 50-52	social perspective of law	7.184
law		study of law	9.78
Alexandrian law	7.180, 183, 183-4 n.76, 188	XII Tables	7.221 n.110
		lease	
ancestral	8.42	agreement	8.30 n.80
Antinomians	7.8	duration of	6.96 n.108
Athenian law	7.147-151, 155 n.69, 169, 176	of animals	8.81 n.7
		leasing	
Athenian law of theft	7.149-151, 150 n.47	agricultural land	6.86-105
		duration of agricultural leases	6.89
Attic juristic vocabulary	7.169	duty of care (Egypt)	6.89
Attic orators	7.151	duty of care (Palestine)	6.89-90
Codex Hammurabi	7.85 n.80	maritime	6.82-85
conservative nature of religious law	7.229 n.155	new vineyards	6.96
		legal	
Demotic law	7.132 n.5	action	8.36
editio actionis	7.178	advice	8.132 n.12, 133 n.13
Egyptian legal norms	7.173		
enchoric law	7.175	altercations	9.118
force of law	8.137	case	9.34
formulary procedure	8.134	charge	7.177
Graeco-Roman law	7.132-147	competence	7.173
Hellenistic	8.42	cost	7.172-173
imperial	8.61	dispute	9.34, 111 n.11
imperial respect	8.136 n.41	entity or corporation	8.58
Jewish law	7.231 n.163; 8.142	fiction	7.173, 215, 225 n.129, 226-227, 227, n.142, 232 n.166
law of contracts	7.167		
law of Greek cities (see νόμος πολιτικός)			
law of Moses	9.89, 91, 96		
laws of slavery (see slave)		formalities	9.118
Lex collegii funeraticii Lanuvini	6.51 n.62	idiom	8.139
Lex Fabia	8.26, 35	jurisdiction	9.45-47
Lex Irnitana	10.150	maxims	7.174
Lex Iulia de cessione bonorum	7.104 n.48, 221, 221 n.110, n.111	notice (ἀπογραφή)	7.177
		opinion	8.42, 133
		plurality of legal systems	7.156, 222 n.111
Lex Iulia de repetundis	7.81 n.59	procedure	9.109
Lex Iulia et Titia	10.149	proceedings	8.136
Lex municipii Salpensani	10.150	of Hermias	7.136-139, 154
Lex portorii Asiae	10.95-109	protection	8.39 n.98
Lex provinciae	7.81, 222 n.111	of travellers	7.88 n.96
Lex Rupilia	10.147	remedies	8.138 n.48; 9.43
Pentateuch law	7.189, 190 n.95	report of legal proceedings	7.189
purity laws	7.192	service	8.133 n.15
royal ordinance/law	7.155, 168, 175, 184, 188, 191, 195,	system	9.43, 50-53, 93, 97, 108

Index 1 – Subjects

terminology	8.130 n.1; 9.55		103-105, 111, 122, 123, 176; 9.71 n.4, 78
terms and concepts	7.152 n.54		
title	7.149		
tradition	8.135	age	7.102
letters		ἀναχώρησις	7.103-105, 103 n.46, 104 n.48
accusation of neglect	7.27-28		
ἀφορμή formula	7.27, 27 n.4, 49, 49 n.3	ἀνάθαυσις	7.102
		ἀρχαί and λειτουργίαι	7.95, 95 n.15
Christian	6.169-177; 10.164-174	ἄπορος	7.97 n.25, 100 n.31, 102, 103 n.46
condolence	8.124		
couriers		cities	7.122
early church	7.50-57	compensation	7.100
reliability	7.28-29	cultivation of royal land	7.140, 141 n.30
travellers	7.26-29, 46, 50, 54	cultic office	7.136 n.23
crossing and sealing	6.172-173	definition	7.93
delivery of Christian letters	7.50	ἐπιτήδειος	7.100
delivery to third person	7.39	ἐξέτασις	7.102
directions for delivery	7.29-43, 38 n.32	εὔπορος	7.93, 100
for return letters	7.42-43	exemption	7.94 n.13, 102-103, 103 n.43
on separate papyrus	7.31-34		
orally communicated	7.43-44	expenses of office	7.97
with address	7.34-41	finding replacement	7.100
distribution of addressed letters	7.34 n.20	fines	7.100, 100 n.31
distribution of types of address	7.34 n.22	guilds	7.123-127
familial terms	7.49 n.2; 10.165, 173	hire of substitute	7.2, 97
		interval of relief	7.102
filial respect	6.157	introduction of liturgies	7.93-94
finding courier	7.27-29	κατάστασις	7.96
finding addressee	7.43	lien on real property	7.97
γραμματηφόρος (see *cursus publicus*)		μερισμὸς ἀνακεχωρηκότων	7.103-4 n.46
identification as Christian	6.173-177	minors	7.102 n.40
inferiors to superiors	7.35	*munera patrimonii*	7.102
introduction	8.125	*munus possessionis*	7.59
letter of authority	7.54	nomination	7.1, 96-101
letter of Claudius Lysias	7.24-25	nominator's responsibility	7.100
letter of Jerusalem council	7.24	oath of office	7.96, 113, 124
letters of introduction	7.55, 90	παράστασις	7.100
letters of protection	7.222 n.112	personal liability	7.94
prescript and address	7.34-36, 35 n.21, 41	πόρος	7.97. 97 n.25
		protesting against	7.101-102
request for a letter	7.29	πρόγραμμα	7.96-97
significance of courier	7.27, 52	pseudepigraphical	8.120 n.11
from soldiers and sailors	7.45-47	public transport	7.58-92
use of middle person	7.43 n.39	official Roman posts	7.93
use of temple	7.43	rotation of liability	7.122
(see also under New Testament letters)		sources of abuse	7.101
Levitical priesthood	9.2	supervision	8.48, 64
liability	7.85, 85 n.80; 8.50 n.19, 58, 99 n.2	term	8.65
		types of compulsory service	7.94-96
lintels	8.156	*vacatio*	7.102
liquidation of assets	8.17 n.33	value of the πόρος	7.97
lists	8.67, 98-100	widening of responsibility	7.98, 100
liturgy	8.25 n. 63, 48, 58, 62, 65, 66, 70, 76, 78, 81, 85, 89, 95,	women and minors	7.102
		Livia	10.66, 67
		Augusta	10.25
		living God	9.38

'living image'	9.36-38	Delphi	6.52, 72-76, 79-81
loan	9.32 n.2, 33, 45-49, 52, 90, 97	economic effects of	6.80
		exploitation of	6.50, 66, 80-81
loans	6.105-111	formal and informal	6.151 n.168
cancellation of	6.107-109	Jewish practice	6.37, 66
interest rate	6.107	origins of sacral manumission	6.73
paramone	6.61	patrons	6.79
local		proportions of sexes released	6.79-81
bourgeois	8.75	sacral manumission	6.70-76
businessmen	8.74	'slave of god' (Delphi)	6.72-73
churches	8.170	'slave of God' (Paul)	6.75-76
civic authorities	8.60	slave's patronym	6.79
clergy	8.170	tax on	6.66
representatives	8.57	Thessaly	6.76-81
logistes	9.106-108, 111	under Zeus, Earth and Sun	6.66
log-linear modelling	6.211	Marcus	10.23
logos	9.10	Marcus Aurelius	9.28, 30
'lord'	10.173	M. Licinius Crassus	10.56
Lord's day	9.108-113, 117	Mariam	10.157-158
loss of identity	8.127	market day	9.113
loss of socio-economic status	7.183 n.76	markets	9.118 n.41
lost sheep	9.55	marriage	6.1-18; 9.49, 50, 62, 64-66, 72, 82, 84-98
Lucius Verus	10.38		
Luke's dating of Jesus' birth	6.31, 118-119, 123		
Lydia	10.26, 116	as agreement	6.12, 14
		bride's guardian	6.5, 15
– M –		celibacy	6.16-17
		consanguinity	6.137
Maccabean	10.74	contract	10.116
Maccabees	10.157	dowry	10.116
Macedonia	10.90	Egyptian marriage	6.6-9
magic	8.156, 167 n.43, 178, 178 n.12; 10.10	in Roman period	6.4-6
		Jewish (*kethubah*)	6.12-18
amulet	8.166; 10.39, 45	Jewish terminology	6.13-14
Ephesia grammata	10.17, 41	*Lex Minicia*	6.17
Jewish	10.46	maintenance of widow	6.2, 13, 31, 31 n.37
powers	8.166 n.37	marital duties	6.3-4, 14-15
spells	8.167 n.43; 10.22	ownership of property	6.3-4, 10, 13
voces magicae and *characteres*	10.21	Roman law	6.4, 14, 15, 16, 17
magical formulae	10.17	social function	6.2-4, 8, 18
magical papyri	10.10	unwritten marriage	6.4, 16, 18
magistracy	8.49, 57, 60, 122; 9.29, 67	virtue in a woman	6.18-19
		vows	6.14 n.21
women	8.49 n.9	marriage settlement	7.193
magistrates	7.79 n. 50, 179, 223, 237, 239; 8.54-55, 59, 60	Mars Ultor	10.28
		martyr	9.109
		Mary	9.29, 50, 66, 119, 121
maintenance of wife	9.92, 94, 97	Masada	10.140-141
Mani Codex	8.174	master	9.16, 47, 59 n.1, 65, 66, 90, 106
manumission	6.63-70; 8.39; 9.71 n.3, 118		
1 Cor.7.21	6.67-70	*mathetai*	10.2
analysis of data	6.73-75	Maximinus	10.7
Christian slaves	6.55	Maximinus Thrax	10.84
cost of	6.66, 74	meal	9.62, 64, 65
		meeting places	9.50

Index 1 – Subjects

memorandum-taker	8.140	life as race	8.119 n.5
menorah	10.155	literary	8.1
merchant	9.59	pagan motifs in Christian inscriptions	
messenger	8.133		8.176 n.3
Messiah	9.58	Mount Gerizim	8.149
Mesopotamia	10.38	movable property	7.147; 8.141
Messianic secret	10.22	mules	10.125
methodological problem	8.159	mummy labels	7.30-31, n.13
metrical inscriptions	8.176	municipal governance	7.94 n.12, 95 n.16, 122, 169
metropolitai	7.94 n.12		
metropoleis of Egypt	8.61 n.70	municipal magistracy	6.136 n.157
metropolites	6.143 n.161; 8.95 n.57	municipal structure	8.61
		musican contests	9.67
midday	9.112 n.13	musicians	8.144
midnight	9.112	mutual obligation	8.84 n.2, 86, 90
Midrash	6.18	Mysia	10.1
milestone	9.23, 24	mystery cult	9.43
Miletus	10.48	mysteries	7.237
militarisation		of Artemis	6.196-201
cursus publicus	7.17 n.51		
public administration	7.38 n.29	– N –	
military colonies	9.24		
military service	9.71 n.3	Nabataea	10.145
mines	10.105	Nabataean	10.142
minor	8.89 n.30	Nag Hammadi library	
miraculous event	8.174	ownership of	6.182-185
Mishnah	9.84, 92 n.15, 94	name	
missing persons	8.100 n.9	as indicator of status	6.62, 149-152
Mithras	8.161 n.19	names	8.122; 10.156
model of Greek city	8.107	Babylonian	8.18 n.36
mohar	9.88-93, 96, 97; 10.151	Egyptian	8.53 n.24
		Jewish	8.53 n.24; 10.156-158
monasticism	8.104, 174		
monetary economy	8.56	naming of child	9.58
monks		nationalistic bias	8.75
orthodoxy	6.182-185	nationality	9.51, 52
ownership of property	6.182-189	neocorate	9.28-31
monogram	8.4, 167 n.39	*neokoros*	9.27, 30
monopolies	9.32 n.2, 33, 39	of Artemis	6.203-206
monotheism	9.2	*neopoioi*	10.30, 48
Montanist	10.160	(Neo-) Pythagorean letters	6.19
moral depravity	8.174	Nero	6.113; 9.87; 10.63, 81, 82, 99
moral teachings	8.178-179		
moral terms	8.108	new covenant	8.179
mortgage	6.92 n.100; 9.32, 33, 48	new creation	8.179
		new Jerusalem	8.165
mortgagee	7.148	new moon	7.193
mosaic	8.163	New Testament anthropology	9.19
Moses	9.37, 89, 91, 96, 99, 100; 10.8, 151	New Testament letters	
		couriers of	7.45
mother	10.173	fictive author	7.44
motif		Claudius Lysias	7.54
aretalogical	8.174	to seven churches	7.54
carpe diem	8.119	prescripts	7.36
death at young age	8.118-119	*salutatio*	7.36
death in foreign land	8.118-119	use of persons of high status	7.45

use of emissaries	7.51-7	*komogrammateus*	8.25 n.63, 37, 64, 91 n.44, 101
use of synagogues	7.45	*logeutai*	8.53
nexus between king and city	8.107 n.1	*nomarches*	8.48 n.5, 65
Nicene Synod	9.68	*oikonomia*	6.19
night revelry	7.181 n.72	*oikonomos*	7.62 n.17; 8.50-51 n.19, 52 n.23, 52-55 n.27, n.33, 61-62; 9.32 n.2, 35, 39
nomads	8.14 n.17		
nomen sacrum	7.48, 242, 247, 248 n.23, 252		
non-territorial association	8.144		
notice	8.11, 13, 24	*phylakitai*	8.19, 20, 21, 22, 25
board	8.111	police officials	8.11
circular	8.23	*praktor*	8.48, 61-62, 65, 66 n.83-86, 67-69, 70-71, 74, 79, 95, 97-98, 100
notification of birth	6.122-123		
as proof of status	6.122, 137-139		
notification of death	6.122		
number of the beast	9.87	prefect	8.61, 65 n.79
numbers	8.160	*presbyteros*	8.64, 66 n.86, 100
numerological speculation (see also isopsephism)	8.165-166	procurator	8.59 n.56, n.59, 153, 154
Nun (Egyptian deity)	10.42	*proxenoi*	8.119
		royal functionary	8.107
– O –		*strategos*	8.11-12, 15 n.22, 23 n.55, 25, 28-31 n.80, 37, 61, 65-67 n.79, 69, 70, 72-73, 86, 91 n.44, 98, 118, 146
oak	8.173		
oath	7.214 n.74, n.75, 215 n.76, 229; 8.50, 50-51 n.19, 101; 9.10, 11, 43, 45, 47, 48; 10.66		
		symbolaphylakes	8.53
Octavian	9.27	*syntaktikoi*	8.47
offence	8.173	*topogrammateus*	8.101
office of bishop	7.107, 109 n.60	*xystarches*	8.32-33
official coercion	7.133 n.7, 221	oil for anointing	6.191
official corruption	6.99 n.114	oppression	8.75
official duty	9.35	oracle/s	8.104; 9.9, 10
official toleration	8.168	oral law	9.37
officials	8.53, 55-6, 130	oral tradition	9.101
aediles	8.26	order of the world	7.226
agoranomos	8.47	ordinal adjectives	6.132
antigrapheus	8.50, 53, 53 n.28, 55, 62	organisation of *vicus*	7.79
		origo	7.30 n.12
archidikastes	8.86	orphans	8.88-9 n.30
basilikogrammateus	8.37, 50, 52 n.22, 61, 65, 91, 91 n.44, 98	orthodoxy and heterodoxy	7.244
		orthography	6.61-62
		Old Testament cult	7.105
bureau of *strategos*	8.11, 23, 28	and the early church	7.107
dekaprotoi	8.49-50 n.13	ossuaries	8.167 n.43
dioiketes	8.50, 61	Ostia	10.155
ephodos	8.53	Otho	10.77, 84
epistrategos	8.61, 65, 71, 72, 73	owner's consent	9.55
governor	8.27, 35, 42, 57, 59, 60, 134	ownerless property	7.137, 146
		ownership of animals	8.81 n.7, 92 n.47
gymnasiarch	8.87, 108 n.2	Oxyrhynchus	10.172
high official	8.133		
hyperetai	8.53	– P –	

Index 1 – Subjects

p-value	8.160 n.15, n.16
paideutai	10.2
paganism	8.177 n.6
palaeography	9.102
Palmyra	10.100
Paphlagonia	10.69
parable	9.35, 36, 55, 65, 66, 103
of the wicked tenants	6.93-105
parable and allegory	7.156-157
definition	6.92-93
paradise	8.178
paraenetic material	8.127
paramone	6.60-63, 66; 7.165, 188-189; 9.90
at Delphi	6.74, 75, 80-81
loans without interest	6.61 n.71
repayment for services	6.61
release from	6.61
services unspecified	6.61
slave of God in Paul	6.75
paratactic καί	6.95 n.105
parental relationship	8.154
parousia	7.194
partner	8.58
partnership	9.47-49, 52, 78; 10.105
Passover	9.113
Pastoral epistles	9.13, 22
patriarchs	8.112
patron	8.103 n.16, 128; 9.15-18, 27, 43, 67, 68, 73, 77, 78
patronage	10.72
patronage and Paul's gentile mission	7.241
patronal practice	9.17
patronymic	9.77
Paul	9.2, 4-8, 11, 17, 18-22, 26, 35, 37, 38, 44, 48, 52, 53, 55, 58, 74, 79, 102, 104, 15; 10.2, 18, 49, 52, 61, 72, 85, 101, 112, 130, 166, 167-168
accommodation	7.90
advice on marriage	6.53
attitude to slavery	6.53-55, 59-60
citizenship	7.90 n.101, 92
conversion	7.88
emphasis on 'gift' of divine grace	10.61
evaluation of status	6.139-140
imprisonment	8.44
letter to Philemon	6.54
manumission	6.70
metaphor of inheritance	6.39
metaphor of the testament	6.42-47
ministry in Ephesus	10.38
renunciation of Jews	7.91
Roman citizenship	6.39, 41, 154-155
slave of God	6.75-76
use of synagogues	7.89, 91
Paul and Seneca	6.53 n.64; 8.120 n.11
Pauline letters	
collection of letters	7.256
collective audience	7.44 n.48
copies of letters	7.255
function of emissaries	7.56-57
function of letters	7.56
lost letters	7.256 n.30
painful letter	7.51, 256 n.30
pastoral epistles	7.245
personal details	7.56
prescript	7.255
Romans 16	7.45 n. 51, 51-52, 255 n.51
widening of audience	7.44
Paullus Fabius Persicus	10.59
payment of expenses	8.13-14 n.17
penalty	7.172-174, 177, 179-180, 184-185, 189, 231; 8.2, 15-16, 15-16 n.24-5, 26, 35, 53 n.28, 54, 65-66, 81, 134; 9.43, 53, 55, 60, 61, 91, 96, 104, 108, 109
for frivolous complaint	7.178
Pentecost	8.178
penthemeros	8.85, 87, 88, 90
Pepouza	10.161
performers	8.22 n.52; 10.49
Pergamum	9.24, 27, 29, 30
persecution	8.143, 165, 171, 179 n.15
of believers	7.195
Persephone	10.43
Persian of the *epigone*	9.59
personal favour	8.19
personal influence	8.25-26, 57
personal injury	7.165
personal relations	9.15
personal relationship	8.154
Pertinax	10.81, 82
Peter	10.166
petition/s	6.96, 99; 7.101-103, 105, 122, 131, 131-147, 164-166, 188, 203-204, 206, 210, 212-215, 217,

	227, 229-230; 8.133, 144, 145, 147; 9. 21, 24, 35, 40, 42-44, 46, 47, 49, 50, 52, 54-56, 60, 63, 106, 108, 109, 115; 10.144	Pompeius	10.56
		ponos	10.7
		pontiff	9.23, 30
		Pontifex Maximus	10.83
		Pontius Pilate	9.41, 52, 53
		poor relief	9.78
		Poseidon	10.17
(see also *libellus*)		possession (oracular)	10.22
addressees of	6.143	possession and ownership	6.33-36, 37, 43-44
form of	6.140-141	postal system/s	
pretence	6.57 n.66	in LXX and NT	7.22-25; 8.80 n.4, 88
social history	6.140-146		
threats and appeal to pity	6.142-143	(see also *cursus publicus*)	
verbal to emperor	8.133 n.21	liturgies/requisitioning	7.12
verbs of	6.145-146	military post	7.47
petitioner	8.133, 144, 145, 147	official postal system	7.49
		Persian Empire	7.2-5
(see also *libellus*)		Ptolemaic Egypt	7.5-13
Petra	10.149, 151	βυβλιαφόροι	7.11
Pharaoh	7.137	efficiency	7.10 n.21
Pharisee/Pharisaism	7.87, 153, 226; 9.100; 10.53	postal station	7.8-11
		ὡρογράφος	7.11, 21
phases of the moon	9.114	Roman Empire	7.13-22, 7.52 n.10
Philemon	10.106, 108, 167-168	posting	8.10, 19, 20, n.49, 24-25, 30-31, 50, 131 n.9, 134-136, n.31, 139, 141
Phoebe	10.117		
Philadelphia	10.3		
Philippi	9.6, 50, 79		
Philo	9.4, 7, 10, 19, 22, 71, 104, 115; 10.6	Potitus Valerius Messalla	9.17
		power of Satan	8.177
philosopher	8.113-114	*Praenestine* calendar	10.55
philosophos	10.2-5	*praetor urbanus*	7.222 n.111
phrourarchos	9.60	praetorian guard	10.74
Phrygia	10.92, 161, 162	praise	8.145
piety	8.116 n.57	*praktoreia*	8.100
Pisidia	10.162	prayer	8.145-147, 167, 178; 9.9, 12, 57, 58, 120
Pisidian Antioch	9.25, 26, 79; 10.55		
planetary control	9.114, 116, 117	preaching of Jesus	7.158
planetary week	9.110, 114-116, 118	prefect	6.142 n.160; 7.13, 19 n. 63, 21 n.76, 63 n.23, 65, n.26, 67, 70-72, n.36, n.39, 80, 84, 102, 122, 126-127, 131, 140, 204, 210, 212, 229; 9.61, 106-109; 10.148
planets	9.114, 115, 116, 117		
Pliny the Younger	9.25		
plurality of laws	6.7 n.11		
Plutarch			
collocation of βιάζεσθαι and ἁρπάζειν			
	7.158		
polis system	8.49 n.13	prefecture of Egypt	10.141
politeuma of Alexandria	9.71	prefectorial *prostagmata*	8.61
political diplomacy	8.110	*presbyterus*	9.2, 15, 68-71, 74
political power	8.5	prescript	8.122, 170; 9.70
politician	9.15, 17	demise of	8.125 n.7
poll tax		Greek and oriental	8.127, n.13
variations in	6.136 n.156	Hebrews	8.127
polygamy	10.143	intitulations	8.127
Pompeii	10.117	James	8.127

Index 1 – Subjects

omission of	8.123
transmission of	8.127
NT letters	8.127
price of crops	8.103 n.15
Priene	10.48, 60
priest	7.239; 8.15 n.22, 23, 108 n.4, 111, 167; 9.2, 4, 20, 28, 37, 39, 41, 51, 52, 67, 71-73, 92, 100, 111, 112
priest of Dionysos	7.237
priestesses in Roman Egypt	6.66 n.77
(see also high-priestess of Asia)	
prison	8.43, 46, 67
prisoner	9.35, 53, 60, 61
private	
capital	9.33
debt	8.77; 9.60, 61
lawyers	8.132 n.12
religious celebration	8.22 n.52
travellers	7.83 n.66
private property	
ownership of animals	8.82 n.13
ownership of land	8.39 n.98
ownership of property	8.47 n.1. 50 n.19, 59 n.56
ownership of real property	7.97
protection of property	8.25 n.61
sanctity of property	8.26
private travellers	7.83 n.66
privilege	9.2, 20, 31, 67, 115
pro- and anti-Roman factions in Palestine	7.153
probability theory	8.159
procedure of execution	7.197-212
against person and property	7.198 n.3
against person	7.184, 218-224, 222 n.111, n.112
imprisonment	7.218-219, 220 n.102, 223-224, 224 n.125
servitude	7.176, 191, 219-224, 224 n.122, n.125
slavery	7.184 n.79, 190 n.96, 191 n. 101, 219-224, 219 n.99, 244 n.125
against property	7.184
ἀγώγιμος clause	7.222, n.112
ἀντίρρησις	7.131, 200 n.9, 202, 204-207, n.31, 208 n.40, n.41, 211-212, n.51, n.55, 214 n.70, 215-216, 229
ἀπογραφη	7.210 n.43
διαστολικόν	7.200 n.9, 202-204, n.14, n.20, n.21, 210 n. 44, 211-212, 215-216
distraint	7.148
ἐμβαδεία	7.200 n.9, 202, n.14, n.18, 208 n.41, 210-211, n.44, n.45, 214, n.71
ἐνεχυρασία	7.131, 198 n.2, 199 n.7, 200 n.9, 201-202, n.14, n.18, 204-208, n.41, 210 n.44, n.45, 210-215, n.51, 230
ἐπικαταβολή or μετεπιγραφή	7.200 n.9
ἔντευξις	7.204, 210, 212, 214
καθάπερ ἐκ δίκης clause	7.215-218, n. 78, n.91, n.92, 222 n.112
καταγραφή	7.200, 202, n.14, 206, 208-211, n.40, n.41, n.45, 214 n.71, 230
kyria clause	7.231 n.164
Lex Iulia (see under 'law')	
libellus	7.205 n.29
loans secured by ὑποθήκη (see types of security)	
παράδειξις	7.198 n.2, 204-206, 211-212, n.51
praxis clause	7.198 n.3, n.4, 200 n.9, 215-218, n.88, n.91, n.92, 221-222, 231 n.164
προσβολή	7.198 n.2, n.3, 205-210, n.32, n.41, n.45, 218 n.92, 227-230
συγχώρησις	7.208 n.41
third party	7.202, 206, 212, 216, 217 n.88, 231 n.164
ὑπόμνημα	7.203, 207, 211-212, n.51
use of torture	7.221 n.107
valuation of property	7.205-206
ξενικῶν πράκτωρ	7.178, 197, 201-202, 204-208, n.29, n.41, 211, n.54, 213-214

	n.75, 217, 220 n.102, 221, 223	notice	8.10, 17, 19, 20, 23, 25, 26, 64; 9.32
procession of laurels in honour of Apollo	7.238	officials	9.26, 108
proconsul	10.92	revenue	8.32
procuratorship	8.155	service	8.85
(see also *procurator*)		spectacles	7.238
professional associations	8.144	suit	9.43
propaganda	9.4, 37, 109	transport	
property base	9.47	Roman Egypt	7.62-72
property of God	8.167 n.43	other provinces	7.72-80
property registration		virtue	8.109
ἀπογραφή	7.204 n.27, 210	publication	8.135
βιβλιοφύλακες ἐγκτήσεων	7.201, 204, 207, 210	of decrees	6.110-111, 115
βιβλιοθήκη ἐγκτήσεων	7.201 n.12, 204 n.27, 210, n.44	punishment	8.1, 2, 4, 40, 41, 54, 173; 9.14, 54
		purple-seller	9.77
διάστρωμα	7.97, 103, 200-201 n.9, 204 n.27, 210 n.44	Pythagoreans	10.4
		Pythagoras	10.6
κατοχή	7.201 n.12, 204 n.27	– Q –	
register of lands	7.114	*quaesor*	9.15, 17
prophetic literature	8.75	quasi-divine honours	9.15
prophets	9.9, 14, 66	Quirinius	6.31, 123, 124, 127, 130, 131; 9.41
propraktikon	6.66		
proselyte	9.73, 77, 79, 80		
Jewish	6.18 n.31	Qumran	9.41, 112
prostagma	9.52	administrative organisation of	6.128 n.147
prostatis	6.24-25		
protective sign	8.166-167 n.39	– R –	
proto-Gospel	7.252		
protocol	7.136, 138, 204 n.23, 211; 9.109	Rabbi Gamaliel II	8.75
		rabbinic literature	9.111 n.11, 116
provision of support	8.172	rabbinic marital formulae	9.84
province	10.95	racial origin	9.51
provincial		ransom	8.15 n.22
cities, prosperity of	9.25	rates of pay	8.53
government	9.26	rebel administration	7.147
officials	9.25	rebirth	8.179
prozbol	6.92, 92 n.100; 7.225-232	receipts	6.107-109; 8.47-48, 53, 61-62, 67, 77, 92
civil or religious	7.229 n.155	receipt of information	7.55
issued over real property	7.228 n.147	reciprocal obligation	6.157 n.176
Prusa	10.1-4	reciprocity	8.46, 55, 57, 109 n.6
prytaneion	7.235, 238		
prytanis	7.233-236, 238; 10.33, 50	church patronage	8.116 n.57
		ethics	8.115
pseudepigraphy	6.19, 22	ideology	8.114
Ptolemaic army	7.142	motifs	8.113
Ptolemaic civil service	7.12	norms of	8.114
Ptolemaic transport system	7.12	parental favour	8.114
public		terminology	8.109, 113-115
advocate	9.29	recourse and redress	8.55
debt	9.33	redirection of document	9.70
entertainment	7.239		

Index 1 – Subjects

regional specialisation	8.155	retaliatory execution	8.2 n.7
registration	8.78, 81, 90-91, 99	revolt	8.146-147
deeds of sale	8.39 n.101	reward	8.10, 13, 15-17,
minors	8.67 n.92		n.17, n.21, n.23,
population	8.39		n.24, 19, 25-26,
sheep	8.81 n.6		31, 45, 51, n.20, 68
wagons	8.93 n.51		n.95
regulation of personnel	8.53	right of execution	6.90-92
reintegration edicts	6.115-119	Egypt	6.90-91
religious disposition	8.75	Palestine	6.91-92
remarriage	10.116	self-help	6.91-92, 98-104
reminders	9.65	risk	8.50 n.19
remorse	8.41	ritual fund	8.146-147
repayment	8.115 n.55	rituals	7.239
repentance	8.41, 173	road accident	7.164
reports	8.65-66	roads	
republican magistrates	9.16	via Campana	7.88 n.94
republican order	8.58	via Egnatia	7.75
repudiation	9.88	via militaris	7.73 n.44
requisition/ing		via Sebaste	7.82 n.61
abuses	7.66 n.29, 67 n.31,	robbery	8.146
	73 n.41, 80 n. 51,	Roman	
	84 n.68; 8.68, 80	administration	
	n.4	perception of	6.141-142, 145
burden of providing	7.80 n.51	citizen	8.95 n.57, 152
exemption	7.82 n.62	citizenship	8.141
for imperial visits	7.63 n.23, 71 n.36	colony at Philippi	7.74
for military *annona*	7.63 n.23	*dominium*	8.142
obligation to supply	7.63 n.19	*equites*	8.76
of goods and services	7.63 n.23	generals and dictators	8.112
penalties	7.67 n.32	influence	8.2
provisions	7.60 n.11	law	8.42, 58, 142
record of expenses	4.67 n.33	legal opinion	8.42
risk of being seized	7.86 n.82	legal terminology	8.130 n.1
ships	7.53 n.17	legal tradition	8.135
(see also under *angareia* and liturgy)		provincial government	7.202
rescript	8.61, 129-147;	testaments	6.38 n.52
	9.68, 109, 115	Romanisation	10.145
archive	8.13, 135 n.31	root fallacy	6.114
authentication	8.131 n.4	rounding of ages	6.30-31
authoritative opinions	8.136	royal office	8.107 n.1
codes	8.136	royal treasury	7.140
composition in Latin	8.136 n.39	rulers	
earliest evidence	8.133 n.15	gentile	8.149
early church	8.142	Graeco-Roman	8.132
epistulae	8.136 n.39	Hellenistic	8.132
legal status	8.136-137, 141	ideal	8.111
posting	8.131 n.9, 135 n.31	munificence of	8.112 n.29
private rescript	8.131	runaway slaves	6.55-60
subscripts	8.37, 73, 101-102,	apprehension of	6.57
	134-136, 135 n.36,	assistance of	6.56
	136 n.39	destinations of flight	6.58
residence of emperor	8.131 n.9, 134	master's reputation	6.58, 60
restraining order	7.144-145	need to explain flight	6.59-60
resurrection	8.176; 9.2, 11, 38,	Paul's letter to Philemon	6.59-60
	53, 104, 117, 120	response of masters	6.57-60

theft of property	6.58, 59	in Graeco-Roman Egypt	6.99 n.115
– S –		self-reliance	9.35
		self-revelation of deity	8.174
		Sempronius Liberalis	6.117
Sabbath	9.111-118	senatorial provinces	8.59, n.56, n.58, 60 n.60
eve	9.113		
limit	7.192	Seneca	10.28, 62, 63
sabbatical year of release	7.225-226, n.131, 228, n.147, n.152, 229 n.155, 230, 232	Septimius Severus	6.117, 148; 9.77; 10.162
		Serapeum	7.135 n.16; 8.14 n.19, 15 n.21; 9.62, 64
sacrament	8.167 n.44, 177-179		
sacrifice	7.238; 1, 2, 6, 37, 67, 109	serfdom (the colonate)	7.104 n.46; 8.103 n.16
to gods	8.142	Sergius Paullus	7.240
saints	9.2	servant	10.166, 167
salary	8.54 n.31, 66 n.83	seven-day week	9.113-117
Salome	10.156-157	Sextus Appuleius	10.59
salutation	8.172	sexual/purity offences	8.173
salvation	9.4, 5	sheep	9.54
salvation history	7.153	shepherd	9.55
Samaria	10.46	shipping contracts	6. 82-86; 7.160
Samaritan religion	8.150	duration of leases	6.83
Samos	10.6	limitation of liability	6.83-85
Samothrace	9.43	shipwreck	9.55
sanctuary	8.173	Sicily	10.26, 147
Sanhedrin	8.112; 9.52, 53, 69, 72, 111	signatures	9.87, 92, 96
		signing of forehead	8.178
Sarapis	9.62, 65	silver *denarius*	10.42
Sardis	9.22, 27, 30, 31; 10.39, 94	Simon Magus	10.13
		singular and plural first and second person	6.170-172
Satan	10.13, 45	sins	8.175
Saturday	9.114, 115, 117	sister	8.171; 10.153, 173, 174
Saturn	9.114-117		
Saul	10.166	Siwah	10.22
saviour	9.4, 16, 28, 30, 31, 36, 104	Sixth Syrian war	7.23 n.81
		slave/s	9.2, 11, 35, 49, 59, 65
schism	8.171; 9.41		
school	10.3	(see also manumission, *paramone* and runaway slaves)	
schoolteacher	10.3		
school exercises	6.23	as metaphor	7.194
'school of philosophers'	10.2	asylum, right of	7.185, 195; 8.14 n.19
scribes	10.166		
scriptures	8.120	authority to punish	8.33
seal	8.131 n.4	branding	8.12 n.10
seasonal work	9.110	capitation taxes	8.92 n.47
seating arrangement	9.65	clubs	7.167
Sebaste	10.162	collars	8.13 n.11
security	8.51, 58	compliance of	6.57-58
Selene	10.42	cost of slave	7.178 n.63, 184
self-help	7.133, 133 n.8, 136 n.20,139, 148-150, 150 n.46, 216, 227 n.143; 8.25-26; 9.59, 108	cruelty	8.36-37, 15 n.20, 39 n.98
		debtor slavery	7.219-225
		definition of fugitive	8.41

Index 1 – Subjects

description of	8.16,17, 20, 24, 27, 39 n.101	damages paid for injury	7.193 n.106
discipline and coercion	6.50, 54	caprice of penalties	7.184 n.78
disease, defect or noxal liability	8.26	collusion to deceive master	7.178
discontent of	6.51-52, 55	corporal liability	7.184
enslavement of fellow citizens	7.190	exemption from prosecution	7.172
escape		legal effects of actions	7.186
financing of	8.34	*litis aestimatio*	7.185-186
incidence of	8.39	*noxae datio*	7.178-179, n 33, 186
successful	8.40 n.103	payment of slaves	7.167
familial relationships	6.50, 79, 188	reprisals against slaves	7.176 n.55
fictitious sale of	6.72	sale overseas	7.173, 175, 176 n.56, 178
fear of new master	8.36	torture	7.167, 173, 176 n.58, 177
fear of punishment	8.36		
flight	8-46, 100	*verberandum exhibere*	7.185-186
as remedy	8.99 n.2	whipping	7.175, 180, 184-187 n.78, n.83
in NT	8.40		
inclination to	8.26	lot of slaves	6.50-52
multiple	8.20, 36, 40	management slaves	6.51
reasons for	8.36	manumission	6.186-189; 7.167, n.17, 168 n.22, 191, 192 n.104, 193, n.107
successful escape	8.40 n.103		
fugitivarius	8.26-27		
fugitive types	8.18		
functions of	8.18 n.37, 39 n.98	master/slave relationship	8.1
funerary inscriptions	6.51-52	control over sexual activity	7.195
harbouring	8.15 n.24, 16, 28, 33, 35	honour	7.195; 10.167
		intervention of government	7.168 n.22, 175, 178 n.64, 195
hiding place	8.36, 45 n.109	intervention of third party	7.195
improvement in lot	7.177	*ius vitae et necis*	7.191
in Christian households	6.54-55, 70	master's complicity	7.173, 177, 179, 186-188
incidence of escape	8.39		
inclination to flight	8.26	master's liability	7.185 n.83
independent journeys	7.167	master's rights and interests	8.19 n.44
influence of Egyptian practice	7.177	master's rights and obligations	7.165, 175-176
joint ownership of	6.79		
legal capacity of	6.50, 66; 7.165-193	relationship to master	6.85; 7.165
ability to reason	7.192	submission	7.195
agency	7.165 n.5, 167, 193, n.105	treatment of slave	7.194
		murder of master	6.57 n.67; 8.1 ff., 2 n.7
as witness	7.167, 176-177, n.58, 192	names of	6.62 n.72
laws of slavery	7.172	New Testament	7.193-196
OT and Judaism	7.189-193	numbers	8.39 n.99
property ownership	7.167, n.14, 193	origins of	6.58
Ptolemaic period	7.166-168	ownership	8.13 n.11, 39
Roman period	7.165-166, 188-189	*paramone*	6.61 n.69
suit against slave	7.167, 172-175	permit of movement	6.60-63
suit for injury against owner	7.177-180	prisoners of war	6.52 n.63
wrong suffered by slave	7.184	rebellion	6.57 n.67
legislation improving lot	6.51	receipt of information	8.19
liabilities and penalties	7.184-188	registration of	7.168; 8.39-40 n.101
appeal against conviction	7.172-175		
as object of revenge	7.185 n.83	runaway slave/s	6.101-104; 7.194
branding	7.173, 175	intention of	8.41-42

pursuit of	8.10-36	tax exemption	6.147-148
receipt of information	8.19	Son of Man	9.102
return of	8.14	*sophistai*	10.2
unclaimed fugitive	8.27 n.72	*soter*	9.16
sale of slave	6.48, 53	soteriological language	9.4
sales tax	7.219	soteriological propaganda	9.4
to another master	8.14	Soteros	10.2
seizing of	8.15 n.21	Souchos	6.71
servitude for debt	7.219-224	soul	9.10, 13, 19, 37, 83, 103
slave of God (Delphi)	6.72-73		
slave of God (Paul)	6.75-76	soup kitchen	8.162; 9.78
slaves of state	6.79	Spain	10.117
status of slaves	7.165-166, 192 n.104	*speculator*	7.58
		spell	10.22
caste status	7.191-192	spirit	9.11, 14, 16, 19, 37, 103
citizen and slave	7.168 n.22, 183 n.76		
		state security	9.47
familial ties	7.189, 191-192	status	8.16, 36, 111, 130, 136 n.39; 9.102
Hebrew slave	7.189		
marriage to free woman	7.167-168	and privilege	7.94
terminology	7.173-174	*epikrisis*	6.132-139
verification of status	8.39-40 n.101	freedmen	6.151-152
witness	8.23 n.57	indicated by name	6.149-152
taxes on slaves	6.122 n.141; 7.219	notification of birth	6.122
terminus technicus σῶμα	6.81 n.94	of early Christians	7.240, 252
slavery (see also slaves)		of women	7.193
moral dilemma of	6.53, 54, 59	Paul	6.139-140
NT attitude to	6.53-55	petitioners	6.143
NT metaphor of	6.53	role of marriage	6.18
Stoic attitude to	6.52-53	soldiers	6.149, 152-154
sleep	8.2	titles	6.175-177
Smyrna	9.6, 23, 25, 26, 27, 29; 10.31	Stoicism	10.2
		attitude to slavery	6.52-53
social categories in cities	7.237	storms at sea	6.85-86
social distinction	9.109	strangers	9.13, 111
social expectations	8.113 n.46	*strategos*	6.42, 56, 113, 114, 116, 129, 141, 142; 7.23 n.80, 41, 50, 61-62, n.17, 68, 70-71, 96, 98, 101-102, 112-113, 121, 123 n.46, 124 n.52, 127, 130-131, 133, 135, 138-139 n.26, 142, 144-146, 163-165, 167 n.15, 170, 174, 180, 203-204, 210-211, 214, 221, 233, 237; 9.47, 60, 106, 108; 10.84, 88
social obligation	9.35, 65		
social order	9.43		
social upheaval	8.40 n.102		
solar deities	8.161 n.19		
soldiers	9.39, 42-44, 54, 55		
Claudius' reform	6.148		
discharge of	6.147-148		
epikrisis	6.135, 148		
expenses (clothing)	6.158-159		
grant of citizenship	6.151 n.171		
Jerusalem garrison	6.159-161		
Jewish	6.167		
letters	6.156-159		
marriage and family	6.148-149, 152-153		
		stratification of ancient society	7.94
pay	6.157-158	striking an *archon*	7.183 n.74
settlement on retirement	6.152-153	Subatianus Aquila	6.117, 118
size of units	6.159-161	subcontractor	8.48, 52 n.22
status advancement of	6.153-154	succession	10.55-58, 69-72
taktomisthoi	6.167		

Index 1 – Subjects

suit for injury	8.35
suits	
actio de peculio	7.165 n.5
actio iniuriarum	7.183 n.75
actio tributoria	7.165 n.5
against slave	7.172-5
against slave's owner	7.177-180
γραφαί, εἰσαγγελίας, φάσεις	7.151 n.48
γραφὴ κλοπῆς	7.150 n.47, 151
γραφὴ λωποδυσίας	7.151
γραφὴ περὶ εὐθυνῶν	7.150 n.47
γραφὴ ὕβρεως	7.151, 151 n.48, 183 n.75
διαδικασία	7.149, n.41
δίκη	7.213, 217 n.91, 218
δίκη αἰκισμοῦ	7.180
δίκη αἰκίας	7.148, 183 n.75, 187
δίκη ἀτίμητος	7.182 n.73
δίκη βιαίων	7.133, n.8, 147-149, n. 35, n.37, 151, 180, 183 n.75
δίκη βίας	7.147 n.35, 148
δίκη βλάβης	7.184
δίκη ἐνοικίου	7.134, n.15, 149
δίκη ἐξούλης	7.133, 136 n. 20, 148-149, n.37, n.41
δίκη κακηγορίας	7.183 n.75
δίκη καρποῦ	7.133, 140, 143, 147, 149
δίκη κλοπῆς	7.149-151, n. 45, n. 47
δίκη λωποδυτίας	7.151
δίκη οὐσίας	7.149, n.41
δίκη σιδήρου ἐπαντάσεως	7.183 n.75
δίκη τιμητή	7.182 n.73
δίκη ὕβρεως	7.183 n.75
summons	7.136, 169, 189, 213-214, n.70, 229; 8.23
Sunday	8.178; 9.106, 109-118
sunrise	9.112, 113
sunset	9.111-113
supernatural event	7.85
supernatural power	8.167 n.44
superstition	8.166 n.38
supervisor	8.48, 62
symbol	8.92 n.48, 93 n.49, 156-157, n.5, 159-161, n.14, n.22, 164-168, n.39, n.43, n. 44, 172, 177-178
chi-rho	8.4, 8, 157 n.5
christogram	8.166-167, n.39
cross	8.166-167 n.39, 167 n.43
staurogram	8.166 n.39
taw	6.166-167 n.39
symbola	8.50, n.18, n.19, 51
synagogue	8.110, 149, 150; 9.26, 31, 69-71, 77-80; 10.154
syncretism	8.161 n.19, 179 n.15
syngraphe	6.107
synhedrion	8.74 n.102
synod of gymnasts and stage performers	8.131 n.3
synods	8.144; 9.67, 68
synoptic gospels	9.100, 101, 111
syntax	8.159
Syria	10.60
Syrian Antioch	10.77

– T –

table fellowship	9.55
talisman	8.167 n.39
tattoo	8.11-12
Talmud	9.37, 38, 87, 90, 116; 10.151
Tannaim	7.226
tax	
absconding	8.67 n.90
arrears	8.48, 54, 65, 66, n.84, 74, 77, 81, 103
assessment	8.53, 55, 58 n.51, 70, 99 n.6
assessor	8.53 n.27
avoidance	8.75
burden	8.103-105
of tax farmers	8.65 n.79
bureau	8.53 n.23
bureaucrat	9.42
capitation tax	8.64, 67-68, 67 n.90, 78, 88-89, 92 n.46, n.47, 93 n.52, 96, 98-100, 103
checks and balances	8.55
chrysargyron	8.67 n.89
collection	8.47-76; 9.52, 71 n.4
of direct taxes	7.93
collectors	8.47-76, 171; 9.43, 47; 10.52-53
control of companies	8.53 n.23
debtors	8.54

delinquents	8.98, 100	trade tax	8.69, 78, 93
direct taxes	7.93; 8.58, 61, 74	taxable property	8.55 n.35
disputed assessment	8.53 n.27	taxation	9.15, 33, 43
donkey tax	8.77-78	absenteeism	6.112-119
economic exploitation	8.75	abuses	6.144-145
efficiency	8.68	ages of liability to	6.121
enkyklion	8.47 n.2	assessment of	6.113-115
exemption	8.91 n.44; 9.67, 68	cancellation of	6.114
farmer	7.114 n. 9, 127, n.61	census declarations	6.121-122, 124
		epikrisis	6.136
wealth and influence of	8.57	exemption of veterans	6.147-148
farming	8.47-76, 95; 9.32, 43, 47, 48	Herod	6.129
		idia	6.113
of indirect taxes	7.93 n.5	immunity from	10.102
ferry tax	8.99 n.3	Judaea	6.129
grievances	8.110	lists	6.126, 136
Hellenistic system	8.54, 74	notification of birth	6.122-123, 137-139
imposition on cities	8.58 n.51		
increases	8.68	notification of death	6.122
indirect taxes	8.58, 58 n.54, 59, 68, 74, 76	on manumission	6.66
		system	10.99
'in kind' tax	9.54	teaching of church	8.177
Jesus' attitude	8.75	*telos*	10.97
Judaea	8.74-76, 49 n.13	temple	7.43, 135; 9.2, 15-17, 24, 26-31, 36, 41-43, 53, 62-64, 106, 112
land tax	7.114 n.4, 128 n.62		
licence tax	8.80-82, 94		
lists	7.114; 8.92, 99 n.5		
loss	8.52 n.23, 69	Jerusalem	8.145
multiple collecting	8.52 n.21	Mount Gerizim	8.149
obligations	8.55 n.35	rivalry	8.149
on property sold	7.210	tenant farmers	8.103 n.15
personnel	8.66	*tesserae*	10.44
pig tax	8.99 n.3	testimony	8.174
poll tax	8.67, n.90, 92 n.47, 95, n.57, 97, 99, n.3, 103	theft	9.43, 55
		Thessalonica	10.2, 73
		Third Syrian war	8.17 n.3
		thug	9.43
praktor	7.93	Tiberius	6.31; 7.65 n.26; 9.7, 11, 22, 41; 10.60, 66
professions	8.67 n.89		
profit	8.50-51 n.19, 52, n.21, n.23, 54-55, 60, 65 n.79, 75		
		Tiberius Caesar	10.25
Ptolemaic Egypt	8.49-57	Tiberius Iulius Alexander	8.153; 9.61
publicani	7.93	tiles	8.157
rates	8.68, 95 n.57	times of necessity	9.7
recalcitrant taxpayer	8.74 n.103	titles	6.158 n.178
receipts for grain	7.117 n.19	brother	6.175-177
records	8.58 n.51, 61	father	6.177
release from	8.130 n.2	master	6.175-177
remission	8.68 n.95	mother	6.177
Roman Egypt	8.61-74	sister	6.177; 10.171
Roman taxation	8.95	titulature	9.23, 24, 29, 31, 36, 37
sales tax	8.51 n.20		
on slaves	7.219	Titus	10.81
salt tax	7.168; 8.99 n.3	tomb	8.118; 9.19, 78, 102, 119
sinners and collectors	8.75		
status	8.95 n.57	*topogrammateus*	9.32

Index 1 – Subjects

Torah	10.154
Torre Nova	10.3
torture	9.53, 109
trade	8.92 n.47
traditional hostilities	8.150
Trajan	6.148; 9.25; 10.74, 77, 81, 84
Tralleis	10.25
transliterated Greek	9.84, 86, 87
transmission of *arete*	7.240
transport	
animals in the NT	7.128
by ship	7.117 n.15, 121 n.30
certificates	7.126 n.56
importance of Rome	7.96
of corpse	7.30 n.13
(see also under grain)	
travail	9.58
travel in the New Testament	7.87-92
treason and acts of war	8.2
treatment of Christianity	
in courts	8.142
tree of life	9.3
trials	8.137; 9.51, 52, 111
tribune	9.53
trumpet (of God)	9.102, 103, 105
Twelve Tables of Roman law	6.111
twenty-four hour day	9.112
twilight	9.113
two natures of Christ	8.158
types of security	7.200-201, 200 n.8, n. 9, 231-2
ἀνανέωσις	7.200 n.9
ἐπὶ κυρίᾳ	7.201
Jewish law	7.231 n.163
ὑπάλλαγμα	7.201, 203, 205, 216
ὑποθήκη	7.200-1, 200 n.9, 203, 210 n.44, 216
Tyrannus	6.197-198

– U –

Ugaritic	10.166
unfair distribution	8.103
unknown Gospel	9.99
unlawful possession	8.147
unwritten marriage	9.95
urbanisation	8.58 n.51
usufruct	6.31, 33-37, 43, 46; 9.89
usuary	7.225, 231

– V –

Valerius Datus	6.117, 118
Vedii	10.103
Vedius Pollio	10.101
vernacular	9.51
Vespasian	9.16, 23
via Campana	7.88 n.94
via Egnatia	7.75
via militaris	7.73 n.44
via Sebaste	7.82 n.61
Vibius Maximus	6.115-119, 126
vigil	8.178
vineyards	6.167
virgin	9.66, 83, 88 n.8, 94, 120, 121
vocative	9.63
vote of gratitude	8.107
vows	6. 14 n.21; 7.238; 9.112

– W –

wagon	8.93
wandering charistmatics	8.105
warrant	8.17, 20 n.49, 30
wealth	10.61
weavers	8.69
'we' passages	7.92
weddings	9.62-66
Wednesday	9.84 n.2, 116, 117
welfare institution	9.77
wells	7.180
widow/s	8.109, 113, 116, 116 n.57; 10.144
destitute	8.113 n.44
wife	9.45, 46, 48, 49, 59 n.1, 83, 84, 88-97; 10.173
as property	6.13-14 n.18
wild beasts and birds of prey	8.1
wills	6.38-39
annulment by others	6.42
annulment of	6.41-47
conditions and regulations	6.39
Jewish legal instruments	6.43-46
Paul's metaphor	6.42-47
ways to revoke	6.42
wine	
medicinal use	6.190-191
wine retailer	9.59
witness	8.173, 174
women	8.48-49, n. 9, 121, 158; 9.50; 10.120
authors	6.19-22
benefactors	7.237
gymnasiarchs	8.49

in public life	6.24-27; 8.49	– Y –	
of means	9.50		
prisoners of war	8.15 n.22	Yahweh	10.11
word of God	9.37		
work contracts	6.95, 164-167	– Z –	
(see also *paranome*)			
		zealot/s	8.75
–X –		movement	7.87, 153-154
		Zenon	6.98-105
xystarchi	10.30	Zeus	9.36, 116

2. Selected Words in Greek, Latin, Hebrew and Aramaic

Greek

ἀγαθῇ τύχῃ	8.156 n.1
ἀγαθός	6.157
ἀγαπητὸς ἀδελφός	6.175
ἀγγαρεύειν	
(see under *angareia* in subject index)	
ἄγγελος	8.165
ἀγέννητος	9.104
ἀγορανομεῖον	8.65 n.79
ἀγορανόμιον	7.208
ἀγράφως συνεῖναι	6.4
ἀγώγιμος	6.8
ἀδελφή	10.165-166, 173
ἀδελφός	6.175, 177; 10.165-166, 173
ἀδίκημα	7.168 n.22, 173, 178, 186
ἀθετεῖ	6.43
αἰγιαλῖτις γῆ	7.140
αἰών	10.85
αἰώνιον	10.81
ἁλιάδες	7.2 n.1
ἁλιαδίτης	7.2
ἁλική	8.99 n.3
ἀμήν	8.158, 161, 166 n.37
ἀμιξία	7.139
ἄμφοδον	6.125; 7.41 n.37
ἀναγράφειν	6.107
ἀνακεχωρηκότες	8.99 n.6
ἀνακοπτέω	10.121
ἀνάκρισις	8.39-40 n.101
ἀναχώρησις	6.62 n.75, 113, 113 n.119, 126, 8.98, 99, 123
ἀνδράποδον	7.173
ἀνδρεία	9.20
ἀνὴρ ἀγαθός	9.6, 20
(ὁ ἔσω) ἄνθρωπος	6.53
ἀνθρωπός τις	9.65
ἀνιππίας	7.12, 12 n.24, 8.88, 88 n.30
ἀντίρρησις	6.90
ἄξιος	6.157
ἀξιῶ	6.141, 145
ἀπαγωγή	7.150 n.46
ἀπαιτήσιμα	8.66
ἀπαίτησις	7.114
ἀπαιτηταί	8.66 n.84, 78, n.1
ἀπεδήμησεν	6.94 n.102
ἀπεργασία	8.85, 88 n.28
ἀπέχειν	6.3
ἀπὸ τῶν γραφέντων	7.207
ἀπογραφαί	8.91 n.44, 92 n.47
ἀποδιδόναι	7.213
ἀποδίδωμι	6.3, 157, 157 n.176
ἀπόδος	9.35
ἀπόδος εἰς οἰκίαν	7.39 n.33
ἀπόδος παρά+	7.39 n.33
ἀπόλυσις	6.61, 61 n.69
ἀπόμοιρα	8.49 n.11
ἀποπομπή	6.11
ἄποροι	6.113-114, 121 n.139; 8.99 n.6
ἀρετή	9.109 n.5; 10.7
ἁρπαγή	7.69, 151, 153, 160 n.85
ἁρπάζειν	7.152, 154 n.65
ἀρχεῖον	10.146
ἄρχοντες	6.99; 9.70
ἄρχων	6.92
ἀρχώνης	8.52, 55, 57, 59 n.58; 9.47, 48
ἀστάνδης	7.2-3 n.6, 4
ἀσχολούμενος	8.47 n.2
ἀστυνόμῳ	8.10 n.2
ἀσωτία	10.7
ἀτελής	8.96 n.59
ἀτιμία	8.54
ἄτιμος	7.168-9 n.22, 183 n.74
αὔριον	9.63, 110
ἀφαίρεσις	6.15 n.25
ἀφορμή	8.126
ἄωρος	10.23
βασιλεία	10.85
βεβαιωταί	8.50 n.19
βία	9.55
βία θεοῦ	6.82-86
βιάζεται	6.98
βιαιοθάνατος	10.23
βιβλιοθήκη δημοσίων λόγων	8.64 n.74
βιβλιοθήκη ἐγκτήσεων	6.9
βλάβης δίκη	6.90
βοηθός	8.53, 66, 162 n.26
βραχεῖα	8.141
βραχεῖα ἀφορμή	8.141 n.49
βύρσης	8.89 n.30
γενητήρ	9.104
γενητής	9.104
γενήτωρ	9.104
γεννάω	8.158
γεννητός	9.104
γραμματεῖς	8.66
γραφή	8.53 n.23, 54, 55; 9.43
γυμνασιαρχίς	8.49
γυνή	10.174
δαίμων	8.118 n.1

δάνειον	6.6	ἕκτον	8.83 n.16
δεδανεικέναι	6.7	ἐκ τῶν θυσιῶν	9.2
δεξιολάβοι	6.160 160, n.181	ἐκφεύγω	9.58
δέομαι	6.141, 145-146	ἐλαϊκή	8.49 n.11
δεσμωτήριον	9.60	ἔλεος	10.72
δεσπότης	6.175-177; 10.173	ἐλεύθερος	8.96 n.59
δημοσία βιβλιοθήκη	6.121	ἑλληνικῷ νόμῳ	6.16 n.27
δημόσιος χρηματισμός	6.107	ἐλπίς	9.4
δημοσιώνης	8.48 n.5	ἐμβαδεία	6.90
διαγράμμα	9.60	ἔνδειξιν	6.115
διαγράμματα	6.90; 9.51, 60	ἐν εἰρήνῃ	8.171
διαθήκη	6.37, 38-39, 38 n.51, 41-47, 46 n.60	ἐνεχυρασία	6.90
		ἐν καιροῖς ἀναγκαίοις	9.7
		ἔντευξις	9.60
διάκονος	9.44	ἐν τοῖς δεσμοῖς	8.43
διαλογισμοί	8.51 n.19, 53 n.23	ἐξειλφότες	8.78 n.1
διαμονή	10.81	ἐξέτασις	6.121
διαστολικόν	6.90	ἐξομολογεῖσθαι	8.173
διάφορον	8.15 n.21	ἐξουσία	6.62 n.74
διέπων	9.116 n.32	ἐξουσιάζω	6.15 n.22
δικαία ἀφορμή	8.141 n.49	ἐπανόρθωσις	9.37
δικαστήριον	7.174, 218	ἔπαρχος	6.160
δίκη	6.90; 9.43	ἐπείκτης	7.50
διοίκησις	8.66	ἐπιγραφή	9.3
δίπλωμα	7.15 16-18, 19, 20, 71-72, 77, 80- 85	ἐπιγένημα	7.266; 8.51, n.19, 52, n.23, 55, 66 n.83
διπλώματα	6.48		
δόγμασιν	6.110-111	ἐπιδέκατον	7.172
δόμα	6.12 n.16	ἐπιδιατάσσεται	6.43
δόξα	9.12; 10.62	ἐπικεφάλαιον	8.92 n.47
δοῦλος Χριστοῦ	6.75	ἐπίκρισις	6.120 n. 127, 125 n.146, 132, 139; 7.102, 192 n.104; 8.40 n.101
δύναμις	8.174; 10.17		
δωδεκάδραχμος	6.138		
δωρεά	8.20 n.45		
ἑβδομάς	9.115	ἐπιπεντεκαιδέκατον	7.172
ἔγγραφος γάμος	6.15 n.25	ἐπίσταλμα	8.33; 9.108
ἐγδεδομένη	6.10	ἐπιστάτης	8.15 n.22
ἐγκύκλιον	8.50 n.19, 51 n.20, 65 n.79	ἐπιστρέφια	10.121
		ἐπιτήρησις	8.64, 65
ἔγδεια	8.52	ἐπιτηρητής	8.48, 62, 65
ἔθνος	9.39 n.2	ἐπίτροπος	9.94
εἰ (direct question)	6.183	ἐπιφάνεια	10.74
εἰ καί	6.69	ἐπιφανής	10.73
εἰκονίζειν	6.127	ἔργα ἀγαθά	6.19
εἰκονισμός	6.125 n.146, 127	ἐργάζεσθε ὡς τῷ Κυρίῳ	6.19
εἰκών	8.16; 9.2, 103	ἔργον θεοῦ	9.102-3
εἰρήνη	8.172 n.7; 9.4	ἐρωτῶ	6.145; 9.65
εἰς	6.157-158	ἐσυκοφάντησα	8.74 n.103
ἐκδιδόναι	6.15	ἑταῖροι	10.3
ἐκδόσιμον	6.39	εὐκοσμία τῆς ψυχῆς	6.18
ἔκδοσις	6.7 n.10	εὔνοια	9.20; 10.103
ἐκκλησία	10.88	εὐργεσία	9.6
ἑκουσία ἀπαλλαγή	6.11	εὑρίσκω	6.183
ἑκουσίως	6.10-11	εὐσέβεια	9.22; 10.35
ἐκτίθημι	6.110	εὐσεβῶς	10.30, 35
ἐκτενῶς	10.30, 36	εὐταξία	6.19

Index 2 – Words

εὐτύχει	6.141	Κρονική	9.117
εὐχαριστία	9.22	κτηνοτρόφος	8.90 n.36
εὐχόμενοι	10.81	κύριος	6.2, 7 n.9, 15, 34, 124 n.143; 9.49, 89, 94
ἐφέστιον	6.115 n.122, 117 n.123		
ἔφηβος	10.48	κύριος ἀδελφός	6.176 n.193
ἔφορος	8.55	κύριος πατήρ	6.176 n.193
ζηλωτής	8.108 n.2, n.4	κωμάρχης	6.129
ἡγεμονίαν	10.79	λαογραφία	6.136 n.156
ἡ κυριακὴ (ἡμέρα)	9.115	λαοκρίσιον	9.51
ἡ τοῦ Ἡλίου λεγομένη ἡμέρα	9.117	λαοκριταί	7.137, 175
ἡλίου ἡμέρα	9.110	λεύκωμα	6.115
θβ	8.164	λογευτήριον	8.53 n.23
θεῖοι λόγοι	9.10, 10 n.1, 12, 13	λοιποῖς	6.16
θεός (= *divus*)	6.133 n.155	λόχιον	9.62
θυγάτριον	10.130	λύκανον	9.63
ἰδία	6.113-114, 115-119, n. 122, n.123, 125-126, 127; 7.100, 103-105, n.46, n.29; 8.99, n.6, 100, n.12, 103	μάγματα	10.39
		μάγος	10.40
		μᾶλλον	6.69-70
		μαντεῖα	9.9
		μάντις	10.69
		μαρτυρίαι	7.176
ἴδιον ὀφείλημα	9.61	μεγαλοφροσύνη	9.20
ἴδιος λόγος	8.66	μεγαλύνομεν	9.121
ἱεροὶ λόγοι	9.10	μεμερικέναι ... μετά+	6.32
ἱερός	6.72	μερίς	9.2, 3
ἰκονισθέντες	6.126	μερισμός	6.113-115, 121; 8.67 n.90, 99-10
Ἰουδαῖοι	8.149		
Ἰσραηλῖται	8.149	μεριτεία	6.34
καθάπερ ἐκ δίκης	6.91	μέρος	9.2, 3
Κακότης	10.7	μετάβασις	6.125-126
κακοῦργοι	9.61	μετοχή	8.53 n.23; 9.47, 48
καλοὶ κἀγαθοί	8.108, 109, 111, 115	μέτοχος	9.47, 48; 10.106
		μέτοχοι	8.52, 53 n.23, 64, 66, 66 n.85
καλοκαγαθία	6.19		
καλῶς ἄν ποιήσαις	6.104	μηνύειν	8.13 n.16
καμηλῖται	7.11, 123	μήνυτρον	8.14 n.17
κατὰ ἄνθρωπον	6.44-46, 44 n.56, n.57	μὴ ὄκνει	9.58
		μήτηρ	10.173
καταγραφή	6.90	μία τῶν σαββάτων	9.115 n.24, 117
κατάστασις	7.213	μισθοπρασία	6.83
καταξίως	10.51	μισθός	6.61 n.71; 8.53
κατ' οἰκίαν ἀπογραφή	6.119	μορφή	9.103
κεκλημένοις	9.65	ναύβιον	8.89
κεκυρωμένην	6.43	νεανίσκος	6.100
κίνδυνος	7.100	Νέρων Καῖσαρ	8.165
κληρονόμος	6.37 n.49	νίκη Καίσαρος	9.9
κοιμητήριον	8.176 n.2	νομάρχης	7.120, n.28, 210, 215 n.75
κοινόν	10.3		
κοινωνία	9.47, 48; 10.106	νόμοι	6.16 n.27, 90
κοινωνοί	10.105	νόμος πολιτικός	7.168, n.22, 172-188, 190, 202
κολάσιμος	8.7		
κόλλημα	6.9, 9 n.13, 121	νομοφύλαξ	7.169, 171-172, 178, 197, 202
κοράσιον	6.49, 61-62		
κρίσις	7.211-212	νοῦς	6.53
κρίτης	6.92	νυμφών	9.66

ξενοκρίται	10.152	προθυμία	9.21
ὁ ἀγαθός	9.6	προίξ	6.2, 2 n.2, 31 n.38;
οἱ δικασταί	7.174, 176		9.94, 95
οἱ χωρὶς οἰκοῦντες	6.63	προνοεῖν	8.113
οἰκογένεια	8.40 n.101	πρόνοια	8.109-116
οἰκοδομή	9.103	πρός	6.10, 157-158
οἶκος	6.2	πρὸς ὥραν	8.43
ὁμολογεῖ	6.38 n.50	προσάββατον	9.115
ὁμολογία	6.32; 10.124	προσαγορεύω	8.126 n.9
ὁμόνοια	6.173-174, 174 n.190; 7.108	προσβολή	6.90, 92
		προσδέχομαι	8.171
ὅμως	6.43 n.55	πρόσδοσις	6.8
ὀνηλάτης	8.90 n.36, 92 n.46	προσηλῶσαι	6.111 n.118
οὐδείς	6.46	προστάγματα	6.90; 9.51
ὀφείλειν	9.97	προστάτις	6.24-25
ὀψώνιον	8.51, 51 n.19	προσφορά	6.4; 8.23 n.59; 9.49, 95
ϙθ	8.157, 161, 161 n.18, n.22, 166 n.37, 169, 172	προτίθημι	6.110
		πρωτοπραξία	6.4, 13
πάλιν	6.98	πρῶτος – πρότερος	6.130
παντοκράτορα	6.175	ῥάχος	6.166
πατήρ	10.165	σάββατα	9.114
παράδειξις	6.90	σάββατον	9.114
παράγγελμα	8.23	σάρξ	6.53
παρακαλῶ	6.145	σὲ μεγαλύνομεν	9.121
παραμονή	6.60-63, 61 n.69	σκέπη	8.122
παραζυγή	8.86 n.27	σπουδή	9.21
παράφερνα	6.3, 4-5	σταθμός	7.4, 73 n.41, 97 n.27
παρασκευή	9.115		
πατελλᾶς	9.78	στάσις	7.108, 108, n.58
πατήρ	10.173	σταυρός	6.109; 8.166 n.39
πεντάδραχμος	8.85 n.26	στέρεσθαι	6.3
περισσεύειν	9.4	στηλογραφεῖν	8.173
περιστερά	8.161 n.21	στηλογραφία	8.173
περίζωμα	8.12 n.8	στρατήγιον	7.170
Πέρσης τῆς ἐπιγονῆς	6.7, 7 n.12, 9; 7.222 n.112	στρατηγός	6.129
		στρατοπέδων	8.153
πιστοὶ λόγοι	9.9-13	συγγραφή	9.48, 52
πιστὸς ὁ λόγος	9.14	συγγραφὴ τροφῖτις	6.6-9
πνεῦμα	9.19	συγχώρημα	6.35
πολεύων	9.116 n.32	συκοφαντεία	8.54
πόλις	6.2	σύμβολα	9.48
πολιτεύματα	7.175, 219	σύμβιος	10.174
πολιτικοὶ νόμοι	9.51	σύμβολον	8.47
πορνεία	6.16	συνήθεια	7.76
πρακτόρειον	8.67	σύνοδος	10.82
πρακτορικόν	8.66 n.83	συντάξεις	9.40
πράκτωρ ξενικῶν	6.90	σχίσμα	7.108-109, 108 n.58
πρᾶξις	6.90-92; 7.219; 10.17		
		σώματα	7.173
πρᾶξις πρὸς βασιλικά	7.219, 219 n.99	σωτήρ	9.4
πρεσβύτεροι	9.69	σωτηρία	9.4, 5; 10.79
πρό	6.157	σωφροσύνη	6.18; 9.20
προαίρεσις	6.174 n.189	τάγμα	7.107
πρόγραμμα	8.23, 62, 64; 9.32	τάξις	7.107
προέθετο	6.115	τέλειος	7.87

Index 2 – Words

τελειοῦσθαι κατ' ἀρετήν	6.18
τέλος	7.127 n.60; 8.81 n.7; 9.4, 10
τέλους ὠνή	8.49
τελῶναι	8.47; 9.47
τελώνης	7.114 n. 9, 127; 8.47-57
τιμιώτατος	6.157
τόμος	6.9 n.13, 121
τοπάρχης	6.129
τοπογραμματεύς	6.129
τύπος	7.24
ὕβρις	7.187
ὑϊκή	8.81 n.7
υἱός	10.166
ὑπέραλλα	8.70.74
ὑπερβάλλειν	7.199 n.6; 9.20, 21
ὑπερβολή	7.199 n.6; 9.4, 21
ὑπέρθεσις	6.114
ὑποθήκη	6.92 n.100
ὑπηρέται	8.66
ὑπογραφή	8.130 n.1
ὑπογραφῆς ἀντίγραφον	8.102
ὑποκείμενα	7.67 n.31
ὑπόμνημα	7.33; 8.61; 9.60
ὑπόμνημα ἐπιγεννήσεως	6.122, 137
ὑποτασσόμενοι ἀλλήλοις	6.19
ὑπόχρεος	7.219 n.99
ὑφίστασθαι	7.199 n.7
φερνή	6.1-18, 2 n.2, 12 n.16; 9.49, 94
φθαρτός	9.2
φιλαλληλία	6.173-174, 174 n.190
φιλανθρωπία	9.20
φιλοδοξία	7.237; 9.20
φίλοι	8.111
φιλοκαλεῖν	6.19
φιλοτείμως	10.30, 35
φιλοτιμία	9.20; 10.35
φόρος ἵππων	8.88 n.30
φόρος νομῶν	8.48 n.5
φόρος	7.127 n.60; 8.81 n.7
φροντιστής	7.214 n.74
φυλακίτης	8.22 n.52
φυλακτήριον	8.167
φωσφόρος	10.42
φωταγωμήτωρ	9.121
φωταγωγός	9.121
χαῖρε	8.124, 125 n.6, 126, 170
χαίρειν	7.35; 8.123, 170
χαίροις	8.124, 125 n.6, 126
χάρις	6.157; 9.4, 21; 10.17, 60, 61, 101
χείρ	7.163 n.1
χειρισταί	8.66
χειραγωγοῦντες	7.88
χειρωνάξια	8.92 n.46
χιάζειν	6.108, 109
κεχιασμένην	6.173
χιλίαρχος	6.160, 160 n.180
χλαμύς	8.12 n.8
χμγ	8.4, 156-168
χρηματισμοί	8.61
χριστιανός	7.248; 10.161
Χριστός	10.10
χωματικόν	8.67 n.90, 89, 92 n.47
χώρα	6.118, 137
ὡρογράφος	7.11, 21

Latin

a libellis	8.131 n.4, 132, 133, 33 n.15, 134, 136
ab epistulis Graecis	8.132-4
ab epistulis Latinis	8.132-3
actio furti	8.35
actio servi corrupti	8.35
adaeratio	8.86 n.27
adiutor	8.153, 154, 154 n.5
aerarium	8.57
aerarium Saturni	8.59 n.59, 60 n.60
album	6.115
annona	6.83
annona militum	8.48
antigrapheus	9.42, 43
apparitor	8.27
assertio in libertatem	8.15-16 n.24
auctoritas	10.57, 70
aureus	10.55
auxilia	6.149, 153 n.174, 159-161
avaritia	6.58
beneficarius	8.152
beneficium	10.59, 102
beneficium abstinendi	6.38 n.52
bona fides	8.138, 141, 141 n.49
causa	8.138
cave canem	10.132
censor	8.57, 57 n.45; 9.23
centuria	7.47
cives Romani	6.127
civitas libera	7.74
clementia	10.63, 68, 72
clientela	9.17
coercitio	9.109

cognitio	8.35, 134; 9.97, 108, 109; 10.146	extra ordinem	9.109
		fama	10.70
cohors equitata	6.160	familiae	7.15 n.39
cohors equitata milliaria	6.160	fideicommissum	6.38 n.52
collegia	7.15 n.39	fides	10.62, 70
collegium funeraticium	6.51 n.62	fiscus	6.83, 113, 118; 7.210; 8.27 n.72, 59 n. 58. 60 n.60
coloni	8.104		
coloniae	8.138		
concilium	8.133 n.17	flamines	10.26
conductor	8.59, 59 n.58, n.59	formula	10.102
coniugium	10.174	fortuna	10.83
conquistor	8.26	fugitivarius	8.25-27
consecratus	9.16	fugitivus	8.41
consilium	8.142	furtum	8.16 n.25
contubernium	7.168	gens Aurelia	9.77
conubium	6.17, 148	geruli	7.17 n.49
conuentus	10.102	gloria	10.70
corpus	6.53	graeca adulatio	9.15
corrector	8.60	grammatici	8.144
crimen capitale	8.35	heres	6.38 n.52
cum mano	6.14 n.20, 15 n.24	honestiores	8.35, 35 n.90
curator	8.60	humiliores	8.35, 35 n.90
curator civitatis	8.60; 9.25	impensae	10.60
curator rei publicae	8.60 n.65	imperator	10.78, 144
curiales	7.19 n.63	imperium	8.137; 10.79, 103
cursores	7.17 n.49	infamia	7.221, n.110
cursus honorum	8.152, 153, 155; 10.72	institutio heredis	6.38 n.52
		interior pars	6.53
cursus publicus	8.133; 10.78	iudicium publicum	8.35
(see also *cursus publicus* in Subject Index)		iuridicus	8.71, 73; 10.150
		ius	8.137
damnatio memoriae	9.24, 28	ius civile	6.38 n.52, 40; 8.134, 138 n.48
decreta	8.137		
decumae	8.57		
decurio	7.19 n.63; 8.60; 10.150	ius Italicum	8.42, 138
		ius praetorium	6.38 n.52, 40; 8.138 n.48
defixio	8.167 n.44; 10.39, 40, 43		
		iusta causa	8.138-139, 141, 141 n.49
diaconus	9.68		
diploma	6.147; 8.80, 80 n.4, 81, 82, n.13, 83, 83 n.16, n.18, 84, 90, 92 n.47, n.49, 94, 130 n.2	iustum initium	8.141
		iustum matrimonium	6.17
		istus titulus	8.141 n.49
		labarum	8.167, 167 n.42
divinus homo	9.16	lapidarius	10.96
divus	6.122, 133 n.155	legatus	10.149
domus	10.72	lex	8.137; 10.95-109
donatio mortis causa	6.38 n.52	(see under subject index for individual laws)	
ecclesia	9.68	lex censoria	8.57
episcopus	9.68	lex provinciae	8.42
epistula	8.131-132, 134 n.23, 135-137, 136 n.39, 139, 142-144	libellus	7.205 n.29; 8.129 ff., 133 n.15, n.18, n.20, n.21
equites	10.103	loculus	8.163
exedra	10.3	longae possessionis praescriptio 8.139	
exemplum	7.136 n.19, 138 n.26		

longi temporis praescriptio	8.137-8, 138 n.48, 141-142	praefectus castrorum	8.153, 154
		praefectus praetorio	8.35
lorica	8.167, 167 n.43	praefectus urbi	8.35
lustrum	8.57	praefectus vehiculorum	8.60
magister privatae	8.31, 31 n.83	praefectus vigilum	8.27
magistri, promagistri	8.57, 58	praenomen	9.17
manceps	8.57-8, 59 n.58	praepositus	9.108
mandata	8.27	praetor	10.145
manumissio inter amicos	6.151 n.168	praetor urbanus	8.42
manumission per epistulam	6.151 n.168	presbyterus	9.68
membranae	7.250, 253	primipilaris	8.153
memorandum	8.17, 19, 20, 37, 45	princeps	10.57, 72, 79
mens	6.53	procurator	8.61; 9.22, 52
militia secunda	6.154	procurator Augusti	8.60; 10.103
milliaria	6.159-161	propositio	8.134
missio	6.147	providentia	8.112
modus	6.38 n.52	publica custodia	8.46
monstratio	7.43	publicani	8.50 n.13, 57-61, 74, 74 n.102, 76; 9.68; 10.97
monumentum Ephesenum	10.96		
munimen	8.167		
munus	8.58	publicum	8.60 n.60
nemo est heres viventis	6.40	pugillares membranae	7.250
nobiles	10.70	quadragesima	8.58 n.54
nobilis	9.20	quaestor	9.17
nomen	9.77	quingenaria	6.159-161
nomen sacrum	7.48, 242, 247, 248 n.23, 252; 8.169, 171	receptum nautae	6.83
		recognovi	8.131 n.4, 132, 133, 135
nomina sacra	6.175	relegatio in perpetuum	8.35
nundinae	9.113, 118	rescripsi	8.132-3
oratio recta	9.109 n.2	rescriptio	8.129 ff.
ordo publicanorum	8.57	responsa	8.132 n.12
otium	10.3	res publica	10.60
pactiones	8.74 n.102	sacerdotes	10.26
pagus	10.173	sacra	6.40
patella	8.162; 9.78	saeculum	10.83
paterfamilias	6.14, 15, 15 n.24, 40; 9.90, 91, 93	saevitia	6.58
		schola	10.3
patrocinium	9.17	scrinium	8.133, 134
peculium	6.50, 66; 7.165 n.5	scripsi	8.135
persona	6.40	scriptura	8.57
pilleus	8.26	senatus consulta	6.110-111
pistrinum	8.46	senatus consultum	8.2, 26
plagium	8.35	senatus consultum Silanianum	8.2 n.7
pontifex maximus	10.83	servus publicus	8.26
portorium	8.59 n.59; 10.95, 99	signum fidei	8.177 n.9
		societas	10.107
potens	10.56	societas publicanorum	8.58-9, 59 n.58, 76
potestas	6.14, 15, 15 n.22, n.24	socii (see also μέτοχοι)	8.57; 10.105
potitus	10.56	soter	9.16
praecipua potentia	9.114 n.21	speculator	7.58
praedes	8.57	spolia opima	10.56
praedia	8.57	statio	10.70
praefectus	6.160	stipendium	6.157; 8.74
praefectus alae	6.118		

subscriptio	8.130-2, 130 n.1, 133 n.18, 134, 136, 136 n.39	הול	9.114 n.23
		החרמו קרן	8.146
		הר	8.149
successor in locum defuncti	6.38 n.52, 40	חשך	9.112
sui heredes	6.40	חליצה	6.12
sui iuris	6.14, 15	חזקה	6.95-98; 7.156
tabulae	7.250	חרם	8.147
tesserae	10.44	כתובה	6.3 n.3, 12-18; 9.88 and n.8; 10.151
testatio	10.145		
tria nomina	6.149-151, 154		
tribunus militum	6.160	לבין השמשות	9.113
tributum capitis	8.58 n.49; 10.103	מהר	6.12, 12-13 n.16, 13 n.17; 9.88
tributum soli	8.58 n.49; 10.103		
turma	6.159	מהר ומתן	9.88 n.7
tutela	10.145	מהיום ולאחר מיתה	6.33
tutor	6.14, 15	מזל שעה גורם	9.116
usucapio	8.138, 138 n.48, 141-2, 141 n.49	מוסר	7.226
		מלוג	6.13; 9.88
vectigal	8.59 n.58; 10.100	משלים	6.105
venerabilis dies solis	9.110, 111	משפח	7.161
verba ipsissima	8.96 n.59	מתנת בריא	6.37, 43-47; 7.156
viaticum	7.47	מתנת שכיב מרע	6.37, 45
vicesima hereditatum	8.59	נימוס	9.84 n.3
virtus	10.70	נשואין	6.18 n.33
vis maior	6.83; 7.85 n.80	עבדך	10.167
votum	10.68	עם הארץ	6.128
		ערב שבת	9.113, 115
		ערובא	9.115
Hebrew and Aramaic		פרן	9.96
		פורנא / פרנה	6.12; 9.84 n.3, 88 and n.8
אב	10.166		
אדון	10.152, 167 (§24)	פרחבול	6.92
אחר שבת	9.115 n.24	פרק	8.146
איתודי	7.230	צאן ברזל	6.13; 9.88
אנוס	7.161	קדש	6.14, 18
אנס	7.161	קדש אדון	10.155
אפותיקי	7.192	קים	9.93
אפיפורים	7.252	קל וחומר	6.69
אפטרפא	10.152	קנה	6.13-15 n.22
ארוסין	6.18 n.33	קרן	8.147
בית דין	6.92	שבת	9.114
בן	10.166	שלום	8.172
בעל	6.13, 13-14 n.18	שלחים	6.12 n.16
גזל	7.162 n.90	שלימן למלקה לך	6.91
דיאתיקי	6.37, 43		
הדנה	9.88, 89		

3. ANCIENT AUTHORS AND WORKS

Acta Pauli et Theclae
3.8-19 — 10.121

Aelian
De natura animalium
1.8, 4.4, 6.25-26, 7.10,
  28-29, 38, 40 — 10.127
8.12 — 6.131
10.41, 45, 11.13, 12.35 — 10.127

Aeschines
Orationes
3.67 — 10.88

Aeschylus
Suppplices
735 — 7.207 n.36
Agamemnon
282 — 7.59, 4 n.13

Aesop
Fabulae
306 — 10.127

Ammianus Marcellinus
15.7.6f., 21.16.18 — 9.68

Andocides
De mysteriis
7 — 9.11

Antiphon
De choreuta
29 — 9.11

Anthologia Latina
1176 — 10.126

Appian
Illyrica
30.88 — 6.62 n.74
Mithridatica
103 — 7.132 n.3
Syrica
38 — 10.89
45 — 10.89

Apuleius
Apologia
42.6-8, 43.3 — 10.24

Aristeas
Epistula
35, 41 — 7.22-23 n.80, 9.70

Aristides, Publius Aelius
Panegyricus in Cyzico
240 — 6.44 n.57
Sancti sermones (*Hieroi logoi*)
1.11 — 6.206

Aristophanes
Thesmophoriazusae
78-80, 834 — 10.88
1029 — 8.1 n.2

Aristophanes Grammaticus
Nomina aetatum 20 — 7.59

Aristotle
Atheniensium respublica
1.13 — 10.122
43.2 — 9.113
43.4-5, 44.4 — 10.88
De caelo
299a — 9.12
De generatione animalium
 — 10.127
De lineis insecabilibus
969b — 9.12
De mortu animalium
 — 10.127
De partibus animalium
 — 10.127
In ethica Nicomachea
(anon.) 54 — 6.44 n.57
4.1 (1119b-1120a) — 10.7
1172a — 9.11
Historia animalium
 — 10.127
Magna moralia
2.12.1 — 8.114 n.50
Parva naturalia
 — 10.127
Politica
A 1254b — 7.191 n.100
1321b — 10.112
Rhetorica
1416a — 9.11

Arrian
Anabasis
2.7.2 — 9.11

Athanasius
Apologia contra Arianos
7.2   9.68
51.4   6.176
Contra Sabellianos
28.112   6.44 n.57
Orationes contra Arianos
2.6, 3.36   9.11

Asconius
Commentarii in Pisonem
13.16-17   10.89

Athenaeus
Deipnosophistae
4.19   6.157
4.359c   10.131
4.630c   6.131, 132
10.63   7.132 n.3
12.518f, 519b   10.127

Augustine
De catechizandis rudibus
26.50   8.167
De vera religione
3.42, 7.20   10.81
Epistulae
88.2   8.144

Aurelius Victor
Epitome de Caesaribus
13.5   7.19 n.62

Barnabas
Epistula
     7.245, 247; 10.8
9.8   8.161 n.21

Basil the Great
De renuntiatione saeculi
     7.159
Epistula ad Libanium
339   8.120 n.11
363, 364   6.176

Caesar
Bellum Gallicum
3, 21   10.68
Callimachus
Hymni
4.89   7.132 n.3

Cato
De agricultura
     10.127
140   9.112
Orationes
44, frag.173 (Malcovati 1955) 7.14

Censorinus
De die natali
23.3   9.113
23 and 24   9.112, 112 n.13

Cicero
De finibus bonorum et malorum
5.1   9.15
65   10.174
De legibus
3.8.18   7.16
19, 29   9.112
De natura deorum
2.27   10.42
De optimo genere oratorum
3.8   10.31
Epistulae ad Atticum
2.1   9.17
5.15.3   8.45
5.21.7   9.16
6.1.13   8.45
6.1.15   10.147
8.15.2   7.73 n.41
9.5.1   7.73 n.41
13.6.3   7.255 n.25
15.11.4   7.16
16.5   7.255 n.25
Epistulae ad familiares
2.1.1   7.28; 9.17
4.4.5   7.73 n.41
5.4.1   7.56 n.22
5.9.2   8.26, 45
6.6.8   10.68
10.1   8.26
13.77.3   6.58; 8.26, 45, 13 n.14
16.5.2   7.15 n.39
Epistulae ad Quintum fratrem
1.1.7   9.16
1.1.19, 20   9.15
1.1.33   10.99
1.2.14   8.45
In Verrem
2.1.13, 32-33   10.148
2.1.44, 114-116, 118   10.147
2.3.105ff   10.99
3.78.181   10.99
Orationes Philippicae
116   10.68

Index 3 – Ancient Authors

Pro rege Deiotaro
8, 33, 37 10.68

Clement of Alexandria
Protrepticus
8 8.120 n.11
1 Clement
1.1 7.108 n.58
1.2 7.55-56 n.20
2.1 7.60 n.11
2.6 7.108 n.58
2.8 7.108
3.2 7.108 n.58
3.3 7.108
3.4 7.108, 110
3.4-4.13 7.110
6.1 7.109
6.4 7.108
10.7 7.55-56 n.20
11.1 7.55-56 n.20
12.1 7.55-56 n.20
14.2 7.108 n.58
16.1-19.1 7.107-8 n.57
19.2-21.9 7.108 n.59
21.1 7.109
30.3 7.108 n.59
31.4 7.107-8 n.57
34.7 7.108 n.59
35.5 7.55-56 n.20
40.1, 2, 5 7.107
41.1, 2, 3 7.107
42.1-4, 5 7.107
42.1-6 7.107
44.1 7.106-7 n.57
44.1-2 7.107
44.1-6 7.106-7 n.57
44.2-3 7.107
44.3-6 7.108
44.4 7.106-7 n.57
44.6 7.109
46.9 7.108 n.58
48.6 7.106-7 n.57
49.5 7.108 n.58, 59
51.2 7.109
53.2 7.106-7 n.57
54.4 7.109
55.1 7.108
55.6 7.106-7 n.57
57.1 7.106-7 n. 57, 108 n.58
59.3 7.106-7 n.57
60.4 7.108 n.59
62.2 7.108 n.59
63.2 7.108 n.59
63.3 7.51 n.9, 54
65.1 7.54

Codex Theodosianus
2.8.1 9.118, n.40
8.5 7.85 n.78
8.5.1 7.66 n.29
8.5.35 7.21
8.5.38 7.19 n.59
8.5.4 7.85
8.5.41 7.85
9.40.16 8.104
12.1.63 8.104
13.5.18 8.150

Columella
De re rustica
10.127

Constitutiones apostolicae
1.6 8.121

Constantine VII Porphyrogenitus
De caerimoniis
318 8.7

Cyprian
Epistulae
70 8.177 n.7
73.5, 10 8.178

Demetrius
Formae epistolicae
21 9.6

Democritus
6.174

Demosthenes
Contra Lacritum
26 7.150
Contra Macartatum
1 7.149 n.42
Contra Nicostratum
11 7.190 n.96
Contra Timotheum
105 7.150 n.45
Contra Theocrinem
19-21 8.15 n.24
De corona
43.62 9.113
92-93 9.2
In Midiam
33 7.183 n.74
44-45 7.150
In Timocratem
202 6.69
Περὶ τῶν πρὸς Ἀλέξανδρον συνθηκῶν
23 7.132 n.3

Didache

	10.8	12.42-43	8.114 n.50
7	8.177	31.54	10.60
8	9.115	37.5	10.79
11.3-6, 12	7.55-56 n.20	45.3	9.11
12.1-5	7.55-56 n.20	50.3	8.112 n.30
13.1-7	7.55-56 n.20		
14.1	9.110	Diodorus Siculus	
15.1-2	7.106 n.54	*Bibliotheca historica*	
15.2	7.109 n.60	1.42.1	6.131
		11.25.1	6.111
		12.26.1, 70.5	6.111
Didymus Caecus		13.19.4	6.111
Commentarii in Job		19.57.5	7.5
6.3-4	9.12	29.10	10.89
		31.18	10.89

Dio Cassius
Historia romana

		Diogenes Laertius	
36.50.2	7.132 n.3	1.59	9.113
37.16-17	9.117 n.33	7.30	8.112 n.37
37.18	9.114, 117		
37.19	9.115 n.32, 117	Dionysius of Halicarnassus	
43.10.3	10.68	*Antiquitates Romanae*	
46.25.2	6.69	3.11.8	10.80
49.22	9.117 n.33	7.66.2	9.11
50.20.6	10.49	9.17.1	6.157
51.19	10.68	9.19.3	9.11
51.20.6	6.203	9.36.2	6.157
51.24.4	10.56	9.59.4	6.157
51.25.1	7.132 n.3		
	7.65 n.26	Dio-Xiph. (see Dio Cassius)	
53.1.1, 2.3	10.57		
53.14	10.93	Epicureus Herculanensis	
54.23.1	10.103	346.4b.7 (Vogliano)	9.4
57.3.1-6	10.71		
57.10.5	7.65 n.26; 8.68	Epiphanius	
59.1	6.42	*Adversus haereses*	
59.1.1	10.79	1.267	8.163
59.6.1	10.79	2.186	8.163
59.6.3	8.132		
60.17	6.154	3.140, 340, 451	8.163
62.4.3	6.69	66.2	10.121
67.3.5	6.157	70.12.3	9.115
68.25.5	6.44 n.57		
69.1-2	10.77	Euclid	
69.9	6.149	*Catoptrica*	
69.16.2	8.60	28	7.207

Dio Chrysostomus
Orationes

Euripides
Helena

	10.2	569	10.42
3.6, 39	10.80	*Phoenissae*	
3.50	8.112 n.30	589	7.207 n.36
3.52	8.112 n.31		
3.127	8.112 n.32	Eusebius	
4.44	8.112 n.30	*Commentaria in Psalmos*	
11.11	7.132 n.3	(Migne, *PG* 23) 496, 621	8.163

De laudibus Constantini
6.5-6, 10-17   8.165 n.33
Demonstratio evangelica
6.13.20   10.81
1.1.11   8.163
Historia ecclesiastica
3.20   6.130
5.16.3   6.181
6.43.2-4, 21-22   9.68
7.11.10   9.68
7.13   8.143
7.24   7.248
Quaestiones evangelicae ad Stephanum et Marinum
     9.115

Vita Constantini
1.11.2   8.162
1.27.1-2   8.162
1.28-31   8.167 n.41
3.6f.   9.68
4.20.1   8.162
4.36   7.250

Eustathius
Commentarii ad Homeri Iliadem
19.247   10.41

Flavius Vopiscus
Vita Saturnini
see Scriptores Historiae Augustae

Formula Bituricensis
9   6.188

Formula extravagans
18   6.188

Fronto
Epistulae ad M. Caesarem
1.6.2   8.137

Gaius
Ad edictum provinciale
30   10.148
Institutiones
1   10.149
1.5   8.137
1.6   10.146
2.43   8.141 n.49
2.46   8.138
4.47   10.148
183, 185, 195   10.149

Galen
In Hippocratis librum
6.17b.190   9.11

Institutio logica
1.5, 17.7-8   9.12
Opera omnia
3.387   9.11
4.440   9.11
9.108, 867   9.11
14.245   9.11

Gellius, Aulus
Noctes Atticae
3.2.4   9.113
3.2.4-6   9.113
3.2.7   9.112
3.2.8-10   9.112 n.13
15.7.3   10.70

Georgius Monachus
Chronicon
5.795   8.7

Gorgias
frag. 11.127, 11a.83   7.132 n.3

Grattius
Cynegetica
     10.127

Gregory of Nazianzus
De spiritu sancto
10   9.11
Carmina quae spectant ad alios
75-98   9.12

Gregory of Nyssa
Contra Eunomium
1.1.338   8.163
In canticum canticorum
6.30   9.10

Heliodorus
Aethiopica
1.22.2   10.33

Hermas
Mandata
8.10   7.55-56 n.20
Similitudines
9.27.2   7.55-56 n.20
Visiones
4.1.2-3   7.88 n.94

Herodas
Mimus
1	10.122
4	6.206

Herodian
Ab excessu divi Marci
1.3.1	6.62 n.74
3.8.5	6.148

Herodotus
Historiae
2.108	8.88 n.30
3.126	7.3, 59
4.84	6.190
5.52.1	7.3
8.98	7.3, 59
8.98.2	7.3

Hesiod
Opera et dies
287-292	10.7

Hippolytus
Traditio apostolica
17	
	8.178
36	8.167 n.44
42	8.167

Refutatio omnium haeresium
4.28.8-9, 41	10.24

Homer
Iliad
2.617-670	6.23
4.349-363	6.23
5.1ff	
13.502	6.131
18.92	6.131
22.69	10.129
27.173	10.129

Odyssea
3.181	10.112
4.280	10.112
6.102-109	10.44
10.216	10.128
14.29-36	10.127
17.290-307	10.127
17.309-310	10.129

Horace
Carmina
2.19	8.174

Iamblichus
De mysteriis
3.13	10.22

De vita Pythagorica
38	8.115 n.53

Ignatius
Ad Ephesios
1.3, 21.1	7.54

Ad Magnesios
2.1, 15.1	7.54

Ad Philadelphios
10.1	7.55
11.2	7.54
13.1-2	7.55

Ad Polycarpum
7.2, 8.1	7.55

Ad Romanos
10.1	7.54

Ad Smyrnaeos
11.3	7.55
12.1	7.54

Ad Trallianos
1.1	7.54
3.2.1	6.45 n.57

Irenaeus
Adversus haereses
1.13	10.23
1.15.5	8.161 n.21, 81
1.18.1	10.81
5.30.1	9.87 n.6

Isaeus
De Apollodoro
40	7.149

De Cirone
2	7.14

De Pyrrho
62	7.149

Isocrates
Aegineticus
12, 15	6.42

Antidosis
280	9.10

Busiris
48	6.69

De pace
1	6.69

Panegyricus
81	9.11

Trapeziticus
58	9.11

Isodore
Etymologiae
1.3.7-8	10.7

Jerome
Epistulae
22.30	8.120 n.11

John Chrysostom
Adversus oppugnatores vitae monasticae
(see *PG* 47, 343)	9.11

De fugienda simulata specie
(see *PG* 48, 1073)	9.10, 11
18.4	6.16 n.30

In epistulam ad Philemonem
1.2	10.119

In epistulam I ad Corinthios homiliae
14	9.11

In Joannem homiliae
2.2	8.120 n.11
38	9.11

In sanctum pascha
52.31	10.81

Josephus
Antiquitates Judaicae
1.33	9.115
3.143	9.115
3.248	9.115
1.54, 70	7.161
2.40	8.112 n.34
4.226	7.161
7.252	10.53
8.42-49	10.13, 4
10.207	7.161
11.12-17, 104	7.22-23 n.80
11.105	9.71
11.123-130	7.22-23 n.80
11.203	7.3, 59
11.273-283	7.22
11.281	9.115
11.345	8.150
12.7	8.150
12.10	8.149 n.3, 150 n.7
12.37	8.112 n.35
12.45-50, 51-56, 138-144	7.22-23 n.80
12.145 f.	10.138
12.160 f.	8.49 n.13
13.10.5.292	6.152 n.172
13.256	8.149
13.74	8.150, 150 n.7
13.78	8.150
13.79	8.150 n.7
14.10	8.149
14.10.12, 20-23, 25	9.115
14.197-198	6.111
15.417	10.137
16.9-10	6.91
16.23	8.118
16.100-101	9.11
16.166	10.94
16.171	10.93, 94
17.195, 202	6.42
18.3	6.128
18.33.1	10.79
18.85	8.149 n.4
18.261-301	10.74
19.213-216	8.149, 149 n.1
19.299	8.154
19.332-334	10.137
19.353	8.154
20.6.2.132	6.160 n.180
20.135	6.163
20.200-203	9.53
20.251	6.128
63-64	9.117 n.33

Contra Apionem
2.20-21, 27	9.115
2.206	8.115 n.55
2.282	9.114
31	10.146

Bellum Judaicum
1.146	9.115
1.146-147	9.117 n.33
1.669	6.42
2.12.6.244	6.160 n.180
2.273	6.91
2.405	6.128
2.426-427	10.146
2.427	6.96 n.109
2.456	9.115
2.571	6.99
3.307	8.149 n. 3, n.4
3.359	6.69
3.67	6.160 n.180
5.99	9.115
5.194	10.137
6.125, 126	10.137
6.250	9.115
6.354	10.146
7.409	10.141

Vita
1-6	6.128, 139
423	8.113 n.42

Julian
Epistulae
36	8.121 n.13

Julius Caesar
De bello civili
1.101.3 7.16
Justinian
Codex
3.12.2 (3) 9.110, 111, 117
4.62.4 10.99
7.71.4 7.222 n.111
10.54.1 9.68

Digesta
1.4.1.1 8.137
1.15.4.1 8.27
1.20.2 10.149
4.9.3.1 6.83
9.2.44-45 7.179 n.68
11.3.1.5 6.56
11.4.1.1 8.26, 27
11.4.1.2 8.26
11.4.1.3, 4, 8, 8a 8.27
19.2.15.1 6.83
19.2.25.6 6.83, 85
19.5.17.4 6.83
21.1.1.1 8.26
21.1.17.1 8.43
21.1.17.12 8.41, 43
21.1.17.4, 5 8.41
21.1.43.1 8.41
26.5.1 10.149
26.5.3 10.150
27.3.1.24 10.150
28.3.6.9 8.134
29.5.1 8.2
39.4.12 10.99
48.18.1, 8, 9 7.176 n.58
48.19.28.16 8.2
48.5.39.10 8.133 n.15
48.15.6.2 6.56

49.1.25 8.134
49.4.1.7, 10 8.134
50.2.3.3 9.77
50.4.3.15 7.95
50.15.1 10.103
50.15.3 6.127

Institutiones
1.8.1 8.15 n.20
1.20 (Pr.) 10.149
1.20.4 10.148
2.6 8.138, 141 n.49
2.6.11 8.141 n.49

Justin Martyr
Apologia
1.29 7.247
1.61 8.178
1.67.3, 7 9.117
1.69 8.143
Cohortatio ad Graecos
8, 35 8.120 n.11
Dialogus cum Tryphone
41.4 9.117 n.36
Oratio ad Graecos
5 8.120 n.11

Juvenal
Saturae
1.102 7.189 n.94
6 10.122
6.653-654 10.127
8 10.72

Lactantius
De mortibus persecutorum
44 8.166 n.39

Lex XII tabularum 1.9 9.111

Libanius
Orationes
2.32 8.104
28.11 9.10
30.8-31 8.104
45.26 8.104

Livy
Ab urbe condita libri
4.46 8.112 n.39
33.19 10.88
37.45-11-18 10.89
43.16.1ff. 10.99

Lucian
Apologia
13 8.112 n.29
De Syria dea
36 9.9
60.12 6.111
Fugitivi
27, 29 8.10
Verae historiae
1.4 8.174

Lycophron
Alexandra
438 10.120

Index 3 – Ancient Authors

Lysias
Orationes
5.3	9.11
7.30	9.11
34.5	9.11

Macrobius
Saturnalia
1.3	9.113 n.16
1.16.9, 10-12	9.112

Manetho
Apotelesmatica
1.329-30	6.131
4.198-200	8.1 n.1

Marcellus
De incarnatione et contra Arianos
Migne, *PG*26, p.1013	6.44 n.57

Marcus Aurelius
Meditationes
9.3.1.1	6.44-45 n.57

Martial
Epigrammaton libri
	7.248 n.27, 250
14.184, 186, 188, 189, 190	7.250

Martyrdom of Polycarp
1.1	7.51 n.9
20.1	7.54

Melissa (ed. Städele)
	6.18-23

Menander
Frag. 186, 349	7.59 n.6
Kock 440	7.60 n.11

Methodius
Symposium
6.5	6.16 n.30

Michael
In ethica Nicomachea
532	9.11

Nemesianus
Cynegetica
	10.127

Nicolaus of Damascus
90F 134	8.118

Oppian of Apamea
Cynegetica
	10.127

Oracula Sibyllina
3.278, 296	9.104

Origen
Contra Celsum
1.62	8.120 n.11
1.71	9.12
7.58-59	8.120 n.11

Homiliae in Lucam
26	8.178

In Jeremiam
4.3	7.248

Ovid
Epistulae ex Ponto
2.8.20-26	10.62
3.1.117-118, 145, 164-165	10.26

Fasti
1.536	10.27
1.640-641	10.26

Tristia
3.1.35-46	10.62
5.2.49	10.62

Palladas (*Anthologia Palatina*)
7.686.6	10.121

Parmenides
frag. 8 ll.50-52	9.12

Paulinus Nolanus
Epistulae
31.3.8	10.81

Pausanias
Graeciae descriptio
4.14.2	10.68
4.31.8	6.204; 10.42
10.4.1	10.112

Pempelus
Fragmenta
	8.116 n. 56, n. 57

Persius
Saturae
3.56-57	10.7

Philo
De Abrahamo
28	9.115 n.28

De cherubim
87	9.115 n.28

De decalogo		3.26	10.127
107-108	9.104	5.149	8.118
111-115	8.115 n.55	8.61	10.127
De fuga et inventione		9.78	10.103
97, 101, 108, 137	9.10 n.1		
174	9.115 n.28	Pliny the Younger	
De Josepho		*Epistulae*	
161	8.112 n.37		10.1
241	9.7	1.10.5-7	10.2
De mutatione nominum		2.4	6.38 n.52
260	9.115 n.28	8.14	6.57-8 n.67
		9.21	6.60; 8.41
De opificio mundi		9.24	8.41
124-5	9.87 n.5	10.1-2	10.83
De praemiis et poenis		10.37-40	9.25
89	10.130	10.44, 50	10.77
De somniis		10.45, 46	7.84
1.147-148, 215	9.10 n.1	10.52	10.84
De specialibus legibus		10.72	7.75
2.5	6.66	10.96	8.142
2.198	9.104	10.97	8.142
3.1	9.10 n.1	10.120	7.80, 84
3.159-162	8.68, 99 n.2	*Panegyricus Traiani*	
De virtutibus			10.83
217	6.44 n.57		
De vita Mosis		Plutarch	
1.174	8.162	*Aetia Romana et Graeca*	
Legatio ad Gaium		207d	7.158
4.26, 8.54	6.62 n.74	271d	7.132 n.3
19.2	10.80	*Alexander*	
51	8.112 n.29	17	7.4
61.1	10.79	*Amatoriae narrationes*	
119	10.74	772e	7.158
141-142	9.22	*Apophthegmata Laconica*	
143-147	9.4	203c	7.158
23.155	6.152 n.172	*Cato Minor*	
203-346	10.74	18	6.131
253	8.112 n.37	*De Herodoti malignitate*	
307	9.53	857a	7.158
315	7.22-23 n.80;	*De defectu oraculorum*	
	10.94	414e	10.22
		De sera numinis vindicta	
Plato		562d	7.158
Gorgias		*De sollertia animalium*	
455b	9.39 n.2	967a	9.11
517b	7.132 n.3	*Eumenes*	
Leges		8.3	8.112 n.37
922	6.42	*Galba*	
Phaedrus		8.4	7.17, 21, 72, 84
254c-256e	9.19	*Lycurgus*	
Respublica		12.2, 82.222	6.157
351c	9.39 n.2	*Moralia*	
		100a	8.88 n.30
Pliny the Elder		138a-146f	10.122
Naturalis historia		479f	8.114 n.50
2.188	9.112, 113	760e	10.41

Index 3 – Ancient Authors

795d and e	10.33	*Maximini duo*	
802f	8.112 n.33	30.4	7.253
Pyrrhus		*Opellius Macrinus*	
14	7.158	13.1	8.137
		Pertinax	
Romulus		1.4	7.84
19	7.158	*Saturninus*	
Quaestiones Romanae		7	7.245
84	9.112	7.8	8.150
Septem sapientium convivium			
2.1	7.189	Seneca	
		De beneficiis	
Solon		2.11.5	8.114 n.50
23	7.158	3.20	7.195-6
Themistocles		*De clementia*	
10.6	10.127	1.4.1-1.5.2	10.63, 73
Pollux		1.18.2	10.103
Onomasticon		1.26.1	6.57 n.67
1.210	8.88 n.30	2.21	10.28
		De ira	
Polyaenus		3.40.2	10.103
Strategemata		*Epistulae*	
7.16.1	10.112	47.5	8.2
		73.10	8.113 n.42
Polybius		107.1	6.58
Historiae			
1.72.6, 5.89.4	6.157	Sextus Empiricus	
15.7.1-2	9.11	*Adversus mathematicos*	
21.17.3-8	10.89	2.35	7.59 n.6
31.2.5-6	10.90		
31.14.3	10.89	Sozomen	
		Historia ecclesiastica	
Polycarp		5.18	8.121
Epistula ad Philippenses			
1.1	7.55-56 n.20	Statius	
14.1	7.54	*Silvae* 4.9.26-19	7.17 n.51, 22
Procopius		Strabo	
Historia arcana		*Geographica*	
30.3-4, 3-5	7.19 n.59	4.1.23	6.206
		4.4.2	10.68
Quintilian		6.2	10.127
Institutio oratoria		6.4.2	6.62 n.74
10.5.4-11	6.23	13.4.5	10.39
		14.1.20	6.196
Scholia in Platonis respublicam		14.1.23	6.197
46	7.148		
		Suetonius	
Scriptores Historiae Augustae		*Augustus*	
Antoninus Pius		31.5	10.71
12.3	7.19, 19 n.63	49.3	7.15
Hadrianus		49.3-50	10.78
4.6, 7	10.77	51	10.68
7.5	7.19 n.63, 21	56.2	10.70
10	6.149	97	10.68
15.1	10.77		

Domitianus
7.3 6.157
8 9.25
Caesar
75 7.16
Caligula
44.2 7.17
Claudius
11 10.27

Tiberius
24 10.71
26 10.25
38 10.68
52 7.65
Titus
10 7.73 n.41

Synesius
Epistulae
4 9.113, 115

Tacitus
Annales
1.7 10.71
1.10 10.103
1.11-13 10.71
1.13.2 10.70
1.17.6 6.158 n.176
1.57, 58 10.68
1.72.1 10.25
2.10, 42 10.68
2.59-61 7.65
2.69 10.68
3.6 10.70
3.38.2 10.57
3.47 10.68
4.15, 37-38 10.25
4.43 10.68
4.55 6.203
4.56 10.25
4.74 10.68
12.60 10.104
13.32.1 6.57 n.67
14.27 10.112
13.50, 51 10.99
14.42-45 6.57 n.67
Dialogus de oratoribus
28 f. 10.122
Historiae
1.11 10.78
1.72 8.5
2.19 8.112 n.39
2.73 7.17
5.4 9.114 n.21
5.9 8.154

Terence
Adelphi
573-584 7.43
713-714 7.43

Tertullian
Ad nationes
1.13 9.114 n.21
Adversus Marcionem
4.19.10 6.129 n.152
Apologeticus
16.9-11 9.114 n.21
De resurrectione carnis
8 8.167
De baptismo
  8.178
15 8.177 n.7
De corona militis
3.3 8.167

Theophrastus
Characteres
93 10.127

Thomas
Gospel of
104 10.130

Tibullus
1.3.8 9.114 n.21
1.3.18 9.116

Ulpian
Digesta
50.15.1.1 10.60

Valerius Maximus
Factorum ac dictorum memorabilium libri
2.8.7 10.62
4.7.5 9.6
6.1 10.27
9.4.8 (ext.) 1 8.113 n.40
12. Tables 6.3 8.138

Varro
De re rustica
  10.127

Velleius Paterculus
Historiae Romanae
2.92.2 10.99
2.124 10.71
2.126.4 10.71

Vitruvius
De architectura
5.4 10.31

Xenophon
Anabasis
2.4.8 10.81
3.1.21 7.189 n.94
5.3.6 6.205
6.4.9 10.81

Cyropaedia
5.3.52 7.207 n.36
8.6.17-18 7.4
De equitandi ratione
 10.127
Hellenica
3.3.1 6.44 n.57
Memorabilia
2.1.21-33 10.8

4. INSCRIPTIONS

Agora
21 J6   8.162

L'Année épigraphique (AE)
(1909) 158   10.60
(1928) 97   8.61
(1934) 143   7.32 n.16
(1936) 1   7.80 n.56
(1950) 170   7.21
(1955) 225   7.21
(1973) 485   7.18, 21-2
(1975) 289   10.27
(1978) 828   10.122
(1991) 1442   10.67
(1989)(1992) 681   10.95
(1993) 1414   10.64, 67

Bulletin épigraphique *(BE)*
(1968) 564   8.150
(1970) 633   8.152 n.1
(1983) 323   7.233-241
(1984) 478   8.117-118

BCH
(*Bulletin de Correspondance Hellénique*)
3.(1879) 443   10.26

British Museum
inv. CM 1995.4-1.1   10.55

BMC (*Coins of the Roman Empire in the British Museum*)
74, 76   10.104
31.118 (Ionia)   10.26
139.348 (Mysia)   10.26

CIJ
1.123   8.109 n.8
1.365   10.155
1.368   10.155
1.663   9.71
1.682   8.110 n.14
1.694   7.89-90 n.99
2.748   9.79
2.964   8.161, 164
2.1400   10.137
2.1404   7.89; 9.69
2.1436-7   8.161, 164

CIL
1.551   7.14 n.34
2.473   10.26
2.1571   10.26
2.5421   10.26
3, p.950   10.107
3.411   8.135 n.31
3.447   10.106
3.4121   9.118
3.5706   10.68
3.7124   10.104
3.7251   7.73 n.44, 81-82
3.12074   6.157
3.13283   8.60
4.1136   10.118
4.3779, 4429, 7037, 9934   7.32 n.16
5.34   8.154
6.1598   7.20 n.67
6.8543   7.18
6.8622   7.84-85 n.76
6.32323   10.69
6.33885   10.77
6.37813   10.4
8.1027   7.16
8.1042-1025   6.160
8.4508   10.98
8.6987   10.26
8.16456   10.26
8.19492   10.26
9.1155   10.26
9.1556   10.104
9.1703   10.103
10.750   10.26
10.1413   10.26
10.6976   7.22
10.7464   10.26
10.8038   10.60
10.8375   10.69
11.3076   10.25
11.6172   10.26
14.399   10.26
14.5347   8.133 n.15
15.7142   7.16, 16 n.44, 82 n.62, 83
16.26   8.155 n.14
16.30   6.161 n.182
16.31   6.159, 160, 161 n.182
16.33   6.157
16.45, 58   8.155 n.14

Index 4 – Inscriptions

CIRB
71	9.79

CIS
2.3.1.3913	10.98

Ditt., Syll.[3]
736	7.184, 185 n.83; 8.15 n.24
880	7.5 n.27
888	7.21, 65, 77 n.49, 80, 105

DocsAug[2]
pp. 45, 46, 55 (*Fasti Ann. Iul.*)	10.68
p. 52 (*Fasti Ann .Iul.*)	10.70
69	10.71
98a	9.4
98b	9.4; 10.60, 61, 73
102b	10.25

DocsFlav
328	10.80

DocsGaius
47	10.82
134	10.74
135	10.82
380	10.104
391	10.148
401	10.81

FD
3.4.301	10.82

FiE
9.1.1.A1, 2	6.197
9.1.1.B12	6.196
9.1.1.B45	6.198
9.1.1.B54	6.198, 200
9.1.1.C1, 2	6.198, 199
9.1.1.D1, 2	6.200
9.1.1.F1	6.199
9.1.1.F3	6.199, 200
9.1.1.F5	6.199
9.1.1.F9	6.201
9.1.1.F13	6.199

FIRA
1.2.23	10.150
1.72	10.60

Fouilles d' Amyzon en Carie (= *Iamyzon*)

GDI
2327	6.61 n.69

GVI
1805	10.6

Iamyzon
(1983) pp. 259-263	6.57 n.67; 8.1

Iaph
5.108	10.49
12.325	10.49
12.920	10.31

IaphrodChr
181ii	8.6

IaphrodJud
pp. 5-7	8.162; 9.73-76

Iassos
8	9.2

ICUR
7.19820	8.176

Icos
391	10.74

Idelos
6.1517	9.7
7.2532	8.149
7.2616	8.149, 150

Ididyma
31	9.9

IegChr
64	8.158

Ieph

1a, 2	6.204; 10.39
1a, 10	6.200; 7.238
1a, 18	10.104
1a, 18b	10.59, 61
1a, 20	6.150, 151 n.167
1a, 24	6.204; 10.40
1a, 26	6.201
1a, 27	6.205; 10.34
1a, 47	6.198, 200
2. 212	6.204; 9.28, 29
2.216	10.2
2.234-5, 237, 241	6.206
2.251	10.73
2.276	6.210
2.300	6.204
2.412	6.179; 10.81
2.424a	6.206
2.429	7.237
2.459	10.59
2.501	6.203
2.504	10.50
2.510a	10.81
2.555	8.111 n.19
2.562	10.131
3.606	10.40
3.613	10.51
3.614b	10.33
3.616	10.4
3.617	10.34
3.619	10.49
3.624, 629	10.51
3.630	10.49
3.637	10.34
3.647	6.203; 9.28
3.650	6.210; 7.238
3.665, 681	10.33
3.683a	10.4
3.712b	6.179
3.722	10.81
3.740	6.203
3.789	10.4
3.857	6.204
3.940, 943, 957, 960	10.50
3.961	10.49
3.980	10.34, 35
3.894	10.34
3.982	10.32
3.987	6.201; 10.32, 34
3.989	6.201; 10.35
3.992a	10.34
3.997	10.32
4.1012	6.196
4.1045	6.198
4.1060	6.198, 199
4.1061	6.198, 199
4.1062	6.199
4.1064	6.199, 200
4.1066	6.179
4.1068	6.199; 10.33
4.1069	6.201
4.1075	6.200
4.1078	6.199
4.1126	10.49
4.1222	10.40
4.1285	8.163
4.1312	6.179
4.1351	10.40
4.1390	8.110 n.15
5.1449	6.197
5.1522	6.205
5.1548	10.2
5.1578a	10.49
5.1595	6.209, 210
5.1655	10.33
6.2004	6.205
6.2039	6.204
6.2113	10.3
6.2245	10.106
6.2261	10.3
7.1.3034	10.35
7.1.3038	6.206
7.1.3039	6.179
7.1.3005	6.204; 10.3
7.1.3059	6.201; 10.32, 34
7.1.3064	9.29
7.1.3065	10.3
7.1.3072	10.33
7.1.3415	6.198
7.2.3901	10.4
7.2.4101	10.2, 98, 103
7.2.4102	6.197
7.2.4340	10.4

IG^2

2^2.838	10.88
2^2.945	10.88
2^2.971	9.7
2^2.1132	8.110 n.11
2^2.1346	10.82
2^2.2391	10.131
2^2.2943	8.150, 151
2^2.3241	10.26
2^2.3449	8.109 n.8
2^2.3741	10.32
2^2.4125	10.103
2^2.10219-10222	8.150

Index 4 – Inscriptions

IG
5.1.235
5.1.1432
5.1.1448
5.1.1564a
7.2.2712
7.2.2713
7.2.4132
9.2.1109
10.2.1.145
10.2.1.789
12.3.175
12.3. 324
12.7.381
12, Suppl.1.124
12.5.590
12.8.439
12.9.191
12.9.211
12.9.239
12.9.905
14.336
14.643
14.1054, 1055
14.1102, 1105
14.1829

IGBulg
4.2015a

IGLSyria
1.230
2.309
2.310a
4.1249
4.1442
4.1443
4.1447
4.1448
4.1452
4.1486
4.1614
4.1632
4.1648
4.1707
4.1789
4.1812
4.1814

10.131
8.110 n.17
10.67
10.131
8.108 n.2
10.103
8.110 n.16
8.111 n.22
10.3
8.150
10.82
10.81
10.26
6.180
6.131
8.150
10.106
8.111 n.21
8.108 n.2
8.111 n.20
8.150
10.131
10.31
10.31
6.179

10.113

8.161 n.20
8.156 n.3, 161
8.161 n.18
8.156 n.3, 160
8.156 n.2, 165 n.32
8.156 n.2
8.162, 164
8.156 n.2
8.156 n.2
8.161
8.156
8.161 n.18
8.156 n.2
8.165
8.156 n.2
8.156 n.2
8.161 n.18

4.1814b
4.1831
4.1957
4.1995
5.1998

5.2179

5.2232
6.2916

IGRR
1.881
1.1142
1.1183
3.1056
3.1171
4.180
4.215
4.249
4.263
4.319
4.349
4.1398
4.1693

IGUR
1.117
2.768

IgalatN
2.44

Ihadrianoi
51-52

Iiasos
150
152
2.416, 417

Iilion
64

Ikaunos
pp. 200-215

Ikeramos
6

8.162, 164
8.161 n.18
8.156 n.2
7.66, 86 n.82
7.18 n.52, 20 n.65, 71-72, 75-77, 80, 84
8.156-157 n.3, 161, 164
8.156 n.2
8.161 n.20

6.72
7.73 n.41
10.98
10.98
10.31
10.26
10.103
10.26
7.238
10.26
10.82
10.82
10.72

10.12
6.179

6.208

10.1, 2

8.110 n.18
9.7
10.106

10.103

10.98

9.7

Ikhargeh		*Imagnesia*	
4 (= *DocsFlav* 328)	10.78, 80, 81	101.46-47	10.48
		239	8.7
IkhiosMcCabe		*Imiletus*	
18	10.80	2.563 inv. 92	10.106
		3.135	10.48
IkilikiaDF			
69	9.4	*Imylasa*	
		1.106	10.36
Ikios		1.119	9.1
	8.118		
		Inikaia	
Iklaudiupolis		1.550	10.2
70	8.117, 118	1005	8.7 n.5
177	9.102		
		Inscr.Cos	
IkolophonMcCabe		391	10.74
4, 6	10.131		
		Insc.Italiae	
IkorinthKent		13.1, 59	10.93
102	10.82		
		Iolympia (IvO)	
ILAfr		149	10.131
301	10.60	160	10.131
ILS		*Ipergamon*	
23	7.14 n.34	8.3.29	6.206
109	10.104	8.3.30	6.204
116	10.25		
119, 120	10.26	*IphrygDB*	
137	10.69	3	6.209
1.318	10.77	5-8	6.208
214	7.73 n.44, 81-2		
1418	6.159	*Ipriene*	
1434	7.22	112	10.36
1677	7.84-5 n.76	231	6.205
1702	7.16, 16 n.44, 82 n.62, 83		
1862	10.106	*IprusaOlymp*	
6870	8.104	13	10.1
8393	10.68	24	10.3
8726-8732	7.43 n.40	17-18	10.1
8727	7.43 n.40		
8731	8.13 n.11	*Ismyrna*	
8794	10.103	2.1.594	10.82
8858	8.60	2.1.616	9.6
9481	8.176	2.1.644	6.206

2.1.657, 696	6.204		
2.1.826	9.23	*MW* (= *DocsFlav*)	
		457	7.71-75, 80
Istratonikeia			
1.272	6.206	*OGIS*	
2.2.1307-8	6.207	90	9.36, 39 n.2
		456	10.62
Itralleis		483	7.179
11	10.25	519	7.66, 86 n.82
		2.598	10.136, 137
Ityre		609	7.60 n.12, 80 n.54
1.160bis	8.163	2.629	10.98
		665	7.16, 18 n.52, 63, 63 n.20, 67-69, 71, 77, 80, 84
JIWE			
1.189	10.155	669	7.221-222; 9.61; 8.42, 110 n.12
2.170	10.155		
		2.674	10.98
JWI		701	7.73 n.41
51.169	10.12	751	8.110 n.13
LBW		*OMS* (Robert)	
6.2145	8.161 n.18	1, p.414	6.207
LIMC		PfuhlMöbius	
2.1.763	10.44	2.2087	10.6
2.2.442-628	10.44		
2.2.669	10.7	*Recueil des inscriptions chrétiennes de Macédoine*	
		5	8.176
Limes de Chalcis		265	8.177
p. 206, no.37	8.161 n.18	291	8.150
MAMA (*Monumenta Asiae Minoris Antiqua*)		*Res gestae divi Augusti*	
6.27	10.127	1.3	8.113 n.41
9.13	10.92	7.1	10.57
9.63	6.207, 208	9	10.68
9.64	6.208	15-16	7.239
		16.1	7.239
McCabe, *PHI Aphrodisias*		25.2	10.56
29	10.82	32	10.62
		34	10.68
Michel, C. *Recueil d'inscriptions grecques*		34.1	10.55, 56, 68
515	10.36	34.2	10.55
541	8.114 n.51		
1011	8.108 n.2	Reynolds, J.M. *Aphrodisias and Rome*	
		8	6.110
Montanist Inscriptions (Tabbernee)			
17, 20, 33, 35, 60-62,		*Roman Imperial Coinage*	
64-66, 76, 81, 87	9.104	1.Galba 96	10.83
3, 4, 5, 72	10.161	1.Tiberius 52	10.83

2.Hadrian 2	10.83	37.958	9.15
2.Hadrian 110, 136	10.83	37.959	9.17
2.Hadrian 319-320	10.83	37.1012	9.9
2.Hadrian 534	10.83	37.1096	9.30
2.Nerva 126	10.83	37.1102	10.69
2.Trajan 148b	10.83	37.1207	9.4
2.Vespasian 88	10.83	37.1210	9.7, 20
		38.340	10.64, 67
		38.1924	10.10, 12
SEG		39.1180	10.95
8.169	10.136	39.1189	10.30
8.170	9.69	39.1205	10.48, 51
8.504a	9.36	39.1618	10.156
8.527	10.36	40.1001	10.103
10.410	9.9	40.1599	10.126
11.948	8.114	41.328	10.64, 67, 68
14.639	10.98	41.971	10.59, 61
15.765	7.164	41.981	10.37, 40
16.754	7.72, 77, 80-81	41.1283	10.126
18.27	8.108 n.4; 10.36	41.1619	10.20
18.633	9.36	42.344	10.64, 67
19.21, 181	10.106	42.916	10.154
19.476	7.72, 77-80	42.1081	10.6
20.651	10.141	42.1692	10.16, 17
22.114	8.111 n.23	44.785	10.131
24.1666	10.12		
26.1392	7.14, 69, 71-73, 80-84	*SIG³*	
		273	10.48
27.1016	8.163	399	8.110 n.11
28.889, 929	6.207	591	8.110 n.18
29.628	10.113	618	8.110 n.18
30.80	8.111 n.20	700	8.109 n.9
30.531a, b	6.79 n.91	734	8.110 n.11
30.1658	10.106	740	8.111 n.21
30.1740	8.165	798	10.68
30.1785	8.163	814	8.111 n.19; 10.62
31.543	6.72	834	9.4
31.577	6.79 n.91	1073	10.31
31.694	8.164		
31.952	10.98, 103		
31.1494	8.5	Sherk, R.K. *The Roman Empire: Augustus to Hadrian*	
32.809-810	8.148		
32.1108	8.164	31	10.60
32.1135	10.59	42b	10.60
33.1266	8.152	43	10.50
34.1259	8.117-118		
34.1666	10.10	Smallwood, E.M. *Documents* (see *DocsGaius*)	
35.593, 599, 600	6.79 n.91		
36.970	9.73		
36.1027	10.95	*SNG* von Aulock	
36.1092	9.22	1872, 1875	10.44
37.198	9.19		
37.859	10.88	Sydenham, E.A., *Coinage*	
37.886	9.28	1117	10.42
37.957	9.7		

Syll.²
694	6.110
764	6.111

Syll.³
814	10.103

TAM (Tituli Asiae Minoris)
2.760c	10.74
3.1.746	10.126
5.1.238	8.173
5.1.185	6.207
5.1.279	10.113
5.1.586	6.208
5.1.598	6.209

Welles, C.B. Royal Correspondence in the Hellenistic Period
63	9.7

ZPE
49 (1982) 191-192	6.208
51 (1983) 80-84	8.145
51 (1983) 105-114	8.106
87 (1991) 157-162	10.59
144 (2003) 264	10.55

5. Papyri

Am.Stud.Pap.		2.648	7.140, 147, 160
23, pp. 329-333	6.147-152	2.665	7.28
23, pp. 357-361	6.140-143	3.719	6.32 n.39, 35, 38 n.50
BGU		3.762	7.63 n.23, 72
1.8	8.67	3.802	7.117
1.15	7.82, 96, 122, 123 n.46, 124-126	3.821	8.125 n.6
		3.831	7.118
1.23	7.67 n.31	3.832	7.200-201 n.9
1.37	7.40	3.845	7.27 n.5
1.77	8.86, 87	3.887	6.48, 49
1.84	7.114	3.888	7.203, 208-209 n.41, 221
1.86	6.31, 35-36, n.45, 38 n.50	3.903	6.114
1.93	7.35	3.908	7.93 n.3; 8.70
1.95	10.116	3.913	6.62
1.115	7.41 n.37	3.921	7.118
1.118	10.116	3.969	7.124 n.49; 8.86, 87, 90 n.36
1.136	8.86, 90 n.36		
1.140	6.148; 10.77	3.993	6.32 n.39, 33, 35 n.44, 38 n.50
1.146	7.189		
1.159	6.117, 118	3.994	6.33
1.168	6.141	3.1009	7.26
1.176	10.82	4.1022	7.100 n.31
1.183	6.32 n.39, 35, n.45, 38 n.50	4.1038	7.201, 204, n.25, 214, 215, n.76, 216, 217 n.91
1.213	8.81, 82, 83 n.16, 84, 85	4.1050	6.3; 9.90
1.251	6.32 n.39, 35, n.45, 38 n.50	4.1055	7.222 n.112
		4.1060	7.140
1.252	6.38 n.50	4.1062	7.2
1.266	7.63 n.23	4.1073	8.130 n.2
1.267	8.137, 141	4.1074	8.130 n.2
1.340	8.61	4.1078	7.28, 39
1.361	7.189	4.1079	7.26, 38 n. 32, 39, 41
2.372	6.114, 117		
2.423	7.46	4.1080	7.35
2.429	7.118	4.1098	6.38 n.50
2.432	7.38-39 n.32	4.1115	7.204
2.435	8.125 n.6	4.1122	6.167
2.451	7.27 n.4	4.1123	9.47
2.467	7.165	4.1126	6.61
2.515	8.70	4.1132	7.208-209, n.41
2.530	10.106	4.1138	7.221
2.562	6.127	4.1139	7.189
2.578	7.202-203, n.14, 208-209 n.41, 216	4.1141	10.81
		4.1153, 1154	6.61
2.594	7.41	4.1157	6.83
2.596	7.38 n.32	4.1187	7.139
2.605	7.35 n.24	5.1.2	7.208-209 n.41
2.619	7.97	5.65-67	7.176
2.646	10.82	5.108	7.123 n.41

Index 5 – Papyri

5.1210	6.39, 107	*CPH*	
6.1217	7.114	55, 70	8.130 n.2
6.1248	7.213, n.63		
6.1249	7.213 n.63	*CPJ*	
7.1564	7.63-64 n.23	6	6.100 n.116
7.1565	8.47 n.3	22, 28	8.150 n.7
7.1566	7.97 n.29, 100, 101, 105	126	7.220, n.101,103, 105, 224-225 n.125
7.1568	7.63-64 n.23		
7.1573	7.208 n.40, 210, 210 n.44, 211, 214 n.71	128 6.100 n.116; 8. 152	6.15; 8.150 n.7; 9.89 7.26, 38 n. 32, 39, 41
7.1574	7.200-202 n.9		
7.1575	7.208-209 n.41	432	9.70, 71
7.1613	7.118	448	8.146 n.4
7.1636	7.118 n.21	513, 514	8.150 n.7
8.1730	7.167 n.17, 168-169 n.22, 195; 8.23	3 Inscr 1436-1437 *CPL*	8.161
8.1741	7.62 n.17	238	10.77
8.1756-1890	8.23	241	9.68
8.1760	7.114		
8.1773	7.134, 136 n.20	*CPR*	
8.1774	7.190; 8.10 n.3, 22, 23, 30	1.27 1.28	6.10 6.38 n.50
8.1836	6.142	5.19	6.157
8.1848	10.117	5.23	6.176
8.1871	9.35	6.4	8.48 n.5
9.1894	8.82 n.12, 83, 84, 85	6.41 6. 80	10.31 7.26, 54 n.19
9.1896	6.167 n.184	7.4	7.95 n.16
10.1993	8.19-22, 25, 45	7.20	6.35 n.46
11.2012	8.111 n.26	7.49	8.164
11.2110	8.82 n.11	10.32	8.157 n.5
12.2133	6.11		
13.2245	6.11	Cowley, *Aramaic Papyri*	
13.2297	7.119	10	6.91
13.2299	7.119	14	9.90
13.2327	8.88 n.28	15	6.13, 16 n.26; 9.90, 91
13.2338	7.208-209 n.41		
14.2376	6.90; 7.197-202, 205-208, 213	18 48	9.90 9.90
14.2377	7.197		
14.2381	6.167	*DJD (P.Mur.)*	
14.2417	7.26, 29, n.8	2.18	6.92, n.100; 9.87
15.2460	7.124	2.19	6.14, 16, 16 n.28, 17
15.2472	6.90; 7.204, n.25, 214, n.71, n.73	2.20	6.14, 15, 16 n.27; 9.89
15.2473	6.90; 7.19	2.21	10.147
15.2475	6.127	2.24	6.90, 96 n.109
15.2476	6.34	2.114, 115	6.92
15.2520	8.79, 81, 83 n.16, n.17, 84	2.116 27.65	6.13 9.93, 94
15.2550	7.119, 120, n.28	27.69	9.90, 92-97

Jur.Pap. (Meyer)
48   7.201-202, 204,
                                    214

Kraeling, *Brooklyn Aramaic Papyri*
2   6.13, 16, n.26;
                                    9.90, 91
4   9.91
5   9.90, 91
7   6.13; 9.90, 91

MChr
16   7.220 n.105
18   7.139
100, 101   7.221
102   7.221-222; 9.61;
                                    8.42, 110 n.12
227   7.221
228   7.204, 211, n.48,
                                    n.54
229   7.211-212, n. 48,
                                    51, 54, n.55, 221
231   7.204-205
289   6.10
306   6.35 n.45
312   6.38 n.50
322   7.105
341   6.83 n.96
373   10.77
381   9.68

MPER
inv. 24552   7.192, 224, 168-
                                    169 n.22, 220
                                    n.102, 103,n106,
                                    224-225 n.125

P.Aberd.
19   7.202, 204-205,
                                    211 n.53, 214 n.71

P.Abinn.
4, 5, 9-15, 17, 18, 33, 43   6.176 n.193
30   6.176
32   6.176, n.193
50   10.121

P.Alex.
27   8.125 n.6
29   8.125 n.6, 126 n.9,
                                    170, 171
inv. 203   7.251

P.Amh.
1.3a   7.50
1.3b   7.248
2.30   7.133
2.33   7.134 n.13; 9.52
2.39   7.26
2.64   8.49
2.70   7.95
2.77   10.99
2.78   7.244
2.92   8.82-84, n.18;
                                    10.106
2.94   9.47

P.Amst.
32b   6.122
40   6.1, 9-11, n.13,
                                    158

P.Ant.
1.32   8.47
1.42   6.166
2.92   6.176, 177
2.93   7.39; 8.126 n.9
2.94   7.54 n.19
2.95   6.176

P.Athen.
66   7.38-39 n.32

P.Babatha
12   10.152
13-15   10.142
14   10.150
15   10.150, 151
16, 18, 27   10.152
28-30   10.142, 145
36-37   10.152

P.Bad.
2.19b   10.106
2.35   7.38-39 n.32, 41
2.36   7.26

P.Bas.
1.7   7.201 n.9
1.16   7.26, 48 n.1, 50;
                                    8.125 n.6, 126 n.9

P.Batav. (see also *P.Lugd.Bat.*)
1.11   8.47 n.2
1.22   8.164

Index 5 – Papyri

P.Beatty Panop.
1   7.1; 8.31, n.82
2   7.1

P.Berl.
inv. 10592   7.82 n.62, 125 n.53
inv. 16546   6.140-143

P.Berl.Frisk
2.1   7.119 n.25, 122

P.Berl.Leihg.
1.1   7.118, n.20, 22
1.2   7.122
1.4   7.118
1.5   7.118-119
1.7   6.113; 7.103 n.46
1.10   7.208-209 n.41, 210-211, 214, n.71, n.74
1.15   8.20, 37, 39
1.16   6.125, n.145
1.17   10.116
2.43 frag. a   7.63-64 n.23

P.Berl.Zill.
6   6.174 n.189

P.Bibl.Giss.
inv. 311   6.42, n.53
inv. 252   10.31

P.Bon.
21   6.57
24   6.167 n.184
44   7.27 n.5

P.Bour.
13   9.47; 10.108
42   7.114, 118 n. 21, 119

P.Brem.
10   7.27 n.4
19   8.125 n.6
56   8.125 n.6

P.Brit.Mus.
1.42   7.35 n.26
inv. 10591   6.34 n.42

P.Brookl.
4, 8   10.114

P.Cair. Isid.
1   8.61 n.70
4, 5   6.30
8   8.61 n.70
66   10.121
72, 73   7.63-64 n.23

P.Cair.Preis.
42   6.32 n. 39, 34

P.Cair.Zen.
1.59003   7.166
1.59015   6.101-104, 171; 8.13-14 n.1719, 20, 36, 37, 45
1.59018   6.100-101
1.59070   8.16
1.59093   7.176
2.59145   7.166-167
2.59187   7.38 n.32
2.59213   8.13 n.13
2.59267   7.167 n.10
3.59369   7.167 n.10, 15
3.59371   7.199 n.7; 9.39, 40
3.59468   7.167 n.10
3.59509   7.62 n.17
4.59537   8.36
4.59613   8.13 n.13
4.59620   8.14 n. 19, 15, 36
4.59653   7.33-34
5.59804   8.36, n. 94, 37
5.59822   8.45
5.59837   8.45

P.Cattaoui
2   6.117

P.Charite
8   10.117
20   8.89

P.Chester Beatty
3, 10   7.244

P.Col.
1 recto 1a-b   8.67
1 recto 2   8.67
1 recto 3   8.67
1 recto 4   7.119 n.25, 121-2, 121 n.31, n.32
2.1 recto 5   7.123 n.47
5.1 verso 4   7.118 n.20
6.14   10.106
6.123   8.133

7.135	7.113			
7.174	7.132 n.2	P.Enteux.		
8.215	7.26, 38 n.32	62		8.150 n.7
inv. 480	7.168-169 n.22, 178 n.64, 219-220, n.99, 220 n.101, 103, 105, 106, 224-225 n.125	69		7.141, 143-145
		P.Erasm.		
		2, pp.137-151		7.121
		P.Erl.		
P.Coll.Youtie		118		8.126 n.9
1. 27	7.118, n.22			
1.51	9.62 n.1	P.Fam.Tebt.		
2, p.449	6.2	7		6.31
		10		6.31
P.Colon. (= P.Köln)		15		8.111 n.24
inv. 10213	7.249-250, n.1	48		10.116
Pap. Colon.		P.Fay.		
12	6.12, 15	11		7.198-199 n.4, 213
		12		7.213 n.63
P.Colt		18b		7.122, 123
7	8.161	20		6.111
		24		6.117
P.Congr.		105		6.158
15.22 col. 3	7.207 n.37	106		7.103
		129		8.125, n.6
P.Corn.		132		9.63
8	9.47	153		8.67, n.92
16	6.125			
24	8.99, n.2, 100	P.Flor.		
52	7.27 n.5, 28	1.1		7.201 n.9
		1.2		7.97-100, n.29
PDM		1.5		7.208-209 n.41
14.1-295	10.23	1.6		6.117, 118
14.30-45	10.24	1.39		7.2
14.65	10.23	1.44		6.61
		1.48		7.211
P.Diog.		1.55		7.108 n.41, 210, 214, n.71
11-12	6.31, 32 n.39, 35 n.44, 38 n.50			
		1.56		7.205, 210-211, 213-214, n.71
P.Dura		1.61, 65		6.108
13	8.74 n.101	1.86		7.203, 200-201 n.9
20	6.61	1.91		7.102 n. 42, 105
30	6.2	1.97		7.204-205 n.27
46	7.38-39 n.32	2.140		8.125 n.6
		2.278		7.63-64 n.23
P.Edfou		2.345		8.125 n.6
270	8.84-85 n.22, 94	3.301		10.116
272	8.84-85 n.22, 94	3.370		10.106
397	8.84-85 n.22, 94	3.382		8.70
446	8.94			
		Pap.Flor.		
P.Egerton		7, pp.147-154		6.194
2	7.244 n.9; 9.99, 101			

Index 5 – Papyri

P.Fouad		3.570	10.12
21	7.22	4.331-332	10.11
26	6.101; 7.132 n.2	4.86-87	10.13
35	6.166	4.88-93	10.23
		4.850-929	10.24
P.Freib.		4.870-875	10.12
4.57	8.25, 126 n.9	4.1227-1264; 1233	10.13
		4.2085-2086	10.45
P. Fuad Univ.		4.2287	10.43
1.6	7.63-64 n.23, 86	4.2302-2303	10.43
	n.83	4.2522-2526	10.43
1.7	9.63	4.2523	10.43
		4.2550	10.43
P.Gen.		4.2711-2730	10.41, 42
1.5	8.25 n.63	4.2715	10.43
1.16	6.117, 118, 167	4.2721-2727	10.43
	n.184	4.2773	10.41
1.37	7.100	4.2780	10.17, 41
1.50	7.35; 8.164	4.2811-2228	10.42, 43
1.55	7.27 n.4	4.3007-3086	10.12, 13, 45
2.95	8.77, 78, 92, n.47	4.3020-3021	10.13, 45
2.108	8.48 n.5	5.1-54	10.23
		5.108, 312, 945	10.11
P.Gen.Lat.		7.220	10.11
1	6.158; 10.141	7.429-458	10.22
4	6.157	7.540-578	10.23, 24
		8.49, 61, 156, 466, 611	10.11
P.Giss.		12.63, 263-266, 285	10.11
1.2	6.2; 7.167 n.14	15.15	10.11
1.3	10.84	17, 71	10.21
1.33	7.211	78	10.41, 42, 43
1.34	7.211, n.54, 212	101.4	10.11
	n.57	101.52	10.12
2.40	6.117, 118	105.1-15	10.11
3.58	8.66	123, 125	10.12
3.69	7.63 n.23		
		P.Graux	
P.Giss.Univ.		2	6.142
1	7.198-199 n.4		
		P.Grenf.	
P.Got.		1.30	7.27
3	7.63 n.23	1.47	7.165; 8.36
		2.14b	7.12, 60 n.11
P.Grad.		2.41	8.61
1	7.168, 168-169	2.43	6.158
	n.22	2.77	7.35
		2.100	8.157 n.5
		2.112a	8.158, n.9
PGM			
1.300	10.12, 17	*P.Gron.*	
1.300-305, 310, 312-313	10.12	10	6.32 n.39, 34
2, p.13	6.131	17	8.125 n.6
3.146, 147, 221	10.11	18	7.27 n.5; 8.125 n.6
3.434-435	10.43		

P.Hal.		5	6.175
1.1	7.134, 134 n.15, 168 n.22, 180-188, n.83, 190, 217-218 n.91, 219, 220 n.106	6 40 45 64	6.175, 176 8.150 n.7 8.125 n.6 8.161, 164
1.7	7.38 n.32, 51 n.9	*P. Hib.*	
1.8	7.38 n.32	1.29	7.167 n.17, 168 n.22, 196; 8.55 n.35
P.Hamb.			
1.9	8.80 n. 4, 81 n.5, 82 n.10, 83 n.16 17 19, 84, 85	1.30 1.30d 1.34	7.205 n.29 7.217 n.91 9.60, n.3
1.16	7.208-209 n.41	1.49	7.38 n.32
1.17	113, 117, 121, n.30, n. 31, 126 n.57	1.54 1.73 1.94, 95	8.22 9.60 8.50 n.18
1.33	7.123 n.46, 124 n.49; 8.91, n.40	1.110 2.197	7.5-13 7.202 n.18
1.83	8.48 n.5		
1.88	7.38-39 n.32	*P.Iand.*	
1.91	8.15, n.22, 20, 36	2.12 6.94	8.125 n.6 8.125 n.6
P.Harr.		7.143	8.92, n.48
1.61	7.168-169, n.22	8.146	6.157
1.62	8.20, 25, 28-30, 32, 45	*P.IFAO*	
1.64	7.2	2.24	6.62
1.68	10.150	3.18	7.210
1.70	6.125		
1.93	7.123 n.46	*P.Ital.*	
1.107	7.26, 50, 248	3.30, 37	6.50
1.112	6.176		
1.132	7.132 n.2	*P.Ketub.*	
1.137	8.30 n.80		9.82ff.
P.Haun.		*P.Köln*	
2.13	6.18-23; 10.122	3.144	6.96, 164-167
2.33	8.125 n.6	3.147	6.10 n.14, 82-85, 158; 7.161
P.Heid.		3.157	6.185-189
2.212	8.10 n.3, 22, 24, 25, 45	3.163 4.186	8.125 n.6 7.23-24, n.81
3.13	6.57	4.188	8.81 n.6
4.292	9.119	5.219	8.47 n.2; 9.32 n.1
4.294	9.120, 121	5.236	8.156 n.1
4.333	8.172 n.7	6.160 6.200	9.35 n.2, 39 n.1 9.33 n.4
P.Hels.		6.201	9.32 n.2
1	9.45, 52	6.255	9.99, 100
2	9.42	6.259	9.40
31	9.54	6.260 6.267	9.39, 40 9.34
P.Herm.		6.268	9.32, 35 n.2, 39
2	6.176	6.280	9.62, 63
4	6.175; 8.126 n.9	7.186	7.23-24, n.81

Index 5 – Papyri

P.Kroll
col. 2   7.62 n.14, 220 n.102, n.103

P.Kron.
50   6.31, 35 n.44, 38 n.50

P.Laur.
1.6   6.83 n.97, 84
1.20   7.37-38
2.41   7.39

P.Leit.
5   7.105
7   7.102 n.42
11   7.96
13   7.115 n.11

P.Lille
1.8   6.142
1.28   7.170
1.29   7.167-180 n.22, 187-189; 8.35
2.1   7.141, 143, n.3, 32, 147

P.Lips.
1.44   8.131, n.3, 132; 9.68
1.104   7.29
1.105   7.35 n.24; 8.123
1.110   7.35
1.120   7.205, 207 n.35, 208-209 n.41

P. Lond.
1.45   7.135
1.131   7.163 n.2
2.220   6.107
2.231   7.35
2.232   7.35
2.234   7.35
2.261   6.126, 127
2.311   6.18 n.31
2.348   7.201
2.357   7.67 n.31
2.401   7.139, n.27
3.846   7.103
3.897   7.42
3.900   7.118 n.21
3.904   6.115-119, n.123, 126
3.908   7.211-212, n. 48, 51, 54, n.55, 221
3.924   7.140
3.1164   6.83; 8.130 n.2
3.1171   7.18 n.52, 66-67, n.28, 80, 84, 86 n.82
3.1177   9.70, 71
5.1658   7.27 n.4
5.1714   6.85
5.1729   6.189
6.1912   8.111 n.28
6.1917   6.171; 8.125 n.6
6.1918   6.171
6.1925   7.27 n.4
6.1927, 1928, 1929   6.171
7.1949   8.16
7.1950   8.16, 22
7.1951   6.58
7.1973   7.10 n.21
7.2052   8.10 n.3, 17, n. 30, 20-22, 25, 36, 45
inv. 2196   6.127
inv. 2420   7.118 n.20

P.Lugd. Bat.
19.21   7.38-39 n.32
20.30   9.40
22.32, 34   6.107

P.Lund
4   7.27 n.5

P.Magd.
6   7.183 n.75
24   7.183 n.75

P.Masada
2.722   10.140

P.Med. (see *P.Mil.*)

P.Med.Bar.
5   8.88-89 n. 30
(see also *Aegyptus* 66 (1986) 24-30)

P.Mert.
2.63   7.39
3.105   6.38 n.50

P.Meyer
20   7.29, 36-38, 40, 42-24, 44 n.47, 46 n.55
21   8.126 n.9

P.Mich.		inv. 241	7.28 n.6
1.18	6.58-59	inv. 5262a	6.144-145; 7.132
1.33	9.35		n.2
1.70	7.168-169 n.22	inv. 5806	6.127
2.121	6.7, 9		
2.123	6.61	P.Mich.Michael.	
2.130	7.248, 251 n.11	27	8.125 n.6
3.170	8.102		
3.171	8.102	P.Mich.Zen. = P.Mich. I	
3.209	6.158 n.178;		
	10.165, 166	P.Michael.	
3.213	7.27 n.5	29	8.126 n.9
3.217	7.27 n.5		
4.223	8.82	P.Mil.	
4.224	8.150 n.7	1.7	6.61
4.360	8.85, 88 n.28	2.33	6.157
5.238	6.61		
5.321	6.34, 38 n.50	P.Mil.Vogl.	
5.322a	6.34	1.26	7.210
5.339	6.9	2.53	8.83, 84
5.340	6.7, 8, 11	2.54	7.95 n.16
6.364	8.47 n.3	3.146	7.208-209 n.41
6.579	6.122	3.193b, 194a and b	10.116
8.467	6.158 n.178;	4.212	8.150 n.7
	10.165	6.266	7.210
8.468	6.158, n.177, 178;		
	10.165	P.Monac.	
8.490	7.26, 38-39 n.32,	1.8	6.32 n.39
	43 n.39, 45, 46	3.45	9.36
	n.54	3.49	9.69, 71, 72
8.491	7.26, 38-90 n.32,	3.52	9.59-61
	45, 46 n.54, 47	3.57	9.57
8.493	7.38-39, n.32		
8.495	7.38-39 n.32	P.Murabba'ât	
8.496	7.27 n.5	18	6.92 n.100; 7.224
8.499	7.27, 28		n.125, 230-232,
8.501	7.54 n.19		n.164; 9.87
8.503	7.26, 46 n.55	20	6.14, 15, 16 n.27;
8.509	7.39		9.89, 91-93, n.14,
8.514	7.39-40, 42		95, 97
8.519	8.126 n.9	21	9.91-93, 95;
10.529	8.70		10.147
10.580	6.114; 8.100, 101,	24	6.90, 96 n.109;
	n.14		7.232 n.165
10.582	7.93 n.4	114	6.92; 7.231 n.164
10.594	8.99 n.2, 4	115	6.92; 9.92-97
11.620	7.113	116	6.13; 9.93-95
11.621	7.41		
11.624	6.176	P. Mur. (see DJD above)	
14.675	7.102-103		
14.676	6.132-137	P.Nag.Hamm.	
15.700	6.5-6	C4	6.184
15.709	8.78, 83, 84, 91, 92	C8	6.184
15.751	7.26, 54 n.19	G63	6.183
15.752	7.26, 28	G64	6.183

G65	6.182-183	2.281-282	6.11
66	8.126 n.9	2.282	6.57
G72	6.182-183, 184	2.283	7.189; 8.23 n.57
		2.284	8.68, 69
P.Neph.		2.285	8.68, 69
1, 2, 8, 10	6.176 n.193	2.286	7.213
12	8.126 n.9	2.294	7.132 n.2
		2.298 verso	8.68
P.Ness.		2.300	7.39, 41
3.89	6.62	2.362, 363	6.108
		3.393, 394	8.68
P.Oslo		3.405	7.251
1.3	6.11	3.472	8.36
2.31	6.11	3.473	7.95
2.33	7.118 n.22	3.483	7.201
2.34	7.118 n.22	3.485	7.200-201 n.9,
2.40b	7.201 n.12		203, 208-209 n.41
2.50	7.38-39 n.32	3.486	7.208-209 n.41
3.79	8.111 n.27	3.487	7.105; 10.150
3.111	6.117 n.123	3.491, 494	6.36
3.160	7.27 n.5	3.498	7.41-42 n.37
		3.500	8.146, 147
P.Oxy.		3.509	7.208-209 n.41
1.30	7.250, 253	3.524	9.63
1.36	8.54, 61	3.525	7.35 n.24; 8.123
1.44	8.47 n.2, 61, 65	3.526	8.125 n.6, 126 n.10
	n.76	3.528	7.27 n.5
1.68	7.204, 211, n.48,	3.529	7.39, 41
	n.54	3.530	7.29
1.76	6.174 n.189	3.599	7.35 n.24
1.106	6.7, 84	3.601	6.42 n.53
1.111	9.63	4.656	7.244
1.112	8.125 n.6	4.705	8.146, 147
1.115	7.35 n.26	4.707	6.167
1.117	7.41	4.708	7.117
1.122	8.125 n.6	4.710	7.11, 12 n.25
1.123	7.26, 27 n.4; 8.12	4.712	7.204-205, 210,
	n.10		216, 207 n.35
1.144	6.84	4.713	6.34
1.155	7.35 n.24	4.714	7.192 n.104
1.158	6.176	4.715	7.124
1.174	8.48, 62	4.728	7.88
1.178	6.42 n.53	4.742	7.38-39 n.32
1.181	9.63	4.746	7.41
1.185	8.47 n.2	4.805	7.29
2.237	6.7 n.10, 15 n.25,	6.888	10.150
	33; 7.41-42 n.37,	6.899	7.103
	201, 222 n.111;	6.900	7.27 n.5
	8.42	6.904	6.69
2.251	8.100, 101 n.14	6.903	7.248
2.251-253	6.114	6.916	8.48 n.5
2.252	8.100, 101, n.14	6.927	9.63
2.253	8.100, 101, n.14	6.932	10.117
2.259	7.221	6.933	7.27 n.4; 8.125 n.6
2.265	6.38 n.50	6.940-942	7.35 n.24
2.281	7.216	6.942, 943	6.176

6.995	8.164	17.1933	6.176
7.1027	7.207, 212	17.2106	6.117 n.123
7.1050	10.31	17.2131	6.141
7.1061	7. 39, 41, n.36	17.2136	6.83
7.1063	8.125 n.6	17.2150	7.39; 8.126 n.10
8.1119	7.95, 100, n.31	18.2182	7.96, 113, 122
8.1121	10.121		n.35, 126, 127
8.1132	6.10, 11	18.2193	8.125 n.6
8.1153	7.27 n.4, 38 n.32	19.2234	7.132 n.2
8.1155	7.40-41	20.2274	8.125 n.6
8.1156	8.125 n.6	20.2275	8.126 n.10
8.1157	6.126	20.2276	6.176
8.1162	8.170, 171, 172	22.2341	10.112
8.1165	6.176	22.2342	10.106
8.1185	8.124 n.5, 125 n.6	22.2347	6.84
9.1189	8.146, 147	24.2413	6.114
9.1193	7.58	24.2414	8.91, 92
9.1203	7.211 n.54	27.2479	6.142
9.1205	6.72	31.2595	7.28, 41
10.1261	7.63 n.23	33.2669	8.100, 101 n.14
10.1266	10.141	33.2674	10.121
10.1282	6.108	33.2675	7.124
10.1296	6.158 n.178;	33.2678	9.63
	10.165	33.2680	10.117
10.1300, 1350	8.126 n.10	34.2710	6.111
12.1409	8.88 n.28	34.2713	7.124
12.1422	8.28, 31, 34	34.2719	7.31-32, n.16, 17,
12.1423	6.57; 8.13 n.13,		34, 38
	32-34	34.2721	6.85
12.1424	6.176 n.193; 8.122	34.2722	7.124
12.1431	7.63 n.23	36.2728	6.176 n.193
12.1438	8.77, 82, 91, 92,	36.2759	6.42 n.53
	n.47	36.2785	8.125 n.6, 126
12.1457	7.63 n.19; 8.82,		n.10, 170-72
	91, 92 n.49	41.2985	8.125 n.6
12.1463	6.50 n.61	41.2986	8.125 n.6
12.1472	7.95 n.16	42.3055	7.248
12.1486-1487	9.63	42.3057	6.169-177, 181
12.1492	8.125 n.6, 126 n.10	42.3067	7.54 n.19
12.1517	8.92 n.46	43.3094	8.125 n.6
12.1579-1580	9.63	43.3150	8.123, 126 n.10
12.1587	8.124 n.5, 125 n.6,	44.3188	7.97
	126 n.10	44.3203	10.2
14.1626	7.63 n.23	45.3240	7.154 n.65
14.1631	6.95	46.3270	10.106
14.1639	7.222 n.112	46.3302	7.132 n.2
14.1643	8.32, 34	47.3333	6.158
14.1664, 1667	8.125 n.6, 126 n.10	47.3336	6.119-120, 124,
14.1675	8.125 n.6		167 n.184
14.1676	7.26	47.3354	6.95
14.1678	7.32, 36-38	48.3396	6.158 n.178;
14.1757	7.27 n.5		10.165, 167
14.1773	7.32, 37-38	48.3407	9.110
14.1774	8.126 n.10	49.3464	6.98
16.1833	7.102, 122, 41-42	49.3468	7.130-132, 208-
	n.37		209 n.41

Index 5 – Papyri

49.3469	8.125 n.6	*P.Petaus*	
49.3477	6.50 n.61; 7.208-209 n.41	28-29	7.32
		30	7.253
49.3482	7.124	44	8.86
49.3491	6.38 n.50	53	8.111 n.25
49.3500	6.2		
49.3507	8.125 n.6, 126 n.10	*P.Petr.*	
49.3510	6.122 n.141	2.2	6.142
50.3523	7.242-244, n.13	2.8	7.134 n.15
50.3555	7.163-165	2.11	7.29
50.3556	8.47 n.4	2.20	7.62, n.17
50.3593	6.62	2.25	7.123
51.3602-3605	7.58 n.2	2.39	7.12 n.24; 8.88-89 n.30
51.3611	8.129-132, 144		
51.3616	8.9-10	2.46a and b	9.48
51.3617	8.9-10, n.1	3.7	7.220, n.101, 103, 105, 224-255 n.125
51.3622	7.2		
51.3623	7.1-2, 49		
51.3638	7.124	3.25	7.213
51.3645	8.122	3.32	7.71 n.36
51.3646	9.66	3.32f	9.39 n.2
54.3747-53	9.106	3.53m	7.12, 60 n.11
54.3759	9.106, 108-113, 109-110 n.7	3.54b	8.88-89 n.30
		3.57a, b	8.50 n.18
55.3781	10.76	3.58c, d	8.50 n.18
55.3796	7.2	3.59b	9.39 n.2
55.3813-3815	6.176 n.193; 10.120, 165	3.110	7.12 n.24; 8.88-89 n.30
55.3815	10.119, 122		
55.3819	8.126 n.10	*P.Phil.*	
55.3781	10.73	1	7.100, 103 n.43
56.3857	8.169, 170, 171, 172; 10.165	10	7.103
		34	8.124 n.5, 125 n.6
56.3858	10.164, 170		
56.3859	6.158 n.178; 10.165, 167, 170-174	*P.Prag.*	
		1.40	10.123
56.3863	8.126 n.10	*P.Princ.*	
563874	10.170	2.20	10.99
60.4087, 4088	7.67 n.33	2.50	8.48
		2.71, 74	8.125 n.6
P.Panop.Beatty		3.165	8.125 n.6
2	10.1201		
		P.Rain.Cent.	
P.Paris		122	8.67 n.89
14	7.132, 136, n.19		
15	7.136-139	*P.Rein.*	
17	10.106	7	7.220 n.105
18	7.38-39 n.32	1.18	6.142
38	7.135	1.47	7.63 n.23
39 recto	7.135	1.48	8.125 n.6
47	7.35	2.135	8.78
61	8.54		
62	8.14-16	*P.Rend.Harr.* (see *P.Harr.* above)	

P.Rev.		10.1176	7.163
	8.49, 53, 54, 61	12.1229	7.124
10₁₀, 14₉, 15₂, 18₂, 22₂	10.106	12.1230	7.192 n.104
col. 34	9.47, 48	12.1237	7.210, 208-209
col.57.4	9.40		n.41, 214 n.71, n.75
		12.1241	7.39, n.32, n.33, 42
P.Ross.Georg.		12.1243	7.102 n.41
2.12	6.121 n.138, 127	12.1276	6.23
3.4	8.125 n.6	13.1331	7.39, n.33, 41
3.6	7.38, n.30, n.31	13.1333	7.86 n.82
3.9	7.27 n.4	13.1334	7.27 n.5
5.8	6.176	14.1401	7.62 n.14, 199 n.7
5.154	6.157	14.1406	7.102 n.42
		14.1412	7.248
P.Ryl.		14.1429	6.176
2.65	7.197; 9.39		
2.115	7.204, 214	*P.Sitol.*	
2.119	6.142	2	7.121
2.141	6.142		
2.144	7.165-166	*P.Sorb.*	
2.154	6.11; 7.217 n.88	1.49	9.35
2.189	7.63-64 n.23		
2.194	8.65, 81, 82 n. 9, 84, 85	*P.Stras.*	
		2.93	7.58 n.3, 62 n.17
2.195	8.86, 89, 90	2.122	6.62
2.235	7.27 n.4	4.239	6.113
3.457	7.244, 248	4.245	7.63 n.23
4.595	8.99, n.2, 100, n.9	4.286	6.176, 177
		8.719	7.38-39 n.32
P.Sakaon			
38, 48	10.121	*P.Tebt.*	
		1.5	6.7 n.11, 167; 7.12, 62, n.17, 93 n.1, 178 n.64, 199-200 n.7, 220 n.102, 103; 9.52, 61, 93
P.Sarap.			
3	7.63 n.19		
25	6.166		
85	7.26		
		1.6	6.98; 7.141 n.30; 9.39 n.2
PSI			
3.207	7.35 n.26		
4.299	7.27 n.4, 35 n.26	1.27	7.114 n.8
4.332	7.63 n.23	1.33	7.60 n.11
5.446	7.19 n.63, 63, 63-64 n. 23, 66, 71, 80, 84, 86 n.82	1.41, 50, 53	6.142
		1.253	7.71 n.36
		2.277, 311	7.118
5.489	7.167 n.10	2.326	10.149
5.549	7.220 n.105, 224-5 n.125	2.356	7.118
		2.364	7.119, 120
6.685	7.103	2.365	7.119
7.732	7.192 n.104	2.377	7.118
7.785	7.63 n.19	2.381	6.31, 38, n.50
10.1108	7.1	2.384	6.61
10.1112	6.125	2.386	6.7
10.1124	7.118	2.409, 422	7.38-39 n.32
10.1126	7.208-209 n.41	2.423	7.35 n.24
10.1134	7.118	2.439	7.105
10.1159	7.95 n.16	2.583	7.46 n.55, 47

Index 5 – Papyri

2.615	7.119	P.Wisc.	7.38-39 n.32, 54 n.19
3.700	7.167 n.17, 169 n.22, 196	2.69	
3.704	7.58 n.3, 62 n.17	2.71, 84	7.26
3.710	7.199-200 n.7		
3.748, 749	9.49, 50	P.Würzb.	
3.776	6.34 n.42	21	7.38-39 n.32
3.779	7.141, 144-145		
3.782, 786, 787	6.142	P.Yadin	
3.814	7.202, 205-206, 208, 210	10	6.15; 9.89, 91-93, 95-96; 10.147
3.818	6.167	11	6.92, n.100; 7.231-232 n.164
		12	10.149
P.Tor.		18	6.12, 13, 15, 16 n.27, 92; 9.88-90, 92-97
1	7.136-139		
2	7.136-139		
3	7.135-136, n.19, 213		
		19	6.46
13	6.7; 7.136 n.1; 7.3; 9.49, 52	21	6.92; 10.145
		37	9.90, 92-95, 97
P.Turner		P.Yale	
17	6.108-109	inv. 1535	6.2
18	6.10 n. 14, 156-159		
		SB	
19	6.63-66, 70	1.25	7.30 n.13
22	6.48-52, 62	1.421	10.84
26	6.66, 70-72	1.761	7.30 n.13
29	6.123	1.1207	7.30
41	6.51, 55-60	1.1214	7.30, n.12
		1.1268	7.31
P.Ups.Frid.		1.2052-2054	7.30 n.13
1	6.2 n.1, n.2, 27, 32; 7.163	1.2133	6.11
		1.2639	7.31, n.14
2	6.8-9	1.3442	7.30 n.13
3	6.105-108	1.3553-3555	7.30 n.13
5	6.137-139	1.3557	7.30 n.13
6	6.60-63	1.3815, 3892	7.31
		1.3924	7.63 n.20, 63-4 n. 23, 64
P.Vars.			
22	7.27 n.5	1.4284	6.117
		1.4516	7.63 n.19
P.Vind.Sijp.		1.5140-5143	7.30 n.12
26	7.41, 50	1.5140-5145	7.30.n.13
		1.5142	7.30 n.12
P.Vind.Tand.		1.5174, 5175	6.189
27	6.31, n.44, n.45	1.5205, 5208, 5216	7.30 n.13
		1.5217	6.148
P.Vind.Worp		1.5275	10.31
15	7.40, 41	1.5538	7.30 n.13
		1.5725	10.31
P.Wash.Univ.		3.6011	7.30 n.13
3	6.148 n.162	3.6155	10.81
13	6.41-42, 43	3.6222	7.27 n. 5, 28, 40

3.6262	7.27 n.5	8.9842	8.92, 92-93 n.49
3.6263	6.158 n.178; 7.28; 10.165, 166	8.10039	9.36
		8.10196	7.105
3.6951	7.208-209 n.41	8.10199	7.102 n.42
3.7181a	7.63-64 n.23	8.10203	7.96
3.7182	7.167 n.13	8.10205	7.115 n.11
3.7202	9.32 n.1	10.10219	10.116
3.7243	8.126 n.9	10.10255	8.170
3.7246	6.111	10.10493	10.31
3.7263	7. 10 n.21	10.10572	6.38 n.50
3.7269	8.170, 172	12.10773	8.126 n.9
4.7375	7.2	12.10786	6.11
4.7379	7.206, 208-209 n.41	12.10803	7.26
		12.10833, 10835, 10836	7.30 n.13
4.7405	7.62 n.17	12.11187	7.30 n.13
4.7427	6.145	12.10888	6.31 38 n.50
4.7432	8.162 n.26	12.11009	8.125 n.6
4.7457	6.111	14.11270	6.137
4.7461	8.67, 99 n.2	14.11279	6.86-89
4.7462	8.99 n.2	14.11277	6.50
5.7559	6.35	14.11374	6.112-115
5.7572	7.38-39 n.32	14.11492	6.176
5.7635	6.176	14.11548	6.11
5.7642	6.157	14.11552	6.83 n.96
5.7708	7.30 n.13	14.11575	6.10
5.7745	9.63	14.11577	6.3
5.7817	7.202-205, n.21, 211 n.53, 214, n.71, 75, 215, n.76	14.11584	7.38-39 n.32
		14.11586, 11587	6.122
		14.11588	8.125 n.6
5.8004	8.125 n.6	14.11652	9.63
5.8033	6.98; 7.141, 145-147, 160	14.11857	7.249
		14.11858	7.249-250, 250 n.4
5.8267	6.111	14.11863	8.70
5.8077	7.30 n.13	14.11881	7.48-49, n.4; 8.126 n.9
5.8299	9.36		
6.9050	7.93 n.4; 8.70 n.99	14.11882	6.176, 177
6.9107	6.176	14.11902	8.69
6.9126	7.30-32, 30 n.12	14.11904	7.115 n.10, 120-121
6.9138	6.176 n.193		
6.9207	8.70	14.12015	7.103-104 n.46
6.9251	7.38-39 n.32	14.12076	7.58
6.9252	7.218 n.92	14.12087	7.132 n.2
6.9315	7.100 n.31	14.12089	7.115-116
6.9328, 9329	7.132 n.2	14.12168	7.112-113
6.9373	6.38 n.50	16.12240	7.208 n.41, 210
6.9376	6.176	16.12334	6.38 n.50
6.9377	6.31, 35 n.44	16.12550	7.33-34
6.9454	7.134 n.15	16.12572	7.39
6.9524	8.125 n.6	16.12663	6.176 n.193
6.9526	10.106	16.12854	9.66
6.9528	6.111	16.12982	7.27 n.5
6.9608	6.176	16.13030	7.222 n.112
8.9642	6.31, 35, n.44, 38 n.50	18.13747	10.112
		22.15203	10.79
8.9683	6.176, 177	30.1608	10.108
8.9740	10.114		

Index 5 – Papyri

Stud.Pal. (= SPP)		382	9.63
4.70	7.123 n.43	395	7.103
15.234	7.251	397	7.95, 100, n.31
20.75.1	7.63-64 n.23	400	7.100
20.167	8.164	405	7.2
22.177	8.83, 83 n.18, 84	450	7.134 n.15
Suppl.Mag.		*O.Brux.*	
2.66	10.20	81-94	7.127
UPZ		*O.Fay.*	
1.3	8.15, n.21	24, 27, 28, 32	7.126 n.56
1.4	8.15, n.21		
1.9, 10, 11	7.135	*O.Leid.*	
1.59	7.26, 198-199 n.4	pp. 1-2, F1901/9,166	6.190
1.65	6.158 n.178;		
	10.165, 1666	*O.Skeat*	
1.71	9.7	2	7.123 n.40
1.112	8.45, 49, 51, 52		
	n.23; 9.40, 48-49	*O.Wilb.*	
1.121	8.14-16, 19, 20,	20	7.2 n.1
	22, 34, 36		
1.124	9.60, 61	*O.Wilck. (= WO)*	
2.160	7.136	392, 395	8.89, 93
2.161	7.136-139	684	8.89, 93, n.52, 94
2.162	7.136; 9.51	1054	8.89, 93, n.51, n.
2.161	7.136-139		52
2.170	7.132, 136, n.19	1057	8.89, 93, n.51, 94
1080	8.94	1091-1125	7.127
1081	8.94	1261	8.89, 93 n. 51, 94
WChr		*ZPE*	
109	9.36	4 (1969) 187-191	10.20
193	9.70, 71	24 (1977) 43-53	7.93
355	7.140	50 (1983) 147-154	6.190
360	7.140, 147, 160	87 (1991) 253-254	10.20

6. BIBLICAL, QUMRAN AND RABBINIC WORKS

Hebrew Bible

Genesis
1:26	9.103; 10.28
1:26-27	9.38
1:28	10.28
2:9	9.3
2:24	6.15 n.22
14:14	7.86
17:17	6.183
20:3	6.13
31:15	6.12 n.16, 13
34:12	6.12, 12 n.16; 9.88, 88 n.7

Exodus
3:6	6.194
3:15-16	6.194
4:5	6.194
12:6, 18	9.113
12:43-44	7.189
16:22, 23	9.115
18:13-27	6.128 n.147
20:4	9.2
20:12	8.115, 116 n.56
20:17	6.13
22:16	9.88 n.7
22:16-17	6.12, 12-13 n.16
22:16, 17	9.88
21:2-6	7.190
21:20-1, 24	7.190
21:26-27	7.190
21:29-32	7.191
21:32	7.190
22:19	8.147
22:22-24	8.116
23:11	7.225
30:11-16	6.128
34:21	9.111

Leviticus
6:16, 26	9.2
22:11	7.90
25:35	7.230 n.158
25:39-43	7.190
25:44-46	7.190
27:28, 29	8.147

Numbers
22:22	7.128
27:8-11	6.43

Deuteronomy
2:19	6.202
2:34	8.147
3:6	8.147
4:28	10.46
5:16	8.115
6:4	10.11
7:2	8.147
10:18	8.116
15:2	7.228
15:3, 9	7.226
15:12-18	7.190
17:17	6.12 n.15
18:1	9.2
20:11	8.172
20:17	8.147
21:13	6.13
21:14	6.13-14 n.18
21:16-17	6.43
22:22	6.13
22:38-39	9.88 n.7
23:6	8.172
23:15-16	6.54
24:1	6.13
24:2	6.16 n.28
24:17-21	8.116
26:16-19	10.11
27:15	10.46
30:14	10.8

Joshua
1:1	7.105 n.53
8:26	8.147
10:28, 37	8.147
15:18-20	6.12-13 n.16
16:10	6.12-13 n.16

Judges
5:3, 5	10.11
6:23	8.172 n.7
19:20	8.172 n.7

Ruth
4:5, 10	6.13

1 Samuel
7	8.146
24:11, 16	10.166
25	8.115 n.55

Index 6 – Biblical Works

26:17, 21	10.166	*Esther*	
18:25	6.12, 12-13 n.16; 9.88, 88 n.7	1:8	7.161
		3:12-14	7.3
		4:17	10.53
2 Samuel		8:3-17	7.22
9:10	7.190 n.95	8:10	7.3
11:14, 15	7.22	9:20	7.22
13:18	7.105 n.53		
19:18	7.105 n.53	*Job*	
		6:34	9.12
1 Kings		12:20a	9.12
1:4, 15	7.105 n.53	30:1	10.130
9:16	6.12-13 n.16		
10:5	7.105 n.53	*Psalms*	
10:24	6.183	1:3	8.158
15:22	7.86	2:6 (LXX)	10.85
18	8.146	4:2	10.27
19:21	7.105 n.53	4:11	10.130
21:8, 9-10	7.22	15	8.173
		23	9.115
2 Kings		32:1-2	10.60
4:43	7.105 n.53	34:20	8.172
5:5-7	7.22	44:7	10.85
5:18	10.53	45:7	9.48
6:15	7.105 n.53	45:10b, 14b (= LXX 44)	6.181
10:2-3, 6	7.22	47	9.115
19:9-14	7.22	55-59	8.173
19:28	10.120	61:9	8.162
20:12	7.22	68:5	8.116
		68:18 (= LXX 67:18)	10.60
1 Chronicles		77:35	8.162
12:18	8.172 n.7	79:6	10.46
24:7-18	6.129	92:1	8.145
27:1	7.105 n.53	91-93	9.115
		100:6	7.105 n.53
		101:27	10.85
2 Chronicles		106:20	10.27
9:4	7.105 n.53	109:1 (LXX)	10.85
17:19	7.105 n.53	115:4	10.46
22:8	7.105 n.53	119:63	9.48
32:9-17	7.22	121:8	8.172 n.7
		124:5	8.172 n.7
Ezra		132:17	8.147
4:11-16	7.22	146:9	8.116
4:13	7.86		
6:14	9.72 n.7	*Proverbs*	
9	6.17	2:17	6.14
9:6	10.54	15:25	8.116
10:8, 14	9.72	17:9-16a	6.181
Nehemiah		*Isaiah*	
10:31	6.17; 7.225	2:2-4	10.134
13:23-28	6.17	3:15	10.12
		5:1-2	6.94

6:8, 11	10.12	*Hosea*	
10:24	10.12	4:7; 9:11; 10:5	10.27
22:13	8.119		
23:1-4	10.134	*Amos*	
25:6-8	10.132, 134	1:9	10.134
34:2	8.147		
37:9-14	7.22	*Obadiah*	
37:19	10.46	14	8.146
40:18-31	10.46		
41:21-24	10.46	*Micah*	
44:9-20	10.46	4:13	8.147
46:5-7	10.46		
48:12-14	10.46	*Nahum*	
49:6	10.134	3:1	8.146
51:5	10.134		
56:1-8	10.134	*Malachi*	
60:4-14	10.134	2:13-16	6.14
61:1	10.14		
66:19-21	10.134	**Apocrypha**	

Jeremiah
2:11	10.27	*1 Enoch*	
3:19	6.40	13:5	10.53
9:7	8.172	62:12-14	10.132
10:25	10.46		
25:9	8.147	*1 Esdras*	
25:22	10.134	6:8-21	7.22-23 n. 80
29:24-32	7.22	7:2	9.72 n.7
48:25	8.147		
50:21	8.147	*2 Esdras*	
		4:17	8.172 n.7
Lamentations		5:7	8.172 n.7
2:3	8.147		
3:42	10.53	*Tobit*	
		1:15	7.86
Ecclesiastes		5:2-3	6.108
4:10	9.48	6:2	10.130
		7:12-14	6.12; 9.88
Ezekiel		7:13	6.15; 9.89
9:4	8.166-167 n.39	8:21	6.12 n.16, 46
16:8	6.14	10:10	6.46
26-28	10.134	11:4	10.130
29:21	8.147		
37	9.104, 105	*Judith*	
39:17-20	10.132	6:16, 21	9.69
		7:23	9.71
Daniel		8:6	9.115
3:31	8.172 n.7	8:10-11	9.71
4:6	7.161		
4:34	8.172 n.7	*Wisdom of Solomon*	
9:19	10.53	2:24	7.110
12:2, 13	9.2	5:5	9.2

Index 6 – Biblical Works

13:8-9	10.46
18:21	7.105

Prayer of Azariah

27	9.120

Sirach

7:28	8.115 n.55
8:8	7.105 n.53
10:2, 25	7.105 n.53
33:31-33	7.189 n.92
46:1	10.81
49:5	10.27

1 Maccabees

14:28	9.72
15:15-24	8.150
15:23	8.149
1:41-42	7.22-23 n.80
8:23-32	7.22-23 n.80
10:18-20	7.22-23 n.80
11:30-7, 57	7.22-23 n.80
12:6-18, 20-3	7.22-23 n.80
12:20-23	7.22-23 n.80
13:36-40	7.22-23 n.80
14:20-23	7.22-23 n.80
14:24c-h (= 15:16-24)	7.22-23 n.80
15:2-9	7.22-23 n.80

2 Maccabees

1:1-10a	7.22-23 n.80
1:10b-2:18	7.22-23 n.80
1:14	6.12-13 n.6
4:5	8.112 n.37
7:7	6.183
9:19-27	7.22-23 n.80
11:16b-21	7.22-23 n.80
11:23-26	7.22-23 n.80
11:27b-33	7.22-23 n.80
11:34b-38	7.22-23 n.80
15:3	6.183

Joseph and Aseneth

10:13-14; 13:8	10.129

2 Baruch

1-4	10.132

T. Isaac

6:13	10.132

Pseudepigrapha

Jannes and Jambres   10.11

4 Ezra

9:19	10.132

3 Maccabees

1:8	9.72
3:12-29	7.22-23 n.80
5:5	7.105 n.53
5:14-16	9.63 n.3
7:1-9	7.22-23 n.80

Prayer of Jacob   10.11

Testament of Dan

5:7-8	7.110

Testament of Solomon

12:4	10.13, 45
17:15	10.74

Qumran

CD

16.13	7.161

IQH

6.25-36	7.158

IQM

1.4	8.147

4Q510, 4Q560, 11Q11	10.11
4Q Lev^B	10.11

Rabbinical Literature
(alphabetical order)

Mishnah

m. 'Abodah Zarah 3.4	10.46
m. 'Arakin 1.1	7.192
m. 'Arakin 5.6	6.15
m. 'Abot 2.7	7.195
m. Baba Batra 3.1	6.97; 7.192
m. Baba Batra 3.2	6.96, 97
m. Baba Batra 3.3	6.95 n. 106, 96, 97

m. Baba Batra 4.7	7.192	m. Ketubbot 2.2	8.142
m. Baba Batra 4.9	6.95 n.106	m. Ketubbot 2.9	6.152 n.172; 7.193
m. Baba Batra 5.1	7.192	m. Ketubbot 1.4	6.152 n.172
m. Baba Batra 8-9	6.43	m. Ketubbot 4.4	6.12, 14 n. 21, 18 n.32
m. Baba Batra 8.1	6.13		
m. Baba Batra 8.7	6.36 n. 47	m. Ketubbot 4.7	9.93
m. Baba Batra 10.4	6.96 n.109	m. Ketubbot 4.7-12	9.92
m. Berakot 2.7	7.192	m. Ketubbot 4.12	6.13, 31 n.37
m. Berakot 3.3	7.192	m. Ketubbot 5.5, 6	6.14
m. Baba Meṣiʻa 1.5	7.193	m. Ketubbot 5.7	6.13, 15
m. Baba Meṣiʻa 1.6	6.92	m. Ketubbot 5.8-9	6.14
m. Baba Meṣiʻa 5.3	6.96 n.110	m. Ketubbot 6.3	6.13; 9.88
m. Baba Meṣiʻa 6.3	7.85, 85 n.80	m. Ketubbot 7.4-5	6.15
m. Baba Meṣiʻa 7.6, 8	7.192	m. Ketubbot 7.6	9.89
m. Baba Meṣiʻa 8.3	7.193	m. Ketubbot 7.6-7	6.13, 15
m. Baba Meṣiʻa 8.4	7.192	m. Ketubbot 7.9-10	6.15
m. Baba Meṣiʻa 9.1-10	6.89	m. Ketubbot 8.1	6.13
m. Baba Meṣiʻa 9.11	6.96	m. Ketubbot 8.5	7.192
m. Baba Meṣiʻa 9.13	6.92	m. Ketubbot 9.1	6.13
m. Baba Meṣiʻa 9.8-9	6.90	m. Ketubbot 9.9	6.12; 7.229 n.155
m. Baba Qamma 3.10	7.192	m. Ketubbot 12.3-4	6.13
m. Baba Qamma 4.5	7.193 n.106	m. Ketubbot 31.1	6.91
m. Baba Qamma 5.6	7.193	m. Ketubbot 13.7	6.97 n.111
m. Baba Qamma 6.5	7.193	m. Kilʼayim 7.6	6.97 n.112; 7.161
m. Baba Qamma 8.3	7.193	m. Megilla 1.2, 3.6, 4.1	9.115
m. Baba Qamma 8.4	7.192-193	m. Maʻaśer Šeni 1.7	7.192
m. Baba Qamma 8.5	7.193	m. Maʻaśer Šeni 4.4	7.193
m. ʻEduyyot 1.6	6.13	m. Nazir 9.1	7.192-193
m. ʻEduyyot 1.12	6.13, 31 n.37	m. Nedarim 8.1	9.112
m. ʻEduyyot 1.13	7.192	m. Nedarim 10.2	6.14 n.21
m. ʻEduyyot 8.2	6.152 n.172	m. Nedarim 11.1-2	6.14 n.21
m. ʻErubin 5.5	7.192	m. Nedarim 11.4	6.14
m. ʻErubin 7.6	7.193	m. Nedarim 11.10	6.12, 14 n.21
m. Giṭṭin 1.4	7.192	m. Nedarim 11.12	6.15
m. Giṭṭin 2.3	7.192	m. Niddah 5.4	6.18 n.32
m. Giṭṭin 4.3	7.226	m. Niddah 5.7	6.14 n.21
m. Giṭṭin 4.4, 5, 6	7.192	m. Niddah 11.10	6.14 n.21
m. Giṭṭin 5.1-3	6.13	m. Peʼah 1.1	8.147
m. Giṭṭin 5.6	6.97 n.112	m. Peʼah 3.6	7.227 n.142, 232 n.166
m. Giṭṭin 7.4	7.193		
m. Giṭṭin 7.5	6.16	m. Peʼah 3.8	6.193 n.107
m. Giṭṭin 9.2	6.17; 7.192	m. Pesaḥim 5.1, 8, 6.2	9.114 n.23
m. Giṭṭin 9.2-3	6.16	m. Pesaḥim 8.1	7.192
m. Giṭṭin 9.3	6.14, 16 n.28	m. Pesaḥim 8.2	7.193
m. Giṭṭin 9.8	6.12, 15	m. Pesaḥim 8.7	7.192
m. Giṭṭin 9.10	6.15	m. Qiddušin 1.1	6.18 n.32
m. Horayot 3.7	6.152 n.172	m. Qiddušin 1.1-6	6.14
m. Horayot 3.8	6.128	m. Qiddušin 1.2	7.192
m. Ḥullin 5.5	7.112	m. Qiddušin 1.3	7.193
m. Kelim 1.8	10.137	m. Qiddušin 1.5	6.95 n.106
m. Kelim 24.7	7.252	m. Qiddušin 2.1	6.12; 9.89
m. Kerithot 1.3	7.192	m. Qiddušin 3.1	9.92
m. Kerithot 2.2-5	7.192 n.103	m. Qiddušin 3.2	6.12; 9.89
m. Ketubbot 1.1	9.115	m. Qiddušin 3.12	6.17; 7.192
m. Ketubbot 1.2	9.94	m. Qiddušin 4.1	6.138; 7.191
m. Ketubbot 2.2	6.97	m. Qiddušin 4.1-7	6.17

Index 6 – Biblical Works

m. Qiddušin 4.4	6.128
m. Qiddušin 4.9	7.14
m. Roš Haššanah 1.8	7.193
m. Sanhedrin 2.3, 5.2, 7.2	9.53
m. Sanhedrin 11.1	7.192
m. Sanhedrin 11.4	6.91
m. Šabbat 1.3, 10, 11	9.112
m. Šabbat 2.7	9.112, 113
m. Šabbat 7.2	9.111
m. Šabbat 15.3	9.112
m. Šabbat 23.3, 4	9.112
m. Šabbat 24.1	9.112
m. Šebi'it 10.2	7.226 n.132
m. Šebi'it 10.3	6.92, 7.226 n.132
m. Šebi'it 10.4	6.91, 92; 7.225
m. Šebi'it 10.5	7.232 n.167
m. Šebi'it 10.6	7.227, 227 n.142, 232 n.166
m. Šebi'it 10.7	7.227 n.142, 232 n.166
m. Šebu'ot 4.12	7.193 n.105
m. Šebu'ot 5.5	7.193
m. Šeqalim 1.3, 5, 6	7.192
m. Šeqalim 8.3	7.193
m. Soṭah 1.3	6.91
m. Soṭah 6.2	7.193
m. Soṭah 8.2, 4	6.96
m. Sukkah 2.1, 8	7.192
m. Ta'anit 2.4	8.146 n.3
m. Ta'anit 2.9	9.115
m. Temurah 6.2	7.192, 195
m. Terumot 3.4	7.193
m. Terumot 8.1	7.192
m. Yadayim 4.4	6.128
m. Yadayim 4.7	7.192-3
m. Yebamot 2.5	7.192
m. Yebamot 4.3	6.13
m. Yebamot 4.7	6.13
m. Yebamot 7.1-2	7.192
m. Yebamot 7.5	6.17
m. Yebamot 11.2	6.6.18 n.31; 7.192
m. Yebamot 12.6	6.12
m. Yebamot 13.1, 2	6.12
m. Yebamot 13.6	6.12
m. Yebamot 14.1	6.15
m. Yebamot 16.7	7.192
m. Zabim 2.1	7.192
m. Zebaḥ 3.1	7.192
m. Zebaḥ 5.5	7.192 n.103
m. Zebaḥ 5.6-7	7.192

Tosefta

t. Baba Batra 9.14	6.47
t. Baba Meṣi'a 7.7	7.85
t. Baba Meṣi'a 9.1-33	6.89
t. Baba Meṣi'a 9.8	6.89
t. Baba Meṣi'a 9.13	6.90
t. Baba Meṣi'a 9.33	6.89
t. 'Eduyyot 1.6	6.13
t. Giṭṭin 5.1	6.97 n.112
t. Ketubbot 3.2	6.152 n.172
t. Ketubbot 4.12	7.231
t. Ketubbot 4.9	6.15; 9.89
t. Ketubbot 4.16	6.95 n.106
t. Ketubbot 12.1	6.13
t. Nedarim 7.1	6.14 n.21
t. Qiddušin 3.7	6.14
t. Qiddušin 4.15	6.17
t. Qiddušin 5.1-13	6.17
t. Yebamot 13.1	6.12, 14

Babylonian Talmud

b. 'Abodah Zarah 54b	10.130
b. Baba Batra 35b	6.96
b. Baba Batra 47a	7.66, 86
b. Baba Batra 135b	6.46
b. Baba Batra 160b-161b	7.230
b. Baba Batra 164a-b	7.230
b. Baba Meṣi'a 78b	7.85
b. Hag. 13a	10.130
b. Giṭṭin 9a	6.37
b. Ketubbot 84a	6.13
b. Ketubbot 51a, 82b	9.93
b. Nedarim 32a	7.86
b. Pesaḥim 112b	9.115
b. Pesaḥim 117a	8.147 n.5
b. Qiddušin 66a	6.152 n.172
b. Qiddušin 69a	7.191 n. 101, 224 n.121
b. Sanhedrin 9b, 41a, 48b	9.53
b. Sanhedrin 101b	7.86
b. Šabbat 34b	9.113
b. Šabbat 156a-b	9.11
b. Soṭah 10a	7.86
b. Yoma 35a-b	7.86

Palestinian/Jerusalem Talmud

y. Baba Batra 3.3	6.97
y. Baba Batra 16c	6.16
y. Baba Batra 3.3	6.96, 97
y. Baba Batra 3.5	6.96
y. Baba Batra 10.1	7.230
y. Baba Meṣi'a 11a	7.85
y. Ketubbot 30b	6.16
y. Ketubbot 4.8.28d	6.15; 9.89
y. Ketubbot 32b	7.214 n.70
y. Kil'ayim 74	6.96
y. Qiddušin 3.4	6.108

y. Sanhedrin 2.6	6.15 n.15, 16 n.29, 46	10:9-14	7.89, 92
		10:25	6.68, 69
y. Šebiʿit 38	7.214 n.70	10:28	9.19
y. Yebamot 15.3.14d	6.15; 9.89	10:34-36	7.154
		11:12	6.98; 7.152-162, 60 n.85; 9.55
Others		11:12-13	7.152
		11:19	8.69
Esther Rabbah (intro. 5)	7.86	11:21, 23	8.174
Leviticus Rabbah 12.1	786	12:10	6.183
Leviticus Rabbah R. 23.5	7.86	12:27	10.13
Leviticus Rabbah R. 27	7.110	12:28	10.14
Mekilta de-Rabbi Ishmael, tractate Nezekin, chapter 3	6.12	12:28-29	7.154
		12:29	7.160
Sipra Deuteronomy 113	7.226	13:58	8.174
Sipra Numbers 134	6.115 n.120	14:2	8.174
Tg. Exodus 21.11	6.14	14:6	10.158
Tg. Isaiah 5.7	7.161	14:22-33	6.86
Tg. Isaiah 21.2	7.161	15:21-28	10.129, 131
		15:22	8.111 n.19; 10.131
		15:24	10.129
New Testament		15:31	8.174
		16:16	9.38
Matthew		16:19	7.154 n.66
1:1-14	10.157	16:21	9.71 n.6
2:1, 3	6.123; 9.41	17:15	8.111 n.19
3:16	8.161 n.21	17:24-27	8.95
5:3	7.154 n.66	17:25	7.127
5:5	7.154 n.66, 156	17:26	8.96 n.59
5:10	7.154 n.66	18:6	7.128
5:17-19, 17-20	7.87	18:12-14	9.55
5:20	7.87	18:17	8.69
5:21-47	7.86-87	18:23-34	7.222-224, n.125
5:25-26	6.92, 99; 7.222-224, n.125; 9.61	18:30	6.99
		19:3	6.183
5:32	6.16	19:9	6.16
5:41	7.66, 86-87, n.81, 82; 8.105	19:12	6.16
		19:14	7.154 n.66
5:48	7.87	19:24	7.128
6:5-9	10.52	19:28-30	9.2
6:13	6.194	20:1-16	8.105
6:25	9.19	20:20-28	6.50
6:30	6.68, 69	21:1-9	7.128
7:6	10.130	21:23	9.71 n.6
7:11	6.69	21:28	6.131
7:13-14	10.8	21:31	8.69
7:22	10.14	21:32	7.157
7:33	10.8	21:33-43	7.156
8:11	10.132, 134	21:33-44	6.93-105
8:11-12	9.66	21:33-46	6.39
8:27	6.85	21:37	6.95
9:10-11	8.69	21:38	7.156
9:18	9.71 n.6	22:1-14	9.66; 10.132, 134
9:27	8.111 n.19	22:34-40	7.87
9:33	8.174	23:8	10.166
		23:12	10.52

Index 6 – Biblical Works

23:13	7.154 n.66	11:16	10.134
23:24	7.128	12:1-12	6.39; 8.105
24:31	9.102	12:1	6.95 n.105
24:42-51	9.66	12:2	7.128 n.62
25:1-13	9.66	12:7	6.37 n.49
25:10, 12	9.66	12:14	7.127
25:21	6.181	12:16	9.3
25:32	6.181	12:40	10.52
26:3, 47	9.71 n.6	13:8	9.7
26:57	9.111 n.11	13:9	6.91
26:63	9.38	13:10	10.132
27:1, 3, 12, 20	9.71 n.6	13:34	6.62-63
27:32	7.66, 86 n.82, 87; 8.105	14:15-24	10.132
		14:29	6.68
27:35	6.159	14:53	9.111 n.11
27:41	9.71 n.6	14:53-72	9.111 n.11
27:51-53	8.174	14:64	9.53
27:62	9.115	15:1	9.53, 111 n.11
28:1	9.115	15:6-15	8.5
		15:21	7.66, 87
Mark		15:24	6.159
		15:26	6.115; 10.129
1:6	7.128	15:33, 38	8.174
1:24	10.13	15:42	9.115
1:25-26	10.14	16:2	9.115
1:27	8.174	16:8	10.79
2:3-12	10.53	16:9	9.115
2:19-20	10.132	18:19	10.85
2:23-8	9.111		
3:11	10.13	*Luke*	
3:23-27	10.14		
3:26	10.13	1:5	6.123
5:6, 7, 8, 9, 10, 11-13	10.14	1:23	7.105
5:22	9.71 n.6	1:26	6.123, 132
4:11	6.202	1:36	6.132
4:41	6.85	1:39-41	6.123
6:2, 5, 14	8.174	1:59	6.132
6:22	10.158	1:46	9.121
6:30-44	10.132	1:47	9.31
7:24	10.134	1:69, 71, 77	9.5
7:24-29	10.126, 127, 129	2:1-2	9.41
7:25	10.130, 133	2:1-3	6.119, 123
7:26	10.129, 131, 133	2:1-5	6.124
7:27	10.129, 133	2:1	6.111
7:28	10.131	2:2	6.131 n.154
7:29	10.133	2:3	6.112-119
7:31	10.134	2:7	6.130
8:1-10	10.132	2:39	6.119, 123
8:23	6.183	3:1	6.31
9:42	7.128	3:12-13	8.74
10:11-12	6.16	3:12-14	8.69
10:25	7.128	3:13	8.105
10:35-45	6.50	3:14	6.158 n.177
11:1-9	6.37	3:23	6.31; 9.41
11:1-10	7.128	3:23-38	10.157
11:4	7.44 n.45	3:24-26	10.45

4:1-2	10.14	15:13	10.7
4:17	10.14	16:16	7.132 n.2, 152,
4:36	8.174		157-158, 160; 9.55
5:26	8.174	16:18	6.16
5:7	9.48; 10.14	16:31	10.132
5:8	10.14	18:1	10.50
5:10	9.48	18:1-8	6.98; 9.35
5:30	10.53	18:8	10.53
6:7	6.183	18:9-14	8.69
6:21	10.132	18:10-14	10.52
6:26-36	10.53	18:11	10.52, 53
6:27-36	10.134	18:11-12	10.52
7:3	9.69	18:12	10.53
7:21	6.194	18:13	10.52, 53
7:29-30	7.157	18:14	10.53
7:34	10.53	18:25	7.128
7:47-48	10.53	18:33	6.132
8:2	6.194	19:1-10	8.69
8:25	6.85	19:2-7	10.53
8:41	9.70, 71	19:8	8.54, 74, n.103,
8:43-48	6.196		105; 10.53
8:46	8.174	19:28-38	7.128
9:22	6.132	20:9-19	6.39
9:38-39	10.14	20:20	10.79
10:4-11	7.92	20:24	9.3
10:17-20	10.14	20:35, 47	10.52
10:34	7.128	22:25	9.6, 15
11:13	6.69	22:25-26	9.4
11:17-18	10.14	22:29	10.85
11:19	10.13, 14	22:44	10.36
11:20-23, 24-26	10.14	22:49	6.183
11:26	6.194	22:54	9.66-71, 111 n.11
11:52	7.154 n.66	22:66-71	9.111 n.11
12:13	6.390	23:13	9.71
12:19	8.119	23:26	7.87
12:28	6.68, 69	23:34	6.159
12:36-38	9.65, 66	23:44	6.132
12:38	6.132	23:48	10.53
12:57-59	6.92	24:1	9.115
12:58-59	6.99; 7.222; 9.61	24:7	6.132
13:15	7.128	24:20	9.71 n.6
13:23	6.183	24:21, 46	6.132
13:24	10.8		
13:28-29	10.134	*John*	
13:30	10.8	1:11	6.119 n.126
13:32	6.132	1:15	6.131
14:1	9.71 n.6	2:1-10	9.66
14:5	7.128	2:14-15	7.128
14:7-11	9.2, 65	2:20	6.62
14:11	10.53	3:1	9.70
14:16-24	9.65; 10.134	4:10	9.37
14:19	7.128	4:20	8.149 n.4
15:1	8.69; 10.53	5	9.100
15:2	8.171	5:14	9.101
15:4-7	9.55	5:35	8.43
15:11-32	6.37		

Index 6 – Biblical Works

6:19	6.30 n.35	8:9-13	6.195
6:23	10.50	8:10	10.13
6:29	9.103	8:13	10.13
6:51	9.37	8:26-40	7.88
6:62	6.183	8:28-29	7.129
7:38	9.37	8:37-39	8.177
7:45	9.48, 71 n.6	8:38	7.129
7:48	9.71 n.6	9:2	7.54
8:11	9.101	9:4-8	7.88
9:6	6.191	9:11	7.44
10:31	9.101	9:15	10.45
12:1	6.157	9:36-42	9.50
12:14-15	7.128	9:43	7.55 n.20
15:4	6.67 n.79	10:1	6.159
16:21	9.58	10:2	9.79; 10.35
18:6	8.174	10:3	6.132
19:23-24	6.159	10:5-6	7.43
19:34-35	8.174	10:7	10.35
20:1, 19	9.115	10:9	6.132; 7.88
		10:22	7.240
Acts		10:23-24	7.88
		10:30	6.132
1:1	6.131	10:38	9.6, 16; 10.13
1:6	6.183	10:40	6.132
1:8	10.13	11:28	9.7
1:14	10.50	12:5	10.36
2:15	6.132	12:10	6.131, 132
2:17, 19	10.45	12:12	9.50
2:22	10.13	12:20-23	6.192
3:1	6.132	12:22	9.15
3:6	9.104	13:2	7.105
3:12	9.22; 10.13, 35	13:3-14	7.240
3:17	9.71 n.6; 10.166	13:4-12	10.13
3:22	10.166	13:5	7.91
3:31	6.194	13:6	10.45
4:5	9.71 n.6, 72	13:6 ff.	10.46
4:7	10.13	13:6-12	6.195
4:8	9.71 n.6, 72	13:8	10.45
4:9	9.16	13:9-11	10.45
4:12	9.4	13:12, 13-14	7.90
4:23	9.71 n.6	13:14	7.91
4:33	10.13	13:16, 26	9.79
5:23	7.36	13:27	9.71 n.6
5:31	10.85	13:43	7.91; 9.79
5:33	9.53	13:46	7.91; 10.132
5:37	6.131	13:50	9.79
5:41	10.52	13:51	7.88
6:8	10.13	14:1	7.91
6:9	7.89	14:5	9.71 n.6
7:8	6.132	14:8-11	10.45
7:12	6.131	14:13	6.209
7:32	6.194	14:15	9.38
7:38	9.37	14:22 ff.	7.92 n.110
8:4-13	10.13	15:22	7.54
8:9 ff.	10.46	15:23	7.54; 8.127
8:9-11	10.45	15:23-29	7.24

15:27	7.56	19:25	10.46
15:30-33, 41	7.54	19:24-27	10.49
16:1-2	10.117	19:26	10.46
16:3	7.91	19:27	10.46
16:4	6.111	19:29, 31	7.55
16:10-17	7.92	19:34-35	10.46
16:12, 13	7.91 n.103	19:35	7.237; 6.204, 205
16:14	9.79	19:37, 40	6.205
16:15	7.55 n.20, 91 n.103; 10.117	19:38	10.49
		20:4	7.55
16:16-18	10.45	20:5-21:17	7.92
16:16-22	6.205	20:7	9.11
16:15, 40	9.50	20:13	7.88
16:34	7.55 n.20	20:18	6.132
16:37	6.154	20:38	7.88
17:1-2	7.91	21:4	7.90, 55 n.20
17:4	7.91; 9.50, 79	21:5	7.88
17:7	6.111	21:7	7.90
17:10	7.91	21:7-8	7.55 n.20
17:12	7.91; 9.50, 79	21:27-32	6.205
17:14	7.55	21:27-23:35	6.159-161
17:17	7.91; 10.84	21:31-33	6.205
17:23	7.88; 9.3; 10.35	21:33	9.53
17:29	10.46	21:35	9.55
18:3	7.55 n.20; 9.50	22:1	10.166, 167
18:4-5, 6	7.91	22:5	7.54
18:7	7.55 n.20; 9.79	22:7-11	7.88
18:7-8, 19-20	7.91	22:22-29	6.154
18:25	7.245	22:24	9.53
18:27	7.55, 55 n.20	22:25	6.154, 183; 9.53
19:1-20:1	10.61	22:25-28	6.153
19:5-7	10.46	22:30	9.53
19:8-9	7.91	23:14	9.71 n.6
19:9	6.197; 10.2, 46	23:15	9.53
19:10	10.3, 46	23:23	6.132, 160 n.181; 7.128; 9.53
19:11	10.13, 45		
19:11-12	6.196	23:24	7.88, 128
19:11-20	10.13	23:25	7.24
19:12	10.46	23:26	7.36; 8.127
19:13	10.13, 45	23:26-30	7.24
19:13-18	10.45	23:29	9.53
19:13-21	10.44	23:32	7.128
19:15	10.46	23:33	7.54, 88
19:15-16	10.45	24:1	9.71 n.6
19:17-20	7.91; 10.46	24:2	8.113 n.42
19:17-35	10.61	24:2-8	9.53
19:18	10.17	24:3	9.22
19:19	6.202; 10.40	24:7	9.55
19:19-20	10.45	24:18-20	9.53
19:19-41	10.45	24:26	9.35
19:20	7.92 n.110	25:3, 9, 11	9.53
19:22	7.55	25:9-11	9.53
19:23-25	10.60	25:15	9.71 n.6
19:23-41	7.123 n.43; 8.5; 9.27; 10.46	25:20	9.53
		26:10	9.53
19:24	10.46, 49, 50	26:12-16	7.88

Index 6 – Biblical Works

26:17	10.45	7:19	7.194
27:1-28:16	7.117	8:4	6.44 n.56
27:1-44	6.85	8:12	6.44 n.57
27:1	6.159	8:18 ff.	9.4
27:19, 27, 33	6.132	8:22	9.58
27:41	9.55	8:29	9.2
28:1-6	10.45	8:31	8.165 n.32
28:7	7.55 n.20	8:38	10.18
28:11	7.117	9:4-5	9.20
28:14	7.55 n.20	9:22-24	6.183
28:15	10.50	9:26	9.38
28:16	8.43	10:2, 3-4	9.21
28:17	10.166	11:12	6.68, 69
28:24, 25 ff.	7.91	11:16	6.68
		11:17-18	10.132
Romans		11:24	6.69
		11:36	10.28
1:1	10.161	12:1	6.146; 9.37
1:2-5	10.27	12:13	7.55 n.20; 10.107
1:3	6.44 n.57	12:17	7.240
1:7	7.45 n.51	13:1-7	6.145; 10.28, 74
1:8	7.53; 10.50	13:3	7.240
1:10	10.50	13:6-7	7.127 n.60
1:14	7.45 n.51	14:6	10.50
1:16	10.132	14:19-20	9.104
1:20-23	10.46	14:20	9.102, 103
1:21	10.50	15:13-33	7.53
1:21-23	10.27	15:18	7.239
1:21a	10.27	15:20	10.35
1:23	9.2; 10.27	15:24	7.55 n.20
2:17-3:20	8.174	15:26-27	10.107
3:5	6.44 n.56	15:27	7.105
3:25	6.115	15:30	6.146
4:1	6.44 n.57	16:1-2	7.51, 55 n.20; 8.171; 9.50
4:7-8	10.60		
5:1, 2, 4, 5, 6	9.4	16:2	10.52
5:3	6.44 n.57	16:4	9.19
5:7b	9.6	16:5, 6, 12-13	9.50
5:9	9.4	16:13	6.158 n.178
5:10	9.4	16:15	9.50
5:10, 15	6.69	16:17	6.146
5:12-21	9.4	16:18	7.194
5:17	6.69; 9.4	16:20	10.18
5:18, 20	9.4	16:27	10.28
6:6	7.194		
6:8	6.44 n.56	*1 Corinthians*	
6:12 ff.	6.53 n.64		
6:16, 17	7.194	1:11	10.117
6:18	6.75	1:18-31	10.52
6:20	7.194	1:2	7.45 n.51
6:22	6.75	1:4	10.50
7:5	10.50	1:8-11	10.28
7:13	9.21	1:10	6.146
7:13-15	6.53	1:11	7.55; 9.50
7:13-25	8.174	1:23	9.2
7:14-25	7.194	2:4-5	8.121

2:6-8	10.18	10:14-22	10.28
2:14	9.19	10:18-22	9.2
3:3	6.44-45 n.56, 57	10:20-21	10.18
3:9 ff.	9.104	11:3	6.15
3:17	9.104	11:7	9.38
4:1	6.202	11:11	6.15
4:6-13	6.139	11:18	7.55
4:8	6.67 n.78	12:13	6.54, 59; 8.44;
4:9-13	10.52		10.112
4:15	6.68, 158 n.178	12:31	9.21
4:16	6.146	14:2	6.202
4:17	7.51, n.9, 55-56	14:7-9	6.43 n.55
5:1-13	9.18	14:18	10.50
5:3	9.19	15:1	10.166
5:5	10.18	15:24	10.18
6:1-11	9.18	15:24-28	10.85
6:13-20	6.53 n.64	15:32	6.44 n. 56, 57;
6:16	6.15 n.22		8.119
6:20	6.75	15:44-5	9.19
7:1-16	6.14	15:45	9.37
7:3	6.14	15:49	9.2, 38
7:4	6.15, 15 n.22	15:52	9.102
7:5	6.15; 10.18	16:2	9.115
7:10-11, 12, 15	6.16	16:3	7.55
7:12-13	6.17	16:10-11	7.55 n.20
7:12-16	6.17	16:12	10.166
7:14	6.18	16:15	6.194
7:20	6.53	16:19	9.50
7:21	6.67-70		
7:22	10.63	*2 Corinthians*	
7:23	6.75; 7.194	1:1	7.45 n.51
7:24	6.75	1:3-14	6.172
7:25-40	6.14	1:19	7.55
7:26, 29	9.7	2:3-4	7.51, 256 n.30
7:29-31	6.17	2:8	6.146
7:31	9.7	2:11	10.18
7:32-35	6.15	2:12-13	7.51
7:35	6.75	2:17	10.108
7:36-38	6.14, n.19	3:1-2	6.180
7:39	6.17	3:1-3	7.55
8:4-6	9.27; 10.46	3:3	9.38
8:5-6	9.2; 10.28	3:9, 11	6.69
8:10	10.28	3:10, 17	9.21
9	10.108	3:18	9.2, 38
9:2	6.68	4:4	9.38; 10.18
9:3-18	7.55 n.20	4:7	9.21
9:8	6.44-45 n.56, 57	4:7-12	10.52
9:9	7.128	4:10	6.53 n.64
9:12	6.68, 69	4:16	6.69
9:13-14	9.2	5:9	10.35
9:25	9.2	5:13	6.68
9:24-27	8.119 n.5	5:16	6.68
9:27	6.53 n.64	5:20	6.146
10:1	10.166	6:1	6.146
10:1-22	9.18	6:8-10	10.52
10:2-3	6.44 n.56		

Index 6 – Biblical Works

6:10	9.7; 10.35	12:18	7.51
6:14	9.48	13:4	9.2; 10.52
6:14-16	6.17		
6:15	10.18	*Galatians*	
6:16	9.38	1:11	6.44 n.56, 57
7:5-7	7.51	1:14	10.52
7:6-7	7.55	2:5	8.43
7:8	8.43	2:9	10.107
7:8-12	7.51, 256 n.30	2:12	7.55
7:12	6.68	2:19-20	10.52
7:13-16	7.51	3:5	10.45
8:1	9.21	3:10-12	8.174
8:4	10.107	3:13	9.2
8:6-7	7.55	3:15-19	6.43
8:8	9.21	3:15	6.37, 41-47
8:9	9.21; 10.35	3:18	6.68
8:11	9.21	3:26-28	6.59
8:12	6.68	3:27-28	6.54; 7.194; 8.44
8:16-24	7.51, 55	3:28	6.15, 152; 10.63, 112
8:17	7.51 n.9	4:1	6.39
8:18	7.51 n.9; 10.166	4:3	7.194; 10.18
8:22	10.166	4:4	9.4
8:23	10.106, 166	4:8	10.46
9:3	10.166	4:8-9	7.194
9:3-5	7.51	4:12	6.146
9:5	7.55; 10.166	4:19	9.58
9:8	10.17	4:23	6.44 n.57
9:12	7.105	5:1	6.75
9:13	10.107	5:7	10.120
9:14	9.21	5:13	6.75
10:1-2	6.146	5:11	7.91
11:1	10.52	6:1	6.69
11:2	6.16 n.30	6:6	10.107
11:3	10.18	6:11	7.51 n.9
11:4-6	10.52		
11:6	6.68	*Ephesians*	
11:7-10	10.108	1:1	7.45 n.51
11:12-23	10.52	1:2	10.60
11:14	10.18	1:6	10.60, 62
11:15	6.69	1:7	10.60, 62
11:16, 17, 21	10.52	1:12, 14, 17	10.62
11:21-23	9.21	1:18	10.61, 62
11:22	6.139	1:19	10.61
11:23	10.52	1:20-22	10.18
11:23-25	9.44	1:21	10.13, 18, 85
11:23-29	10.52	2:2	10.18
11:24	7.91	2:3	10.62
11:24-25	6.154	2:4	10.61
11:25	7.88 n.92	2:5	10.60
11:26	6.85; 7.88	2:7	9.21; 10.60, 61, 62
11:26-33	9.7	2:8	10.60, 62
11:30-33, 31	10.52	2:9	10.62
12:7	10.18	2:11-19	10.62
12:12	10.45	2:11-21	10.63
12:13-18	10.108		
12:17-18	7.55		

2:20	10.62	3:4-11	10.52
3:2	10.60	3:5-6	10.52
3:7	10.61	3:5-8	6.139
3:8	10.60, 61, 62	3:5	6.128
3:9	6.202	3:17	6.172
3:10	10.18	4:1	9.2
3:16	10.61, 62	4:2, 3	6.146
4:1	6.146; 10.52	4:2-3	9.50
4:7	10.60, 61	4:4	7.48
4:7-16	10.62	4:6	10.51
4:8	10.60	4:8	8.115
4:9-10	10.18	4:8-9	7.240
4:24	6.209	4:10	7.48
4:27	10.18	4:15, 18	10.107
4:29, 32	10.60	4:15-18	10.108
5:15-6:9	10.63		
5:18	10.7	*Colossians*	
5:21	10.62	1:3	10.50
5:21-6:9	7.191 n.100	1:5	6.110
5:21-33	6.15	1:7-8	7.55
5:21, 22-6:9	6.19	1:10	10.52
5:27	6.19	1:12	9.2
6:1-4	7.240	1:12-13, 13-15	6.110
6:5	6.53, 55	1:15	9.2, 38
6:5-9	7.194; 8.40	1:16	10.18
6:8	10.50	1:18	9.4
6:9	8.40	1:23, 27-29	6.110
6:11, 12	10.18	2:8, 10	10.18
6:16	10.18	2:13-14	6.115
6:21-22	7.51, 55-6	2:13	10.18
6:22	7.51 n.9	2:14	6.105-111
6:24	10.60	2:15	10.18
		2:18	6.209
Philippians		2:20	10.18
1:1	7.45 n.51	3:10	9.38
1:3, 4	10.50	3:11	10.112
1:5	10.106	3:17	10.50
1:20	6.53 n.64	3:18-4:1	6.19; 7.191 n.100
1:27	10.52	3:18-19	6.15
2:5-11	10.52	3:22-4:1	7.194; 8.40
2:6-8	6.140	4:1	8.40
2:7-8, 9-11	9.2	4:7-8, 9, 10	6.110
2:10	10.18	4:7-9	7.51, 56
2:17	6.69; 7.105	4:7-10	7.55
2:19	7.52	4:8	7.51 n.9
2:19-23	7.55	4:10	7.55-56 n.20
2:25-30	7.51, 55	4:12	8.45; 10.51
2:28	7.51 n.9	4:14	10.112
2:29	8.171	4:15	9.50; 10.117
2:30	7.105	4:16	7.56, 256 n.30
3:1	7.48		
3:1-4:20	6.172 n.187	*1 Thessalonians*	
3:2	10.130	1:2	10.50
3:4	6.68, 69	1:9	9.38
3:4-6	7.239	2:1, 9	10.166

Index 6 – Biblical Works

2:2-3	7.52	4:7	10.35
2:12	10.52	4:8	8.43; 10.35
2:13	10.50	4:9	6.180; 9.14
2:15-16	7.91	4:10	9.38
2:17-3:13	7.54	5:1	10.167
2:18	6.172; 7.53; 10.18	5:1-8	8.109, 109 n.6
2:19	9.2	5:3	8.113
3:2-6	7.55, 56	5:3-16	8.113, 113 n.44
3:5	6.172; 7.53; 10.18	5:3	8.115
3:11	10.113	5:4	8.113 n.46, 114, 115, 116; 10.35
4:1	6.146; 9.102	5:5	8.116, n.57
4:4	6.53 n.64	5:8	8.109, 112 n.38, 113, 114, 115, 116, n.56
4:10	6.146		
4:11	10.35		
4:16	9.105; 10.18		
5:3	9.58	5:10	7.55-56 n.20
5:12, 14	6.146	5:10-14	10.122
5:17	10.50	5:15	10.18
5:27	6.172; 7.53, 56	5:18	7.128
		5:23	6.190
2 Thessalonians		6:1-2	6.19; 7.195; 8.40
1:3	10.50, 166	6:2	6.175; 9.16
1:5	10.52	6:3	9.14
1:11	10.50	6:3, 5, 6	10.35
2:1	6.146	6:11	10.35
2:3-4	10.74	6:21	6.171
2:5	6.172; 7.54		
2:7, 8	10.74	*2 Timothy*	
2:9	10.18	1:13	9.14
2:13	10.50	2:3-4	6.149
2:15	7.56	2:5	9.2
3:3	10.18	2:6	7.115
3:9	7.240	2:13	9.14
3:12	6.146	2:16	7.127
3:17	6.172; 7.54	2:26	10.18
		3:5	10.35
1 Timothy		3:12	10.35
1:1	9.31	3:15	6.180
1:3-4	7.55	3:16	9.37
1:14	9.14	4:3	9.14
1:15	6.180	4:8	9.2
1:20	10.18	4:10, 12	7.55
2:1	6.146	4:13	7.250, 255 n.26
2:2	10.35	4:20	7.55
2:3	9.31	4:22	6.171
2:8	10.51		
2:8-15	6.19	*Titus*	
2:9-12	10.122	1:1	10.35, 161
3:1	6.180; 9.14	1:4	6.171
3:2	7.55-56 n.20	1:5	7.55
3:6, 7	10.18	1:6	10.7
3:14-15	6.68 n.82	1:8	7.55-56 n.20
3:15	9.38	1:9	6.180; 9.13
3:16	10.35	2:1	9.14
4:1	10.18	2:2-10	6.19

2:3	7.194	10:12	10.85
2:3-5	6.22; 10.122	10:20	9.37
2:8	9.14	10:31	9.38
2:9-10	7.195	12:2	9.120; 10.85
2:12	10.35	12:8	9.48
3:1	6.145		
3:3	7.194	12:22	9.38
3:8	6.180; 9.14	12:25	6.68
3:12	7.55	12:28	10.85
3:13-14	7.55-56 n.20	13:19	6.146
3:15	6.171	13:22	6.146; 10.166
2:1	9.8, 14		
3:8	9.14	*James*	
		1:1	7.36; 8.127, 128; 9.70
Philemon		1:2	10.166
	8.40-45	1:12	9.2
1-2	9.50	3:3	7.128
4	10.50	4:14	8.43
6	6.171	5:14	6.191
8-9	10.167-168		
9, 10	6.146; 8.43	*1 Peter*	
10	8.43		
12	7.51 n.9, 52	1:1-2	7.44; 8.127
13	8.43	1:3	9.38
13-14	8.43	1:3-6	10.122
14	7.194	1:22	10.36
15	8.43	1:23	9.37
15-16	6.60, 175; 10.63	2:4-5	9.38
16	7.194; 8.44	2:11	6.146
17	8.41; 10.106	2:13-17	6.145
17-20	10.108	2:14-15	7.240
18	8.40	2:18-20	6.53; 7.195; 8.40
18-19	8.41, 42	2:18-3:7	6.19
19	8.40	3:3-5	6.19
22	7.55-56 n.20; 8.45	3:14	6.69
23	8.45	3:18-22	10.18
		4:4	10.7
Hebrews		4:9	7.55-56 n.20
1:3, 8	10.85	4:11	6.68
1:9	9.48	5:1	6.146
1:11	10.85	5:4	7.140; 9.2
2:3	9.5	5:9	10.166
2:10	9.5; 10.85	5:14	8.172 n.7
2:9a, b	9.2	6:12-20	10.18
3:1, 14	9.48		
3:12	9.38	*2 Peter*	
4:12	9.37		9.22
5:9	9.5, 48	1:1	7.44; 8.127
6.4	9.48	1:3, 6, 7	10.35
8:1	10.85	1:6-7	7.240
8:6	7.105	2:9	10.35
9:14	9.38	2:16	7.128
9:21	7.105	2:19	7.194
9:28	9.5	2:22	10.130
10:11	7.105		

Index 6 – Biblical Works

3:11	10.35	7:10	9.5
3:15	7.256	9:7-9	7.128
		9:9	7.129
1 John		9:16-19	7.128
2:12-14	10.167	11:15	10.85
		11:17	10.50
		12:1-6	9.58
2 John		12:10	9.5
10-11	7.55-56 n.20	13:14-15	9.2
		13:18	8.161 n.21, 165; 9.87
		14:9-11	9.2
3 John		15:7	9.38
3	7.55	16:2	9.2
5-8	7.55-56 n.20	16:5	6.209
6	10.52	17-18	6.145
10	7.55-56 n.20	18	10.122
15	8.172 n.7	18:3	10.120
		18:13	7.128-129
Jude		19:1	9.5
1	7.44; 8.127	19:7-9	9.66
1.20	10.51	19:11-21	7.128
3	6.146	19:20	9.2
		20:4, 6	9.2
Revelation		20:5	6.131
1:8	8.161 n.21	21:1	6.131
1:10	9.102, 110	21:2	6.16 n.30
2:10	9.2	21:5	9.14
2:13	9.27	21:6	8.161 n.21
3:11	9.2	21:12	9.3
4:1	9.102	21:17	8.165
4:9-11	9.2	22:6	9.14
6:2-8	7.128	22:15	10.130
7:2	9.38	22:19	9.3